Aspects of Multilingualism in European Language History

Hamburg Studies on Multilingualism

The Hamburg Studies on Multilingualism (HSM) publishes research from colloquia on linguistic aspects of multilingualism organized by the Research Center on Multilingualism at the University of Hamburg.

Volume 2

Aspects of Multilingualism in European Language History
Edited by Kurt Braunmüller and Gisella Ferraresi

Aspects of Multilingualism in European Language History

Edited by

Kurt Braunmüller

Gisella Ferraresi

University of Hamburg

John Benjamins Publishing Company

Amsterdam / Philadelphia

∞ TM The paper used in this publication meets the minimum requirements of American National Standard for Information Sciences – Permanence of Paper for Printed Library Materials, ANSI Z39.48-1984.

Library of Congress Cataloging-in-Publication Data

Aspects of multilingualism in European language history / edited by Kurt Braunmüller, Gisella Ferraresi.
p. cm. (Hamburg Studies on Multilingualism, ISSN 1571-4934 ; v. 2)
Includes bibliographical references and index.
1. Multilingualism--Europe--History. 2. Languages in contact--Europe--History. I. Braunmüller, Kurt, 1948- II. Ferraresi, Gisella. III. Series.

P115.5.E85A83 2003
306.44'6'094-dc22 2003062909
ISBN 90 272 1922 2 (Eur.) / 1 58811 446 5 (US) (Hb; alk. paper)

John Benjamins Publishing Co. · P.O. Box 36224 · 1020 ME Amsterdam · The Netherlands
John Benjamins North America · P.O. Box 27519 · Philadelphia PA 19118-0519 · USA

The production of this series has been made possible
through financial support to the Research Center on Multilingualism
(Sonderforschungsbereich 538 "Mehrsprachigkeit")
by the Deutsche Forschungsgemeinschaft (DFG).

Table of contents

Introduction

Kurt Braunmüller and Gisella Ferraresi

Multilingualism in European language history: The default case

The political history of the 19th and 20th centuries and the ideology of 'one state – one nation – one language' have given rise to the idea that monolingualism has always been the default or normal case in Europe and more or less a precondition for political loyality. Facing this situation, it has been overlooked that the vast majority of the world's population – in whatever form or conditions – is multilingual. This is quite obvious when we look at the linguistic maps of Africa, Asia or Southern America at any given time.

Minorities and their languages have, however, sometimes formed a problem for nation-states in Europe because they seemed to represent an alien factor with respect to the nation they were part of and the official language in this nation-state. Minorities were often considered potentially illoyal. For this reason, they were prosecuted in some cases; in others, they played only a minor or even a suppressed role in these countries.

Such a close connection between *language* on the one hand, and political *loyality* and personal *identity* on the other did not become evident before the end of the 18th century. One could, for example as a German national, have a leading function as a minister or civil servant in tsarist Russia or in the kingdoms of Denmark or Sweden without being stigmatized for one's origin. Taking over such functions as a "foreigner" (in the sense of a speaker of a minority language) was not seen as anything special or exceptional either. Your foreign mother tongue was neither a handicap, nor was it considered deviant in one way or another. Especially the upper classes and the court circles often used foreign languages in internal as well as in international communication. They quite often wrote private letters in non-native languages and sent their children abroad in order to get acquainted not only with other countries, their cultures and businesses but also with foreign languages. Being monolingual would have been the non-normal case in the upper layers of the European societies of those times.

Emperor Frederick II of the Holy Roman Empire, for example, was more fluent in Italian and other vernacular or neighbouring languages than in German. The polyglot Emperor Charles V is quoted as saying, "I speak Spanish with God, Italian to women, French to men and German to my horse." King Frederick the Great of Prussia clearly preferred French to German – not only when writing letters to his friend Voltaire. In other words, the use of languages other than that of the main population was by no means anything special for the middle and upper classes in Europe in the centuries before 1800.

But not only individuals were multilingual. The official language of the Danish army was German until 1773, and the language of the Roman (catholic) church has ever been Latin instead of Italian (or any other language). The common linguistic basis for diplomacy and international correspondence was French.

In the Middle Ages, the boundaries were even more fluid. Thus McKitterick says about the Romance-German bilingualism of the Carolingian period: "It is hardly likely that monolingualism was the norm except among particularly isolated social groups or in remote areas [...] We may [...] throughout the early medieval period in the areas dominated by the Franks, be dealing with a largely bilingual or even polylingual population as far as the spoken word is concerned" (McKitterick 1989: 7–8). Such generalizations, however, cannot be assumed without further specification. In fact, as for the Carolingian reign in the 8th and 9th centuries, the above statement can only hold for some regions in the West, and there certainly was no kind of general bilingualism. Diastratic varieties on the one hand and substratum/superstratum relationships between the different spoken languages on the other should be distinguished. But such a differentiation is more often than not of an artificial nature, since what we face here as our object is a continuum and not a distinct set of case studies.

Hellgardt, at the end of his article about multilingualism in the Carolingian reign, relates an anecdote about abbot Ekkehard I of St Gallen, who was widely known both for his charitable disposition and his linguistic skills. He once ordered a servant to bath an overweight paralitic, which the man did with difficulty and some chagrin. The lame patient complains about the temperature of the bath in his native Rhaeto-Romanic: "Cald, cald est!" The assonance between Romanic *cald* 'warm' and German *kalt* 'cold' leads his German-speaking attendant, maybe deliberately misunderstanding his protestations, to pour more hot water, until his charge can no longer bear the heat, climbs out of the tub and tries to run away, thus revealing his lameness as feigned. Then the

Latin narrator goes to some length to describe how the multilingual abbot reprimands the monolingual servant as well as the monolingual impostor in their respective languages, thus showing his readers both the workings of European multilingualism and its limitations.

There are many other examples of individual, societal or functional multilingualism in Europe.

One reason for the existence of these forms of multilingualism was that it was simply a necessary precondition for mastering the various tasks in everyday life (e.g. the need for using languages other than one's own in the fields of trade, jurisdiction, the church or in book-keeping). Examples are the Hanseatic merchants in the High and Late Middle Ages, the middle and upper classes in Britain after 1066, Venetian bankers or the Fuggers in Augsburg (in southern Germany). They all were (or became) multilingual – but no one would ever have had to emphasize this fact. It was just normal. Therefore there is little evidence to be found in (written) sources which stresses the fact that a certain person was multilingual or that the command of a *lingua franca*, like Latin or any other language for a specific purpose, was mandatory for a certain job. A lack of such linguistic skills would, by contrast, have been worth mentioning.

Mastering two or more languages, however, does not mean that the persons in question were 'perfect' bilinguals who could manage all situations in their lives in any of the languages they knew. Receptive bilingualism, functionally restricted multilingualism or the command of a foreign linguistic variety as a *lingua franca* were absolutely normal. Nobody would ever have expected to know other languages 'perfectly' (whatever that may mean in detail). This expectation seems to be a quite modern idea when discussing issues of bilingualism or multilingualism in general. Diglossia, i.e. the functional distribution between a written H-variety (often a standardized language) and a spoken L-variety or vernacular, functional multilingualism in general, the use of a *lingua franca*, e.g. as a language of instruction or administration, or the command of an academic language was a natural part of everyday life and guaranteed that one could master the various domains of work, trade and religion without greater problems. The main point was to achieve effective communication e.g. at the workplace and not a 'perfect' multilingualism in every respect.

We have to bear in mind these once rather self-evident facts when we deal with aspects or problems of multilingualism in former times.

But the study of multilingualism in history is not only of historical or social interest. It allows us to gain considerable insight into some linguistic phenomena which have still not been completely understood, as it is the case with language change. Which role do language contact and multilingualism play in this field? Can we state that language change is favoured particularly or even exclusively in a situation of contact? And if this should be true, which grammatical fields are mostly subject to change?

In the late 1980s a small group of linguists at the University of Pennsylvania who were eager to reconcile the generative framework with the sociolinguistic methods of Labov tried to show, especially for English, that syntactic change is due to language contact.

According to their strong hypothesis, multilingualism is an innate property of the human being, and linguistic change is due to a competition among different grammars, one of which eventually gets the better of the others (Kroch 1989; Pintzuk 1991). For the subsequent years, this 'competition' hypothesis was defended by only a minority of linguists, until in the last few years various approaches have tried to deal with the topic of language change from a perspective of language contact.

These are, however, rather sporadic enterprises. There have not always been well-defined methods and criteria which would specify in which of the principal fields of grammar one would have to to look for possible effects of language contact. The first problem one encounters in historical linguistics consists of the fact that we can only make generalizations on the basis of the available data, which most of the time are – due to chance – very limited and possibly not representative of the language under investigation. Which language is really meant when we use written material which is not necessarily the reproduction of oral speech? We do not want to enter into the discussion on the relationship between written and spoken language here. It is not rare, however, for the historical linguist to meet the conviction that the effort to draw generalisations and the attempt to be predictive about linguistic change are only chimerical, since a language is only a by-product of a social communicative need (Coseriu 1974:23):

> Die Ratlosigkeit angesichts des Sprachwandels und die Tendenz, ihn als unechtes, durch "äußere Faktoren" hervorgerufenes Phänomen anzusehen, sind im Grunde der Tatsache zuzuschreiben, daß man von der abstrakten – und folglich statischen –, vom Sprechen getrennten und als *etwas Fertiges*, als *ergon* betrachteten Sprache ausgeht, ohne sich wenigstens zu fragen, was die Sprachen sind und wie sie wirklich existieren und was eigentlich ein Wandel in einer Sprache bedeutet. Daher auch die Stellung des Problems des Sprachwandels in Kausalbegriffen, denn die Veränderungen in den von der Intentionalität jedes Subjekts losgelösten "Sachen" werden gerade "Ursachen" zugeschrieben. Die Sprache jedoch gehört nicht zum kausalen, son-

> dern zum finalen Bereich, zu den Erscheinungen, die durch ihre Funktion bestimmt werden.

How can we resolve this paradox? In order to delimit the scientific object a certain grade of abstraction is necessary. De Saussure's distinction between *langue* and *parole* tries to account for this problem. According to de Saussure (1916: 38), change does not take place in the system itself, but in its use: 'tout ce qui est diachronique dans la langue ne l'est que par la parole', since the system itself is invariable. The written records, where 'diacronic change' can be observed, are only a cross-section of single synchronic individual uses and consequently, in this view, diachronic linguistics cannot exist: it is only the linguist who attributes reality to the completed change, since the time span of data to be considered is a subjective choice; in any case, what is registered is the use, not the system. Another problem, recognised by Coseriu (1974), lies in this distinction between system and use. When an innovation begins to spread among a community after having been introduced by a single individuum, it becomes – in de Saussure's view – a fact of the language. It is not clear in de Saussure's theory, however, exactly how a process in the use becomes a process in the system.

At a more abstract level, Chomsky (1986) proposes to distinguish between I(internal)-language and E(external)-language, the latter being the individual and concrete spoken language and the former the abstract system of rules which regulates the use. It is the I-language that is the object of linguistic research, at least in generative terms. But this concept is not unproblematic either, since, seen from the surface, an abstract language might not even seem to exist, as there is such a great amount of variation in the individual uses of the language in question.

It is clear, however, that the only access we have to the I-language goes through the E-language, and the first step to get closer to a more abstract level of explanation is to analyse the data we have for a grammatical phenomenon of rather limited scope, while we restrict ourselves to comparing languages which are historically related in order to keep the variation minimal. The heuristic value is entailed by proposing strong hypotheses that can be rigorously scrutinized on a large empirical basis, as it is the established method in the natural sciences. An example is the question whether phonology might possibly be a part of the grammar where, in a situation of language contact, one should find either reciprocal or monodirectional influence of the involved languages. In this respect, the contribution by Rindler Schjerve claims that the phonology of Italian and Sardinian – in contrast to e.g. the lexicon – does not seem to be subject to mutual influence; instead both languages keep their own phonological systems quite distinct. Different results are produced by Vella's paper, according to which Maltese phonology has been influenced by different languages. Furthermore, one might ask whether syntax is absolutely impermeable in this sense, and which kinds of semantic change are probable, to give only a few general examples.

All of the aspects mentioned above are present in the study of multilingualism. Often we deal with language pairs which consist of related languages (e.g. Spanish and Portuguese, Italian and Sardinian, German and Danish). There are still many contact situations where field work can be done; thus multilinguistic long-term studies provide the ideal case for observing languages in the course of changing in a fashion similar to that of creolistic studies. Sociolinguistic and pragmatic factors play also a significant role which can be relatively well established; this is made obvious by the fact that all of the following essays give an overview of the social (historical) situation in their respective introductions.

The following ten contributions deal with various aspects of multilingualism in Europe and present newly collected data from different perspectives.The aim of this volume is to give a state-of-the-art account of a number of contact situations in Europe – some of them well-known, others less familiar – especially from a historical point of view, without delimiting a particular theoretical framework. As one can see through the reading of these articles, the richness of topics and data which one discovers in the research of multilingualism is surprising. And we hope to have succedeed in re-awakening some curiosity in the reader.

We start our journey through Europe in the north-west, in the British Isles, where we focus on the region's maritime background. Then we turn to northern Europe and have a look at how multilingualism worked in three towns, namely Flensburg on the Danish-German border, Bergen in western Norway, which represented one of the main trading centres of the Hanseatic League, and finally Vyborg, formerly situated in the border region between Finland and Russia. We continue our journey with an excursion to the linguistic history of Sweden and a political-historical visit to Lithuania in the Baltic region. The next stop is central Europe, where we will be concerned with the influence of Latin on written German. In southern Europe, we first visit the Iberian peninsula in order to view the relationship between Portuguese and Spanish from the Middle Ages onwards, before we carry on to Sardinia, where we will, on the background of that island's checquered history, look into the present situation of diglossia between Sardinian and Italian. Last but not least we shall stop at another Mediterranean island, namely Malta, whose unique geohistorical position gives rise to some consideration of the phonology of its native Maltese.

The contents of the contributions

David Trotter's contribution aims at demonstrating that not only business and trade communication in medieval England was multilingual. He assesses Bertil Sandahl's monumental three-volume work on *Sea Terms* (1951–1982), which says that the sea terms employed in medieval England could be classified according to their linguistic origins. In Trotter's view, the situation was a completely different one: shipping was an international activity linking countries and not separating them. Therefore, ship-type terminology was consequently international, i.e. ship-form names were used irrespective of their provenance across all linguistic boundaries. (A precondition for Trotter's new approach was therefore a change in methodology). These and other terms suggest the existence of an international shipping lexis comprising not just medieval England but the North-Sea area as well as the Biscayan and the Mediterranean regions. Therefore he finds it pointless to try to distinguish e.g. between Middle English and Anglo-Norman French items as this is the case in Sandahl's collection. Trotter convincingly shows that all his data on shipping terminology stem from a time when multilingualism constituted the maritime reality and that shipping terms could be embedded in various matrix languages (cf. also Laura Wright's seminal investigation [1996] into the sources of London English based on documents of business writing around the Thames between 1270 and 1500). On top of that, Trotter also succeeds in showing that Anglo-Norman speakers were able to converse with speakers of other French dialects, based on interdialectal communication. This is an important observation for studies in the linguistic history of French, too.

Elin Fredsted investigates some important parts of the linguistic history of the city of Flensburg in northern Germany on the border with Denmark (predominantly) in the 19th century. In this city, not only two national languages, standard [High] German and Danish, meet but also two vernaculars, Low German and Southern Jutish (Sønderjysk), a Danish dialect which was used in oral communication without being connected to national identity or ideology until the middle of the 19th century. After a short introduction to the history of the various languages of the duchy of Schleswig since the Middle Ages, the paper focusses on two case studies based on letter correspondence between citizens of Flensburg and their relatives in Denmark. The analyses concentrate both on phenomena of everyday multilingualism and on contact-induced language usage where four linguistic varieties are involved. Fredsted shows in detail how language usage, stilistics and the involved language varieties on the one hand correlate with social factors and the writers' formal education on the other. This essay represents a fundamental study of the language history of a border region which describes and analyses various aspects of multilingualism in language use in informal written communication. Furthermore, the linguistic form of these private letters comes very close to spoken language use, which we otherwise have no access to. The main focus of this study is not only the linguistic analysis of contact-linguistic features in lexis, morphology and syntax but it also points out the close coherence between the choice of an individual linguistic variety and the gradual nationalization of the ideology of language in the 19th century.

Agnete Nesse's investigation, a summary of her doctoral dissertation, is concerned with an explanation of how a number of specific linguistic features in the urban dialect of Bergen, a famous Hanseatic trading place situated in the west of Norway, have come into being. As opposed to most earlier, more or less descriptive attempts to come to grips with the Low and High German influence on the local dialect of Bergen, Nesse draws insights from recent studies in language contact and language change, principles of interdialectal communication and sociolinguistic theory (cf. especially the discussion of the question whether we are faced here with a form of double diglossia). Her contribution presents a synthesis of modern language contact theories with analyses of partly unpublished sources related to Bergen in the late Middle Ages and especially in early modern times. The main focus lies, as in Fredsted's paper, on grammatical changes, i.e. on the analysis of morphological and syntactic features such as the use of the infinitive markers *te* and *å*, the use of the ending in the past form of 'weak'/regular verbs *-et*, grammatical gender, the use of the periphrastic genitive with *sin* 'his' and finally the use of the definite article *-en* in connection with proper nouns. She succeeds in showing that the grammatical features just mentioned still play an important role in the contemporary dialect of the city of Bergen. Whereas only few Low German loan words are still in use, the respective grammatical features have survived. This study documents how substratum features due to intensive language contact between genetically closely related languages come into being.

The third paper on multiple language contact in northern European cities is by Finlandswede **Marika Tandefelt**, who introduces the reader to the various aspects of multilingualism in the formerly eastern Finnish city of Viborg/Viipuri/Vyborg, now part of Russia, situated to the west of St Petersburg. The main point of this essay, a condensed version of a much larger study, is to demonstrate how normal and how necessary it was to have a sufficient command of the four languages frequently used in this city: Finnish, Swedish, German and Russian. The emphasis of this presentation lies on a general description of the historical and societal conditions for such a multilingual trading place in a border region through the centuries but it also presents detailed lexical analyses of the multilingually sourced vocabulary of the citizens of Vyborg. The author is able to show how multilingualism is connected with certain linguistic domains in everyday life and how this situation was seen by the various administrations over the course of time. The lexical part of this survey presents data from the language use of 65 inhabitants of Vyborg who all are more or less acquainted with these four linguistic varieties. Interestingly enough, the data also show, among others, translinguistic wordings, special calques and even deviant normative language usage with respect to the respective source languages.

Björn Wiemer's contribution gives a thorough account of the research on and an overview of the literature about the complex multilingual situation on the territory of the Grand Duchy of Lithuania (GDL) in the period from the 15th century up to 1939. The region under investigation here is a part of a larger linguistic contact zone, the so-called 'Circum Baltic Area', or CBA. The present paper discusses the historically varied circumstances under which multilingualism (multidialectalism) existed in the south-eastern sector of this area. Thus it is concerned not only with the sociolinguistic complexities of the border regions of Lithuania and Belarus but also has to deal with some neighbouring parts of present-day Latvia and Poland. The author observes a considerable number of isoglosses, to be found in a certain area of the GDL, that seem to cross the "genetic" borders between the involved varieties and thus point to a situation of ancient language contact between East Slavic and East Baltic. Since the paper includes the indirect discussion of phenomena of convergence and interference, one of its main goals can be seen as a caveat to researchers to more carefully sift information on multilinguism/multidialectism from historical, demographic, ethnical or political factors. Wiemer concedes that the sociolinguistic panorama depicted here must remain unsatisfying, as reliable information on language can be only partially obtained or inferred indirectly. Nevertheless, the present contribution succeeds in synthesizing both a number of findings scattered around in the literature at present, and some results of recent linguistic/sociolinguistic research that enable the author to gain considerable insight into the multilinguistic situation in some parts of the GDL.

Lars Wollin's article deals with the situational and social variation in the history of the Swedish language (in Sweden). It sets out to trace linguistic variation and consciousness of linguistic variation. He sketches the diversity basically by choosing one typical example from each century, starting in the 19th century and ending up in the late Middle Ages. The first three examples are quotes from comments of famous grammarians. The data for the 16th century are, however, taken from different versions of Bible translations. The final destination of this journey back to the Middle Ages lies in the 15th century, where Wollin discusses two typical cases of text revisions from the famous monastery of Vadstena, where the nuns of the order of St Birgitta created one of the bases for the foundation of the modern Swedish written language.

The main point of this contribution is an inquiry into stilistic variation and stratification in language as well as a description of the use of linguistic styles (from vulgar to highly educated) as registers for specific communicative purposes described in terms of diglossia. Wollin also demonstrates how internal variational multilingualism is closely connected with social features. One aspect when dealing with the use of various registers in the Reformation Bible is the question whether we are faced with a mix of two standard varieties. The "Revelations" written by members of the monastery of St Birgitta are discussed in close connection with their Latin source texts. Wollin is able to show how different styles (or registers) and stylistic norms were used when rendering these texts into contemporary Swedish. His investigation of religious texts concludes with an analysis of two divergent texts in the Pentateuch paraphrase where one manuscript shows achaic and the other a more modern lexis.

Diana Chirita investigates the thesis put forward by Otto Behaghel that the rules for word order in modern (written) German texts can be traced back to the impact of Latin and its stylistic norms of writing. She discusses in detail all the arguments and counterarguments on the basis of the research available, both for German and Latin word order. Chirita succeeds in showing that Behaghel's thesis is the most probable way of explaining the verb-last rule in German subordinate clauses since the late Middle Ages. The argumentation is based on the fact that Latin-German bilingualism was the default case of the educated middle and upper classes in the 15th and 16th centuries, when Latin was considered the norm in writing, especially in official language use. Special emphasis is laid on the stilistic norms of the chanceries. Chirita concludes with Hammarström (1923) and others that originally subordination was only rudimentarily developed in German and that its increased use was triggered by Latin models. The impact of the chancery language use on other styles was considerably due to the very high prestige of that official norm.

The article contributed by **Ana Maria Martins** deals with syntactic splitting between Portuguese and Spanish after the 16th century. The paper is concerned in particular with clitic placement during and after a period characterized by Spanish-Portuguese diglossia in Portugal's court circles of the 15th and 16th centuries. It shows that after postverbal clitics in (unmarked) main clauses had been gradually and eventually almost completely lost by the 16th century, Portuguese and Spanish developed differently with respect to this clitic order: in Portuguese, verb-clitic order reappears from the 17th century on and becomes the only possible pattern of clitic placement in unmarked main clauses, while Spanish stabilizes the clitic-verb order and loses completely the postverbal clitic placement in main clauses, even in verb-initial sentences. The author claims a correlation to hold between this difference on the one hand and the (apparent) loss of VP ellipsis in Spanish in the 17th century on the other; she ultimately sets out to show how this correlation between seemingly unrelated empirical facts can be explained on an abstract level within the minimalist framework.

After a short historical overview of the bilingualism in 15th- and 16th-century Portugal, the first part of the paper is concerned with the diachronic development of clitic placement in Portuguese and Spanish. The second part presents interesting empirical data concerning VP ellipsis in both languages and shows the correlation between the availability of VP ellipsis and the occurrence of postverbal placement of clitics in Modern Romance languages. In order to account for this correlation in a minimalist framework, the author – adopting Laka's (1990) abstract functional Σ-phrase, the functional head of which encodes polarity features, i.e. affirmation, negation, modality – claims that Σ bears a strong V-feature in Old and Modern Portuguese as well as in Galician, whereas in Modern Spanish and other Modern Romance languages the V-feature of Σ is weak. From this property, together with a number of further assumptions, the variation in Portuguese and Spanish clitic placement can be derived.

In her paper on language change in Sardinian, **Rosita Rindler Schjerve** considers the actual state of this minority language, which has been recognised as an official language of Italy only recently, in order to arrive at a general conclusion about the grade of convergence between Sardinian and Italian. To this purpose, she brings together her previous work on language contact and bilingualism in Sardinia. After a short historical survey of the different populations who occupied the island over the centuries (from Romans to Catalans), the author presents the interesting results of a micro-sociolinguistic investigation which shows the functional distribution of Sardinian and Italian. Sardinian has undergone many structural changes, expecially in the last two decades. In particular the lexicon is subject to relexification from Italian. The syntax seems to be influenced by Italian, too, whereas phonology and morphology are impermeable in this respect. However, although Sardinian is a viable language, which is used even for informal communication among young people, it is only Sardinian that is receptive for Italian influence, while, interestingly enough, the contrary does not happen. The patterns of code-switching observed by Rindler Schjerve are characteristic of unstable diglossia situations where the communicative means within a bi- or multilingual community are enriched by the possibility of conversing in any of the involved languages. Still the non-dominant language is subjected to a strong converging pressure which can lead to complete convergence or even to its disappearance, but also to language change, as it is the case of Sardinian. In its central part the paper presents a sample of new data collected among families in a rural area of Central Sardinia between 1991 and 1995. A first interesting conclusion here is that the patterns of code-switching are not due to chance but are the result of a conscious choice, which can be analysed in terms of social identity on the one hand and from the perspective of discourse analysis (e.g. topic marking, turn-taking etc.) on the other. A third type realised within sentence boundaries constitutes a separate type, which has to do with 'communicative norms of bilingual use'. In order to bolster her claim, the author develops a differentiated typology of code-switching with various subtypes. Another result suggests intrasentential code-switching in particular to be the locus of language change; it further claims that this type of code-switching can be differentiated on the basis of class.

In its overall conclusion, the paper conveys the idea that Sardinian can be considered a language between maintenance and change.

Alexandra Vella's main goal is the comparison of the sound system of Maltese with those of Moroccan (North African) Arabic and Lebanese (Eastern) Arabic on the one hand, and of Palermo Italian on the other. Previous literature – which the author evaluates in her paper – has suggested that Maltese has some features in common with Maghreb Arabic with regard to morphology, while its phonology is more similar to that of Levantine Arabic. Moreover, she also considers to what extent Italian has had an influence on Maltese phonology, as has been suggested by others. Maltese is shown to have a Semitic base with extensive borrowing both from English and from various Romance languages. According to her findings, the categorisation of Maltese as being closer phonologically to the Levantine rather than the Maghrebian dialects seems to be correct. Nevertheless, an influence of Italian can be observed in the phonological system, too. Concentrating on intonation in particular, Vella claims that the similarity of Maltese to Lebanese Arabic is quite clear. More striking, however, is the fact that whereas Palermo Italian behaves differently from both Maltese and Lebanese Arabic in the intonation of late focus questions – being in this respect remarkably similar to Moroccan Arabic –, the three languages show similar intonational patterns in late focus declaratives. This result can be traced back to the unique situation of language contact in the central Mediterranean. The author calls for more work on this kind of effects, which might help to better exemplify "the melting pot effect on languages in contact".

Finally, we would like to thank, first of all, our authors, who participated enthusiastically in this project; it was a great pleasure to collaborate with them. Then we are grateful to the SFB 538 'Mehrsprachigkeit' (Research Center on Multilingualism), University of Hamburg, for their original suggestion to produce a volume of the present kind, and for supporting our efforts. Our special thanks go to the anonymous reviewers of the articles, who did the work but did not receive the honour. We also thank Beata N. Zaide and Martin Hilpert, M.A. for their assistance with copy editing and checking the linguistic forms of the contributions. We hope that this collection of essays will help to intensify the discussion about multilingualism in European language history.

References

Chomsky, N. (1986). *Knowledge of language.* New York: Praeger.

Coseriu, E. (1974). *Synchronie, Diachronie und Geschichte.* München: Fink.

Kroch, A. (1989). Reflexes of grammar in patterns of language change. *Language variation and change, 1*, 199–244.

McKitterick, R. (1989). *The Carolingians and the written word.* Cambridge: CUP.

Pintzuk, S. (1991). Phrase structure in competition: variation and change in Old English word order. Ph.D. Dissertation. University of Pennsylvania.

Wright, L. (1996). *Sources of London English. Medieval Thames vocabulary.* Oxford: Clarendon Press.

Hammarström, E. (1923). *Zur Stellung des Verbums in der deutschen Sprache.* Lund: Håkan Ohlsson.

Sandahl, B. (1951, 1958, 1982). *Middle English Sea Terms.* Uppsala: Almqvist & Wiksell. [vol.1 = Sandahl 1951; vol. 2 = Sandahl 1958; vol. 3 = Sandahl 1982].

Saussure, F. de (1916/1972). *Cours de linguistique générale.* Paris: Payot.

Oceano vox: You never know where a ship comes from

On multilingualism and language-mixing in medieval Britain

David Trotter
University of Wales Aberystwyth

> Par mer vindrent de tutes parz
> E en dromunz e en chalanz
> E en esnekes e en hallos,
> En bouces, en barges par tros,
> Mil niefs en une compaignie.[1]
>
> (Kjellman 1935: vv. 2029–2032)

In these five lines of the late 12th-century Anglo-Norman life of St Edmund are seven ships' names.[2] Not in itself unusual in a passage like this, describing an invasion fleet en route across the North Sea to attack Edmund in his kingdom of East Anglia: but of these seven names, two are from Latin (*barge*, *niefs*), two (*bouce* and *esneke*) are Norse, one is from Greek via Latin (*dromon*), one (*chaland*) from medieval Greek, and the last (*hallos*) derives, depending on whom one believes, from Anglo-Saxon, Middle Dutch, or Arabic.

1. Ships, trade and language

This short passage exemplifies the multilingualism of shipping terminology in medieval England. Ships are by definition international in function. The sea, in the Middle Ages, however frightening travel across it may have been, was not a barrier between people but a means of contact. Ships brought trade; trade meant contact; and contact meant that people had to find ways to communicate with each other, and probably had to learn at least little bits of each others' languages. Renovation and repair work carried out in ports on passing vessels, many of which must have been foreign, similarly implies communication between ships' captains and shipwrights. The radical solution in such circumstances is to invent a pidgin; the less dramatic, and maybe easier, way is to acquire enough of your trading partner's language to be able to deal with him. A case in point is perhaps the wine trade between west Wales and Portugal and Gascony (Lewis 1913; Lloyd Gruffudd 1992): the surviving documentation is in Latin, but that of course means nothing (Clanchy 1993), and it seems on the face of it inconceivable that Gascons and Portuguese learnt Welsh or conversely, that wine-merchants in Carmarthen spoke Gascon and Portuguese, so we are left, by a process of elimination, with communication most plausibly taking place in what was effectively the *lingua franca* of French. From the Portuguese wine trade Anglo-Norman, and then English, acquired the "pots of osey" examined so brilliantly by Freeman (1997). Similarly, the *Port Books* of Southampton record a wide range of merchandise being imported, from geographically dispersed sources, and again, the only likely language available to all parties must have been French in which, at least for 1435–1436, the records are kept (Rothwell 1999). Yet these records of medieval business transactions are by no means as monolingual as they appear at first sight. The Southampton books contain a number of Italianisms (Foster 1963: xiv) and the accounts for 1439–1440, although predominantly in Latin, contain numerous English and French words (Cobb 1961: lxx). Earlier customs accounts from Exeter (Kowaleski 1993) display similar patterns. Ships' names are usually French even in Latin documents, but not invariably, or rather, they cannot invariably be attributed unerringly to French alone: in November 1319, a ship called *le Long Batel* of Southampton docked in Exeter in 1319, as did *le Lang Bot* of Dartmouth (Kowaleski 1993: 178–179). One ship, from Bayonne, which docked in August 1320, is listed as "la nau Sancti Michaelis" (Kowaleski 1993: 177) – which is presumably how the captain or owner described it to the clerk. Whether it is the same ship which is listed as "la neof Seynt Michel" six months later, in March 1321 (Kowaleski 1993: 194), is unclear. Laura Wright has assembled sufficient evidence for it to be no longer in doubt that business and trade communication in medieval England was a multilingual affair. And shipping and ship-building records, also a form of business record, are likewise multilingual. The question, then, is why; what this tells us about the language of shipping and ship-building; and what it can tell us, at another, more social or sociolinguistic level, about the nature of multilingualism in medieval England.[3]

It has been suggested that "More than most other words, sea terms have a tendency to migrate from one country to another, and [...] a technical innovation adopted from abroad was frequently known by the foreign name that went with it" (Sandahl 1982: 3); and as we shall see, this can lead (and did lead) to significant and numerous migrations of words from the Mediterranean to the North Sea and (at an earlier period) vice versa. The same authority comments, of the Middle English period, that (compared to those for Old English) "the sources are more numerous, more detailed, and almost embarrassingly technical. The most striking feature of the Middle English nomenclature as compared with that of the earlier period, is the great percentage of loan words" (Sandahl 1951: 21). These quotations come from Bertil Sandahl's pioneering three-volume study of *Middle English Sea Terms* (published over a thirty-year period), since when (and apart from which) remarkably little serious work has been done on the subject.[4] Perhaps the feeling is that Sandahl has said it all; and, indeed, as far as detailed etymological and chronological commentary on the lexis of shipbuilding in the Middle English period is concerned, he probably has. Yet there are gaps in Sandahl's work, most conspicuously, perhaps, in its firmly philological methodology, in his concern to determine etymology and provenance of words, and to attach them firmly to particular languages (both achieved on the basis of predominantly formal criteria). As the quotation above implies, the underlying assumption is that we can sensibly talk about separate lexicons of (say) French or English in the 15th century; and thus that the notion of "loanword" actually has meaning in texts of this type. This is quite apart from another discussion which could be held about whether (if we accept that these are some form of linguistic import) we are dealing with loanwords or (as may well be the case) with single-lexeme switches generated by code-switching phenomena and rules (Trotter 2003a). So, for example, the article **houne, hune** (Sandahl 1958: 46–47) observes of this word (held to derive, in both OE and OF, from ON) that:

> It is noteworthy that [...] ME. *houne* occurs in AN. documents, and it is clear that the ME. word must have been influenced to some extent by the OF. [i.e.: AN] one. But the spellings with *ou*, and the subsequent development into late ME., ModE. *hound*, do not indicate that *houne* entered the language via Old French. F. *hune* early acquired the sense "top" which is apparently unknown in England (N. 1. states that "OF. *hune* would have given ME. [ü]").

This is all very well if it is the etymology of the word which is at issue (although such categorical statements as these require a faith in the regularity of historical phonetic developments, and in the reliability of manuscript sources and scribes, which I have some difficulty in sharing). But from our point of view, it is more important to note the texts (multilingual) in which the word is used, and perhaps also the existence of the compound: "clavis vocatis *hounenaill*" in a Latin text from c. 1337–1339. A significant feature of the documents which Sandahl prints *in extenso* (and of those of which he prints only in excerpts) is the nature of the language-mixing which occurs in them. In texts whose matrix language is Latin, technical terminology tends to be Anglo-Norman; in texts (rarer) basically in Anglo-Norman, the sea terms tend to be Middle English. This is a curious situation and not an immediately explicable one. If the technical lexis used by mariners and shipwrights was in Anglo-Norman in Latin documents (and the use of the vernacular of record makes sense), why could the same lexis not then be left in Anglo-Norman when the text as a whole was couched in that language? Sandahl draws the following conclusion (Sandahl 1951: 23):

> It is interesting to observe that Middle English sea terms are regularly employed in Anglo-Norman documents instead of French terms. The cases where the particulars of an account are in Anglo-Norman are of special importance in this connection. The inference is that at least from the end of the thirteenth century onwards the language of the sailors was English, and to all appearance had been for a considerable time.

The last hypothesis is not unreasonable and may account for at least some of the Middle English sea terms of ultimately Anglo-Norman provenance which appear to have developed specifically maritime senses only once they had passed into Middle English, such as *garland* or *latchet* (Sandahl 1958: 41, 49). It might be added that (quite apart from the possibility that the data available to us are incomplete) it is by no means unknown for Middle English to preserve attestations of originally Anglo-Norman words which significantly antedate the Anglo-Norman, or for that matter French, evidence (e.g., the Franco-English compound *privschip* in the *Ancrene Wisse* is nearly a century earlier than any known use of *priver*/*privé* in French, insular or continental, cf. Trotter 2003a). But if Sandahl's analysis is correct, it leaves still the problem of the greater number of documents which are in Latin, and where the technical terms are in Anglo-Norman. Are we to accept that such texts would not have been understood by the sailors, being (maybe) only accessible to (and perhaps intended only for) the ships' owners, or the ships' captains? Perhaps this is an indication of the implicit hierarchy of the three languages concerned, which is well documented elsewhere, but in terms of text-types, and register of the documents, there is no sign that the Anglo-Norman documents are aimed at a different readership from those to whom the Latin ones are apparently addressed. And when we look more closely at some of the more problematic etymological conundra in Sandahl's study, it is clear that the underlying distinction (necessary to his argument) between English and Anglo-Norman lexical items is in many cases unsustainable. So, for example, *harpoun*, supposedly a derivative of Germanic *harpa* "clamp, cramp", is attested in a text whose matrix language is Latin but in which it is impossible to decide whether the word *harpoun* itself is English or Anglo-Norman ("in factura de *harpouns* balengere predicte", Sandahl 1951:63). *Loof/luff* is more or less simultaneously attested in the two languages (Sandahl 1958:53–62). *Cule-rudder*, "stern-rudder" (a technological innovation) is explained by Sandahl (1951:116) as a form of Anglo-Norman *cul*, which in this context surfaces only in Latin documents (surely itself suspicious), and is otherwise unknown in Anglo-Norman; but no comment is made on the Dutch source in which the seemingly indistinguishable *kuelroeder* is attested before 1275 (Sandahl 1951:120).

Another study contains a vast quantity of detailed information on the construction of sailing ships from PRO and French sources (Bernard 1968:282–294), much of which is redolent of (and in some cases identical with) Sandahl. Jacques Bernard, in his monumental study of *Navires et gens de mer à Bordeaux*, comments on the phenomenon from a more broadly European perspective:

> Il est bien évident que ces caractéristiques et ce progrès qu'enregistrent la nomenclature et le dénombrement des appareils de la nef anglaise du XIVe et du XVe siècle n'étaient nullement l'apanage de celle-ci, et, sous des termes parfois différents, mais souvent semblables, se manifeste, et quelquefois jusque dans la Méditerranée, si puissamment originale pourtant, l'unité de toute la façade maritime de l'Europe. Ce qui est "tref", "lof", "estay", "raque", "trousse", "penton", "brache", "aussière", "poulie", "gadde", "escoppe", "pucheur", en Normandie, reste "tref" et "lof", ou devient "*stay*", "*rakke*", "*trusse*", "*pendant*" ou "*peyntyng*", "*brassey*", "*haunser*", "*pulley*", "*gate*", "*scope*" et "*spuchour*", en Angleterre, "treu", "estay", "trossa", "polige", en Méditerranée. Dans les "*... acubus pro velo*", qui figurent à l'inventaire d'une nef anglaise, on reconnaît les "*agulles de veles*" d'une nef catalane, et les "especs" du "vindas" normand n'ont pas grand chemin à parcourir pour rejoindre les "*spekes for the wyndas*" du navire anglais, ou même les "*aspes*" du "*guindar*" de la nef catalane, parenté de termes qui traduit la parenté des choses. (Bernard 1968:1, 292–293)

2. Multilingualism and the lexis of shipping

I am increasingly convinced that the perspective adopted by both these authors is in the end wrong. This is not to detract from the very considerable merits of two outstanding scholarly works which contribute massively to our knowledge of the Middle Ages. But it is erroneous to attempt this type of classification of vocabulary into different languages, especially in England, because the distinction itself is not supported by the documentary evidence (indeed, it is undermined by it), and because there is a very strong case for arguing that the separation of these languages at the lexical level, which is really all we are concerned with here, does not correspond to medieval reality. And so, too, not surprisingly perhaps, we find that ship-building documents from this part of France are themselves multilingual: Sandahl cites B.M. Add. 17364, an account (c. 1350) of repairs to galleys and spinaces at Bayonne, with French (or Gascon) words in the Latin matrix language (Sandahl 1982: 22). This fits exactly with the abundant evidence from south-western France generally of language-mixing in non-literary documents of all sorts (Trotter 2003d).

Bernard devotes a substantial section to the terminological difficulties associated with ship-identification in the international port of Bordeaux (Bernard 1968: 1, 237–241). Now Bordeaux is not (despite appearances) as inappropriate a parallel with England as it might look. Especially under the English administration of Gascony (which lasted for very nearly three centuries), the linguistic and sociolinguistic situation in this part of France was not dissimilar to that in England, with Latin, French, Gascon and at least some (though probably very little) Middle English all involved (Baldinger 1960; Trotter 1997, 1998a). There is evidence of specifically maritime terminology moving from England to Gascony in the form of the (apparently) English tax of *quillage*, which was introduced on the Gironde (Trotter 2003e). Moreover, for historical and political reasons, Bordeaux traded extensively with England, as well of course as with the Mediterranean and with the northern cities of the Hanseatic league. So some at least of what Bernard concludes about Bordeaux is likely to have some relevance for England. He points out (for example) that even nowadays, ships (or boats) may be named after the style of rigging, by the shape of the hull, by their function (for example, by the type of fish they are used for catching), or by their place of origin. These are, then, competing, overlapping, and not always consistent taxonomic principles which can and do easily baffle the non-specialist. The problem is no different in medieval sources, and there is no reason to suppose that all medieval scribes were versed in matters nautical any more than (say) modern accountants or journalists are. Nor is the position obviously different in places other than Bordeaux; and it is doubtless exacerbated by an element which Bernard does not mention, namely the less precise nature of much medieval terminology (cf. Rothwell 1962) – together, of course, with the more prosaic difficulties of deciphering and interpreting the textual evidence we have. Thus, for example, it is far from easy always to attribute a specific sense to the most common term for "ship", which may be *nau*, *nef* or *navis*, according to the language used (Bernard 1968: 1, 271). The question, of course, is whether the authors of the texts did indeed have in mind a specific, technical sense at all.

Nonetheless, and perhaps more immediately pertinent to this study, one point which does emerge very clearly from Bernard's survey is that the majority of ship types which can be identified from the Bordeaux records are themselves pre-eminently international. Bordeaux was an international port which traded throughout Europe and ships came from everywhere in the known world. Flemish galleys put in to Southampton and Sandwich (Bernard 1968: 1, 243); whalers (*baleiniers*) were found on the Thames and off the coast of Portugal (Bernard 1968: 1, 247–248); the *flouins* of the Garonne (Bernard 1968: 1, 259) reappear in England, or something going under the same name does (Wright 1996: 142; Rothwell 1984: 171); pinnaces are recorded in English ports from Normandy, Brittany, and Spain, and occasionally from Bordeaux too (Bernard 1968: 1, 265). In other words, ship forms were themselves international. Bordeaux is not unique: the records from Exeter and Southampton both furnish evidence of trade, and thus of visiting ships, from all over western Europe. It follows that there must have been a degree of internationalization of construction technique to permit *"l'unité de toute la façade maritime de l'Europe"*, together with dissemination of the terminology used to describe it, used during the processes of ship-building and repair, and used, presumably, by the sailors themselves.

Before turning in greater details to the implications of this statement both for the interpretation of the textual evidence from medieval England, and for what it may be able to tell us about multilingualism in medieval English shipyards (and beyond), it should be said that multilingualism is far from unique to England even if (certainly as far as the French element is concerned) it is particularly the English documentation which has attracted scholarly attention. As much is implied in Bernard's comments. To be sure, England is a slightly unusual case in that it brings together Germanic and Romance elements; but, outside the world of shipping, even that is not an isolated case. There is copious documentation which shows that the same type of pattern occurred, and was indeed the norm, in Flanders and Lorraine, both areas where Romance and Germanic were in long-standing and productive contact (Coutant 1994; Giry 1877; Mantou 1972; Trotter 2003c). That the evidence is conveniently disregarded in histories of French which aspire to chart the seamless progression from Latin to modern French via monolingual central French (the fictitious "francien") speakers does not make it any the less real. But the Mediterranean offers a similar, copiously documented, and extremely confusing parallel. Clearly, the Mediterranean was not only the source of the major shipbuilding innovations from late Antiquity through to the Renaissance (galleys, carvel construction, non-square sails), but also, inevitably, of much of the terminology too; and much of that terminology is not so much multilingual as (more simply) unlocalizable: it is often impossible to attribute the lexis of maritime affairs with certainty to any of the irresponsibly promiscuous and apparently interchangeable languages used in Mediterranean ports from east to west. The uncertainty faced by anyone (e.g. Trotter 2003b) attempting to determine the source-language (for example) of French nautical terms, which may come from Genoese, Occitan, or north Italian, or all three, either in linear sequence or in more complex fashion, all transmitting a lexis which may be Arabic, Greek, or Turkish, or again, some combination of the three (Minervini 1996, 1998; Vidos 1960, 1965), is very real; and it is mirrored by the similar situation which Hispanists face with regard to ships' names in the Iberian peninsula (Eberenz 1975). It is impossible to study this material without reaching the inescapable confusion that the modern urge to impose order and clarity on this mêlée of forms and languages is about as likely to succeed (and about as safe) as an attempt to determine the precise racial origins of the denizens of Genoa's waterfront on a rowdy Saturday night.

Whilst the overwhelming majority of shipping terms in English are of (broadly) Germanic origin (Norse, Dutch, Anglo-Saxon), some are French, and it is with the English-French contacts that this study will primarily be concerned. The French borrowings are necessarily later than some at least of the Germanic loanwords into Old and Middle English: the Old Norse element, for example, antedates the Norman Conquest. Having said that, the importance of cross-Channel contact before the Conquest should not be underestimated: the existence in French itself of a series of Anglo-Saxon terms, notably for the main points of the compass (north, south, east, west) as well as of the word for "boat" itself (< OE. *bāt* + Latin-Romance diminutive *-ellus*), makes the point. These crucial maritime terms are a striking example of what Sandahl calls "Channel words" (Sandahl 1982: 3), part of the "fairly homogeneous core of terms that were common to the seafaring language of all the Germanic nations", including French in France and in England (ibid.).

Sandahl observes that "The [English] sea terms that go back to French are of a different type. As far as can be ascertained, very few of them of are originally nautical. Apart from a certain number of Old Norse loan words the French nautical vocabulary is largely of Mediterranean origin, but only very few of these southern words have found their way into English." (Sandahl 1951: 23). One such is the isolated survival of *calfater* and *calfatyngge* (the latter a typical A.-F./M.E. hybrid with English suffix appended to French root, cf. Rothwell 2000; Trotter 2003a). It sheds interesting light on the realities of historical, human and thus language contact across the Channel and – in this case – far beyond. *Calfatar* ('to caulk') originates in Arabic *qalfāta* and (in the West) is first attested in Genoa, in Latin, in 1213;[5] transmission to Italy seems to have been via Byzantine Greek rather than directly from Arabic (FEW 19,81b). The transmission of the word into French is variously explicable: the FEW suggests via ports in Provence (FEW 19,81b), Fennis (1995) offers a range of options: "En ce qui concerne le français, *calfater* vient d'une langue méditerranéenne qui est tantôt le génois (textes de Rouen, *Chron. de Savoye*, 1443, 15e s.), tantôt l'italien de Chypre (ca 1320), tantôt l'occitan (1459, 1541, 1547–1550, etc.), tantôt l'italien (ex. litt.)" (Fennis 1995: 455; cf. Fennis 1978: 271–275; Gebhardt 1974: 244). It is perhaps noteworthy that the earliest localized French attestation of any of the related words, in the event the substantive *calfat*, "ouvrier chargé de calfater", is from Rouen in 1296 (Fennis 1995: 451), where the *clos des galées* had been established in the late thirteenth century.[6] Of the Clos des Galées, Vidos observes that it was an ideal locus for transmission of vocabulary: "le lieu de rencontre des constructeurs, armateurs, charpentiers, maîtres de hache, calfats et marins français et méridionaux, surtout génois, de 1294 à 1419" (Vidos 1960: 4). His argument is that bilingual Genovese shipwrights invented an equivalent of their native word in "French".[7] Sandahl comments that the language of the *Compte du Clos des Galées* "has many affinities, especially regarding the technical terms, with that of the AN. and L. accounts kept in England" (Sandahl 1958: 84 N. 2). Amongst other things, the point here is that (despite oft-reiterated but unsupported assertions to the contrary)[8] Anglo-Norman was not cut off from its continental cousin (de Jong 1988, 1996; Möhren 1997; Trotter 1998b, 2003c). The parallels between documents in Rouen and documents in London are (from this perspective) not a surprise: they are, rather, to be expected.

Whether Vidos's hypothesis (and it is no more) is the exact explanation for the transmission of *calfatar* to Rouen (and thus to French) is immaterial: the point (for our purposes) is that a multilingual working environment is the perfect opportunity for words to be passed between languages. Caulking (if that is the sense we are dealing with, rather than the more general and possibly etymologically distinct "waterproofing")[9] is a feature above all of carvel construction (where planks abut rather than overlap); and carvel building is a technique which first developed in the Mediterranean. In the North Sea and English Channel boats and ships appear, traditionally, to have been clinker-built, with carvel construction coming in only in the later Middle Ages, as a result of Mediterranean influence. The indications seem to be that the Anglo-Norman *calfater*[10] and the hybridized *calfatyngge* made their way across the Channel from Rouen. In any case, the word exemplifies language contact at a practical, everyday level, and belies the notion of Anglo-Norman and French existing in isolation from each other.[11]

3. Multilingualism and ships' names: Some specific examples

To return, then, to some of the data in Sandahl's *Middle English Sea Terms*, and in particular, to two aspects of this: firstly, the names for ships and boats (the international nature of which has already been indicated), and secondly, the documentation which he publishes as "text appendices" (Sandahl 1982: 133–165). Sandahl chooses not to deal with the lexis of ship types themselves, which is a pity: many of these (from the point of view adopted here), repay closer investigation. There is an important preliminary study of a number of them (necessarily river-going vessels) in Wright (1996: 138–152). Here I will single out only three, two of whose names appear to be (perhaps inextricably) related. The first of the ship-types is *halop*, encountered in England and in Gascony (Bernard 1968: 1, 298); the second, *hulke* (Bernard 1968: 1, 299), a word also attested in the Baltic and the North Sea. *Halop* (DEAF H 105) is probably ultimately from Arabic; it has a Gascon form *falop* which could be interpreted either as hypercorrection for *halop* (initial *h-* being a stigmatized Gascon feature, with the result that scribes sometimes inadvertently change etymological *h-* to *f-*, Baldinger 1958) or as evidence of the greater proximity of this form to the supposed etymon Arabic *falūwa* (FEW 19,42b; cf. Arveiller 1974: 452–455; Baldinger 1998: 398). The word is quite well documented in Gascony but there is (DEAF) only one known Old French attestation. What is harder to explain is how this word (essentially localized in Gascony and apparently referring to a version of a *felucca*, a three-masted, lateen-rigged light sailing ship from the Mediterranean) should have made its way into the Anglo-Norman life of St Edmund (of Abingdon). It is, however, attested in British medieval Latin (DMLBS 246c **calupus**). But the Latin sources from Britain are potentially misleading: two come from the Gascon Rolls, and the third, from the Close Rolls, is a document (composed at Jedburgh) which discusses reparations payable to the vassals of Didacus Lupi de Haro, lord of Biscay, for "goods and wares" taken in their *calepo*, (mis?)translated by the *Calendar of Close Rolls* as "sloop" (CCR 1296–1302: 220). It is possible that the word for the ship was simply the one used by the complaining Biscayans. In other words, all the supposedly British Latin attestations are effectively to do with Gascony or north-western Spain. They do not really substantiate the case for reading the Anglo-Norman *hallos* as a form of the (mainly Gascon) *halop* / *falop*.[12] To an already complex picture needs (perhaps) to be added *chaloupe* / *shallo(o)p* / *sloop*, attested respectively in 1699, 1578 and 1629 in English. English *sloop* appears to come from Dutch *sloep* (not attested before the sixteenth century) but that word is probably itself from French *chaloupe* (TLF 5,470b and DEAF H105); the less plausible case for a derivation from **skala* via OF *eschalope*, "nut-shell" (FEW 17,84a and Fennis 1995: 524) is semantically and chronologically problematic (why would OF *eschalope* < **skala* disappear from the documentary sources and resurface in Brittany and Gascony in the 16th century with a hitherto unattested sense?). Bernard (1968: 351) argues that *chaloupe* is a relatively non-specific term in Gascony and along the western French seaboard, raising the suspicion that we are dealing here with several types of ship (strictly speaking, distinguishable to the specialist, but with features in common which allow the non-specialist to group them all together), as well as a number of etymologically distinct words whose form converges to generate further confusion. One such added confusion is the possibility (both semantically and formally) that the (thus far) sole known OF attestation is in fact a form of *hulk*; the *Anglo-Norman Dictionary* glosses it, following Kjellman's own interpretation, as "transport vessel (?)" (AND 349a). It appears (as we saw at the beginning of this essay) in the midst of a list of ships: "Par mer vindrent de tutes parz E en dromunz e en chalanz E en esnekes e en hallos, En bouces, en barges par tros, Mil niefs en une compaignie" (EdmK 2031). Possibly the last line indicates that these could all be subsumed under the generic and thus unhelpful term "niefs". *Dromunz* (from Greek via Latin: FEW 3, 163a) are fast sailing-ships, *chalanz* are often smaller, possibly flat-bottomed vessels (from medieval Greek: FEW 2^1, 633b); an *esneke* (the word is ON: FEW 17, 159a) is a "schnelles Raubschiff" as the FEW defines it; *bouces* (ON again: FEW 1, 667a and 15^2, 47b) are big, broad ships; *barges* (< Latin *barca*, FEW 1, 251a) can be either sea-going vessels or ferry-boats (Wright 1996: 138). In short, the context is not conclusive: what we have here is a list of different ships, the intention of which is to build up a picture of an impressive and fearsome fleet, possibly made more so by the diverse origins of the vessels in which the enemy embarks. What we can say without fear of contradiction is that these five lines reveal at once the multilingual nature of Anglo-Norman (and so, English) shipping vocabulary: Norse, Arabic, Greek, Latin, Romance "en une compaignie". Of greater interest perhaps is a source seemingly unknown to the DEAF, namely the Exeter customs books referred to above, whose editor hints at (but does not resolve) the issue of identification of the *halop* (Kowaleski 1993: 18 N. 97). The attestations in these documents are as follows (page-references are to Kowaleski 1993): 1288 "*halop* de Seynt Servan" [Saint-Servan, Landes] (48); 1288 "la *halop* de seynt Nicholas" (48); 1298 "le *halop* de Sancto Nicholao" (57); 1299 "le *halop* Seint Nicholas" from Le Vivier [Ille-et-Villaine] (59); 1313 "le *holhop* Seint Nicholas" (68); 1304 "la *holhop* Seint Pere" of "Moun Doun" [Mont-Dol, Brittany?] (82); 1304 "la *hol-hop* Seint Nicholas" of Le Vivier (84), and again in 1305 (92, 98) and 1306 (107); 1310/1311 "la *holoc* de St Lowis" [Le Vivier?] (120); 1311 "la *holhop* de St Lowys" (121); 1312/1313 "la *holhop* Seint Lowys" of Le Vivier (126); 1313 "le *holhop* Seynt Nicholas" (128); 1318 "le *hollok* Seynt Sampson" [Guernsey?] (163, 169); 1319 "le *hollow* Seynt Sampson" (172); 1321 "le *holoc* Seynt Johan" of Guernsey (199); 1321 "le *hollouw*" of Seynt Malloc [St Malo] (200). All these are patently sea-going cargo ships. Their provenance is varied: Brittany, the west coast of France, Guernsey. The form of the word sometimes but not always suggests a final *-c* or *-k*, but St Malo comes out as "Seynt Malloc"; other instances of it are more compatible with the form in *-op*. What appear to be the same ships can be recorded using either form ("la *holoc* de St Lowis" in 1310/1311, a page later "la *holhop* de St Lowys" in 1311). In theory, the orthographic and phonetic overlap between *halop/haloc/hulk(e)* should be relatively easily resolved on the semantic level since the *hulk(e)* was a much larger vessel altogether. In practice, it is not so simple. The MED also has a number of forms listed under **hulk** (H 1023b) which seem similar to those in the Exeter accounts: "le Holoc" 1227; "Hulloc" 1227; "le Hulluc Sancte Marie de Barbefle" 1230. This word, which DEAF derives from MDu. *hulke*, is also widespread with forms (probably derived from the French word) in Italian, Gascon, Catalan, and Spanish (DEAF H 712). In Anglo-Norman, Middle English, and British medieval Latin, it has forms which (if they are genuinely distinct from those of *halop*, above) are certainly easily confused with them: A-N *holoc, hollok*. The (apparently ME?) form *hulk, hulke* is attested in Anglo-Norman documents (Wright 1996: 145). DMLBS **1 hulcus** (1182a), like the MED, suggests the word is originally Anglo-Saxon: this implies that its emergence in Anglo-Norman and British Latin is more plausibly from Anglo-Saxon than from Dutch. OED (**hulk**^{2}) states rather unhelpfully that it is "a word of early diffusion among the maritime peoples of Western Europe, of uncertain origin". Finally, as a last twist to an already complicated story, the earliest Anglo-Saxon attestation of *hulc* is in Aelfric's glossary, where it glosses (Classical Latin) *liburna*, translated by the DMLBS (1604a) as "light sailing-vessel, ship".

Again, in other words, there is evidence (not easily disentangled) of the international nature of shipping lexis and of the extent to which medieval England was part of a much wider maritime world, recipient as well as provider of terminology, and a trading-post between Germanic and Romance. The third ship (or boat) name is *hakebot*. As the word suggests, this too is originally Dutch (< *hoecboot*), and (unlike *hulk*) rare (conceivably because of the potential for confusion with *hake* (the fish), of unknown etymology, DEAF H 93, OED H 27, DMLBS 1131b *acca, haka*). Nevertheless, it is used in both Latin and Anglo-Norman documents, although (with one exception, Wright 1996: 144) always apparently in a Dutch and Flemish context – neither the boat nor the word, it seems, have ever been properly naturalized into English.

Finally, let us turn to the documents printed by Sandahl as a series of "text appendices" (Sandahl 1982: 133–165). These texts, and the hundreds of excerpts printed throughout the three volumes of his study, are a concrete demonstration of the reality of multilingualism at the level of records. I have already suggested above that in them, distinguishing between Middle English and Anglo-Norman words is often a hopeless (and for that matter, pointless) task. We can usually identify a matrix language, mainly Latin, but quite often Anglo-Norman – although why one language is chosen over the other is not always obvious. Possibly (if mundanely) it simply had to do with the competence or predilections of an individual scribe. Irrespective of the matrix language, though (and of course it would later become English), the documents are all characterized by consistent and persistent language-mixing. Naturally, this affects almost exclusively nouns, the element most commonly involved in code-switching (or borrowing). Most striking of these is Sandahl's Appendix 3 (Sandahl 1982: 143). He observes (Sandahl 1982: 134) that the main interest of this document is that its sea terms are in Anglo-Norman, and contrasts it with Appendix 4 (Sandahl 1982: 144–148) which follows the normal practice (for Anglo-Norman documents) of giving sea terms in English. But this is (in both cases) a simplification of what is in reality a more complex situation and one which raises once more the question of how (and indeed whether) identifications of discrete languages can be made in the case of lexical items in texts of this type. Appendix 3 (from 1342–1343) thus contains the following words which appear on the face of it to be English: *bowspret*; *bowlyn*; *rak*; *stetynges*; *boys*; *worp'* [?]; *tailhoke* (glossing "aliud Crouk ferr'"); *gordynge*; *bedowe* (glossing "crouk ferr"' again); *tripode*. It also (even more interestingly) has a number of words where it is extremely difficult to say which language they are in (not least because of the abbreviation and suspension system used). These include: *bonet*; *trusses*; *polys*; *mast*; *harpeners*; *spoung'*. Finally, there is a hybrid compound of the type identified by Rothwell (2000): *boiscordes* ("buoy-ropes"). These are nearly all (to quote Sandahl) "highly technical terms in actual, competent, connective use" (Sandahl 1982: 133); and the scribe moves from one language to another with ease, fluency, and no sign whatever of any concern that his text might not be understood. In Appendix 4 (from 1347–1359), sea terms are supposedly in English. So, for example, there are listed "xxxij. milers de menue spykyng rondnayl" (Sandahl 1982: 145) but the text continues immediately in Anglo-Norman: "... et autres menues clowes de ffer". These various nails are "pur tylater hurdiser halborder et autres diverses overaignes". The first two operations are authentically "French" (Trotter 2001); the third is again a hybrid, an English noun morphologized into an Anglo-Norman verb. Nonetheless, overall, the document does show a high level of anglicization in lexis, and the majority of the technical terms are indeed English, not Anglo-Norman; but the question must remain, of the extent to which such vocabulary, in a text of this type, would really have been perceived as being "borrowed" from English, as opposed (quite simply) to being the appropriate technical lexis for discussing such matters. There is again no sign of the scribe suspecting that his choice of lexis might create problems; and we can only assume that in practice it did not. Medieval shipwrights and those concerned with the commercial operations associated with shipping were clearly accustomed to dealing with words in all three of the languages of medieval England. Just as medieval shipwrights and port officials were accustomed to encountering (and working with, and on) ships from all over Europe, so they must have been used to terminology drawn from all over the known world. *Les mots et les choses*, as always, need to be looked at together.

Notes

1. 'By sea they came from all parts / And in sailing-ships and in boats / In swift skiffs and in transport ships / In busses, in barges in droves / A thousand ships in one company.'

2. I am very grateful to Professor William Rothwell for confirming the context of the passage, and for supplying me with the variant reading from the Manchester (Rylands) MS. of the text, which reads as follows: "Par mer vindrent de tutes parz / En dromunz e en canarz / E en sneckes e en hallos, / En buces, en barges e par tros ..." (Manchester, John Rylands

Univ. Lib., Fr. 142, f.22v). The word *canarz* (here, a type of ship, not a duck …) is ON: see AND 374b **kenard**, FEW 16,336b **knarri**.

3. This study will be largely concerned with England *stricto sensu*, partly for reasons of space, partly because of the author's incompetence in the languages of the rest of medieval Britain. However, there is no reason to suppose that the position would be fundamentally different elsewhere in Britain. Welsh, certainly, appears to have numerous loanwords for shipping terms; whether from Middle English or Anglo-French is, as usual, uncertain.

4. Dr Lisa Jefferson, at the time employed as an HRB-funded Research Assistant on the *Anglo-Norman Dictionary* project (on which see now www.anglo-norman.net), embarked in 1997/1998 on an investigation of the subject, initially based on Sandahl, but with the ultimate aim of revisiting the PRO documents which he excerpts. This work was not, however, completed and no use has been made of it in the present study.

5. GdfC 8, 412b; FEW 19, 80b; BattAl 1, 666a; Battaglia 2, 509b; MltW 2, 49 ***calafates**; DMLBS 244a **calfatare** (with a curious reference to OF *chaufeter*, unrecorded in Gdf or TL, though cf. **chaufete** Gdf 2, 97b, related to heating not caulking). [Abbreviations for dictionaries are decoded in the references.]

6. See Chazelas (1977) and Bréard (1893).

7. Wansbrough (1996: 165) identifies the same phenomenon in the (rather earlier) Ottoman chancelleries: "The nautical lexicon exhibits of course a borrowed technology whose agents were (mostly) identifiable Greek and Italian mariners/engineers recruited to Ottoman service […]. The jargon facilitated naval projects, whether ship-building or warfare".

8. For example: Dor (1994: 65, 71). This is an important point: the process is two-way. Not only was Anglo-Norman not cut off from the Continent; Continental French also continued to have contact with Anglo-Norman. Histories of French need also to embrace Anglo-Norman.

9. Cf. Fennis (1995: 455), etymological notes on **calfater**, indicating that possible candidates are Arabic *qilf* "bark", *qafr* "asphalt", *kufr* "pitch". The last two in particular would plausibly generate the same form in Latin or Romance and the first is not necessarily (given the extraordinary transmogrifications of Arabic words into unrecognizable Romance and Latin reflexes) distinguishable. Whether (once the Arabic etyma had filtered through to Romance) the distinction supposedly maintained in the original Arabic remains watertight (and for that matter, whether it is recoverable from the textual evidence) is a moot point. Finally, most commentators refer also to the possibility of contamination (no doubt facilitated by the practice of heating up the pitch used for caulking) with CALEFACERE.

10. *Calfater* is cited by Sandahl (1951: 23) and Sandahl (1982: 5) as one of half a dozen "Mediterranean words" in English nautical terminology. It appears also in London in documents concerning the Thames (Wright 1996: 162).

11. For this word, see Rothwell (1998: 163).

12. Unfortunately, the variant MS has the same form of the word. See N. 1, above.

References

AND = Rothwell, W. et al. (Eds.). (1977–1992). *Anglo-Norman Dictionary*. London: Modern Humanities Research Association.

Arveiller, R. (1974). Addenda au FEW XIX/1 (abar–qubba): 5e article. *Zeitschrift für romanische Philologie, 90*, 449–482.

Baldinger, K. (1958). Die hyperkorrekten Formen als Konsequenz der Scripta im Altgaskognischen. In H. Weinrich (Ed.), *Romanica (Festschrift für Gerhard Rohlfs)* (pp. 57–75). Halle/S.: Max Niemeyer.

Baldinger, K. (1960). Lexikalische Auswirkungen der englischen Herrschaft in Südwestfrankreich (1152–1453). In W. Iser (Ed.), *Britannica. Festschrift für Hermann M. Flasdieck* (pp. 11–50). Heidelberg: Carl Winter.

Baldinger, K. (1998). *Etymologien: Untersuchungen zu FEW 21–23. Band 2 zu FEW* 22^1, 22^2 *und 23* [Beiheft zur *Zeitschrift für romanische Philologie*]. Tübingen: Max Niemeyer.

Battaglia = Battaglia, S. et al. (1961). *Grande dizionario della lingua italiana*. Turin: Unione tipografico.

BattAl = Battisti, C., & Alessio, G. (1950–1957). *Dizionario etimologico italiano*. Florence: Barbèra.

Bernard, J. (1968). *Navires et gens de mer à Bordeaux (vers 1400 – vers 1550)* [Ecole Pratique des Hautes Etudes – VIe section: Centre de recherches historiques. Ports – Routes – Trafics XXIII]. Paris: S.E.V.P.E.N.

Bréard, C. (1893). *Le Compte du Clos des Galées de Rouen, 1382–1384*. Rouen: Société de l'Histoire de Normandie.

CCR 1296–1302 = *Calendar of Close Rolls preserved in the Public Record Office, of the reign of Edward I, vol. IV (A.D. 1296–1302)*. London: HMSO (1906).

Chazelas, A. (1977). *Documents relatifs au clos des galées de Rouen et aux armées de mer du Roi de France de 1293 à 1418* [Collection de documents inédits sur l'histoire de la France, Section de philologie et d'histoire jusqu'à 1610, 11]. Paris: Bibliothèque Nationale.

Clanchy, M. (1993). *From Memory to Written Record: England 1066–1307*. Oxford: Blackwell.

Cobb, H. S. (Ed.) (1961). *The Local Port Book of Southampton for 1439–1440*. Southampton: University Press.

Coutant, Y. (1994). *Middeleeuwse molentermen in het graafschap Vlaanderen. Terminologie du moulin médiéval dans le comté de Flandre*. Tongeren and Liège: George Michiels.

DEAF = Baldinger, K. (1971–). *Dictionnaire étymologique de l'ancien français*. Tübingen and Laval: Max Niemeyer and Presses de l'Université Laval.

de Jong, T. (1988). L'anglo-normand du 13e siècle. In P. van Reenen & K. van Reenen-Stein (Eds.), *Distributions spatiales et temporelles, constellations des manuscrits. Etudes de variation linguistique offertes à Anthonij Dees à l'occasion de son 60me anniversaire* (pp. 103–112). Amsterdam: John Benjamins.

de Jong, T. (1996). Anglo-French in the 13th and 14th Centuries: Continental or insular dialect? In H. Frede Nielsen & L. Schøsler (Eds.), *The Origins and Development of Emigrant Languages. Proceedings from the Second Rasmus Rask Colloquium, Odense University, November 1994* (pp. 55–70). Odense: Odense University Press.

DMLBS = Latham, R. E., Howlett, D. R. et al. (1975–). *Dictionary of Medieval Latin from British Sources*. Oxford: British Academy.

Dor, J. (1994). Langues française et anglaise, et multilinguisme à l'époque d'Henri II Plantagenêt. *Cahiers de civilisation médiévale, 37*, 61–72.

Eberenz, R. (1975). *Schiffe an den Küsten der Pyrenäenhalbinsel: eine kulturgeschichtliche Untersuchung zur Schiffstypologie und -terminologie in den iberoromanischen Sprachen bis 1600.* Berne and Frankfurt/M.: H. Lang and P. Lang.

Fennis, J. (1978). *La Stolonomie et son vocabulaire maritime marseillais. Edition critique d'un manuscrit du XVIe siècle et étude historique, philologique et étymologique des termes de marine levantins.* Amsterdam: John Benjamins.

Fennis, J. (1995). *Trésor du langage des galères.* Tübingen: Max Niemeyer.

FEW = Wartburg, W. von (1922–). *Französisches etymologisches Wörterbuch*, Bonn, Leipzig and Basel: Zbinden.

Foster, B. (Ed.). (1963). *The Local Port Book of Southampton for 1435–36.* Southampton: University Press.

Frahm, W. (1914). *Das Meer und die Seefahrt in der altfranzösischen Literatur.* Göttingen, Dissertation.

Freeman, M. J. (1997). 'Pots of osey': Portuguese wine in late medieval England and its place of origin. In St. Gregory & D. A. Trotter (Eds.), *De mot en mot: Aspects of medieval linguistics. Essays in honour of William Rothwell* (pp. 17–36). Cardiff: University of Wales Press.

Friel, I. (1995). *The good ship: ships, shipbuilding and technology in England 1200–1520.* London: British Museum Press.

Gdf, GdfC = Godefroy, F. (1880–1902). *Dictionnaire de l'ancienne langue française et de tous ses dialectes du IXe au XVIe siècle.* Paris: Vieweg.

Giry, A. (1877). *Histoire de la ville de Saint-Omer et de ses institutions jusqu'au XIVe siècle.* Paris: Vieweg.

Kjellman, H. (1935). *La Vie seint Edmund le Rei, poème anglo-normand du XIIe siècle.* Gothenburg: Kungl. Vetenskaps- och Vitterhets-Samhälles Handlingar.

Kowaleski, M. (1993). *The Local Customs Accounts of the Port of Exeter 1266–1321* [Devon and Cornwall Record Society, N.S. 36]. Exeter: Wheatons.

Lewis, E. A. (1913). A Contribution to the Commercial History of Mediaeval Wales. *Y Cymmrodor, 24*, 86–188.

Lloyd Gruffydd, K. (1992). Wales's Maritime Trade in Wine during the Later Middle Ages. *Cymru a'r Môr (Maritime Wales) 15*, 7–42.

Mantou, R. (1972). *Actes originaux rédigés en français dans la partie flamingante du comté de Flandre (1250–1350). Etude linguistique.* Liège: George Michiels.

MED = Kurath, H. et al. (1956–). *Middle English Dictionary.* Ann Arbor, MI, University of Michigan.

Minervini, L. (1996). La lingua franca mediterranea. Plurilinguismo, mistilinguismo, pidginizzazione sulle coste del Mediterraneo fra tardo medioevo e prima età moderna. *Medioevo Romanzo, 20*, 231–301.

Minervini, L. (1998). Il mare come mezzo di diffusione linguistica: la circolazione in area italiana della voce catalana *aiòs*. *Zeitschrift für romanische Philologie, 114*, 599–605.

MltW = Prinz, O. et al. (Ed.). (1959–). *Mittellateinisches Wörterbuch bis zum ausgehenden 13. Jahrhundert.* Munich: Beck.

Möhren, F. (1997). Unité et diversité du champ sémiasiologique – l'exemple de l'*Anglo-Norman Dictionary*. In St. Gregory & D. A. Trotter (Eds.), *De mot en mot: Aspects of medieval linguistics. Essays in honour of William Rothwell* (pp. 127–146). Cardiff: University of Wales Press.

Rothwell, W. (1962). Medieval French and modern semantics. *Modern Language Review, 57*, 25–30.

Rothwell, W. (1984). Glimpses into our ignorance of the Anglo-Norman lexis. In I. Short (Ed.), *Medieval Textual Studies in Honour of T. B. W. Reid* (pp. 167–179). London: Anglo-Norman Text Society.

Rothwell, W. (1998). Arrivals and Departures: the Adoption of French Terminology into Middle English. *English Studies, 79*, 144–165.

Rothwell, W. (1999). Sugar and Spice and All Things Nice: From Oriental Bazar to English Cloister in Anglo-French. *Modern Language Review, 94*, 647–659.

Rothwell, W. (2000). Aspects of lexical and morphosyntactical mixing in the languages of medieval England. In D. A. Trotter (Ed.), *Multilingualism in Later Medieval Britain* (pp. 213–232). Cambridge: D. S. Brewer.

Sandahl, B. (1951, 1958, 1982). *Middle English Sea Terms*. Uppsala: Almqvist & Wiksell [vol. 1 = Sandahl 1951; vol. 2 = Sandahl 1958; vol. 3 = Sandahl 1982].

TL = Tobler, A. & Lommatzsch, E. et al. (1925–2002). *Altfranzösisches Wörterbuch*. Berlin and Wiesbaden: Steiner.

TLF = Imbs, P. et al. (1971–1994). *Trésor de la langue française*. Paris: CNRS.

Trotter, D. A. (1997). *Mossenhor, fet metra aquesta letra en bon francés*: Anglo-French in Gascony. In St. Gregory & D. A. Trotter (Eds.), *De mot en mot: Aspects of medieval linguistics. Essays in honour of William Rothwell* (pp. 199–222). Cardiff: University of Wales Press.

Trotter, D. A. (1998a). Some lexical gleanings from Anglo-French Gascony. *Zeitschrift für romanische Philologie, 114*, 53–72.

Trotter, D. A. (1998b). Les néologismes de l'anglo-français et le *FEW*. *Le Moyen Français, 39–41*, 577–636.

Trotter, D. A. (Ed.). (2000). *Multilingualism in Later Medieval Britain*. Cambridge: D.S. Brewer.

Trotter, D. A. (2001). *Le clou tillart*: régionalisme normanno-picard en ancien français? *Revue de Linguistique romane, 65*, 369–380.

Trotter, D. A. (2003a). The Anglo-French lexis of the *Ancrene Wisse*: A re-evaluation. In Y. Wada (Ed.), *A Companion to 'Ancrene Wisse'*. Cambridge: Boydell & Brewer (forthcoming).

Trotter, D. A. (2003b). Contacts linguistiques à l'intérieur de la Romania: Langues romanes et français/occitan. In G. Ernst et al. (Eds.), *Manuel de l'histoire des langues romanes (HSK)*. Berlin: de Gruyter (forthcoming).

Trotter, D. A. (2003c). Not as eccentric as it looks: Anglo-French and French French, *Forum for Modern Language Studies, 40* (forthcoming).

Trotter, D. A. (2003d). *Si le français n'y peut aller*: Villers-Cotterêts and mixed-language documents from the Pyrenees. In D. J. Cowling (Ed.), *Conceptions of Europe in Renaissance France: a Festschrift for Keith Cameron*. Exeter: Exeter University Press (forthcoming).

Trotter, D. A. (2003e). Langues en contact en Gascogne médiévale. In F. Campos (Ed.), *Actas del XXIII Congreso Internacional de Lingüística y Filología Románica, Salamanca, 2001.* Tübingen: Max Niemeyer (forthcoming).

Vidos, B. E. (1939). *Storia delle parole marinaresche italiane passate in francese. Contributo storico-linguistico all'espansione della lingua nautica italiana.* Florence: L. S. Olschki.

Vidos, B. E. (1960). Le bilinguisme et le mécanisme de l'emprunt. *Revue de Linguistique romane, 24,* 1–19 [reprinted Vidos 1965: 295–310].

Vidos, B. E. (1965). *Prestito, espansione e migrazione dei termini tecnici nelle lingue romanze e non romanze. Problemi, metodo e risultati.* Florence: L. S. Olschki.

Wansbrough, J. E. (1996). *Lingua Franca in the Mediterranean.* Richmond: Curzon Press.

Wright, L. (1996). *Sources of London English: Medieval Thames Vocabulary.* Oxford: Clarendon Press.

Wright, L. (1997). The records of Hanseatic merchants: Ignorant, sleepy or degenerate? *Multilingua, 16,* 339–350.

Wright, L. (2002). Code-intermediate phenomena in medieval mixed-language business texts. *Language Sciences, 24,* 471–489.

Language contact and bilingualism in Flensburg in the middle of the 19th century

Elin Fredsted
University of Flensburg, Department of Danish Language and Literature

1. Introduction

The region known from the 14th until the early 20th century as the Duchy of Schleswig is situated between Holstein in the south and Jutland in the north. For centuries it has been a region of transmission and language contact between the Saxonians in the south, the Jutish people in the north and the Friseans in the west. The city of Flensburg is situated in the centre of the Duchy of Schleswig, from 1920, however, directly on the border between the two nation-states Denmark and Germany. Flensburg is linguistically interesting because of (a) a longitudinal language contact situation between several varieties of Germanic languages, (b) two language turnovers during the last 700 years, (c) long periods of medial diglossia, (d) a multitude of language convergence phenomena and (e) societal and individual bi- and multilingualism.

2. The linguistic situation of Flensburg from the Middle Ages until the 19th century

Taking a very broad survey of the linguistic situation in Flensburg, the following languages were represented in the course of the centuries from about 1200 until 1800: South Jutish (oral and written), Latin (written), Low German (written and oral varieties), High German (written and oral), Standard Danish (written) and possibly also Frisean (oral).

The Danish dialect South Jutish seems to have been the dominating language in the 13th and 14th centuries. Dating from about 1300 we have some very important and famous manuscripts written in a South Jutish variety of Medieval Danish: (1) The charter of the city of Flensburg (Flensborgs Stadsret) from 1284 – originally written in Latin but ca. 1300 translated into South Jutish in order to be read aloud once a year to the citizens. (2) From the same period we have a manuscript of the so-called Jyske Lov ['Jutish Law'] issued in the year 1241 by the Danish king Valdemar. The manuscript of Flensburg dates also from about 1300 and is one of the oldest complete versions of this famous legal text written in a distinctly South Jutish variety of Medieval Danish. (3) The manuscript of the "Sct. Knuds Gilde Skraa" ['The charter of the Sct Knuds Guild'] is about one hundred years younger. This manuscript is a written text version of a much older (but now lost) text.

Apart from these very spectacular legal manuscripts most of the administrative texts of the early Middle Ages are written in Latin. So, until the middle of the14th century, we find a stable situation of medial diglossia with South Jutish as dominating vernacular and Medieval Latin as the dominating written language of the administration and the church.

This linguistic situation changes, however, towards the end of the 14th century: As a consequence of the dominating role of the merchant- and town-union of the Hansa in the region of the Baltic Sea and of immigration of trade- and craftsmen from the south (especially from Westphalia) medieval Low German expands to the north rapidly and becomes the language of trade, craft and administration in the larger towns of the Duchy of Schleswig, including Flensburg. In its written form it is oriented to the administrative language of the leading Hansatown Lübeck, in its oral form, however, it is said to contain many remnants of South Jutish. So, at the beginning of the 15th century, you find the Lübeck variety of Low German as written standard, South Jutish among the lower classes and Low German among the higher classes as oral varieties (Schütt 1921). The social advancement made Lower German the official, useful and prestigeous cultural language of both the local and the immigrated upper- and middle-class citizens, whereas the South Jutish city language became a vernacular only spoken by the common people (cf. Bock 1952).

That Low German took over so rapidly from Latin as the dominating administrative language is also due to the fact that the German Chancellery in Copenhagen started to use the language of the Hanseatic chancellery in its communication with the town administration of Flensburg towards the end of the 14th century (Schütt 1921:63). So Low German substituted Latin as the medium of written communication between the central administration in Copenhagen and the local administration of Flensburg. Only few political or private documents of the 15th century are written in Danish. Low German is absolutely dominating in council documents, charters of the guilds, official correspondence and the correspondence concerning the trade of the city (e.g. 12 council documents from the 15th century, see Schütt 1921). The leading position of Low German is manifested in the translations of the charter of the city into Low German in 1432 and 1492. Also during the reign of the Danish King-Dukes Christian I (after 1460) and Hans (1481–1513) the German Chancellery in Copenhagen used only Low German in its correspondence with the town administration of Flensburg. An exception is the short reign of King Christian II (1513–21). During the years 1517–1521 the German Chancellery used Danish in written communication. The reason was political: Christian II allied with the peasants and the citizens against the gentry and the Hansa, and therefore he deliberately used the language of the common people. The spoken variety of Low German in Flensburg showed convergent forms with South Jutish. In his dissertation from 1933 Bock designates the language variety of this region in general as "Low German on Danish substratum" (better: South Jutish substratum, Bock 1933). Bock shows convergences in pronunciation, vocabulary and syntactic constructions. The oral bilingual character of the city led to mutual convergences between these two closely related varieties of Germanic languages. Although the town administration and the educated upper classes wrote and spoke a 'pure' Low German, the Low German vernacular took over features of the 'defeated' South Jutish language and was 'infected' with the so-called Jutish disease ("die jütische Erbkrankheit", Sach 1899).

For the same reasons the Danish language of Flensburg was of low esteem: In the well-known foreword to his translation of David's Psalms (1531), the Danish humanist Christiern Pedersen warns against the, as he claims, unintelligible translation from Flensburg, in which Danish and German are mixed. Also the philologist Ole Borch writes in his dissertation from 1675 "Nostri Flensburgenses inter Danicam & Germanicam lingvam ambicunt, neutri propemodum similes, qvia utriqve. Qvod & ad omnia Nationum diversarum confinia solenne" (Pontoppidan 1745: 34).[1] The reasons for these negative judgements could be (1) that – then as today – people from east Denmark (Christiern Pedersen was born in Helsingør) had difficulties in understanding South Jutish which differs considerably from the dialects on the Danish islands, and (2) that the town dialect of Flensburg actually had been heavily influenced by Low (and later High) German. Even nowadays there exists a large common vocabulary of South Jutish and Low German (Fredsted 2002a).

But already from about 1540 the position of Low German as a prestigeous written variety declined. Just like the German Chancellery in Copenhagen had promoted Low German as administrative language at the end of the 14th century, it established High German as a new dominating written language from the middle of the 16th century. This development started about 1540 and was completed in 1665 (Schütt 1919). From ca. 1570 the council chancellery and the district chancellery of Flensburg followed the linguistic example of the Copenhagen administration and used High German for their external communication. Internally – in the local correspondence – the same clerks held on to Low German as written standard (Schütt 1919). The language of law, school and church as well as that of the trade and craft in Flensburg remained Low German, and this language actually reached its zenith in Flensburg around 1570 (Bock 1952).

Nevertheless, High German expanded in the following years, especially as the two local chancelleries used High German more and more for internal communication in the city at the end of the 16th century. In the lower courts of justice Low German dominated until the beginning of the 17th century (Schütt 1919).

The church changed to High German much later than the administration. The Lutheran reformation (1528–36) had taken place in Low German and so this language held a strong position in religious life for a short period. In 1635 a Manuale Ecclesiasticum was published in Low German and remained in use until Olearius' High German "Kirchenbuch" ['Churchbook'] was published in 1665. The school language was very much a parallel to the church language. In the year 1566 the "Flensburger Gelehrtenschule", a grammar school, was founded. The language of instruction was Latin, of course, but in the lower classes Low German. In 1623 the headmaster of the school, Johannes Moth, published a Low German "Compendium Biblicum" which – together with his Low German-Latin textbook – remained in use until 1638. That year the superintendent of the church, Stephan Klotz, prohibited the use of Low German school books at the Flensburger Gelehrtenschule. Other schools of the city, too, were obliged to use High German as the language of instruction.

So at the end of the 17th century we largely find a language patch-work of the following kind: South Jutish remained the vernacular of the common people in town and in the surrounding rural regions. Actually the loss of prestige of Low German could possibly have eased the pressure on South Jutish. Low German was spoken by the people of craft and trade in the city, whereas church, school, administration and cultural life was dominated by High German as the new high variety. We might suppose, however, that many individuals were bi- or even trilingual with at least a receptive competence in two or three of the above mentioned languages.

3. The nationalist period of the 19th century

The rise of nationalism in the years after the Napoleonic wars had far-reaching consequences for the political and linguistic situation of the Duchy of Schleswig. The dynastic states were – one by one – substituted by national states in which it was supposed that there existed a correspondence or even an identity between people, nation and state. These ideas were in the first place carried into the region of Schleswig from outside.

This principle had previously been formulated by philosophers of the late 18th and early 19th century in Germany such as Fichte ("Reden an die deutsche Nation", 1807/08) and formerly Herder (1744–1803) in "Über die neuere deutsche Literatur" (1768) and "Abhandlung über den Ursprung der Sprache" (1772). These ideas of identity between people, nation and state became part of literature and historical writing all over central Europe in the first half of the 19th century in the so-called Romanticist period.

However, it also strongly influenced the concept of language because language was seen as one of the most important parts of national identity. In "Reden an die deutsche Nation" (1807/08) Fichte wrote (and I translate freely):

> Those speaking the same language are – long before any form of human intervention – connected by invisible bonds by nature itself. These people understand one another and continuously improve their comprehension of each other: they belong together and form an indivisible entity. Such a community cannot assimilate other people of different origin and language, and cannot mix with them without some confusion and without disturbing the gradual process of its own development. (Fichte 1807/08/1978: 207)

Johann Gottfried Herder had previously claimed that language – one's mother tongue – is the individual manifestation of one's national character. So Herder stressed the close connection between language and national character, and he, furthermore, claimed (about 150 years before Sapir and 185 years before Whorf) that language is the tool which forms (and determines) the content of human thought. When you speak a certain language, you will also follow the way of thinking of this particular language. The language forms the thesaurus of all human thought. This makes the national language so important, it even makes the language a conditio sine qua non for your national identity. Further, there must be – according to Herder – a correspondence between national character and language. The new ideas that the state was not only a territory of a monarchy but was the home of the nation – this view had numerous political consequences, particularly in a linguistically diverse region as the Duchy of Schleswig.

Nationalist circles in Copenhagen regarded with great concern how 'Danish' (i.e. South Jutish vernacular) in the regions southeast of Flensburg (Angeln) was gradually substituted by Low German during the first half of the 19th century. The consequence was a national(ist) language policy and a language planning which was aimed at (1) stopping further expansion of Low German to the north, middle and west of Schleswig, (2) introducing Danish as the official standard variety in the regions where South Jutish vernacular was still spoken, partly spoken or had been spoken until recently. After 1811 several language instructions – mainly concerning school language – were released. These regulative efforts culminated after the First Schleswigian War[2] (1848–1850) in the so-called language rescripts (1851) as Standard Danish was made compulsory as language of school and church in parishes of Middle Schleswig and around Flensburg where South Jutish was supposed to be the dominating oral language.

But the interest in language as a symbol of national identity also found influential representatives among intellectuals of this region. Just to mention one example: In 1837 a professor of law at the university of Kiel, Christian Paulsen (who was born in Flensburg) published a small book in Danish: "Det danske Sprog i Hertugdømmet Slesvig" ['The Danish language in the Duchy of Schleswig']. The main thesis of this book is that the language of a people and a nation is its most sacred property (Paulsen 1837: 9). Paulsen further claims that Danish (i.e. Standard Danish) must become the language of school, church, court and administration in the regions of Schleswig where Danish (i.e. South Jutish) is spoken. Thus a strong claim of correspondence between vernacular and official language was formulated which – seen from a historical point of view – had no real tradition in this region characterised by long periods of medial diglossia. Apart from that Standard Danish was a new high variety whose oral and written forms were just as 'unfamiliar' as High German had been 300 years earlier. Not many people of this region actually mastered oral or written Standard Danish.[3]

The language rescripts of 1851 inevitably resulted in a language conflict, especially in the region southeast of Flensburg (Angeln), where Low German had become the dominating vernacular during the first half of the 19th century. A well-documented example of a language struggle in the city of Flensburg is the conflict about the position of the Danish (Standard Danish) language in the curriculum of the Flensburger Gelehrtenschule:

After the First Schleswigian War 1848–1850 a reorganisation of the grammar schools in the Duchy of Schleswig took place: In the grammar school in Haderslev in the north, Danish became the medium of instruction, in the grammar school of Schleswig in the south, German was used as medium of instruction, whereas the Flensburger Gelehrtenschule in the middle was obliged to use both German and Danish as medium of instruction. In 'modern' words: the Flensburger Gelehrtenschule had to function as a bilingual school. This demand of a bilingual pedagogy was supposed to support the bilingualism among the students and enable them to study both at the German university of Kiel and at the Danish university of Copenhagen. The purpose of this bilingual education was to guarantee Danish-speaking teachers, priests, lawyers and civil servants in the northern, South Jutish-speaking part of the duchy.

In the year 1851 a bilingual school was quite a challenge, as there existed neither literature on bilingual education nor did the school authorities of Flensburg have any practical experience on this. So the new Danish headmaster of the school, Simesen, had to work out a curriculum which put German and Danish on equal footing. As Bent Søndergaard concludes in his analysis of this curriculum (Søndergaard 1984) it was – also from a present point of view – a very respectable and well considered curriculum which headmaster Simesen developed. Nevertheless, his efforts to make Standard Danish a language equal in status were met with much hostility by the majority of the German speaking population of Flensburg. In a discussion about the language curriculum of the Gelehrtenschule in the city council the 'Danish' representatives of course defended the language policy of the school, but the critical comments from one of the 'German' representatives, P. E. Petersen, are worth noting:

> Zu der Anschauung, dass das Wohl des Gesamtstaats erfordere, dass die dänische Sprache bei uns eingeführt und eingeprügelt werde, kann ich mich niemals erheben. Im Gegenteil! Wir waren gute Dänen mit unseren deutschen Zungen, das haben wir 1848 wahrhaft bewiesen! Aber wenn man uns nicht mehr als Dänen anerkennen will mit unserer deutschen Sprache – gut – dann sind wir es nicht! [...] Es ist traurig, dass man auf diese unglückselige Idee, die Danisierung des Herzogtums, gekommen ist.
>
> (Quoted after Søndergaard 1984: 71)[4]

This quotation gives a very good impression of traditional Schleswigian attitudes towards language and identity, even in the year 1851: There does not necessarily exist any correspondence between language and nationality. You could be a Danish loyalist German-speaking citizen just as you could be a South Jutish-speaking German. The idea of correspondence between language and nation was not rooted in this region at this time, and this also explains why the efforts of language policy and language planning from Copenhagen were doomed to fail. The linguistic and political reality was much more complicated and diverse than the central power in Copenhagen was able to grasp.

4. Language use in Flensburg in the middle of the 19th century

Considering the typical medial diglossic situation it might seem impossible to find reliable data about language use in Flensburg in the 19th century, since no oral data are available. To conclude anything from official documents, newspaper articles or any printed material would be misleading. Only "inofficial", unprinted material may be considered as fairly valid data, when we want to get an impression of how people in Flensburg in the middle of the 19th century actually spoke and wrote. For that reason I have searched for private letters, business letters and diaries. In my search I found the archives of two Flensburg families from the 1840s, 1850s and 1860s. These archives chiefly consist of letters of some historical interest, and that is the reason why these letters have been put into archives by the local Danish library. But these letters are also very interesting from a linguistic point of view, because they give a good impression of the language use of the middle and upper class citizens of Flensburg in the middle of the 19th century.

4.1 Case study 1: The family Christiansen-Fromm

The first family archive consists of letters from the married couple Christian Carsten Christiansen and his wife Mette Louise (born Fromm) to her parents living in the South Jutish-speaking region north of Schleswig (Halk by Haderslev, after 1920 belonging to Denmark). The earliest letters date back to 1846, the latest from 1857, and so these letters describe the years before and after the first Schleswigian war 1848–1850. Christian Carsten Christiansen (1816–1888) was a wealthy distiller and merchant, who bought grain from the farmers and also used the waste product from the distillery to raise cattle. He had strong business relations with his father-in-law who was a wealthy farmer and owned large areas of fertile land, a large cattle breeding and dairies (Henningsen 1996).

Most of the letters are partly private, partly business letters dealing with the social life of Flensburg, family matters and prices of spirits, grain and cattle. The building activities of the family in Flensburg are also described in great detail. From a linguistic point of view the letters are interesting as they reveal quite a lot about language choice and language use.

Except for a few quotations in Low German, Christian Carsten used High German as matrix language in his letters to his father-in-law. Nevertheless it is a quite unconventional High German language with many features of language contact. When Christian Carsten wrote to his mother-in-law, he wrote in Danish. After 1852 Mette Louise wrote to her parents mainly in Standard Danish (she had a Danish private teacher as a child), but her Standard Danish is also very much influenced by her South Jutish mother tongue. In the following I am going to make a detailed linguistic analysis of language contact phenomena in the letters of both Christian Carsten and Mette Louise. My intention is to analyse and comment on deviations from High German and Danish standard. Some of these deviations (e.g. spelling mistakes or slips of the pen) might of course be accidental and are therefore not interesting. Other deviations are clearly due to language contact. However, in some – particularly lexical – cases it will not be possible to point out exactly, which languages are involved, because e.g. deviations from High German might be due to either Low German influence or South Jutish influence or to South Jutish influence on Low German. Pursuing this question is futile, because it is impossible to prove the direction of influence scientifically, even if you are familiar with all the varieties involved in a certain language contact. In a longitudinal and very close language contact situation lexical influences are mutual and may change direction many times in the course of the centuries. It makes more sense to develop a concept of a common regional lexicon and idiom which can be used in all the three language varieties (Low German, High German and South Jutish)

4.1.1 *Christian Carsten Christiansen's letters in German*

In order to give a short impression of the language of the letters in German, I will quote a typical letter from Christian Carsten to his father-in-law: [1854 15.1]

> *Eben habe ich 20 Stk. Quien zu 70 Rb verkauft, die in 14 Tagen wegsollen. Nun sollte ich aber aus und kaufen, und wollte ich wohl nach Forballum. Wenn du Zeit hast und mit auf willst um mal zu sehen wie Preis dorten im Winter haben, so schreibe mir erstens, um ich nach dir herunter kommen soll oder du hierher. Da die Wege quer übers Land von da aus gewiss nicht besonders sind, wäre es wohl besser wenn du hierauf kämst.*
>
> 'I have just sold 20 heifers for 70 taler, they will be sent away in two weeks. Now I must go out and buy and I would go to Forballum. If you have got the time and want to come with to see what prices [are paid] there in the wintertime,

then write to me in the first place, if I am going to come down to you or you up to me. Since the roads across the countryside [from east to west] surely will not be well, it would be better if you came up here.' [literal translation]

Lexicon

In order to understand the above quoted letter you have to reorganise your notion of the directions "up" and "down": Although Flensburg is situated about 55 km south of Halk (where his father-in-law lived), people from North Schleswig traditionally went "up" to Flensburg, because the city was the centre of the region. For that reason Christian Carsten wrote *nach dir herunter* and *du hierauf* ('down to you' and 'you up [to me]').

Lexically you find words which are transferred from South Jutish and/or Low German. In the letter above you see *Quien* (High German: *Färse*, E.: *heifer*) and the use of *um* (High German *ob*, E. *if*) just as in South Jutish.

Remarkable is the use of the modal auxilary verb *sollen* as a kind of universal modal verb used to (a) denote future time (*in 14 Tagen wegsollen*, 'will be sent away in two weeks', *nach dir herunter kommen sol*", 'if I am going to come down to you') (HG: *werden*). Compare also: *so hat es auch keine Not, wenn es auch noch etwas mehr kosten soll* (28.11.1852) ('it is no trouble if it will be more expensive'), (b) as substitute for the High German modal auxilary *müssen* (meaning 'must') (*nun sollte ich aber aus und kaufen*, 'I must go out and buy'). Compare also: *und sollen noch 16 Räder und 4 Axen zu und Steine um den Schienen an zu befästigen* (16.6.1854) ('and further 16 wheels and 4 axles and stones are necessary in order to fasten the rails').

This use of *sollen* is clearly modelled on South Jutish and Low German and even today a very characteristic feature of the language in Flensburg. Additionally *sollen* is often used (c) as a substitute for High German *wollen* or *möchten* e.g. in utterances like *Wir sollten mal bei dir vorfragen, ob du Lust hättest* (19.6.1856) ('we would like to ask you, if you would like to').[5]

Other verbal expressions from South Jutish are:

> *Ich muß aus und sehen zu das.* (27.1.1855) (SJ: *se te*, HG: *dafür sorgen*, E: *see to*) and *der Winter will beibleiben* (20.2.1853) (SJ: *bliw ve*, HG: *anhalten*, E: *continue*), *die 12* [*Quien*] *bleiben gehen zum September Monat* (19.7.1853) (SJ: *bliwe gangen*, HG: *bleiben*, *the 12* [*heifers*] *will stay until September*). Clearly South Jutish are also expressions in Christian Carsten's letters like *Flüttag* (20.10.1852) (SJ: *fløtdaw*, HG: *Ziehtag*, E: *day of move*), *und bin ich bange für, daß ich für Buchweitzen verlegen werden sollte* (4.6.1856) (HG: *ich befürchte...*, E: *I am afraid that I could be in shortage of buckwheat*).

Other idiomatic expressions are in accordance with both Low German and South Jutish idioms:

> *Da ist also nichts bei zu thun* (21.11.1852) (HG: *Da kann man nichts machen*, E: *You can't do anything about it*), *So will viel Geld zu* (4.12.1852) (HG: *Viel Geld ist nötig*, E: *Much money is needed*), *letzt in der Woche* (9.1.1853) (HG: *Ende der Woche*, E: *at the end of the week*), *wozu soll das werden, wenn diese Dürre beibleibt?* (25.5.1853) (HG: *was wird daraus...?*, E: *what will be of it, if this drought continues?*)

It is worth noting the numerous verbal constructions in Christian Carsten's letters with *bei sein* and *beibleiben*. This indicates that he consciously has a category of durative aspects in his language (comparable to the English *-ing* form):

> *es scheint ja aber so als wenn dieser Winter beibleiben will* (20.2.1853) 'It seems as if this winter is going to continue'.
> *Nun bin ich bei von meinen Brantwein zu verkaufen* (26.6.1853) 'I am selling some of my spirits'.
> *Wenn die Dampfschiffe nur beibleiben von Hamburg nach England zu gehen* (18.12.1853) 'If the steamers continue to sail from Hamburg to England'.
> *Mit unseren Rademacher gesprochen, der ist bei und machen eine Zeichnung* (22.3.1854) 'Have talked to our wheeler, who is making a drawing'.
> *jetzt sind wir bei und lassen eine Einrichtung machen* (3.11.1854) 'just now we are making an installation'.
> *wir sind jetzt bei von den alten Vorrath auszuräumen* (29.5.1856) 'we are removing the old supplies'.
> *Wir sind jetzt schon bei den Schiffer auf den Hause zu legen* (27.9.1856) 'We are slating the roof of the house'.

This could be inspired by the South Jutish durative aspect in the verbal expressions *væ ve å, bliw ve å.*

Inflectional morphology

In comparison with High German and Standard Danish, Low German in general but especially South Jutish are characterised by reduction of inflectional morphology. In South Jutish all inflectional morphemes consisting of a schwa have been deleted such as plural-*e* in nouns, weak inflection of adjectives with -*e* and the infinitive marker. The nouns have two genders, but only two cases (nominative and possessive, like in English). The regional Low German variety shows a merger between nominative and accusative, so it is not surprising that the case system of the Flensburg town language of the 19th century is characterised by some confusion concerning the case system of High German, too.

In fact, the deviations of inflectional morphology concern first and foremost the High German case system, partly also the gender system. Deviation of verbal inflection (personal and temporal conjugation), however, seems to occur more at random. Generally speaking, we find a tendency towards a three-case system (nominative, accusative and genitive) instead of a High German four-case system (nominative, accusative, genitive and dative). In addition to a trend to use dominantly two cases (nominative and accusative) one will find variations of genitive and possessive expressions (see below). The use of the accusative is very frequent, in particular after the following prepositions, which in High German govern the dative:

> **mit:**
> There are numerous examples in the letters, but here only two, one with a noun and one with a pronoun in the accusative.
> *Mit den Kornhandel geht es auf und nieder* (9.3.1854) 'It goes up and down with the corn trade'.
> *Man war aber gar nicht recht zufrieden mit mich...* (Chr.Chr. 5.8.1856) 'They were not quite satisfied with me'.

With the next prepositions there are a lot of examples in the data, too, so that it cannot be considered as a misspelling or slip of the pen, but creates a linguistic pattern.

> **bei**
> *Mit den Milchwagen geht es bei den vielen Schnee der gefallen ist nicht so ganz gut.*(Chr.Chr. 8.1.1857) 'With the milk wagon it does not work very well with the amount of snow that has fallen'.
> **von**
> *so habe ich doch die 4 Kühe von dich zu 40 Rb a Stück verkauft* (Chr.Chr. 5.1.1854) 'so I have sold the 4 cows from you for 40 taler each'.
> **nach**
> *Ich habe schon heute gleich um nicht der letzte zu sein ein Gesuch nach unsere Ministerio abgehen lassen* (Chr.Chr. 4.12.1852) 'in order not to be the last one I have sent an application to our ministry today'
> **zu**
> *Ganz hätte ich beinahe vergessen zu den großen Pferdehandel zu gratulieren* (Chr.Chr. 2.2.1855) 'I almost forgot to congratulate you on the big horse deal'.
> **vor**
> *Polizeimeister Garlieb, welcher vor kurzen in Copenhagen sich längere Zeit aufgehalten hat* (Chr.Chr. 21.11.1852) 'Chief constable Garlieb, who recently stayed in Copenhagen for a while'.
> **aus**
> *Aus deinen lieben Brief vom 18. habe ich ersehen, daß du ....* (Chr.Chr.

20.10.1852) 'From your dear letter from the 18th I have recognised that you...'.
hinter
ich habe nemlich noch immer Hoffnung gehabt etwas von dem Grundstück hinter unsern Hause zu erhalten (Chr.Chr. 21.11.1852) 'I still had hopes to get a part of the piece of land behind our house'.

The dative, however, frequently occurs in idioms and collocations such as

zu billigen Preisen (Chr.Chr. 2.2.1855) 'at cheap prices'; *auf dem Markt* (Chr.Chr. 5.8.1856)'on the market'.

In the data I found one example of High German postposed genitive:

Heute sind wir mit dem Ausgraben des Kellers fertig geworden 'Today we finished the digging of the celler'.

In possessive constructions the High German postposed genitive is seldom used. It is substituted by a preposed enclitic *s*-genitive (as in South-Jutish) *Meines Nachbars Mühle ist auch zu kaufen* (Chr.Chr. 21.11.1852) (HG: *Die Mühle meines Nachbarn ist auch zu kaufen* 'My neighbour's windmill is to buy / to be bought, too') or by the so-called Garpe-genitive, which is known to be used in colloquial language in the whole Northsea area (North-West-Germanic: Low German, Frisian, Dutch, Norwegian, West-Jutish and occasionally in South-Jutish) *wir bekommen es bei Fritz Christiansen seine Ziegelei* (Chr.Chr. 21.2.1855) 'we get it from F. C.'s brickyard'.

Syntax

A very characteristic feature of the syntax in Christian Carsten's letters is the frequent use of conjoining infinitive constructions with *und* where High German generally (and Low German in the southern part of Schleswig and in Holstein) would expect a syntactically embedded infinitive construction with (*um*) *zu* in High German, *to* in Low German. This syntactic phenomenon is well known in Low German of the regions of Middle Schleswig and Angeln where the vernacular had previously been South Jutish (Lau 1975). So it can be regarded as a linguistic feature which has "survived" two matrix language turnovers in the High German city language of Flensburg. In South Jutish vernacular and in Standard Danish speech the infinitive marker *at* (HG *zu*, E *to*) and the conjoining conjunction *og* (HG *und*, E *and*) have merged to [ɔ] so that on the one hand infinitive constructions (with *at*) as well as conjoining sentences (with *og*) are introduced by [ɔ] in speech. Here are a few examples from the letters:

> *Nun sollte ich aber aus* ***und kaufen*** (Chr.Chr. 15.1.1854) 'Now I must out and buy',
> *und deshalb höher taxieren zu lassen deucht mir ist nich wert,* ***das man das haben soll und sprechen über*** *(das du nicht Geld bekommen kannst ohne höher Taxiren zu lassen)* (Chr.Chr. 27.9.1856)
> 'and it does not seem worth while to me to let estimate higher, that they shall have that and speak about (that you cannot get the money unless you apply for a higher estimate)'.
> *Gestern war ich in der Fahrt* ***um und kaufen*** *Buchweitzen* (Chr.Chr. 17.2.1854) 'Yesterday I was busy to and buy buckwheat'.

The "double" construction with *um* and *und* is remarkable here, but nevertheless the conjoining construction governs the word order of the sentence (with postposed object). At the syntactic level the word order pattern from South Jutish neutralises the difference between conjoining and embedding in connection with the use of *und*. HG would have (*um*) *zu* with an embedded infinitive construction and obligatory final position of the non-finite verb. The use of *und* instead of *zu* (Low German *to*) and a North Germanic sentence structure and word order clearly coincide: When the South Jutish conjunction [ɔ]/*und* disappears and is replaced by HG (*um*) *zu* or LG *to*, the South Jutish sentence structures and word orders disappear simultaneously and are replaced by German word order with final position of non-finite verbs which can be seen in the following example with both constructions:

> *Ich habe jeden Tag so viel zu tun, jetzt sind wir bei* ***und lassen*** *eine Einrichtung machen* ***um*** *die Maschine auch den Spühl rühren* ***zu lassen***. (Chr.Chr. 3.11.1854) 'I am so busy every day, now we are at it and have a gadget installed in order to let the machine stir the 'Spühl' [the waste product of the distillery]'.

In this use of *und*-constructions the High German variety of Flensburg shows a clear correspondence with North Germanic languages and English: *at* → [ɔ] (*with a merging of sounds in Danish and Norwegian with og*) *and to* → *and* in spoken English .

Concerning bi- or multilingualism we can conclude from the letters that Chr. C. Christiansen predominantly spoke and wrote a Flensburg variety of High German later known as "Flensburger Petuh". He understood and was able to quote Low German. The letters do not reveal much about his productive competence in this language. He was also able to write short messages in Danish and from his wife's letters we know that he wanted to attend a language course in English. In the middle of the 19th century Flensburg was situated directly on a language border between Low German south and east of Flensburg and South Jutish to the north and west. Dominating in the city itself was the Flensburg variety of High German as represented by Christian Carsten Christiansen. Low German was, however, still the language of the craftsmen and the common people as documented in quotations in Christian Carsten's letters:

> *Der alte Lüt Andersen besah sie [die Balken] letz Tag und meinte "Dat mut man sagen dat ist wat Solides!"* (Chr.Chr. 6.7.1856) 'The old L.A. inspected the rafter the other day and meant "That is really something solid!"'.

4.1.2 *Mette Louise Fromm's letters in Danish*

Apart from two short messages in Danish written by Christian Carsten, the Danish letters are in the hand writing of his wife Mette Louise who was born in 1827 in the South Jutish-speaking region in the north of Schleswig. From 1846 onwards, she was sent to Flensburg in the winter time in order to learn good city manners, enjoy herself and – if possible – also to find a wealthy husband (which she did). In 1852 she married the wealthy bachelor Christian Carsten Christiansen (Henningsen 1996). Her letters date from her early years as a light-hearted girl (1846) to her years as a business woman, wife, mother and caring daughter (1856). Until 1852 she wrote in German, after 1852 mostly in Danish. Only her letters in Danish will be analysed here.

A relevant question is: To which extent does Mette Louise's language represent a variety of the town language of Flensburg? In the middle of the 19th century, we must presume, the old South Jutish town dialect of Flensburg had almost died out. Those people in Flensburg who spoke South Jutish, were mostly persons who came in from the northern and western outskirts of Flensburg – farmers and domestic servants who brought their own South Jutish country dialect into town. Even today you occasionally hear South Jutish spoken in Flensburg, no longer the original town dialect, but North-Schleswigian South Jutish of 'immigrated' persons (like myself). So Mette Louise is no representative of the original Flensburg South Jutish vernacular, but one of the numerous people from the northern and western outskirts of Flensburg who have brought their own mother tongue with them and who have gradually assimilated to the High German vernacular of Flensburg.[6] Reading Mette Louise's letters written in Standard Danish orthography you literally 'hear' her South Jutish dialect through her written language.

Lexicon

Of course Mette Louise's South Jutish language manifests itself through her vocabulary. She uses regional, non-standard lexemes in many of her letters. Some examples of non-standard lexemes are:

> *Men med brændevinen er det dobbelt slem, den er slet ikke til at sælge....., og det lidet der gaar af til en* ***sælle*** *pris* (M.-L. 30.3.1854) 'But with the spirits it is twice as bad, you can't sell it...., and the little you sell goes away to miserable price'.

and later in the same letter:

> *Med kornet hører jeg nok ogsaa nok det er ogsaa* ***flaut*** *her*; 'With the corn [trade] it is also faint/slack here, I hear'.
> *... nu er det Gudskelov ganske og aldeles* ***over.*** (M.-L. 2.1.1855) 'now it is quite and totally over, thank God!'
> *Tredje pinsedag, hvor her* ***immer*** *er en græsselig* ***schau,*** *da er der fest (en* ***art folksfest****) paa Kobbermøllen...* (M.-L. 8.7.1854) 'The third day of Whitsun, where there is always a terrible fun here, then there is a festival (a kind of public festival) on the K.'.

In the last example we actually find three languages involved: Standard Danish as the matrix language, lexical items of South Jutish (*schau*), lexical items common to South Jutish and German (*immer*) and loan translations from German (*art* and *folksfest*).

Morphology

In her morphology I find some instances with a preposed article remarkable (like South Jutish and German) where Standard Danish would have the enclitic article (*skibet*): *Chr., Hagen, Detlef Jürgensen og den tilkommende capitain Ellinger ere i Lübeck for at bese* ***det skib.*** (M.-L. 11.8.1853) 'C.H, D.J and the future captain E. are in Lübeck to inspect the ship'. Her categorisation of countable versus non-countable nouns is also South Jutish, as South Jutish treats some designations of materials as countable nouns (e.g. *soup* and *porridge*). So she uses the countable quantifier *mange* ('many') as attribute to *yeast*: *vi levere mange Gjær nu* (M.-L. 3.11.1854) ('We deliver much yeast now').

Syntax

A syntactic feature, too, reveals Mette Louise's dialect, i.e. the position of the past participle after the object: *Vi har endda og temmelig hø bjerget i disse dage,* (M.-L. 18.6.1854) 'we have gathered in rather much hay these days'). Standard Danish would have the past participle in front of the object: *bjerget temmelig meget hø.*

Codeswitching

A characteristic feature of Christian Carsten's letters is that he never codeswitches except for quotations. Louise, however, codeswitches now and then as in the following letter:

> *Har faaet besked om Jeres snarlige besøg. Eben fällt mir ein, meine liebe Mutter wünschte so gerne die Ständer versammelt zu sehen, worauf Ihr vielleicht nun rechnet, aber die erste Sitzung wird erst nächsten Mitwoch und ob dann freier Zuschau gleich ist, weiss ich nicht. Könntet Ihr aber Euch nicht so einrichten, das wenn dieses der Fall wär, Ihr den einen Tag länger bleiben könntet, denkt nun darüber nach.*
> *Dürfte ich dich, meine liebe Mutter, nicht wieder um ein Paar Käse bitten, oder komme ich zu oft, und den noch ein Paar Knäuler Hedengarn, Blaargarn til at stoppe på vores gamle gjærposer med, jeg saa nok sidst du havde endnu meget blaargarn.* (M.-L. 29.9.1853)
> ([**In Danish**] 'I have received message about your coming visit. [**CS to German**] It just occurred to me that my dear mother would very much like to see the assembly of the representatives of the estates gathered, which you might now expect, but the first assembly will be next Wednesday and I don't know whether you have free admission. Couldn't you arrange it so if this were the case you could stay one day longer, think about it.
> Dear mother, may I ask you for a couple of cheese, or do I ask too often, and then also a couple of ball[**CS to Danish**]s of 'Hedengarn', darning flax to mend our old yeast bags, when I was there last, I saw you had much darning flax left.').

In the first case it is a matter of intersentential codeswitching and this is not very spectacular. In the second case, however, the codeswitching seems to take place 'inside' the German word *Knäuel* ('ball') which has Ø-plural in German. But here it is provided with a Danish inflectional plural morpheme *-(e)r* like the corresponding Danish word *nøgle-r*. The real 'trigger' of the codeswitching is, however, the following proper noun or 'trademark'. Louise asks her mother for a particular kind of darning flax, the name of which she only knows in Danish (*Hede(n)garn, blårgarn*). It is typically a cultural motivation for codeswitching.

The question is, why Louise codeswitches and Christian Carsten does not? The explanation could be that Louise with South Jutish as mother tongue lives in a more bilingual situation in Flensburg than Christian Carsten does and consequently uses a bilingual's language modes. Besides, she is also in a 'double' medial diglossic situation as she does not have any written variety of her mother tongue at her disposal. So she constantly has to choose between two written standards which more or less 'suit' her communicative needs.

4.2 Case study 2: The family Mechlenburg-v. Bentzen

The archive of the family Mechlenburg-v. Bentzen mainly consists of (a) letters from Auguste v. Bentzen (born Mechlenburg) to her parents, owners of the 'Löwenapotheke' in Flensburg (from the years 1844–1850), (b) the exchange of letters between Auguste (in Flensburg) and her husband, captain of horse Jens Otto Paludan v. Bentzen, on duty as a colonel in the Danish army in the Second Schleswigian War (1864), (c) Auguste's memoirs written for her daughter Christine[7] and (d) a few business letters written by v. Bentzen.

Auguste writes in High German, her husband's private letters are in Standard Danish, but his business letters in German. In the letters from Auguste to v. Bentzen the daughter Christine often sends her father greetings in Danish. Concerning the distribution of language in the family we can conclude that Auguste's mother tongue is High German. Auguste went to Denmark in 1848 during the First Schleswigian War in order to join her husband. In her letters she tells her parents that she has hired a Danish-speaking maid in Denmark who could also function as an interpreter. During the First Schleswigian War (1848–1850) she lived at various places in Denmark, where she must have learned some Danish. We also know from her memoires that she had visited the public school for girls run by the (mainly High German speaking) Herrnhuter in Christiansfeld in North Schleswig. v. Bentzen's mother tongue is Copenhagen Standard Danish, but since many of the officers of the Danish army before the Schleswigian Wars were members of the gentry of Schleswig–Holstein, High German was a well known language in the Danish army in the first half of the 19th century. The children seem to have been bilingual speakers of High German and Standard Danish. From the letters we know that the two boys visited the Flensburger Gelehrtenschule until 1864 (in the years of the bilingual curriculum). After the victory of Prussia-Austria and the strict Germanizing of public life and schools in the Duchy of Schleswig Auguste hired private teachers for the boys. Later the eldest son was sent to an acquainted pharmaceutical chemist in the north of Jutland. The family was nationally engaged for the Danish 'Helstat' which means that they represented the opinion that Schleswig-Holstein should remain united with the Danish monarchy. When v. Bentzen was challenged by the leader of the Schleswig–Holstein rebellion, the Prince of Noer, to decide which side he wanted to be on in 1848, he immediately spurred his horse and rode to the north. In contrast to the first case study we here have a family directly involved in the militant national conflicts concerning the Duchy of Schleswig.

For a linguistic analysis of the language of Flensburg, Auguste's letters to her husband during the Second Schleswigian War (1864) and her memoirs written for her daughter Christine some years later are of considerable relevance. To give an impression of Auguste's language here is a short excerpt from a letter dating from the 12th of March 1864:

> *Nun sind die Kinder ziemlich wohl, aber erst wurde Christian Carsten ein paar Tage krank, dann fiel Thue und hatte sich ein tiefes Loch auf den Kopf gestoßen, welches ich noch täglich verbinden muß, nun zuletzt wurde Christine einen Morgen so plötzlich krank, ich wußte garnicht was ich aufstellen sollte, sie war mehrere male nach einander ganz ohnmächtig, ich kriegte Dr. Hansen, denn Valentiner ist noch immer selbst krank, es kam nur durch diese Zeit hervorgebrachte Gemüthsbewegung, wir alle leiden sehr dabei, welches nicht zu verwundern ist, nun nachdem sie 2 Tage zu Bett gelegen, ist es wieder besser. Man hat hier viel aufzupassen in dieser Zeit kannst du glauben. Dabei diese ewige Angst und Unruhe um Dich, macht meinen Kopf mitunter so mürbe, daß ich nicht weiß wohin ich soll.*
>
> 'Now the children are fairly well, but first Chr. was ill for a couple of days, then Thue fell and knocked a deep hole in his head, which I have to bandage up daily, now finally Christine suddenly fell ill one morning, I did not know what to do, she fainted several times in succession, I got doctor Hansen, because Valentiner is still ill himself, it was due to the affects of these days, we all suffer from it, which is not surprising, now having lain in bed for two days, she is better again. I have a lot here to look after at the time being, you know. Moreover, this permanent fear and anxiety about you, makes my head now and then so weary that I don't know what to do.'

What is striking in this text are German re-lexifications of Danish idioms: *was ich aufstellen sollte* (SD: *hvad jeg skulle stille op*, HG: *was ich anfangen sollte*, E: *what to do*; quite common in LG, too: *opstellen* but not with this abstract reading), *Man hat hier viel aufzupassen* (SD: *Man har meget at passe på*, HG: ... *viel, worum man sich kümmern muss*, E. *a lot to look after*),[8] *kannst du glauben* (SD: *kan du tro*, HG: *schon*; E: *you know*). The use of case and preposition in the phrase *ein tiefes Loch* <u>*auf den Kopf*</u> (HG: *am/im Kopf* 'in his head') is not in accordance with HG, but it is difficult to explain this deviation as a language contact phenomenon. Another deviation which is more in accordance with the trend to avoid the High German genitive is *einen Morgen* (HG: *eines Morgens*, E: *one morning*). Typically colloquial north German is the use of *kriegte* as ordinary main verb *ich kriegte Dr. Hansen* (HG: *bekam*, *I got doctor Hansen*).

Lexicon

In the lexicon we find some clearly regional phrases from Danish South Jutish as *Fremden-Schlafstube* (AvB 18.4.1864) (from South Jutish *fremmed* in the meaning of 'guest', HG: *Gästezimmer*, E: *guest room*). Also some of the field names are South Jutish, e.g. *die Lücken* (AvB 5.7.1864) (SJ: *æ lyck*, LG: *de Koppel*, HG: *die Weide*, E: *the pasture*). The use of *sollen* as universal verb is in accordance with the data of case study 1. Here are just two examples of many:

> *nun soll ich Mauerleute hier haben* (AvB 18.4.1864) (HG: *werde*) future time ('I am going to have bricklayers here')
> *Christine und ich waren hin mit großen Kleider Körben mit Essen für die Soldaten ...da soll was zu* (AvB 5.7.1864) (HG: *da muß schon was aufgetischt werden*, 'C. and I were there with big laundry baskets [with food]... a lot has to be served').

Morphology

Auguste uses a High German four case system, and the few confusions of gender (not frequent) and case (more frequent) may not be due to language contact. Other morphological phenomena are, however, due to predominantly Low German influence, i.e. the use of Garpe-genitive as possessive:

> *unsere Mammsell ihr Vater und Schwager sind beide abgesetzt* (AvB 5.7.1864) ('our maid's father and brother in law were both thrown out')

and occasionally Low German plural forms as in: *mit den Mädchens* (AvB 5.7.1864) ('with the girls').

Syntax

In Auguste's letters and the memoirs we find one characteristic syntactic feature, which is not in accordance with High German: Frequently she violates the High German syntactic rules of final position of the infinite verb(s) (past participles and infinitives) and the rule of final position of finite verb in subordinate clauses:

> *Du hattest mir ja gesagt davon in Schleswig.* (AvB 12.3.1864) 'you had told me about it in Schleswig'; *Du schreibst, ich sollte Jacob behalten nach Mai,* (AvB 18.4.1864) 'you write that I should keep Jacob here after Mai'.
> *...und sind so gar keine zu bekommen, die helfen könnten in der Apotheke* (AvB 18.4.1864)
> 'you get absolutely nobody who could help in the chemist's store'.
> ... *worin ich Dir erzählte von Schleswig* (AvB 18.4.1864) 'in which I told you about Schleswig'.

Concerning verb position her language is clearly influenced by North Germanic syntax in accordance with South Jutish and the Scandinavian languages. Another very typical feature is the use of prepositions as verb particles placed towards the end of the clause in front of local and temporal adverbs. This is not possible in standard High German syntax, but quite common in colloquial High German in northern Germany, in Low German, South Jutish and the Scandinavian languages in general:

> *viel geht natürlich zu, in dieser Zeit* (AvB 12.3.1864) 'much gets broken these days'.
> *Da lag Møllerup ganz nahe bei,* (AvB: Lebenserinnerungen) 'Then M. was near by'.

What is syntactically noticeable is that Auguste does not use any conjoining *und*-constructions as substitute for embedded High German infinitive-constructions. An explanation could be that these *und*-constructions are regarded as colloquial style as early as in the 19th century (just like today),[9] and Auguste seems to avoid a colloquial style very consciously in her letters. Accordingly she always addresses her husband with his surname.

Compared with the German letters in case-study 1 there are far less regional linguistic features in Auguste's letters. As mentioned above it is doubtlessly a question of style and register, but it is equally a question of class and education. Whereas the family Christiansen-Fromm can be considered a wealthy self-employed and self-made family without more than an average education, the family Mechlenburg-v.Bentzen is an educated upper-class family – he the son of a counsellor of justice, she the only child of a pharmaceutical chemist and later owner of the parental chemist's store.

Although the data show some variation concerning quantity and quality of language contact phenomena, it is symptomatic for the language situation of the town of Flensburg that you will find less influence of vernaculars and less influence of language contact in the written language of well-educated people because they are more familiar with the written standards.

5. Concluding remarks about monolingual and bilingual linguistic behaviour

Until now I have analysed language contact phenomena on the basis of deviations from standard languages which can be explained through influence from other languages and/or vernaculars. To conclude I would like to change the perspective from the language system to the language users differentiating with regard to language behaviour.

Typical features of a bilingual linguistic behaviour are: (1) Translinguistic wordings in the sense of using lexical items from another language as "quotes" or as loan translations, (2) classical codeswitching. A bilingual person will have two languages that could both be potential matrix languages for a clause, if the bilingual person is sufficiently fluent in both languages. In classical codeswitching there is one structurally dominant matrix language, but the bilingual person will choose one matrix language out of two candidates.

Features of a monolingual, but contact-induced linguistic behaviour are (1) translinguistic wordings, in this case mainly belonging to a (historically and culturally developed) common regional lexicon and (2) bilingual convergence. In Flensburg, convergence is a result of longitudinal language contact and/or a (not fully completed) matrix language turnover. The result is a kind of composite matrix language (Myers-Scotton 1998).

But you will find no codeswitching if the language user is monolingual or if his/her linguistic proficiency is only sufficiently developed in one language so that there is but one dominating candidate for a matrix language. If you have a composite matrix language then two or more varieties provide the input to the frame. But even so they do not provide equal input. One language is always the dominant structure for the frame.

If we look at the data analysed in Sections 4.1 and 4.2 we find individuals with rather different language behaviour: **Mette Louise Fromm** (the Danish letters in case-study 1) is a bilingual person with South Jutish as her dominant oral variety. She writes in Standard Danish and High German, she codeswitches between the two standard varieties and produces clauses with translinguistic wordings. Her Standard Danish is also characterised by morphological and syntactic convergence with South Jutish. What makes her language behaviour complicated (but nevertheless typical for persons who speak a non-standard variety) is the medial diglossia: Her written language does not match her oral vernacular. As a bilingual person she has two candidates for matrix language, when she writes, but none of them really suits her dominant oral language variety. **Christian Carsten Christiansen** (the German letters in case-study 1) and **Auguste v. Bentzen** (case-study 2) both show monolingual, contact-induced language behaviour: They do not codeswitch (or only use "flagged codeswitching" as quotes). They have the Flensburg variety of High German as their absolutely dominating candidate for a matrix language. This matrix language, however, must be characterised as a composite matrix language consisting of input from Low German and South Jutish, but High German dominates the structure of the frame. In their language we find distinct elements of the two vernaculars, not only in the lexical structures, but also as underlying structures in syntax and in morphological patterns. This may be explained by a not fully completed matrix language turnover from South Jutish to Low German and from a South Jutish induced Low German to High German.

This composite language structure seems to have fossilized in Flensburg to a certain degree in the 19th century. At the end of the 19th century and in the first half of the 20th century this language variety became famous as "Flensburger Petuh", a jargon which was used for comedian performances. This partly artificial jargon is a concentrated code-mix. For speakers and non-speakers of Petuh it is nowadays partly a kind of humorous shibboleth and partly an in-group jargon for the "native" citizens of Flensburg. The humour lies in the concentration and the exaggeration of code-mix. These "artificial" texts in Petuh are written by people who wanted to make a humorous travesty of the particular Flensburg idiom whose authentic forms have been described above.

The code-mix of the 19th and the early 20th centuries has gradually been reduced to integrated loan translations and idioms. The explanation runs as follows: the increasing roofing of the H-variety High German prevails over the other varieties. The other varieties (South Jutish and Low German) have gradually been reduced to a "supply lexicon" for the local German population of Flensburg. Nevertheless, in colloquial speech you now and then hear features of the original Flensburg variety of High German.

Unpublished data

Personal archives of Dansk Centralbibliotek, Flensburg:

Bentzen, von: Briefe der Familien von Bentzen, Rübner, Mechlenburg (1842–1899). Dansk Centralbiblioteks Arkiv, Flensborg, p. 180–181.

Christiansen, Christian C.: Briefe an Asmus Fromm aus den Jahren 1846–1857. Dansk Centralbiblioteks Arkiv, Flensborg, p. 402.

Notes

1. "The citizens of Flensburg nowadays vacilate between the Danish and the German language, because (their language) is not really equivalent with any of them, but with both of them. This is usual at all places where different nations meet."

2. The First Schleswigian War (1848–1850) was a civil war in which the revolting SchleswigHolsteinian movement was conquered by the Danish army.

3. Not even Chr. Paulsen himself! Professor H. N. Clausen, who had met Chr. Paulsen in Kiel, wrote: "He did not speak Danish fluently" (Foreword by Lausten-Thomsen to the reprint Paulsen 1837/1941: 3).

4. "I can never share the view that the welfare of the state in its territorial entirety [i.e. the Kingdom of Denmark and the Duchies of Schleswig and Holstein] requires that the Danish language is made compulsory and forced upon us. On the contrary! We were good Danish citizens with our German tongues, we have proved that truly in 1848! But if we are not recognised as Danish citizens with our German language any more – well – then we are not Danes any longer! [...] It is sad that this fatal idea of 'Danizing' the duchies has arisen."

5. Not represented in these data is the use of *sollen* as a substitute for HG *möchte gerne / würde gerne* in utterances like *Ich soll ein Schwarzbrot haben* ('I would like to have a brown bread').

6. Today about 90% of the national Danish minority of Flensburg has High German as home language and a variety of Standard Danish as institutional, mainly school language. This variety of Standard Danish is characterised by many language contact features of High German in lexicon, syntax and pronunciation. You might call this variety "Danish on German substratum".

7. Christine married the pharmaceutical chemist J. Heinrich Carstens who was licensed to found a chemist's store in the town of Jels in North Schleswig. My greatgrandfather built the house with the chemist's store, and the daughter of Christine and Heinrich Carstens, Elfriede Marie, and my grandmother were acquainted for more than eighty years!

8. Later in the same letter she also uses "aufpassen" with the Danish semantic intention of 'look after' (HG: *sich um etwas kümmern*): *Ich passe beide Stellen so gut wie möglich* 'I look after both places as good as possible'.

9. *Und*-constructions substituting embedded infinitive-constructions are, however, still in use in Flensburg nowadays. In spring 2002 an employee at the campus dining hall told me: *Es lohnt sich nicht und kochen drei essen* ('It is not worth while and cook three dishes').

References

Bock, K. N. (1933). *Niederdeutsch auf dänischem Substrat: Studien zur Dialektgeographie Südostschleswigs*. Copenhagen: Levin & Munksgaard.

Bock, K. N. (1952). Flensborgs sprogforhold gennem tiderne. In *Festskrift til L. L. Hammerich på tresårsdagen* (pp. 62–72). Copenhagen.

Dyhr, M. & Zint, I. (1985). Vorüberlegungen zu einem Projekt 'Sprachvariation in Flensburg'. *Kopenhagener Beiträge zur Germanistischen Linguistik, 23*, 91–104.

Fichte, J. G. 1807/08. *Reden an die deutsche Nation*. Hamburg (reprint 1978).

Fredsted, E. (2001). Parallelføring af nært beslægtede sprog. In P. Widell & M. Kunøe (Eds.), *8. Møde om Udforskningen af Dansk Sprog* (pp. 83–93). Århus: Nordisk Institut.

Fredsted, E. (2002a). The decline of a minor language. In Th. Stolz & J. Sherzer (Eds.), *Minor Languages. Approaches, Definitions, Controversies* (pp. 41–57). Bochum: Brockmeyer.

Fredsted, E. (2002b). Om sprogmodus – teoretiske og didaktiske overvejelser. In J. Cramer, O. Togeby, & P. Widell (Eds.), *M/K – Mod og kvindehjerte. Festskrift til Mette Kunøe 5. november 2002.* (pp. 263–281). Århus: Modtryk.

Fredsted, E. (2003). Flensburger Stadtsprache: Sprachkontakt und Sprachwandel. In H. H. Munske (Ed.), *Deutsch im Kontakt mit anderen germanischen Sprachen* (pp. 31–54). Tübingen: Niemeyer.

Henningsen, L. N. (1996). Til sognefoged Asmus Fromm i Soed: Breve fra fru brændevinsbrænder C.C. Christiansen i Flensborg 1846–1857. In L. N. Henningsen (Ed.), *Søndrjyske Årbøger 1996* (pp. 111–146). Aabenraa: Historisk Samfund for Sønderjylland.

Herder, J. G. (1772). *Abhandlung über den Ursprung der Sprache.* Stuttgart (reprint 1997).

Laur, W. (1975). Der Infinitiv mit 'und' statt 'zu' im Schleswigschen. *Muttersprache, 85*, 299–309.

Laur, W. (1983). Sprachen und Sprachformen in Angeln. *Jahrbuch des Heimatvereins der Landschaft Angeln 1983*, 11–21.

Menke, H. (1996). 'Ich bin ein Däne und spreche Deutsch'. Zur Sprachgeschichte und Sprachenpolitik im deutsch-dänischen Grenzraum. In Marti, R. (Ed.), *Sprachenpolitik in Grenzregionen* (pp. 137–161). Saarbrücken: SDV Saarbrücker Druckerei und Verlag.

Myers-Scotton, C. (1998). A way to dusty death: the matrix language turn over hypothesis. In L. Grenoble & L. J. Whaley (Eds.), *Endangered languages* (pp. 289–316). Cambridge: CUP.

Paulsen, Chr. (1837/1941). *Det danske Sprog i Hertugdømmet Slesvig.* Tønder: Sønderjydsk Maanedsskrift's Nytryk Nr. 1 (reprint 1941).

Pontoppidan, E. (1745/1943). *Erik Pontoppidan om det Danske Sprogs Skiæbne udi Sønderjylland eller Slesvig.* Haderslev: Sønderjydsk Maanedsskrift's Nytryk Nr. 2 (reprint 1943).

Sach, A. (1896–1907). *Das Herzogtum Schleswig in seiner ethnographischen und nationalen Entwicklung I-III.* Halle/S.

Schütt, O. (1919/1985). *Die Geschichte der Schriftsprache im ehemaligen Amt und in der Stadt Flensburg bis 1650.* Hamburg: Helmut Buscke Verlag (reprint 1985).

Schütt, O. (1921). Flensburgs Sprache. *Schleswig-Holsteinisches Jahrbuch 1921*, 63–67.

Søndergaard, B. (1984). Dansk og tysk som undervisningssprog i Flensborg mellem de to slesvigske krige. Et forsøg med tosproget undervisning. *Uddannelseshistorie* (pp. 31–86). Copenhagen.

Written and spoken languages in Bergen in the Hansa era

Agnete Nesse
Bodø Regional University, Norway

1. Introduction

Bergen is located on the Western coast of Norway. With approximately 250,000 inhabitants, it is the second largest city in the country. In this article I will discuss the history of the dialect of Bergen in light of contact between Norwegians and the German colony of merchants that existed in the city from approx. 1350 until approx. 1750.

The dialect of Bergen differs from other Norwegian dialects in several respects. First of all, the distance between the dialect of the city and those of the surrounding rural areas is larger than for any other Norwegian city. Second, there are grammatical traits in the Bergen dialect that may be found in other varieties of Norwegian but only as social variables. For instance, the merger of the masculine and feminine gender is part of high-status speech in other Norwegian cities and exists as a remnant of the old Dano-Norwegian mixed language. In standard Danish, the masculine and feminine genders merged during the period 1450–1600 (Pedersen 1999), and as Danish became an increasingly important norm for Norwegians, this merger was one of many features that made its way into high-status Norwegian speech. The majority of the population had, and still has, a three-gender variety.

But in Bergen, there is no social differentiation when it comes to this feature. In fact, most people from Bergen only have a very vague idea concerning which nouns are feminine in other dialects, although they do know that other dialects have the (feminine) ending *-a* on words for which Bergen has the (masculine) ending *-en*. This leads to hypercorrect forms such as the form *Cocen Colen* (used jokingly) for the drink *Coca Cola*. Another important marker is the past tense of class one of the weak declension ("a-verbs"), in which both the Bergen dialect and Dano-Norwegian have the ending *-et*, in contrast with most other varieties of spoken Norwegian, which have either *-e* or (most commonly) *-a*. Again, while *-et* is a high-status variant other places in Norway, in Bergen it is the only possibility.

It has been a problem for dialectologists to explain these features of the Bergen dialect, since they are common to both the high and low variety, and thus cannot be regarded as "non-dialect". There is also no reason to say that Danish influence was any stronger in Bergen than in other Norwegian cities. Therefore, the solution was to find phonetic explanations, without asking the uncomfortable question of why these phonetic processes only took place in Bergen.

If you ask Norwegians the reason for the "strangeness" of the people of Bergen in general and their dialect specifically, you will be told that the international history of the city and the fact that it was Norway's largest city and the most important centre of commerce for centuries account for their strange language and self-confidence – especially their "Bergen-confidence". The memory of the German Hansa merchants is held in high esteem in the city, helped by the fact that some of the buildings where they lived and worked at *Bryggen* 'the harbour' still exist in the heart of the city.

So why haven't dialectologists looked more closely at the history of the city? Why haven't they considered the international flavour of the city and the existence of a German colony at Bryggen as important inputs to the grammar of the present dialect? There are two reasons for this. The first is the troubled history of Norway, marked by the 500-year-long union with neighbouring countries. The humiliating fact that in the late Middle Ages Norwegians gave up their own written language and started writing Danish instead has led to an almost frantic search for the "real" Norwegian language. And since some of the linguistic traits typical of the Bergen dialect were similar to Danish, it was important to claim that these features existed before this union so that it could be claimed that they were not the result of Danish influence. This meant that they would have to have emerged before 1300, and "sympathetic" searches in sources from this period produced evidence for the old age of the Bergen dialect. This evidence must be questioned today. The important point here however, is that the dialect was also claimed to have developed before contact with the Germans started.

The second reason is the neo-grammarian paradigm that was the basis for the work of both dialectologists and historical linguists in the first half of the 20th century. Most research on the history of the Bergen dialect was carried out by Mikjel Sørlie (1938, 1950), but others, like Amund B. Larsen and Gerhard Stoltz (1911–1912) have also contributed. As Jahr (1999) shows, there was no theoretical underpinning for the neo-grammarians to use to analyse results of language contact other than loans. And since these grammatical features so specific to the Bergen dialect do not exist in German, they could not, one assumed, be the result of German-Norwegian contact. For example, how could a three-gender language like Old Norwegian and a three-gender language like Middle Low German produce the two-gender system of the Bergen dialect?

It was not until the (post World War II) development of theories of dialect and language contact that it was possible to look at the "strangeness" of the Bergen dialect anew. Mechanisms like *levelling* and *simplification* and evidence from research around the world showed that contact between different linguistic varieties could result in much more than loans from one language to another.

This is not to say that there has been no awareness of Low German influence on Norwegian. This influence has been strong and has been recognised by everyone dealing with the history of Norwegian, as well as of the other Scandinavian languages. A large part of Scandinavian vocabulary has Low German origins, and since some Low German word formation elements (e.g. *-he(i)t*) became productive in the Scandinavian languages, even original Scandinavian words may contain Low German elements. In Norway this has been important in language politics, since Nynorsk (New Norwegian), the standard developed in the 1800s with a strong purist component, has tried to exclude Low German elements as much as possible.

It has also been recognised that the Low German linguistic material has had two ports of entry into Norwegian. One was through the Danish (mostly written) standard, which represents the "change from above" direction of loans, which Norwegians came into contact with in churches and in all official documents. The other port of entry came through the Hansa merchants, especially in Bergen, and this has to a larger extent been considered to be "change from below" since it came through German merchants' and sailors' contact with Norwegian merchants, sailors, fishermen and farmers. But so far no one had looked at the sociolinguistic situation in detail, nor had anyone considered the grammatical features that distinguish the Bergen dialect from other Norwegian dialects as the result of contact before Jahr suggested that this might be the case in his first article on the topic in 1995 (English version 1999).

My work has been to analyse the sociolinguistic situation in Bergen in order to find out how intense the contact between the Norwegians and the Germans was, how long it lasted, and what kind of code they used when they spoke to each other. The theoretical framework has included theories of linguistic contact, such as Weinreich (1953), Thomason and Kaufman (1988), and Trudgill (1986), and historical linguistics, where Milroy (1992) and Nevalainen and Raumolin-Brunberg (1996) have been especially important. Methodologically, I have relied on the hermeneutics side of philology, as well as sociolinguistic methods related to historical material.

The main data base is a large corpus of written material from the 1300s–1700s, all of which is written in Bergen, but in four different written languages: Norwegian, Low German, Danish and High German.

2. The Norwegians and the Germans

2.1 The Hansa era in Bergen

One problem in using the term 'Hansa era' is that it is known all over Europe (at least in the Northern parts) as the period from approximately the 1200s–1500s. By the early 1500s, the Hanseatic League was losing its strongholds in the North. However, it is important to note here that the Hansa era in Bergen does not coincide with this time frame.

Even though German merchants came to Bergen to trade as early as the 1100s, it was not until the mid 1300s that a Hansa *Kontor*[1] was established in Bergen. This organisation, with its headquarters in Lübeck, and later in Bremen, monopolised the crucial trade of fish from Norway and grain and salt to Norway. Other goods were also traded both ways, but both politically and economically there is no doubt that fish, grain and salt were the most important commodities traded. This was so successful for the Hansa league that they did not give up their *Kontor* ('trading office') until 1756, after 400 years of trade.

Thus, when I claim that important features of the Bergen dialect developed during the Hansa era, it does not mean that they arose before 1500. On the contrary, it is clear that, whereas German loan words were already plentiful in Norwegian in the 1300s, most of the grammatical alternations of the Bergen dialect did not develop until the 1500s. We must seek the reason for this in the way Bergen society was organised; in addition to the difference in how quickly loanwords are adopted compared to the slow pace of grammatical alternations. Even though Bergen had a German-speaking minority in its midst for 400 years, there was relatively little integration between the Norwegians and the Germans, perhaps apart from the last 100–150 years when the situation was normalised. By "normalised" I refer to the fact that the German merchants more often took Norwegian citizenship, married, and then traded as regular Norwegian subjects.

The lack of integration between the groups during most of the Hansa period was due to the way the Hansa league organised their Kontors. We find more or less the same situation in the other three major foreign settlements, in London, Brügge and Novgorod. One important factor was that the Hansa Kontors consisted of single men. In Bergen there were as many as 2,000 of these single German men, and at times they amounted to as much as 1/5 of the overall population. This enforced celibacy we can assume had less to do with morals than with organisational and economic matters. Making sure the merchants did not marry Norwegians assured that their wealth did not stay in Norway, but was channelled back to Germany and to the trade there.

In addition to celibacy the self-regulation of the Hansa Kontor in Bergen served to separate the groups. In the city's official records, the absence of any mention of the Germans is almost total; if one did not know that there was an additional set of Hansa Kontor records, which dealt with the internal affairs of the Kontor, one would think the Germans in Bergen never got into any trouble. In fact, more of the records from the Hansa Kontor than from Bergen society in general have been preserved, partly due to the fact that the German area, Bryggen, did not burn down as often as the rest of the city did. The Germans had strict fire-prevention regulations, a very important one being that they only heated very few of their houses and prohibited open fires in the vast majority of their quarters.

The two groups went separate ways in other areas of life as well. The Germans had their own churches from the 1400s onward, not because of any religious differences: in the 1400s they were all Catholics. The German churches in Bergen became protestant in 1527 (Clausen 1998: 104), and the Norwegian churches in 1536. The official reason for having different churches was that this was necessary because of the language, although it may be the case that isolation in itself was looked upon as favourable, not by the Norwegians, but by the Hansa headquarters. Trade, the foundation of the whole society, was also divided up. The Germans dealt with the export of fish and the import of grain and salt, and foreign trade lay almost exclusively in their hands. But they were not allowed to handle domestic trade, and they were also not allowed to sail their ships to the North of Norway to the fisheries of Nordland and Finnmark to collect the fish. Such restrictions on the movements of the Germans also secured Bergen's position as the centre of trade for most of Norway, even though the most important reason for the restrictions was to secure an income for Norwegian traders.

The fact that fishermen from the Northern part of Norway travelled all the way to Bergen with their fish and depended economically on selling it in Bergen in order to survive in the cold North has left cultural traces that still can be found in the North. Linguistically, they were influenced by the Bergen dialect, and more German loan words can be found in that part of the country than for example in the East (Skancke 2001). The amount of church artwork from the Northern part of Germany found in Northern Norwegian churches shows us both the route of cultural influences, and the fact that trade also brought wealth to groups of Norwegians in the far North.

I have searched through a variety of sources from Bergen for the period in question in order to find contacts between the groups that were not restricted by regulations. Obviously, in those days, if they did not intermarry and did not meet at work or in church, there weren't that many domains left in which mutual friendship could evolve. But there were some possibilities. The Norwegians were invited as spectators to some of the initiation rites that the German apprentices had to undergo when they first came to Bergen. Some of these initiation rites were rather violent, others had more of a resemblance to a small carnival, and must also have been a welcome entertainment for the Norwegians. Still it has been argued that these initiation rites served to point to the German identity of the members of the Kontor, and to strengthen their isolation from the rest of Bergen society (Clausen 1998: 106–109).

Our sources also inform us of shooting competitions in which both groups participated. This parrot-shooting was a tradition originating from France (Clausen 1998: 97), that all groups of the society took part in. From time to time the highest officials of the German colony would be invited by the leading Norwegians to festive occasions such as weddings and baptisms. And of course, the fact that a number of children were born of German fathers and Norwegian mothers means that the contact at times must have been rather intimate.

All in all, we can say that the organisation of Bergen society involved a clear division between the Germans and the Norwegians. However, since people are after all social animals, they found ways of meeting that became an important bridge – also linguistically – between them. And this leads us to the issue of the languages spoken in Bergen at the time. Was there a mixed language? Were people bilingual? Was one of the groups bilingual and the other monolingual? Firstly, we will take a look at Norwegian and Low German, and the relationship between these languages, and Danish and High German respectively.

2.2 Double diglossia?

When the Hansa Kontor was first established in Bergen, both Norwegian and Low German were used in writing. Norwegian was one of the first native languages of Northern Europe to be used instead of Latin in official documents, and due to the strength of the medieval Norwegian state and to emigration of Norwegians to England during the Viking era, the language was used over a wide area in North-Western Europe in the Middle Ages. Low German, although taken into official use somewhat later, spread through the trade of the Hansa league to a large area, which means that at the beginning of the Bergen Hansa era, both Norwegian and Low German were prestigious languages used in writing as well as in oral communication.

This situation did not last through the whole period in question. The various unions between the Scandinavian countries in the late Middle Ages, ending with a stable Danish-Norwegian union, saw Norway as the weaker member, politically as well as culturally. Danish and Norwegian are closely related languages, often viewed as two dialects of one common Scandinavian language. Because of this, the language shift in Norway was not abrupt but took place over several hundred years. Danish elements became more and more prominent in the written language of Norwegians from the 1300s onward. At the time of independence from Denmark in 1814, Norwegians who were literate, i.e. the elite, had learned to write perfect Danish, abandoning almost all traces of Norwegian dialect in their writing. But even though the Norwegians learned to write Danish, most of them never started speaking it. A small elite used a Dano-Norwegian mixed language, but the vast majority of the population continued speaking Norwegian in its various dialects. During the first centuries of the Dano-Norwegian union, we do find traces in the sources of something that could have evolved into a modern Norwegian written language, but after 1600 they more or less disappeared. The Swedish-Norwegian union from 1814 to 1905 left no linguistic traces in Norwegian, one reason for this is that even if Norway was now politically united with Sweden, the cultural ties to Denmark were still much stronger than those to Sweden.

One could perhaps describe the relationship between Danish and Norwegian in Norway during the greater part of the union as diglossic. Danish was then the High language, used in all formal situations such as in church and in court, and in all writing. Norwegian was the spoken language used by everyone, but it was only used in writing for folkloristic and humorous literature, such as poems for weddings, rural comedies etc. (Venås 1990). Bergen was no exception to this, and the fact that such a large part of the population was German did not alter the position of Danish in the city.

The "destiny" of Low German was in many ways the same as that of Norwegian. When the power that had supported the use of a language, in this case the Hansa league, had weakened, another language took over the status of the written language. The struggle between Low German and High German in Germany is not the topic here; an overview can be found in for example Menke (1992). Of course, the relationship between Low and High German in Bergen mirrored the situation in Germany. In both countries there was a large time-span extending from when High German took over in the first domains, until it was used in all written language. The Low German sources from Bergen show the same adoption of High German features as the Norwegian sources do for Danish features. This happened little by little, and different writers didn't always adopt the same features. Thus there is great variation. After 1580, due to the arrival of a new Secretary,[2] High German became the language of official correspondence emanating from the Hansa Kontor in Bergen. But for internal use, Low German was still the main language for another hundred years.

One of the most telling examples of the strong position of Low German in Bergen dates from 1629 (Archiv der Hansestadt Lübeck, Alte Senatsakten, Danica no. 702 a). The Secretary, Caspar Heigenius, always wrote his correspondence in High German. But in this one case he did not write the letter himself, but translated a letter from Danish into German for a group of Norwegians. The letter is addressed to Lübeck, and Heigenius did not translate it into High German as one would expect, but into Low German. Why? There are two possible answers, and one does not exclude the other. One possibility is that the choice of language was a strategic one: addressing the council in Lübeck in the old language of the Hansa league and Lübeck would help promote their cause. Another possibility is that writing the letter in Low German was the choice of the Norwegians. After several hundred years of contact with Low German, they may very well have considered Low German to be the "real" German language; in addition it was probably the one German language they could understand, even if they were not able to write a letter in it.

Diglossia in Bergen was a linguistic situation that applied to all citizens as time passed and the two older languages ceased to be used in official documents, as well as in official speech. High German and Danish became the High varieties, and Low German and Norwegian became the Low varieties. German and Norwegian were never in a diglossic relationship. The two groups had separate institutions and used separate languages. Our next question therefore is this: How did the Norwegians and the Germans communicate with one another?

2.3 A kind of bilingual community?

A bilingual community can have many different faces. All inhabitants can be bilingual, one group can be bilingual and another monolingual, a mixed code can be established, etc. Trying to find out what kind of bilingual community – if any – existed in Bergen 500 years ago means that written sources have to be interpreted both in the light of what languages they are actually written in and what can be read between the lines about language use in that society.

The sources from Bergen are unambiguous concerning the above-mentioned. Both when reading the contents and when analysing language use, it is evident that contact between the Norwegians and the Germans was limited. We can assume that for the majority of the population (the Germans and the Norwegians), the most common speech acts involved speaking their own language.

This means that the need to have an active competence in the other language was limited. We know for certain from the information we have about translating, that a small group of people were bilingual. High officials from both the German and the Norwegian sectors translated letters for ordinary people, and it is evident that they also knew the different varieties: High and Low German as well as Danish and Norwegian. But this only holds true for a relatively small elite. There is no evidence that common people had an active competence in "the other" language of the city.

Suggestions have been made in the past that some sort of mixed language, even a pidgin language, may have existed in the city, and historically the Bergen dialect is a kind of creolised pidgin. But the sources give us no evidence that a mixed code of any kind ever existed. That a "new language" did not arise in Bergen can probably be explained by the strong consciousness of the Norwegians and Germans in Bergen concerning which group they belonged to. A mixed language that is used as a mother tongue often arises owing to the need for the speakers to show a new common identity. Bakker and Papen (1997) describe Michif as a language that arose owing to the need for a "new" group to build their new, common identity by means of a mixed language. Thomason and Kaufman (1988: 228–233) also discuss this, and it makes sense that the separate identities of the groups in Bergen helped keep the languages apart.

Another point is that it has been claimed that code switching could serve as evidence that the population were actively bilingual, not just passive. But just as with code mixing, no trace of code switching is to be found in the written sources. Even the single example of code switching from Bergen reported by Jahr (1999: 135) has been proved to be inauthentic. It involved code switching between Dano-Norwegian and High German in a document from 1632, published in 1877. As showed in Nesse (2002: 143–146), the code switching was not part of the original document, which was written in German only by the Hansa Society in Bremen. The 'code switching' was simply a technique used by the publisher (Nielsen 1877) in order to shorten the document. Only that which Nielsen considered crucial to the content was cited in the original language, German; the rest appeared in Dano-Norwegian. This was a rather common practice among publishers of medieval documents, for example the publishers of *Hansisches Urkundenbuch*, a collection of Hansa documents. How this technique worked, can be ilustrated by the following (original text in bold letters):

> *Published edition, 1877*
> Den ældste Frachsherr skal da aftakke og en anden vælges i hans Sted. **Es mögen auch die Herren Älterleute und Frachtherrn diese Zusammenkunft aus bewegenden Ursachen mit Essen und Trinken wohl vermindern.** De udeblivende skulle straffes **auf sechszehn Grote.**
> *Original manuscript, 1632*
> und soll alsdenn der Elteste Frachtherr abkiesen und von den Elterleuten Eltesten und Frachtherren einen anderen in seine Stelle wiederumb erwhlen, es mugen auch die Herrn Elterleuthe und Frachtherren diese Zusammenkunft aus bewegenden Ursachen mit Essen und Trinken wohl vermindern, nicht zu wenigen aber soll sie, wie auch die Kiesung auf vorbenannte Zeit gehalten, die Ausbleibende aber auf sechzehn Grote gestraffet werden.
> [(lit.) and must then the oldest Frachtherr retire and by the Aldermen and Frachtherren another be elected in his place. The Aldermenn and Frachtherren may, if needed, supply the gathering with only little food, but not too little, if the election is to be carried out in the right way. Those who do not attend, will be punished by sixteen groten.]

Not only did the publisher produce a shorter text, we see that he also standardised the German of 1632 in order to be closer to the German standard language of 1877.

Other – authentic – examples, or even information of any kind of code switching do not exist. The Germans wrote in German, first Low German, later High German, and the Norwegians wrote first in Norwegian, and later in Danish. In the cases where, as I mentioned, Norwegians issued a letter in German or the Germans issued a letter in Norwegian or Danish, we usually have information about the translation process. Even in the documents from court cases in which both groups were represented, nobody felt the need to say in what language(s) the negotiations should be carried out.

There is one document, however, written in Bergen in 1521, that can shed some light on how this was managed (*Diplomatarium Norwegicum* VIII, No. 501). The court case revolves around a fight that took place between (Norwegian) soldiers from the fortress and men from the Hansa Kontor. The representative for the soldiers was Jørgen Hansen, a Danish official in charge of the fortress on behalf of the Danish king. The representative for the Germans was the alderman, one of the top officials at the Hansa Kontor. The document is a long one, and the whole discussion is reproduced in Danish. What is interesting for us is the difference between how Jørgen Hansen's speech and that of the alderman are reported: Jørgen Hansen's is reproduced as direct speech, whereas the alderman's is indirect speech.

First Jørgen Hansen is heard:

> Thalede tha forne Jorien Hansson till oldermandhenn mett therres selscop thesse efftterne ord. Her oldermand oc gode mend alle etther ær well witterligtt huarledes meg ær scked naged forstacket pa wor nadigste herres wegne ...
> [Spoke then the previously mentioned Jørgen Hansen to the aldermen and their company these reported words: Mister Alderman and all good men all know well how something wrong has happened to me on behalf of our merciful Lord (sc. the king) ...]

Then the alderman:

> Gaff tha oldermanden thisse efftherne klage och sager pa Jorien och hanss tienere. Fførst att nw j sommher nagen stwnd forlede(n) kom ther nogher aff Joriens om natter tiid på gadhen mett spentte stolbuer och helbordher och sloge och sckøde på therres thienere och ...
> [Gave then the Alderman this reported complaint and cases against Jørgen and his servants: First that now in the summer a while ago, some of Jørgen's people came during the night on the street with aimed bows and halberds and hit and shot at their servants and ...]

Why has the writer chosen this strategy? It may be that he was taking sides in the case and wanted to show that Jørgen Hansen was trustworthier than the alderman. But I prefer another explanation to this question. The shift between direct and indirect speech most likely reflects the fact that during the hearing, Jørgen spoke Danish and the alderman spoke German. This would have been "standard procedure" in Bergen at that time, because we know for certain that Jørgen knew Low German – he translated several letters between the languages. So he could have spoken Low German if he had to, if this had been the common way of doing things. But it wasn't. Most likely this reflects the fact that the normal situation in Bergen during the Hansa era was for the members of each group to use their own language.

This must mean that the linguistic situation can be described as passive bilingualism: the Norwegians understood Low German, but most of them did not speak it, and the Germans understood Norwegian, but most of them did not speak it. Why and how had this situation arisen? The suggestion has been made (Braunmüller 1995; Jahr 1999) that Low German and Norwegian were so similar that mutual understanding was easy without learning the other language, and that communication between the groups can be compared to that between Scandinavians today. Scandinavians (Norwegians, Swedes and Danes) do communicate with each other by using their own languages because the languages are so similar that they are no harder to understand than a very different dialect from their own country.

Of course, our only way to examine whether or not this was the case between Norwegian and Low German in the Hansa era is through written sources. In addition to the problems this gives us, the notion of *similarity* is a difficult one. Is it a strictly linguistic measure, where we look at the likeness of vocabulary and grammatical systems? Or is it tied to the existence of mutual understanding? The two do not have to coincide – understanding is affected not just by similarity but also by attitudes, willingness etc., and those factors cannot be discovered just by examining linguistic structure. Neither my own investigations nor Warter's (1995) more quantitative investigations on the similarity between Low German and Danish or Swedish can convince us that the languages were readily understandable for speakers of the other group.

My hypothesis is that Norwegian and Low German were not mutually intelligible per se, and this means that "similarity" is not the reason behind the special sociolinguistic situation of the city. It did take some learning on both sides to understand the other language. For the people of Bergen, understanding Low German was a natural part of their upbringing. For the Germans in Bergen, who for the most part entered the city as teen-aged apprentices, learning how to understand Norwegian was part of the new life that they had to adjust to when they arrived, and probably not the hardest one.

In addition to learning to understand the other code, they developed over the centuries a way of communicating with each other that involved two main strategies. One was using loan words from the other group's language. Examples of Low German loanwords in Norwegian are plentiful, of local Bergen loans one could mention MLG *bôm* 'tree' that was used in the compounds *pratebom* ('talking tree', sc. a tree with a circular bench attached to it, where people could sit and talk) and *vippebom* (a kind of elevator for goods), whereas the normal word for "tree" remained Norwegian: *tre*. Norwegian loans in the MLG texts written in Bergen are also common, like *husmor* ('house wife', but meaning female servant), *kleve* 'small room' and *dyrr* 'expensive'.

In addition to using loan words, there has been a strategy of altering their own grammar in a way that would facilitate understanding, e.g. by preferring analytic constructions to synthetic ones. The new periphrastic genitive construction that evolved in the Bergen dialect due to contact with MLG is a good example of this. Since the old case markings merged and became harder to analyse for others than the native speakers, the need would be felt for constructions that were less ambiguous. A genitive construction such as the example from *Bergen Rådstueprotokoll* from 1592: *Henndrich Wishane part* ('Henndrich Wishane's part') has no genitive marker, since both Old Norse nominative *Wishana* and genitive *Wishanu* had been reduced to *Wishane*. The Danish strategy of importing *-s* to these words, since other nouns already had *-s* as genitive ending, was not applied in Bergen. Instead they were inspired by the MLG construction using the personal pronouns *sin* (m.) and *ehr* (f.) to express possessive genitive, and the result was constructions such as the one we find from aproximately the same period: *Jacob Christiernson sine vidnesbyd* ('Jacob Christiernson's testimony'; see 3.1 for some more about this construction).

When we combine these two strategies, using each other's words and altering the grammar so it becomes easier to understand, the step towards creating a common code, a mixed language, is not large. Why didn't this happen?

To find the reason for this, we must again look at the social conditions. The two groups were distinguished from each other in so many ways, e.g family life, work, churches etc., that they never forgot who belonged to which group. And if we view language use as a symbol of the society in which it is used, the use of separate codes in Bergen reflected the separation of the groups. Of course, they could have learned each other's languages actively, and they could have developed a mixed code, but they didn't. They were equal but different, and so were their languages.

3. Grammatical changes

3.1 Introduction

There are a large number of grammatical features in the Bergen dialect to look at from a language contact-perspective. Jahr (1999: 124–125) has a list of 9 different dialect features that may involve contact between the Germans and Norwegians in Bergen, which include phonological, morphological and syntactic features. I have restricted my main research to five features, two syntactic and three morphological. My reason for excluding phonological features is that they cannot be easily traced in the written sources, due to the great variation in spelling. For example, it is hard to trace the opposition between long and short vowels in the texts. This applies especially to short vowels and long consonants in stressed syllables (*venn*, *droppe*, *komme* 'friend, drop, come') in the Bergen dialect, as opposed to long vowels and short consonants in the neighbouring dialects (*ven*, *dråpe*, *koma* 'dito'). In modern written Norwegian length is marked on the consonant, whereas Danish has had a history of marking the length on the vowel. In the texts from the period in question, there are traces of both systems, and it can be hard to interpret how the pronunciation was.

The morphological and syntactic features are easier to analyse from written material. In addition to the features that I present in this article, I have looked at the infinitive marker *te*, the use of the ending *-et* in the past form of weak verbs of class one ("a-verbs"), and the periphrastic genitive with *sin*. The infinitive marker, which varies between *te*, *å* and *og* in present-day Bergen dialect, was *at* in Old Norse. The main reason for the occurrence of *te*, which is also a preposition in the dialect, as an infinitive marker, must have been the likeness to the pattern in Middle Low German, where the infinitive marker *to* is homonymous with the preposition *to*. This system is also found in English, where the infinitive marker *to* is homonymous with the preposition *to*, as well as in High German (*zu* – *zu*). The infinitive marker *te* in Bergen (which spread to other West-Norwegian dialects) is not to be regarded as a direct loan from MLG, the form in the MLG texts from Bergen is always *to*, never *te*. But the German system has been adopted through the course of contact.

The past tense *-et* is according to Jahr (1999) the result of a compromise between the Norwegian and Low German endings for the past tense and participle. The Norwegian pattern is to have the same ending in both forms, either *-a* or *-e*. Low German had *-ede* in the past tense and *-et* in the participle. The people of Bergen then chose the German participle ending and the Norwegian pattern, using *-et* in both the past tense and the participle.

The periphrastic genitive with *sin* is without doubt the feature that has received most attention from both Norwegian and other scholars. The construction exists in a variety of Germanic languages and has been analysed both in a grammatical perspective (e.g. Fiva 1987; Poulsen 2002) and from a more historical perspective (Torp 1973; Norde 1997). My contribution has been to point out the different choices the Norwegians in Bergen had between different analytic genitive constructions in the 1500s and 1600s, and the fact that the one used today (*Kari sin bok*) seems to have arisen among the common people, whereas the construction used by the upper classes, which was a "correct" translation of the German construction (*Kari hennes bok* < LG *Kari ehr Bôk*), died out. The surviving construction uses the reflexive pronouns *sin* (f./m.), *sitt* (n.), *sine* (pl.) instead of the personal pronouns. The reflexive pronoun in its masculine (and feminine) form is identical to the Low German masculine personal pronoun *sin*. So an expression like LG *Peter sin Bôk* has been translated to the similar sounding *Peter sin bok*, instead of the correct translation *Peter hans bok*.

The grammatical changes that I am going to discuss here are both morphological and have in common the fact that they led to an increase in the use of the ending -*en*, which was an extremely common ending in the Low German used in Bergen. We can look at an example from a Low German letter, written in Bergen in 1490:

> Jen**nen** wil**len** als notwert schol**en**, dat de mog**en** vthreding**en** krig**en**, vnde nicht werd**en** gantz vordoru**en** dorch de grot**en** teringe.
>
> (Willebrandt 1748:49)
>
> [for the sake of those who are going North, so they get supplies, and do not become totally destroyed by the great sickness].

We see that the ending -*en* in the Middle Low German example is used in pronouns (*jennen*), verbs (*scholen*), adjectives (*groten*) and nouns (*vthredingen*). This ending is also used in other Norwegian dialects, as the suffixed definite article in masc. sg: *båten* 'the boat'. But in the Bergen dialect, also nouns that were feminine in Old Norse receive this ending: *boken* 'the book', as do the definite form of proper nouns: *Knuten* 'Knut-the'. It was also common until the beginning of the 20th century that all past participle forms ended in -*en*: *Karen war slagen* 'Karen was beaten', whereas modern dialect has *Karen var slått*. Even if the ending -*en* was not applied in exactly the same way in the two languages, the result of the changes was that the languages had more in common.

3.2 The merger of the feminine and the masculine genders

Old Norse had three genders, feminine, masculine and neuter, and so does modern Norwegian. Whereas Standard Swedish and Standard Danish have undergone a reduction from three to two genders, both of the Norwegian written languages have three genders – at least in principle. In practice, the minority language, Nynorsk, is a three-gender language, and the majority language, Bokmål, is usually a two-gender (common and neuter) language, with only a relatively small portion of feminine nouns being marked as feminine (sometimes referred to as a two-and-a-half-gender language). The reason for this strange gender-mix in Bokmål, is that Bokmål in fact is the old Dano-Norwegian language (with two genders), revised in a Norwegian "direction". And most people seem to prefer a rather conservative way of writing, even though official politics has been to make people write more the way they speak.

Since many Norwegians choose to use only the common and neuter gender while writing Bokmål, and since a small group of people in cities like Oslo speak a variety with only to genders, we must say that a two-gender system is not at all unique in Norway. What makes the situation in Bergen so special is that there is no social differentiation between a high-status variety with two genders and a low-status variety with three genders, as was (and to some extent still is) the case in other Norwegian cities. All varieties of the Bergen dialect have only two genders, and this has led linguists to assuming that the reason for this two-gender system in Bergen must be something other than Danish influence during the union between the two countries.

The most common explanation (Sørlie 1938, 1950) for the merger of the feminine and masculine gender in the Bergen dialect has been a phonetic one. In Old Norse, one important feature differentiating the feminine and masculine gender was the opposition between short *n* for the feminine and long *n* for the masculine. The indefinite article was *ein* (f.) / *einn* (m.), and the suffixed definite article was *-in* (f.) / *-inn* (m.), for example *sólin* 'sun-the' (f.), *bátrinn* 'boat-the' (m.). In all other Norwegian dialects, *n* was reduced in both genders, so that there is now no *n* for the feminine (*ein* > *ei* 'a', *sólin* > *soli*, *sola* 'sun-the') and there is a short *n* for masculine (*einn* > *ein* 'a', *bátrinn* > *båten* 'boat-the') (the other changes will not be commented upon here). In the Bergen dialect, so the explanation goes, this reduction of *n* only took place in the masculine gender, thus leading to the two genders merging. Why this should happen only in Bergen has not been explained, and we can state that the phonetic explanation is little more than a description of what happened.

Research on linguistic contact has shown that gender is a feature that is often altered in contact situations. Weinreich (1953:45) discusses which strategies European immigrants from countries with gender-based languages adopted when they accommodated to English in the USA. English loanwords, when used in their native language, would often be assigned the same gender as the word with the same meaning in the native language. An example is the English word *boiler*, which was assigned the masculine gender by the German immigrants, probably because the German word *Kessel* was masculine. It is also important in these cases which gender is the most productive (or the default gender) in the native language.

The Scandinavian languages have several examples of a change in grammatical gender. One of the most unusual is the reduction and redistribution found in some West Jutland dialects (Pedersen 1999: 100). The dialects now have two genders, one for countables (such as *barn* 'child') and one for mass nouns (such as *sne* 'snow'). In the Norwegian and Swedish dialects that have had close contact with the Finnish and/or Sami languages, there has, in the most extreme cases, been a complete loss of gender (see Jahr 1984; Huldén 1972).

The merger between the masculine and feminine gender evolved a slow process in the Bergen dialect. Pettersen (1991) has shown that there is no evidence that either the indefinite article or the suffixed definite article had merged for nouns in the 1200s as claimed earlier. His analysis of official letters and documents from the period 1450–1550 shows that the merger can be dated to the late 1400s.

But, even if the endings were the same, can we say that the dialect of Bergen had no opposition between the masculine and the feminine gender after that? This brings us to the question of congruency. Even if in the 1500s articles and adjectives no longer showed any difference between the feminine and the masculine gender, one category kept the gender for another 100 years, namely the anaphoric pronouns *hun* 'she' and *han* 'he'.

I have studied three different sources from the 1500s quantitatively in order to investigate the use of these anaphoric pronouns. Were *hun* and *han* used? If so, were they used according to the old rules – that is, was *hun* used for old feminine nouns and *han* for old masculine nouns, or were the pronouns used randomly?

The sources are: the diary *Mester Absalons Dagbok* (Iversen 1963) from 1552–1572 written by a priest from Bergen, the chronicle *Bergen Fundas* (Sørlie 1957), most probably written in the late 1550s, but existing today as transcripts from the 1600s; and a city protocol *Bergens Rådstueprotokoll* from 1592–1594, the oldest one of its kind that we have from Bergen (the protocol has not yet been published in its entirety, the original is in Bergen Statsarkiv).

In the diary, it is obvious that the writer does have a feeling for feminine and masculine gender, even though it is not marked on the nouns, articles or adjectives. Anaphoric pronouns are not a very frequent feature in either spoken or written language, but the author consistently uses the correct pronoun according to the old feminine and masculine gender system. It is also interesting that when he uses Middle Low German loanwords such as *gierighed* (< MLG

Giricheit (f.) 'stinginess') and *dagger* (< MLG *Dagge* (m.) 'dagger'), he uses the same gender as the word has in Low German. The conclusion must be that the author does distinguish between the feminine and the masculine gender.

Bergen Fundas also has instances of *hun* and *han* as anaphoric pronouns, but in this source it is evident that the author does not know which words used to be feminine and which were masculine. A word like *by* (m.) 'city' is referred to both with *hun*, *han* and the new form *den*, which later replaced *hun* and *han* in Danish, Norwegian Bokmål and in some Norwegian dialects to refer to both feminine and masculine nouns.

In the city protocol, there is no use of *hun* and *han* as anaphoric pronouns, only *den* is used. That means that the writer not only does not make any distinction between feminine and masculine nouns at any level, but also follows the pattern of the Danish written language in the use of *den*. In the Bergen dialect, this did not happen. Instead, the result of the gender merger was that not only did feminine nouns follow the masculine declination; *han* also became the anaphoric pronoun for all non-neuter (fem. and masc.) nouns. Only female persons can be referred to with the feminine pronoun *hun* in the Bergen dialect today. Even feminine animals like *ku* 'cow' will normally be referred to by the masculine *han*. And even though this is very different from all other Norwegian dialects, and different from both the written standards, a sociolinguistic study carried out in the early 1990s showed that this was not a very salient variant in the dialect. *Han* was used in 82%, the competing variant *den* only in 18% (Nesse 1994: 149), and the young people used *han* just as often as the older people.

The terms *simplification* and *levelling* (Trudgill 1986) are useful in describing how contact between German and Norwegian may have led to the merger of gender in the Bergen dialect. Simplification refers here to the fact that grammatical reduction has taken place. Trudgill (1986: 102–106), based on Omdal (1979), uses the Norwegian dialect of Høyanger to show how dialect contact can lead to increase in regularity of noun declension. In the language contact of Bergen, the process has gone even further and the dialect has both merger of gender and increase in the regularity of noun declension. Levelling, described by Trudgill (1986: 98) as a process where marked variants are replaced by unmarked variants, is an as important factor in this process, since it increased the use of the ending *-en* that emerged as a linguistic "meeting place" for the two groups. Both varieties had the ending, MLG used it more than Norwegian, and the Norwegians increased their use of the ending in their own language as a part of the accommodation process.

In order to get the full picture, however, we also need to bring in the reduction in cases. Old Norse was a four-case (nominative, accusative, dative, genitive) language, whereas Modern Norwegian does not distinguish between cases for nouns. The reduction in cases took place during the same period as the reduction in differences between the feminine and masculine noun declension in the Bergen dialect. In addition, the number of declension classes fell, all in all a massive reduction in morphology.[3]

There are still some Norwegian dialects where the dative is in use, but most of Norwegian has seen a reduction from four cases to one for nouns. In many Norwegian dialects, declension classes for nouns were reduced to one or two per gender. Thus the reduction from three to two genders in the Bergen dialect is part of an overall, morphological reduction process that took place in Norwegian in the late Middle Ages. The reason why this simplification went further in Bergen than elsewhere in Norway, apart from the contact areas in the North, can be found in the German-Norwegian contact.

I see the development from three to two genders in the Bergen dialect as a two-phased process. The first phase co-occurred with the reduction of cases and classes of declension in Norwegian in general. In this phase, the indefinite article, the suffixed definite article and adjectives became the same for feminine and masculine nouns. For a period of time, maybe as long as a hundred years, the anaphoric pronouns *hun* and *han* were the only markers of feminine and masculine gender. By the end of the 1500s, people were no longer able to attach *hun* and *han* to nouns of the correct gender, and *han* took over in speech while *den* took over in writing. In addition, at the start of the new century the written language, in its Danish form, was becoming more standardised, leading in general to fewer dialect traits in writing, even in the writing of Norwegians.

3.3 Suffixed definite article on proper nouns

In Old Norse, proper nouns were treated as other nouns in the sense that they were given endings according to declension class and case. With the disappearance of case and the reduction of declension classes, proper nouns ceased to be declined. What arose instead in many dialects was the use of the personal pronoun before the proper noun, as in *ho Kari* / *a' Kari* 'she Kari', *han Knut* / *n' Knut* 'he Knut'. In some dialects today this is obligatory, that is, you can't use a name without the pronoun, as evidenced in examples like *ho Gro* (former Prime Minister Gro Harlem Brundtland) and even *han Jesus* 'he Jesus'. In other dialects the pronoun is used in much the same way as the suffixed definite article on nouns – to show that the person/thing/fact is known to both interlocutors.

The Bergen dialect does not have this use of the personal pronoun before a proper noun, neither as the obligatory variant nor as a stylistic variant. In this dialect, proper nouns are treated the same as common nouns, that is, when a person is not familiar to the speaker and/or listener, an unmarked form such as *Kari*, *Knut* is used, and when the person is known, the suffixed definite article is used: *Karien*, *Knuten*. Surnames can also be declined, so that a person called *Kari Vik* can be called both *Karien* and *Viken*, but not at the same time. Calling a person just by their surname has been more common for men than for women, so naturally also the definite variant on surnames is used more often for men.

Even though proper nouns were declined in Old Norse, there is no reason to believe that this is a feature that has survived from Old Norse into the modern Bergen dialect. There is a long period of time between the last Old Norse example of declined proper nouns and examples of the new variant. In fact, declining proper nouns like common nouns arrived so late that they are not easy to find in the written sources at all. By the time this feature developed in the Bergen dialect, the (Danish) norm for the written language was more standardised than before, and dialect features were used less frequently. In addition to this, the fact that declined proper nouns are only used in this dialect when both interlocutors know the person in question and are a trait of informal language use makes it less likely that they will be used in formal writing. But we still have the possibility of finding out how this came about with the help of sources from the 1500s and 1600s.

It must be mentioned, though, that other scholars have pointed to other connections to German than the one I am going to propose here; e.g. the fact that German has the definite article before proper nouns, as in *die Grete*, *der Johan* (Pettersen 1989: 213). But as was mentioned earlier, there is an equivalent Norwegian construction in which the personal pronoun appears in front of the proper noun: *ho Kari* 'she Kari', and what we need to explain, is how the contact with German led the people of Bergen to use another construction than this. The *ho Kari*-construction is also older than the one we find in Bergen (Hanssen 1976: 7).

Another idea that has been put forward is that the Bergen variant is a borrowing of the Low German diminutive suffix *-ken* used on proper nouns, as in *Johanken* 'little Johan' (Torp 1973: 144). But the Bergen variant is by no means a diminutive suffix; it is used at least as often for adults (especially men) as for children. There is, of course, the possibility that the German diminutive suffix has been redistributed as a definite marker, but sociolinguistically this explanation does not work. Even though some of the men living at Bryggen were as young as 15 years old, as far as we can interpret the sources, their social structure left little room for human relationships that would encourage the use of the personal diminutive suffix. And in order for the people of Bergen to use it, even as a redistributed form, they would have to have heard it quite often, and this seems unlikely to have happened. Therefore, we should look for another explanation.

In a city like Bergen, there was a great diversity of occupations. In addition to traders of all kinds, and all the domestic workers, there were a variety of craftsmen with different titles, many of Low German origin, such as *Kypper* (< LG *Kuper* 'barrel maker'). In the two oldest city protocols from Bergen, from 1592–1594 and from 1663, we can clearly see that a man's name and his title were both used to refer to him. Look at this example from 1593:

> Och derforudenn haffuer for_ Morthenn innbrudh sig Vdi **Johann Kyppers** hus oc om Natterthidh staalett aff **Kypperens** pung oc hans quindes pung som beløb sig thil 7 mrk 12 sk.
> [And in addition has the before mentioned Morthenn broken into Johann Kypper's house and during the night time stolen from the Kypper's wallet and his woman's wallet that counted to 7 mrk 12 sk.]

The married women are described as belonging to their husband using both his name and his title: *Beritte Steffens quinde* 'Beritte Steffens woman', *kannegyderens hustrw* 'the wife of the pewterer' (*kannegyder* < LG *kannen-geter*).

Since a title is a common noun, it is not strange that it is declined. When titles gradually came to be used as personal names it wasn't a far call for them to also be declined. We can assume that people first started declining names that originally were titles, then other last names and then later still, first names. This change led to a simpler grammatical system than other Norwegian dialects have. Instead of marking familiarity for proper nouns using pronouns and for common nouns using the suffixed article, all nouns, including proper nouns, were declined in the same way. This seems to be a typical example of the process of simplification: the grammatical system becomes more regular, with fewer exceptions to the main rule.

Also, we see that this change led to an increase in the already frequent ending *-en*, an ending that must have been the most unmarked at the time. A levelling process would favour this ending, as we have seen, both with the merger of genders and with the use of the suffixed article on proper nouns. There were other places in Norway where many different occupations were carried out, even though Bergen was probably the place with the greatest diversity. So the reason this linguistic feature only developed in Bergen must be because of the sociolinguistic conditions in the city, that is, contact between Norwegian and German. The use of the suffixed article on proper nouns now also occurs in the rural area South of Bergen, and these three-gender dialects use the feminine ending *-o* : *Kario* and the masculine ending *-en: Knuten*. We must assume that the use of this grammatical feature in these dialects was influenced by the Bergen form.

Unlike other results of contact between Norwegian and Low German in the Bergen dialect, the use of the definite suffixed article on proper nouns does not occur in all varieties of the dialect: it belongs to informal style, and to some degree to the low variety. There has not, however, been any sociolinguistic research investigating this feature, so we cannot assess its frequency precisely. But there is no evidence to suspect that young people use the definite suffixed article on proper nouns any less frequently than older people, so it can't be considered a threatened feature.

4. Summary

We can sum up by saying that the grammatical features in the dialect of Bergen that developed during the city's Hansa era (1350–1750) are still important features of the dialect. Whereas very few of the Low German loan words specific to the dialect are still in use, the grammatical features have survived. Since our written sources also show us that these grammatical changes occurred at a later stage than the loanwords entered the language, we have here an example of the difference between the lexical and grammatical level with regard to language contact: vocabulary is more easily acquired, but also more easily lost.

Notes

1. A Kontor was a privileged German settlement run by the Hanseatic League. Apart from the one in Bergen, there were three others: in London, Brügge and Novgorod.

2. The Secretary was the highest official in the Hansa settlement. He was appointed by the board of the Hanseatic League, and was usually educated at a school of Law (Bruns 1939).

3. In the modern Bergen dialect, all non-neuter nouns (apart from a few exceptions to the rule) are declined in the same way:

	indefinite sg.	definite sg.	indefinite pl.	definite pl.
non-neuters:	– / -e	-en	-ar	-ene
neuters:	– / -e	-e	– / -ar	-ene.

References

Bakker, P. & Papen, R. A. (1997). Michif: a mixed language based on Cree and French. In S. G. Thomason (Ed.), *Contact Languages. A Wider Perspective* (pp. 295–364). Amsterdam and Philadelphia: John Benjamins.

Braunmüller, K. (1995). Semikommunikation und semiotische Strategien. Bausteine zu einem Modell für die Verständigung im Norden zur Zeit der Hanse. In K. Braunmüller (Ed.), *Niederdeutsch und die skandinavischen Sprachen II* (pp. 35–70). Heidelberg: C. Winter.

Bruns, F. (1939). *Die Sekretäre des Deutschen Kontors zu Bergen. Det hanseatiske museums skrifter* 13. Bergen: John Grieg.

Clausen, A. S. (1998). The Lübeck Edition. The creation of a digital edition Featuring *Spillene* A Hanseatic tradition in Bergen. Universitetet i Bergen.

Fiva, T. (1987). *Possessor Chains in Norwegian.* Oslo: Novus.

Hanssen, E. (1976). Nominalsyntagme av typen *Han Asbjørn* i mellomnorsk. *Norskrift, 11,* 1–8.

Huldén, L. (1972). Genussystemet i Karleby och Nedervetil. *Folkmålsstudier: meddelanden från Föreningen för nordisk filologi,* 47–82.

Iversen, R. (Ed.). (1963). *Dagbok og oration om mester Geble.* Oslo-Bergen-Tromsø: Universitetsforlaget.

Jahr, E. H. (1984). Language contact in northern Norway. Adstratum and substratum in the Norwegian, Sami and Finnish of northern Norway. *Acta Borealia, 1,* 103–112.

Jahr, E. H. (1995). Niederdeutsch, Norwegisch und Nordisch. Sprachgemeinschaft und Sprachkontakt in der Hansezeit. In K. Braunmüller (Ed.), *Niederdeutsch und die skandinavischen Sprachen II* (pp. 125–144). Heidelberg: C. Winter.

Jahr, E. H. (1999). Sociolinguistics in historical language contact: The Scandinavian languages and Low German during the Hanseatic period. In E. H. Jahr (Ed.), *Language Change. Advances in Historical Sociolinguistics* (pp. 119–140). Berlin and New York: Mouton de Gruyter.

Larsen, A. B. & Stoltz, G. (1911–1912). *Bergens bymål.* Kristiania [Oslo]: Bymålslaget.

Menke, H. (1992). Monolingual – bilingual – lektal. Die Zweisprachigkeit des niederdeutschen Kulturraumes aus historischer Sicht. In J. A. van Leuvensteijn & J. B. Berns (Eds.), *Dialect and Standard Language* (pp. 221–255). Amsterdam: North Holland.

Milroy, J. (1992). *Linguistic Variation & Change.* Oxford: Blackwell.

Nesse, A. (1994). *Kollektiv og individuell variasjon i bergensdialekten.* In *Talemål i Bergen* 5. Målføresamlinga, Nordisk institutt, Universitetet i Bergen.

Nesse, A. (2002). *Språkkontakt mellom norsk og tysk i hansatidens Bergen.* Oslo: Novus.

Nevalainen, T. & Raumolin-Brunberg, H. (1996). *Sociolinguistics and Language History.* Amsterdam and Atlanta: Rodopi.

Nielsen, Y. (1877). De dudesche Kopman unde de Norman. Et nedertydsk Skrift fra det femtende Aarhundrede, indeholdende en Samtale mellem en Nordmand og en tydsk Kjøbmand i Bergen, – tilligemed Oplysninger om de gamle Bergerfarer-Kollegier i Lübeck og Bremen og deres Arkiver in *Forhandlinger i Videnskabs-Selskabet i Christiania Aar 1876* No. 8. Christiania: Jac. Dybwad.

Norde, M. (1997). *The History of the Genitive in Swedish. A Case Study in Degrammaticalization*. Universiteit van Amsterdam.

Omdal, H. (1979). Høyangermålet – en ny dialekt. In L. Vikør & G. Wiggen (Eds.), *Språklig samling på folkemåls grunn* (pp. 75–77). Oslo: Novus.

Pedersen, K. M. (1999). Genusforenkling i københavnsk. *Danske Folkemål, 41*, 79–105.

Pettersen, E. (1989). Einige Bemerkungen zum Schicksal niederdeutscher Entlehnungen im Norwegischen. In K. Hylgaard-Jensen, V. Winge, & B. Christensen (Eds.), *Niederdeutsch in Skandinavien II* (pp. 212–219). Berlin: Erich Schmidt.

Pettersen, E. (1991). *Språkbrytning i Vest-Norge 1450–1550 II*. Bergen: Alma Mater.

Poulsen, M. (2002). Meinem Vater sein Haus – Konstruktioner med resumptivt possessivpronomen i tysk og beslægtede sprog. Aarhus Universitet.

Skancke, K. (2001). *Mellomnedertysk påvirkning på nordnorske dialekter*. Skrift Nr. 3 fra prosjektet *Språkhistoriske prinsipp for lånord i nordiske språk*. København: Nordisk Ministerråd.

Sørlie, M. (1938). Om opphavet til Bergens bymål. *Maal og Minne*, 125–136.

Sørlie, M. (1950). *Bergens eldste bymål*. Bergen: J. W. Eide.

Sørlie, M. (Ed.). (1957). *Bergens Fundas*. Bergen: Beyer.

Thomason, S. G. & Kaufman, T. (1988). *Language Contact, Creolization and Genetic Linguistics*. Berkley–Los Angeles–London: University of California Press.

Torp, A. (1973). Om genitivsomskrivinger og –s- genitiv i norsk. *Maal og Minne*, 124–150.

Trudgill, P. (1986). *Dialects in Contact*. Oxford: Blackwell.

Venås, K. (1990). *Den fyrste morgonblånen. Tekster på norsk frå dansketida*. Oslo: Novus.

Warter, P. (1995). Computersimulation von Wortverstehen am Beispiel mittelniederdeutsch-skandinavischer Sprachkontakte. In K. Braunmüller (Ed.), *Niederdeutsch und die skandinavischen Sprachen* (pp. 71–124). Heidelberg: C. Winter.

Weinreich, U. (1953). *Languages in contact. Findings and Problems*. [Publications of the Linguistic Circle of New York 1.] New York and The Hague: Mouton.

Willebrandt, J. P. (1748). *Hansische Chronick*. Lübeck.

Vyborg

Free trade in four languages

Marika Tandefelt
Swedish School of Economics and Business Administration, Helsinki

1. Vyborg: A multilingual city

Political borders do not correspond, as we know, with the borders between different languages and cultures. There are many language areas that spread across one or more political borders so that a language that is the language of the majority in one society can at the same time be the minority language in one or more neighbouring countries. We also know that especially cities often are the meeting place for languages and cultures. Here a permanent resident who represents the local language comes into contact with immigrants and visitors who represent languages and cultures that are not rooted in the milieu but still can take root. More important than political borders are sometimes economic cycles and other social circumstances, which put people into motion. But the political borders are not without importance. Especially in a long-term perspective it is possible to see how changes in the power relations in a particular milieu have an effect on language users and thereby also for their language. Political power gives access to prestigious domains and the chance to assert language and cultural rights. Perhaps it is in reality only economic power, which can compete with political power, when it concerns the power and prestige of a language?

Vyborg, which today is a city in Russia, has a nearly seven-century-long history as a Swedish, Russian and Finnish border city. The border between what is today Finland and Russia has been fixed by seven different peace treaties, which all in some way have affected the castle and the city of Vyborg and its inhabitants (see map on p. 86). Regardless of how the border has been drawn since the building of the castle in 1293 (the city was chartered in 1403) the inhabitants

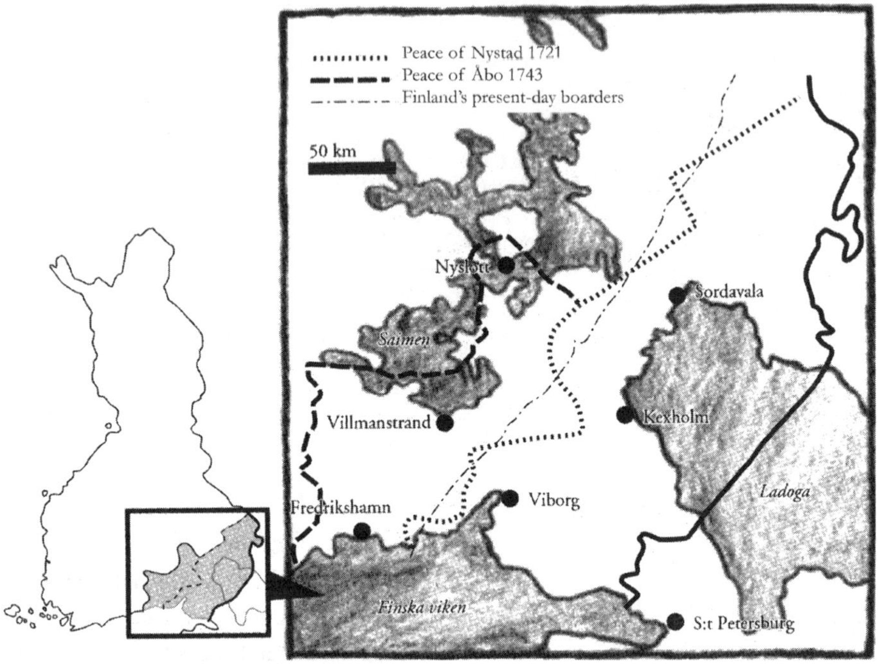

in the surrounding area have represented different languages and cultures. The city's favourable location for trade has been reason enough for the permanent population to remain and for new inhabitants to move in also during changing political conditions. This multilingual and multicultural city environment ceased to exist in 1944 when the city was emptied of its then Finnish but multilingual inhabitants. Vyborg became a Russian city through the Treaty of Paris in 1947 and in this way for the first time in its history a monolingual milieu. The conditions for the earlier lively foreign trade disappeared and the role of the city today is insignificant. On the other hand the memory of Finland's through the ages most cosmopolitan milieu has not faded. The lost Karelia with the central place of Vyborg has over the years gained nearly mythical proportions. To distinguish the historical city that I will be discussing from the city of today, I shall from here on out use its (probably Scandinavian) name *Viborg* (in Finnish *Viipuri*).

Just because several language groups occupy a milieu does not necessarily mean that multilingualism is the rule among the inhabitants. It is quite possible to think that the groups live segregated from each other and that a few individuals function as contact persons and border crossers thanks to their skills in several languages. Another possibility is that multilingualism is widespread among the population but that only one language (or possibly two) has importance on the level of society. Regardless of whether multilingualism most of all characterizes the milieu as a whole or instead only concerns separate individuals, changes will still happen over time. Both a language and the way of using a language live and develop. The process of change can be fast if it is a question of radically different conditions (for example as the result of a war), but it can also be drawn-out if it is influenced by conditions that lead to slower changes in the milieu (for example as a consequence of economic conditions).

Viborg with its long multilingual history offers a possibility to study both radical and slow changes with the consequences for the dominant relations between the city's four languages – Finnish, Swedish, German and Russian – and for the pattern of language contacts between the inhabitants. It has been possible to collect information about the languages and the use of languages from Finns who earlier lived in the city even if today they are very old. Such a study (Tandefelt et al. 2002) has recently been published and in this article I shall present some of the results of this study.

I shall take up two themes of which the first will be given more attention than the second shall. Firstly, I shall describe how the position of the languages in society and within different domains has changed over the centuries. Here I shall first of all build upon the historical literature but also on some writings of the time where the relation between the languages in Viborg has been commented. Needless to say the knowledge of the 20th and the 19th centuries is more solidly based than that of earlier centuries. The material in the town archives was partly lost in the last war. The historical framework is, however, absolutely necessary in order to be able to understand what role the different languages and the city's multilingualism has played in the life of the inhabitants of Viborg. Secondly, I shall present the word and phraseology lists for the four languages that I have collected from earlier inhabitants of Viborg and which they take to have been characteristic of the linguistic multiplicity in the city during the decades before the Second World War. The material consists of answers to questionnaires and interviews as well as to some degree older word lists. A summary of what may be taken to be basically characteristic of Viborg from the late 13th century to the middle of the 20th century concludes the article.

2. The Karelian border region

In Össeby-Garn (in Uppland in Sweden) stands a runic stone from the 11th century in memory of Sigsten who died in Viburgum. The stone is a reminder that the eastward expansion of the Swedes is older than the crusade (1293) which lead to the building of Viborg castle and the shortly thereafter growth of the city of Viborg on the point to the east of the island of the castle. The area around the discharge of the River Vuoksen was of interest to all who wanted to carry trade with Novgorod, and they were many. Swedes, Germans, Finns, Karelians and Russians met here both in battle and to trade.

The Peace of Nöteborg in 1323 established a political border, which despite some attempts remained fixed for centuries. It divided Karelia into a western (Roman and German, catholic and Swedish) and an eastern (Byzantium and Slavic, Orthodox and Russian) part. Viborg quickly took a central position both as Sweden's important strategic eastern outpost and as an important place of trade with the possibility of controlling the trading between the Bay of Viborg and Lake Ladoga. As a free city outside the Hanseatic League Viborg was of special interest to the merchants of the continent. The Dutch, Balts and especially the Germans traded through Viborg and at times settled there. By sailing under the flag of Viborg a German resident was not subject to the restrictions of the Hanseatic League (Tandefelt et al. 2002: 16f.).

Politically Viborg was a border zone that time and again constituted a danger for its inhabitants but from an economic point of view was exceptionally attractive. The possibilities for commerce meant that the city was multilingual and multicultural from the very beginning. Viborg was in addition to Åbo [Turku] the most important city in the eastern Finnish half of Sweden and one of Sweden's largest cities. Even in later times in the Grand Duchy of Finland and the Republic of Finland Viborg was one of the foremost cities in Finland. When Viborg became a Russian city after 1944 Viborg was the second largest city in Finland after Helsinki. By all accounts, from the very beginning Viborg was marked by its multilingualism. Both the inhabitants of Viborg and the surrounding area were conscious that in term of language and culture Viborg was different from other Finnish cities.

3. Viborg and the Kingdom of Sweden

"Det hus heter Wiborg och ligger öster" ('This house is called W. and situated in the east') it says in the so-called Eric Chronicle, which among other things describes the crusade against Karelia and the founding of the Castle of Viborg in 1293. According to the Chronicle the Swedes had two objectives: to convert the heathens and to hold their ground against the Novgorod. In point of fact securing the trade route of the Neva was the most important motive (Tandefelt et al. 2002: 16f.).

Until 1403 when the city received its charter, the population of Viborg was under the ruler of the castle who in turn was under the Swedish king. Finland (or what was to become Finland) was a part of the Kingdom of Sweden until 1809 even if Viborg and the whole southeast of Finland came under the Russian tsar already one hundred years earlier. During the Swedish period the ruling language was Swedish, but not only Swedish. German was also heavily represented in the city in the person of both the mayors (at any one time there were three mayors) and the city councilors. It was the same in other Swedish cities at the time. Russian was a language that one first of all came into contact with in connection with trade. Interpreters and translators between Russian and Swedish were at the castle. Finnish was the language of the majority but the Finnish speakers were primarily the small burghers and those one step below them in the social hierarchy.

There is no direct information about to what degree and in which context the different mother tongue inhabitants of Viborg interacted. Especially the paucity of knowledge about the inhabitants who did not belong to the bourgeoisie and about the majority of women makes it difficult to know anything more specific about the interaction between the language groups. However it does not seem too farfetched to claim that contact between the different social strata and mother tongues must have taken place in for example work relationships and work communities of various kinds. Labourers and tradesmen moved to the area to build the castle and the walls surrounding the city. Merchants needed apprentices, porters, coachmen and farmhands and the wives of the bourgeoisie needed servant girls and wet nurses. The labour that was recruited in the nearby surrounding countryside and further away must have been Finnish speaking.

It is probably fair to conclude that all those with Swedish, German or Russian mother tongue to some degree must have come into contact with the Finnish language. But it is still nearly impossible to ascertain who learned and used whose language. In all likelihood this was the reigning siuation until at least the end of the 16th century (Tandefelt et al. 2002: 21f.).

If a Finnish speaker wanted to engage in foreign trade, German was a precondition and knowledge of Russian was in all likelihood an advantage. If on the other hand one intended to seek a post with the crown it was the Swedish language which counted even if many of the leaders in the castle are said to have had some grasp of Finnish. Many Finnish speakers in Viborg were probably forced to learn an additional language which may have lead to a change of language in a later generation. That Finnish was not a language in which one could receive a formal education gave added reason to study languages if the position required book learning. The Swedish speakers already mastered the ruling language so that further language skills were not obligatory even if they were useful. Probably one learned to read German or understood the kind of spoken German that one came into contact with. The German speakers who did not permanently set up residence in the city but only remained temporarily to engage in trade probably remained monolingual. Their and the Swedish speaking inhabitants of Viborg's ability to understand each other's language probably was sufficient to meet their needs.

It is clear that the Swedish, German and Russian speaking permanent or temporary residents of Viborg constituted a minority relative to the much larger Finnish-speaking majority. The different language groups did not live segregated from each other. It is therefore not unlikely that from a quite early period the Finnish language offered a path of least resistance – a kind of local *lingua franca* – at least in informal and everyday situations. As the *lingua franca* in international commercial contacts the German language was without rival and its importance grew further with the increase of German speaking traders during the greater part of the 17th century.

The domains where the Swedish language could make itself counted were above all the school and the church, which at that time actually was part of the same domain. The official school language was in the 16th and 17th centuries, just as it had been in the Middle Ages, Latin. Still there was a need to fall back on another language and that was Swedish. The teaching of the catechism in Swedish was permitted and translations from Latin to Swedish were introduced. The teacher was allowed to use Swedish in their teaching and their Swedish proficiency was noted. The result was that those boys who had some other mother tongue than Swedish learned Swedish in addition to the knowledge of Latin which the school was primarily intended to teach. The Parish of Viborg was again established in 1618, which further strengthened the position of the Swedish language. Although the language of administration and the courts was officially Swedish, this was not slavishly followed. The court records of the period show that is was assumed that contending parties had a sufficient knowledge of Swedish and German as well as in certain cases Finnish to be able to manage a trial that took place in one or more languages (Tandefelt et al. 2002:24–35).

Towards the end of the Swedish period, Viborg was still an actively three-language milieu. Finnish, Swedish and German were regularly used even where those who used them had some other mother tongue. In addition the inhabitants of Viborg also had a passable knowledge of Russian even though the permanent resident mother tongue Russian speakers were probably too few to constitute a separate language group. The need for knowledge of Russian arose from commerce and politics.

4. The Viborg governorship

Viborg capitulated to the Russians in 1710 and the Peace of Nystad in 1721 only confirmed a situation which already had taken place. By the Peace of Åbo [Turku] in 1743 the area that already had come under the Russian Tsar was extended. The rest of Finland remained as a part of the Kingdom of Sweden until 1809. The initial effect of the conquest was the paralysis of the city. Part of the population deserted the city; part of the population was taken prisoner. But Viborg was still a port city that met the needs for foreign trade even if it lay within the immediate orbit of the new Russian capital of St. Petersburg. From the point of view of the conqueror the importance of the city was political and not economic (Tandefelt et al. 2002: 35f.).

The entire conquered area was formed into a governorship and Viborg became the seat of government. The previous language of ruler ship, Swedish, was changed for a new language which became German and not Russian as had perhaps been expected. The governorship of Viborg was lead from 1735 with the same language as the other conquered Baltic Sea provinces. Viborg was in a way seen as a German city similar to Riga, Reval and Narva. The German influence on the German culture in St. Petersburg in the court and the Tsar's family was also of no small importance. In Viborg German became the language of the council and a German parish was again founded in 1743 and a German school in the middle of the 18th century. Towards the end of the 18th century the school system was successfully reformed and Viborg became a city famous for its schools with German as the language of instruction.

Although the language of administration was German, all correspondence with the rulers in St. Petersburg had to take place in Russian. Swedish was still in use but only locally. What were now needed were civil servants who could work in German and Russian even if their mother tongue was Swedish so in the beginning translators were used. Civil servants who did not know Russian but needed a translator could receive a reprimand that it was the duty of a subject to learn Russian. The 1780s witnessed an increase in the use of Russian as the language of the administration and the court. In 1798 studies at Swedish or foreign universities were forbidden so that studies at the Swedish language Academy in Åbo [Turku] were no longer permitted. Those ministers of the church and teachers who were to work among Swedish and Finnish inhabitants of Viborg subsequently had German or Russian as their language of higher education.

The inhabitants of Viborg adapted to their new role as subjects of the Tsar. The oath of fealty and homage which was given with every accession to the throne, the celebration of the days of festivity of the family of the Tsar and not least the visits of the regent strengthened the bonds of loyalty. The number of Russian speakers in the city and its immediate surroundings increased. The Russian military were stationed in the city and housed in barracks or quartered with the people of Viborg. Improvements to the earlier defense works and the construction of new military fortifications brought in new workers. Russian became the language everybody in one situation or another came into contact with. Russian became ever more important in commerce and the use of Russian became more visible in both popular and highbrow culture as impressions from "the big world" reached Viborg through guest performances from St. Petersburg. Even if the contacts with the Russians of the capital were not so frequent, the Russians from St. Petersburg set the fashion for the society people of Viborg (Tandefelt et al. 2002: 47f.).

The German language became quite simply a bridge between the ruling Russians and the city. For the Russians the Swedish language was the language of the enemy and the Finnish language was not yet a language normally used in official or political circles. German had more or less completely taken over the earlier domain of Swedish. Swedish no longer locally had any official position but was only used within the home and at church. This could not but help to have an effect on the kind of Swedish spoken in the city.

To the above account should be added that contacts with Swedish speakers in the rest of Finland could be maintained even though there was less of a need than earlier. Contacts with Sweden shrank. This meant that the contact with monolingual Swedish speakers or with mother tongue Swedish speakers became weaker which must have also contributed to a weakening of language skills on all levels.

The Vice-Governor of Viborg Nikolai Henrik von Engelhardt wrote to the Tsarina Catherine the Great in Paragraph 32 "Von den Sprachen" ('About the languages') of the report *Die Beschreibung des Russisch Käyserlichen Gou-*

vernements von Wiburg ('The description of the Russian imperial government of W.') that

> [...] Swedish is for the most part badly spoken, the vocabulary is mixed with that of many other languages, especially German, and that not only the vocabulary but also the pronunciation and dialect differ very much from correct Swedish. Still the best Swedish is spoken in Fredrikshamn, German in Viborg and Russian in Kexholm. Finnish is the common language of the peasants, both of the Karelians and the other Finns and is also spoken by the people of rank (von Engelhardt 1973/1767: §32; my translation from German).

Von Engelhardt's father was a German born physician in St. Petersburg, his mother was the daughter of a Swedish-speaking merchant in Viborg and his wife was from one of the known and later Germanized families in Viborg. One can therefore surmise that he had the qualifications for making a judgment about broken Russian and impure Swedish. The comment of von Engelhardt about the widespread knowledge of Finnish confirms the impression that Finnish was the common bridge or *lingua franca* of the surrounding area. With exactly which variety of Swedish the Vice-Governor compared the Swedish of Viborg, one cannot of course know. Already at this time the Swedish used in Finland to some extent differed from the Swedish used in Sweden. It is therefore difficult to draw any conclusions about the local pronunciation or the local "way of speaking". The Swedish language was, in other words, strongly mixed in terms of vocabulary whereas no comparable comment is made about German. The level of German was high in Viborg whereas the inhabitants of Frediks-hamn, a town to the west near the border to Finland had a good command of Swedish and the inhabitants of Kexholm, a town in Eastern Karelia on Lake Ladoga had a mastery of Russian. The differences certainly corresponded with the frequency with which the inhabitants of these towns came into contact with the three languages. At the same time it shows that the roots of the German language were deepest and most firmly planted in Viborg (Tandefelt et al. 2002: 45f.).

5. Viborg and the Russian Grand Duchy of Finland

The victory of Russia over Sweden in the war of 1808–1809 in the long term resulted in great changes for Viborg and the governorship. In that war Sweden lost all of Finland, and a period of more than 600 years of Swedish-Finnish history ended. Under the Russian Alexander I Finland became a Grand Duchy within the Russian Tsardom. The earlier Swedish constitution was to remain in force and the religion and legal rights of the people was to be respected. This meant that Swedish remained the language of government. When the Governorship of Viborg was united with the rest of the Grand Duchy in 1812 Swedish also became the language of officialdom in Viborg (Tandefelt et al. 2002: 56f.).

The biggest change for the German speakers in Viborg was the dissolving of the Governorship and the incorporation with Finland. Even if the German-speaking group was small (363 persons or 12.5% of the population of the city) German was still the dominant language as the language of officialdom had been conducted in German and the language of instruction in the schools had been German. For the German speakers in Viborg the city was however not only a city in Russia but also a part of the large German speaking area to which the whole of the German speaking Baltic belonged. Their cultural roots were embedded in this area and the uniting meant that they became in a sense uprooted. The German speakers shared a religion but shared neither their origin nor their language with the rest of the people in the new Grand Duchy of Finland. Likewise the local customs differed from those of the other less cosmopolitan areas in the Grand Duchy. The people of Viborg looked towards St. Petersburg, the remaining Finns at first to Åbo [Turku] and then quickly to the new capital of Helsinki.

On 29 July 1808 and 7 February 1809 Mademoiselle Sofia Adelaïde von Hauswolff writing in Swedish recorded in her travel diary the following impressions of her visits to Viborg:

> [...] Several languages are spoken here by nearly everyone. There are three religions here – Lutheran, Russian Orthodox and Roman Catholic – but not many of the last. The first two are nearly of equal size which means that German and Russian are the mother tongues: one could even believe that it is French.
> [...] Every better person speaks four or five languages, French, German, Swedish, Finnish and Russian; but it would appear that Swedish will entirely cease to exist after this generation. By the age of eight to ten the children know four languages – but not Swedish (von Hauswolff 29th of July 1808 and 7th of February 1809, my translation from Swedish).

The visit to Viborg was brought about by von Hauswolff's accompanying her father as a prisoner of war, which took father and daughter on a journey from Helsinki via Viborg to Novgorod and back, by the same route. During her stay of many months in Viborg in the early spring of 1809 she witnessed the weakening military moral of the Finnish side in the face of the victories of the Tsar's soldiers. The travel diary records that not only her Russian but also her

German circle of friends welcomed the successes of the Russian army. She herself had “Finnish leanings” and grieved when Finland, the then eastern part of Sweden, was conquered. Her observations on the languages of the society circles in Viborg confirm the report of the Vice-Governor von Engelhardt half a century earlier. Of note is that the children no longer were learning Swedish. The change of language had taken place just when there was once again a fundamental change in the language environment (Tandefelt et al. 2002: 57f.).

In the Viborg of the 19th century Swedish again became the language of officialdom. The position of Swedish was strengthened with the founding of a Provincial Supreme Court in the city in 1839 and with the language of instruction in the gymnasium becoming Swedish in the 1840s. In six decades the number of Swedish mother tongue speakers increased fivefold from 412 in 1812 to 2261 in 1870. Approximately one third of these individuals were persons of rank, i.e. individuals with a certain economic and cultural capital. The Swedish language group grew in size on account of the movement from Sweden and the rest of Finland. In this way was reestablished the contact with mother tongue speakers of Swedish, which in all probability revitalized the language of the Swedish speakers of Viborg. The German and Swedish speaking families intermarried and by the 1840s Swedish began to replace German as the language of social intercourse in educated circles. At the same time it should be noted that unlike with the German language, the Swedish language was not a language that was exclusively used by the haute bourgeoisie. People with Swedish mother tongue were also to be found among the small burghers and among the common working people (Tandefelt et al. 2002: 61f.).

The Finnish speaking population also increased fivefold during the same period from 1279 in 1812 to 6845 in 1870. The growth of the city brought more job opportunities. On the other hand the new situation barely led to any changes or improvements for the Finnish speaking population. It was not until the end of the 19th century that representatives of the Finnish speaking population began to play a role in the business life of the city. Upward social mobility still meant a change of language from Finnish to above all Swedish.

The Finnish language on the other hand was clearly the means of communication in situations where no other common language was available. In Viborg even the educated classes had a greater need of Finnish than in the more western parts of Finland. Some decades later the Finnish language and culture became the object of a growing interest, which after the 1870s slowly lead to a confrontation between Swedish and Finnish harbouring some clear traits of a language conflict. The second half of the 19th century was characterized by the Finnish language beginning to complement and displace the Swedish language from its prestigious domains. Finnish was consciously being refined for use in greater and more demanding domains.

6. Viborg and the Republic of Finland

The decades before and after 1900 were characterized by a serious of dramatic domestic and international events that slowly lead to the independence of Finland in 1917. The new Act on the Constitution in 1919 stated that Finnish and Swedish were the official languages of the nation and the first Language Act in 1922 specified the language rights and the way in which the language status of the municipalities was to be established. It was also stated that the country had two state religions, Lutheran and Orthodox, and that freedom of religion was guaranteed by the Constitution. Officially Viborg became a Finnish-speaking city with a Swedish-speaking minority in addition to the Russian- and German-speaking minorities. The language of officialdom became Finnish while the schools and the churches continued to operate in the two official national languages as well as in Russian. The German language parish continued to operate with the church building and meetinghouse being shared with the Swedish speakers. In German-Swedish families it happened that the members of the older more German-speaking generation were members of the German language parish and the younger more Swedish generation were members of the Swedish language parish (Tandefelt et al. 2002: 137f.).

Many of the people from Viborg who were contacted for the research on the language environment of early 20th century Viborg were old enough to have experienced this period of change in the history of Finland. To this should be added the experience of the Second World War of these people and their families, for Finland the Winter War from 1939 to 1940 and the Continuation War from 1941 to 1944. The population of Viborg was twice evacuated. With the final movement of the border a total of 400,000 individuals were displaced and finally permanently settled further west in new milieus in Finland.

The 65 respondents in the research were born between 1896 and 1936. In 1991 and 1992 when the questionnaire was administered, a number were also interviewed, many years had passed since they had been members of the language community which they were being asked to describe. The responses concerning language attitudes, the multilingualism of different generations, the use of language in different situations etc. are not presented here. Instead an attempt is made to catch a glimpse of what appears to characterize the words and expressions from the four languages that the respondents said were typical of the popular idiom of the people of Viborg (Tandefelt et al. 2002: 145f.).

The respondents in the research on which this paper is based strongly believed that the lexical material they delivered was characteristic of only Viborg. It is not so. The loan words and expressions from German, Finnish and Russian which were reported to be Viborg Swedish can also be found in the idiom of other towns in Finland where there was a variegated language milieu as is to be expected. A city does not constitute a closed milieu; the language variety of a city is influenced by the expressions of people who move in from other areas to live in the city for a longer or shorter period of time. Even the most permanent residents who have lived in the same city for generations move around and bring back expressions from other places. A city has pronounced social differences, which mean that the language or languages vary according to the speaker's social position and activity. For this reason the idiom of a city is variegated.

The lexical material, which forms the basis for this study, consists of 411 words and expressions in the four different languages of the city of Viborg. The division into different languages presented quite a headache. It is clear for example that many of the Russian loan words have entered Viborg Swedish and Viborg German via Finnish and the Finnish dialects in the area. The strong Russian influence on the Finnish of the area is referred to as early as in the beginning of the 19th century. It was not always obvious how to categorize mixed loan words or clearly joking expressions consisting of elements from two languages. By dividing the material into the four languages it nevertheless was possible to arrive at an understanding of what the loans represented, that is to say which domains or activities had resulted in the loans.

7. Viborg Swedish

The number of Swedish words and phrases, which the informants regarded as characteristic of the Swedish used in Viborg, amounted to 12% of the total material. Before reviewing the variations in the Swedish material it needs to be noted that the Swedish that has been and is used in Finland is not identical with the Swedish used in Sweden. What is called Finland Swedish is one of the five regional varieties of the Swedish language. The differences (lexical, syntactic, morphological, phonetic and pragmatic) that are characteristic of the Swedish in Finland are of varying age and are to be found to varying degrees in different kinds of style. Finland Swedish sounds more different than it is in written form where sometimes there is very little to reveal that the writer comes from Finland. Both spoken and written Finland Swedish is fully comprehensible in Sweden and in the other Nordic countries (see bibliographies in Beijar, Ekberg, Eriksson and Tandefelt 1997 or McRae 1999). For this reason the analysis makes a distinction between Finland Swedish and standard Swedish, i.e. those that are common to the whole Swedish language area. By dialect is understood a Finland Swedish dialect (Tandefelt et al. 2002: 173, 179f.).

Among those words and expressions that the respondents stated were typical of Viborg Swedish are to be found both Finland Swedish and standard Swedish expressions. Among the words are Finlandisms that have died out such as *aska om* ('to deal with'), *abuscha* ('to reserve exclusively for oneself') and *bestyrelse* ('board'). Here are also to be found expressions that are still in use such as *firabel* ('extra job'), *hud* ('failure in test'), *kuppa* ('to pinch'), *krimskinn* ('Persian lamb coat') and *fnasig* ('niggardly'). A few words are from dialects such as *bisi* ('old man') and *duljor* ('clothes'). Some of the words are standard, but informal, Swedish such as *haffa* ('to catch somebody'), *gurgel* ('quarrel'), *sjabbig* ('shabby') and *hippa* ('teenager party'). In general it can be said that the words that have been categorized as Swedish or Finland Swedish reflect the activities of youth such as going to the cinema, visiting with friends, playing games and going to parties. The Viborg Swedish material gives a taste of a little older Swedish, especially Finland Swedish, vocabulary (Tandefelt et al. 2002: 184f., 217f.).

8. German loans in Viborg Swedish

The German part of the total material is the same size as the Swedish material, which is 12%. To establish a division between the Swedish and German material was not easy. In addition to mixed language material, also the presence of loans from German, that are in general to be found in Swedish, had to be dealt with, e.g. *Mischmasch* ('hotchpotch') in modern standard Swedish and some Finland Swedish words such as *Schlafrock* in older Finland Swedish for 'dressing-gown'. A great part of the listed words are not Standard German. A number of the expressions moreover have the appearance of German but are constructions that are either seriously or jokingly used. Such expressions are *keine Brosche* for 'no hurry' (derived from Swed. *ingen brådska*), *die Wäsche* for 'lady's handbag' (derived from Swed. *väska*, but also used as a German loanword for 'laundry') and *rote Kinder* for 'red cheeks' (*kinder* in Swed. meaning 'cheeks', but in Germ. 'children').

In some cases it is clear that the respondent has wanted to give the local pronunciation such as *Åuflåuf* for *Auflauf* that is 'soufflé'. It was not possible to establish more indications of a regional pronunciation but a number of comments suggest that one has been aware of the proximity to Baltic German idioms. A few examples show that the respondent has spelled the word in a Swedish way, perhaps to give the word a more Swedish pronunciation such as *strisel* for *Striezel* ('cinnamon bun'). In a few cases changes to a Finnish pronunciation can be noted such as *kutser* for *Kutscher* ('coachman'). In such cases it can be concluded that the word was a well-integrated part of the language into which it had been taken.

In comparison with the Viborg Swedish material the German material includes more phrases, idioms and collocations. There are nearly as many phrases as words. Shorter expressions as *für jeden etwas* ('something for everybody'), *kurz und gut* ('in short'), *so wie so* ('inasmuch') are frequently mentioned. Longer phrases given by the respondents are often common German idioms such as *was der Bauer nicht kennt, das isst er nicht* (litterally translated: 'the farmer does not eat what is unknown to him'), joking constructions such as *darf ich Ihnen den Kopf einschlagen* with the meaning 'can I offer you a cup [cf. Swed. *kopp*, but also Low German *Kopp* 'head' ~ Standard German *Kopf*] of coffee?' and phrases from German language school books such as *so ist es im Lande der Riesen* used approximately for 'that's the way it is, I am sorry to say'.

There are strikingly many collocations that the respondents remember in German in comparison with the other three languages collocations have been loaned from. The German loans do not represent any particular period in the life of the respondent nor any particular activity or register. What is most visible is the teaching at school: German was usually the respondent's first foreign language at school. Such was then the case not only in Viborg but also in the secondary grammar schools and gymnasiums in all of Finland at the time (Tandefelt et al. 2002: 191f., 219f.).

9. Finnish loans in Viborg Swedish

The Finnish contribution to the total material collected is a little larger than the Swedish and German material, which is 19%. The flow of loan words between Swedish and Finnish has moved back and forth over the centuries not only in Viborg but also in Finland. Some of the Finnish loans have also been used in Viborg German. The Finnish list includes words such as *hantuukki* ('towel'; cf. Swed. *handduk* and Germ. *Handtuch*), *kahveli* ('fork', cf. Swed. *gaffel* and

Germ. *Gabel*), *sååssiskååli* ('sauce boat', cf. Swed. *såsskål*), *tivaletti* (Swed. *toalett* meaning 'dress') and other examples of what is often called 'kitchen Finnish'. The list also includes established often everyday lexical Finlandisms such as *kalja* ('small beer'), *kokko* ('Midsummer fire') and *punkki* ('tick'). A number of the words are mixed loanwords that is a combination of elements from the two languages, such as *lutikkapulver* or *lutikspulver* ('bug powder' from Finn. *lutikka* and Swed. *pulver*), *träpulikka* ('small piece of wood' from Swed. *trä* and Finn. *pulikka*), *happanbröd* ('sour ryebread' from Finn. *hapan* and Swed. *bröd*) and *nattpajtu* ('night-shirt' from Swed. *natt* and Finn. *paita*). These words have been used when speaking Swedish but not Finnish. Also Viborg German has incorporated a number of Finnish loan words by assigning them a gender and definite article in German – Finnish nouns do not have a gender and the definite article does not exist. For example *die Borkane* is used for the Finnish *porkkana* ('carrot'). Some words also have the stamp of Eastern Finland or Karelian words such as *akkuna* for the standard Finnish *ikkuna* ('window'), *kohvi* for *kahvi* ('coffee') and *tassi* for *teelautanen* ('saucer').

If one were to describe with one word the language domain of the Finnish loan words then the word that first comes to mind would be *home*. It is a question of words used in the kitchen and the nursery, at the dinner table and in the laundry, where one has more often engaged in small talk than conversed and deliberated. The vocabulary listed by the respondents has above all been that used by women and children and it easy to surmise that the words have been used when speaking kitchen Finnish rather than Swedish. Swedish and Finnish have rubbed shoulders within the private and informal arena, at the same time while through their different social roles the speakers have lived in different worlds (Tandefelt et al. 2002: 198f., 221f.).

10. Russian loans in Viborg Swedish

The Russian part of the material is striking. Of the total number of words and phrases the respondents recalled 57% are Russian. The amount of Russian is large, especially considering that Russian was the mother tongue or home language of a small number of the respondents. Among the rest of the respondents only a small number were old enough to have gone to school during the Russian period when not only was Russian learned as a foreign language but also used as the language of instruction for some subjects. In other words a clear majority did not have any formal instruction in Russian. They had in passing just picked up some Russian. Loans from Russian seem to have been frequent not only in Viborg Swedish but also in German and in Finnish. Some of these loans are still in use both in Finnish and in Finland Swedish but they belong to an informal everyday register and are not used in writing (see for instance Bergroth 1928; af Hällström & Reuter 2000).

It would however be misleading to state that use of Russian words was unique to Viborg. The use of Russian words has occurred and still occurs in milieus where Russian has been and still is a home language. But it is still true that the Russian vocabulary of individual people from Viborg has been quite rich and that the use of Russian loan words has been quite common. The inhabitants of Viborg have not only met Russian speaking people from Viborg but also had the occasion to meet Russian visitors to the city and the surrounding countryside during the summers when many Russians from St. Petersburg visited their *datscha* (or *datja* meaning 'summer residence'; in Russian дача). Of relevance here were also the close living contacts with the Russian language and culture that had one-hundred-year-old roots that went deeper in Viborg than elsewhere in Finland.

As has already been stated, many Russian loan words have been borrowed via Finnish or an Eastern Finnish dialect. They have entered in parallel as well as through German. Evidence of this movement can be found in the variant forms of transliteration in the research material. Where the respondent has not been accustomed to using the Cyrillic alphabet, the homemade transliteration mirrors the differences between the original Russian and Swedish or Finnish pronunciation. I have used the transliteration of the respondents here together with the original words in Russian.

Variations in the transliterations used by Swedish and Finnish speakers are related to the existence of certain sounds in Swedish or Finnish. For the Russian word for a hired coachman (Russ. извозчик) Swedish speakers used *iswoschik, issikka* and *vossikka*, whereas Finnish speakers used only *issikka* and *vossikka* as the *sje*-sound does not exist in Finnish and is replaced by an *s*-sound. Another example is the transliteration of the Russian word биться for the English verb 'hit' in the children's game in which a hard boiled Easter egg is broken by hitting it against another person's egg, that is *litsa, plitsa, plitscha* and *blitsa.* In this case Finnish speakers used the transliteration *litsa* whereas the Swedish speakers used all four transliterations. The explanation is that Finnish does not use a double consonant at the beginning of a word and does not readily use a voiced plosive *b*.

The inability to distinguish between the singular and plural form of Russian words also gives evidence of not knowing Russian. For example the use of the plural form of the word for 'pancake' *blini* instead of the singular form *blin*

(Russ. блин) or the use of the plural form *pitski* for 'matches' instead of the singular form for 'match' (Russ. спичка). In a number of instances it is clear that the meaning given for a Russian word is based on a misunderstanding or a shift of meaning. *Niesnaju* (Russ. не знаю) means literally 'I do not know', but was used meaning 'fool'. Also the proper Russian word *durak* (Russ. дурак) for 'fool' is mentioned. On the other hand an intentional and ironic shift in meaning might well be the case when the Russian word for freedom *svaboda* (in Russ. свобода) is explained to mean 'confusion' or 'chaos'.

Judging from the humorous Swedish expression *flickuschki* for 'girls', the suffix *-schki* has been used as a common Russian marker for creating a humorous word based on the Swedish noun *flicka* ('girl'). The word *stobakoff* has been used by Finland Swedes for 'idiot'. Here it is the suffix *-off* which gives the word a Russian touch. In other words, there is evidence of certain creativity in the mixing of Russian elements with other languages. Likewise among the Russian loan words there are many older Finland Swedish expressions some of which are still in use today such as *birs* ('cab stand'; биржа), *butka* ('jail'; будка), *fortuschka* ('airing panel'; форточка), *karonka* ('party'; коронка), *lafka* ('shop'; лавка), *torakan* ('cockroach'; таракан) and *pränika* ('medal'; пряник). Originally the last word – *pränika* (or *prenika*) – was used in Finland Swedish (and in Finnish) both in its original Russian meaning (which is 'gingerbread biscuit'), and as a humorous word for 'medal'. There is of course a certain resemblance in form between the two objects. Today *pränika* solely means 'medal' in Finland Swedish and Finnish and the original much more trivial meaning is totally forgotten (see Bergroth 1928: 304; af Hällström & Reuter 2000: 134).

Some Russian phrases and shorter expressions were also used. The informants have mentioned *a vot* for agreeing with somebody ('nice' or 'good'; А вот), *puskaj* meaning 'okey' (Russ. пускай), *tschort vasmi* (Russ. Черт возьми) for 'fuck you', *sorovno* or *soromno* (Russ. все равно) for 'it is all the same to me', greetings such as *kak poschuvaite* (Russ. как поживаете?) for 'how are you' and so on.

The Russian loan words belong to many domains. Loan words from the Russian kitchen are still today used not only in Finnish, Swedish and German but also in other languages and milieus. A further domain, which has many loan words, is the world of work. The use of Russian words for a number of trades points to an interaction between non-Russian and Russian speakers even if it is not possible to draw any definite conclusions about the actual language of interaction. All in all the Russian words not only represent a wider spectrum than the other languages but also dominate the total research material (Tandefelt et al. 2002: 203f., 224f.).

11. Ein echter Wiburger geht auf allen Vieren

The collection of over 400 words and expressions in the four different languages Swedish, German, Finnish and Russian gives a good picture of the variegated language milieu in which there was no fear of borrowing when one felt that one was missing the right word or expression. According to the reports of the respondents and other observers, it was common that a conversation in Viborg *gick på alla fyra*, that it 'walked on all four legs', that *Ein echter Wiburger geht auf allen Vieren.* One started a conversation in one language but was all the time prepared to use another language by either switching to or borrowing words from another language. Apparently there was no language puritanism or performance anxiety. One both dared and wanted to use languages of which one only had an elementary command. The likelihood that one would succeed in making oneself understood was still sufficiently high (Tandefelt et al. 2002: 214f.).

The survey of the local historical roots of the different languages shows that the diversity of languages was a legacy that was made good use of in Viborg. The common feature is the use of Finnish as the language of the majority, together with the use of the language of the various minorities, Swedish, German and Russian. The changing dominant position of especially Swedish and German but also of Russian shows that the number of speakers is not the deciding factor. Political power and economic benefit can provide a language minority with the opportunity not only to survive but also to rise in a polyglot environment. Finnish became the *de facto* majority language in Viborg after it had assured its political and economic position. Characteristic of Viborg was that as the only cosmopolitan milieu in Finland with centuries of a tradition of exposure to many languages, one understood how to prize rather than eliminate the multitude of languages even when there was a change in the balance and dominance between the four languages.[1]

Note

1. I would like to thank Alexander Paile for his expert help with the Russian language and Finn Nielsen for the translation of this article from Swedish.

References

Beijar, K., Ekberg, H., Eriksson, S., & Tandefelt M. (1997). *Life in Two Languages.* Espoo: Schildts.

Bergroth, H. (1928). *Finlandssvenska. Handledning till undvikande av provinsialismer i tal och skrift* (2nd edition). Helsinki.

von Engelhardt, N. H. (1973[1767]). *Die Beschreibung des Russisch Käyserlichen Gouvernements.*

von Wiburg. [Suomen historian lähteitä VIII.]. Helsinki: Suomen Historiallinen Seura.

von Hauswolff, Sofia Adelaïde (1808/1809). *Journal hållen under Resor i Ryssland då jag följde min Far, i Dess fångenskap. År 1808 och 1809* [copy of a not published journal in the National Archive of Finland].

Hällström, Ch. af & Reuter, M. (2000). *Finlandssvensk ordbok.* Esbo: Schildts.

Karjala. Historia, kansa, kulttuuri. (1998). P. Nevalainen & H. Sihvo (Eds.). Suomalaisen Kirjallisuuden Seuran Toimituksia 339. Helsinki.

Klinge, M. (1996). *Finlands historia 3.* Espoo: Schildts.

Lagus, G. (1893–1895). *Ur Wiborgs historia.* Wiborg.

McRae, K. D. (1997). *Conflict and Compromise in Multilingual Societies. Finland.* Helsinki and Ontario: The Finnish Academy of Science and Letters and Wilfrid Laurier University Press.

Ruuth, J. W. (1906). *Wiborgs historia I och II.* Helsinki.

Tyrgilsmuseets tidsskrift för minnen från Wiborg. (1973/1974). Helsinki: Tyrgilsmuseet r.f.

Tandefelt, M. et al. (2002). *Viborgs fyra språk under sju sekel.* Espoo: Schildts.

Viipurin kaupungin historia I–V. (1974–1982). Helsinki: Torkkelin Säätiö.

Dialect and language contacts on the territory of the Grand Duchy of Lithuania from the 15th century until 1939

Björn Wiemer
Constance University, Germany

1. Introduction

The main task of this paper is to give a comprehensive overview of the quite varied historical and social circumstances under which multilingualism (multidialectalism) existed in the south-eastern edges of a larger linguistic contact zone, which recently has been baptised the 'Circum Baltic Area' (CBA); cf. Dahl/Koptjevskaja-Tamm (1992, 2001). I will concentrate more on the period after the partitions of the Polish-Lithuanian Commonwealth (the First Rzeczpospolita or 'Rzeczpospolita Obojga Narodów') at the end of the 18th century and stop with the outbreak of World War II. I will thus leave out questions related to the consequences of Soviet policy and language planning in the post-war period. Actually WW II has proven to be more than just a hallmark in the history of the described contact area; in many respects it caused a total restructuring of the sociolinguistic situations and, thus, the contact conditions of the populations that are at stake here. An inclusion of these changes and their linguistic manifestations would by far exceed the limits of this contribution. Due to considerations of space I have also decided to elaborate more extensively on the specific contact conditions of the chosen area rather than to supply an explicit account of these conditions in terms of the most recent literature on language contact in general.

For the same reasons I have to refrain almost entirely from the discussion of structural features shared by some or all varieties at stake here; reference to the literature will also be selective. There have been several publications critically surveying in a similar vein the territory and the time span chosen here.

The most recent ones to mention are Čekmonas (2001a, 2001b) and Zielińska (2002b). However, in these studies a focus is put either on Polish ('północna polszczyzna kresowa'; see Sections 3, 4.5 and 5) or on Russian (mainly the speech of the Russian Old Believers; see 4.1). In general, a serious drawback of the bulk of studies published on language varieties and devoted to sociolinguistics and contact conditions on the territory of the former Grand Duchy of Lithuania (GDL) is the fact that most of them do not focus on multilingualism as such, but instead on a variety (or a number of varieties) of one particular language. Often descriptions and analyses are provided on the background of some contact varieties (with only casual knowledge of the latters' structure and peculiarities), but as a rule analyses of the single variety chosen are conducted almost exclusively from the perspective of the respective standardised language (roof variety). The consequences of such narrow approaches (even in fieldwork) are that (a) the reasons and mechanisms of structural convergences in the involved varieties are still understood poorly and often described insufficiently, and (b) the study of the sociolinguistic background of convergent changes (innovations vs. preservation, re-analysis of archaic features etc.) has remained fragmentary and restricted.[1] In particular, from the existing literature we usually cannot infer much (if at all any) reliable information about the chronology and specific nature of language contacts from (otherwise obvious) results of structural interference stated post factum. These complexities still have to be unravelled. The mentioned desiderata cannot be overcome by this single contribution. Nonetheless, I will try to give a kind of synthesis of facts and observations which, unfortunately, appear to be scattered around different places until now. I will also add some results from most recent linguistic and sociolinguistic research inasmuch as they help to shed some light on the pre-WW II situation in some regions of the former GDL (see Section 6).[2]

Furthermore, it may be wortwhile to stress that for the contact zone chosen here it proves especially difficult to give an objective picture of the sociolinguistic situation even as for the more recent past. The reason is that questions concerning linguistic contacts very seldom have been kept apart from matters of an ethnic, archaeological, demographic or political nature. Even questions of settlement and migrations in the GDL and the neighbouring regions, have often been mixed up with questions of ethnic or religious identity and, even more so, with purported linguistic usage.[3] In fact, many correlations exist between religion, ethnicity and language use, but these correlations are by far not always as straightforward and reliable as many researchers seem to assume. This problem is delicate with respect to the ethnic self-esteem of 'Lithuanians' vs. 'Poles' and the reality of language use behind them as well as with the role Catholic vs.

Orthodox faith have played in the self-conception of 'Belarusians' (for the latter cf., among others, the detailed account by Sipovič 1973 on the second half of the 19th century). The problem becomes even more delicate given the fact that in the GDL (as in many other political formations of that time) notions like 'nation' and 'national (vs. linguistic) awareness' did not exist to the same extent as in modern societies; on this topic cf., first of all, Niendorf (2003: Ch. 3) and Suchocki (1983).

Consequently, many statements that have been lanced with respect to the ethnic and linguistic identity of certain groups of people must be met with great caution; more often than not they allow little or no reliable inferences about language use (in particular, about multilingual and multidialectal usage) in the respective periods and areas. We have to keep this principal caveat in mind at all times. I therefore wish to stress that attributes like 'Lithuanian', 'Polish', or 'East Slavic', which might be and are used as indications of either linguistic or ethnic (or political) entities, will here by default be employed as *linguistic* designations. This contribution should be read as a synthetic overview, in which an attempt is made to reconstruct *linguistic* usage, i.e. the functional and social range of Slavic and Baltic varieties. If not stated otherwise, place and country names correspond to the present political situation.[4]

The languages discussed here at length will be varieties of Lithuanian (Baltic), Belarusian and Russian (East Slavic), and Polish (West Slavic). For reasons given in the preceding two paragraphs I will not dwell on the so-called *mowa prosta* (lit. 'simple speech') or *język tutejszy* (lit. 'the language from this region', "the here-ish language"), which is basically an uncodified and largely undescribed Belarusian vernacular spoken in the border region of contemporary Belarus, Lithuania and Latvia. To dwell on this topic would mean opening another can of worms, for which I want to refer the reader to the papers (Wiemer 2003; Wiemer in prep.). Suffice it to say here that *mowa prosta* ought not be confused with *Prosta Mova*, which will be discussed in Section 2. *Prosta Mova* was based on vernaculars which were to be incorporated into the Belarusian dialect continuum, but its provenance, functional range and sociolinguistic status are by no means comparable to those of the *mowa prosta* referred to since the late 19th century and spoken until our days.

Other languages than those just named will be accounted for only marginally.[5] Among these languages Yiddish played a significant role in the former GDL (until WW II). For instance, under Czarist rule 5/6th of the Jews of that area lived in towns, where they often formed an absolute majority (see the census data analysed by Guthier 1977: 40–61). The percentage of Jews fluent in at least one of the other main languages of the places where they lived was very high. For information on the peculiar contact situation and multilingualism of Jews in the territory of the GDL the reader may be referred to the concise account in Jacobs (2001:288f., with further literature) and the detailed introduction of Lemchenas (1970).

The relevant territory at stake here corresponds to the Aukštaitian part of Lithuania (approximately from Kaunas and Panevėžys to the east), Letgalia (south-eastern Latvia), the western part of the Vicebsk district of Belarus (the region around Braslaŭ / Pol. Brasław / Lith. Breslauja,[6] Druja down to Pastavy / Pol. Postawy / Lith. Pastovys) and the entire border area of contemporary Belarus and Lithuania, which includes the northern Belarusian dialects; see Map 1.

2. The Lithuanian–Belarusian transition zone as a centre of structural convergences

I have narrowed down the territory for the subsequent discussion in particular because this smaller area belongs to the strips of land situated on both sides (for some 100–200 km) of the contemporary border between Lithuania and Belarus (see Map 2). This border reflects a somewhat fuzzy transition zone between the Belarusian (East Slavic) and Lithuanian (East Baltic) language territories, in which most intensive (and complicated) linguistic and ethnic contacts have taken place and which roughly coincides with the historical centre of the Grand Duchy of Lithuania. This border reflects also the line at which the long-lasting ethnic and linguistic assimilation of Balts by Slavs, and the replacement of East Baltic by East Slavic, have come to a stop.[7] We can say that this zone constitutes one of (probably) three larger areas showing some particularly outstanding structural isoglosses in the eastern part of the CBA, which justifies singling them out as centres of convergence zones. The other two areas are: the overlap of structural isoglosses in modern Latvia and Estonia, and the Pskov-Novgorod region of Russian dialects. The former has already been singled out as the center of a "linguistic landscape of convergences" (Germ. 'linguistische Konvergenzlandschaft') by Stolz (1991) and Wälchli (2000), the latter has recently been described by Čekmonas (2001c) on the basis of a larger areal and historical background, so that the reader may be referred to these studies. The latter region can also be regarded as the northern prolongation of the area which forms the topic of this contribution. The reason is that the region around Pskov and Novgorod showed quite intensive (though not entirely reconstructed) contacts in trade, policy and by migration (in both directions) from approx. the 4th century AD onwards (cf. Sedov 1994: 9–11). It seems plausible to assume that the structural convergences in eastern and southern Lithuania and northern Belarus resulted from intensive language contacts particularly during the existence of the GDL and in the preceding centuries; for lingustic features shared by northern Belarusian dialects and Russian dialects of the Pskov-Novgorod region cf. Avanesaŭ et al. (1968: 223–230). Among the people who have advocated this view is Bednarczuk (1993, 1994), who mentioned eight features from the phonology, morphology and syntax of practically all varieties in the former GDL: (a) expansion of the palatalization correlation, (b) tendency to unify the vowel structure of words, (c) pronunciation of [v] instead of [u̯] and vice versa, (d) (tendency towards) loss of the neuter gender, (e) a whole set of common morphemes in nominal derivation, (f) tendency of developing an aspect system based on stem derivation, (g) predicative possession expressed by an adlative construction (compare Russ. *u* 'at' + GEN), (h) use of active anteriority participles in resultative constructions.

3. The political and linguistic situation before the partitions (until end of 18th century)

The Grand Duchy of Lithuania came into existence during the Middle Ages as an agglomerate of East Baltic (and possibly East Slavic; see Note 8) tribes, which were rather loosely united in a hierarchical structure of tribal chiefs and dukes. During the 13th and 14th century a feudal, confederate system arose within Lithuania proper and the regions of Novahrudak and Polack.[8] From the end of the 12th century the territory controlled by Lithuanian (and possibly East Slavic; see Note 8) leaders expanded quite continually to the south and to the east, i.e. into areas which, by that time, from a cultural and linguistic viewpoint had already become entirely or predominantly East Slavic.[9] For this reason the GDL increasingly became a multi-ethnical and multilingual state, in which Lithuanians themselves clearly remained in the minority, East Slavs (basically the predecessors of Belarusians and Ukrainians) in the majority. According to Ochmański (1990: 58), the entire territory of the GDL in the second half of the 13th and during the 14th century amounted to approximately 800,000 km^2, but only about 10% of this territory (its north-western part) was, at that time, ethnically Lithuanian (East Baltic). Only in *these* terms might it be appropriate to speak of a Polish-Lithuanian-*Ruthenian* commonwealth. The East Slavic gentry (the boyars) can be assumed to have been Polonised linguistically and culturally from the midst of the 15th century nearly as fast as the Lithuanian gentry. Although for some particular periods we cannot be sure whether Lithuanians or East Slavs constituted the majority in the political élite,[10] we know that a gradual cultural Polonisation was the consequence of the growing political and economical role played by the gentry of East Slavic origin in institutions of the GDL (cf. Lojka 2001: 82ff.; Sahanowitsch 2001; Suchocki 1983: 73ff.). That ethnically and linguistically East Slavic peasant population which later was to become Belarusian and Ukrainian did not play any significant role and was politically suppressed (cf. Sipovič 1973; Guthier 1977).[11]

However the circumstances may have been, the real proportions between Slavic and Lithuanian speaking inhabitants of the GDL have not been ultimately clarified either. All the more, we do not have any basis for more precise judgements concerning the percentages of bi- and multilingual inhabitants (first of all these were peasants) and the type of their multilingualism (massive or rather individual?, which languages/dialects?, diglossic situations?, code-mixing? etc.). In the 15th century – under Vytautas, who reigned as (Grand) Duke of Lithuania in 1392–1430 – the GDL reached its largest size: it extended in the north from the Baltic Sea in Žemaitija (Samogitia) to the south down to the Black Sea between the Dnestr and the Dnepr', at the west it bordered with Ducal Prussia (later East Prussia) and Poland, in the east it included, for some time, the lands of Brjansk and Smolensk (Lojka 2001: 84; Ochmański 1990: 86); see Map 1. As a consequence of the baptism of Jogaila (Pol. Jagiełło) and his marriage with the Queen of Poland Jadwiga in 1386 Poland and Lithuania became politically a personal (or dynastic) union.

The most crucial linguistic fact to elaborate on here is that Lithuanian was not a language of administration used by the authorities. At least since Vytautas' time (see above), but probably much earlier, documents were written in an East Slavic variety which soon was to become a kind of *lingua franca* of the GDL. This variety has been variably called either 'Old Belarusian' or 'rus'ka mova' (cf. Čekmonas 2001a: 81), 'Prosta Mova' (cf. Moser 1998) or 'West Russian Chancellory Language' (cf. Stang 1935).[12] Though its structural basis was clearly East Slavic, with time it was more and more influenced by Polish. The name 'Prosta Mova' refers instead to its status during the 16th–17th centuries. Uspenskij (1987: 261) argued that this name has to be interpreted as an equivalent of 'lingua rustica'. Recently, however, Moser (2002: 225) questioned this explanation on the basis of a thorough historico-philological analysis. Anyway, from a sociolinguistic viewpoint 'Prosta Mova' could best be characterised as a koiné, insofar as it certainly was not the native tongue of anybody who used it, but it was taught at schools and used in all spheres of life except for liturgy

(Moser 1998: 13–20; Žuraŭski 1982: 20–31). Its sociolinguistic status was very peculiar and has to be adequately understood in the context of its time: on the one hand, Prosta Mova stands in opposition to a "high", Church Slavonic variant, on the other hand, it was clearly distinguished from the "uncultivated, low" vernacular of the East Slavic peasants. The famous Lithuanian Statutes from 1529, 1566 and 1588 were written in this language; they announced that official documents had to be formulated in it. It is not clear whether this formulation testifies that in the 16th century this early Belarusian ('Ruthenian') variety still firmly stood as an accepted (and even prescribed) medium of official communication (cf. Bieder [3]1998: 123), or rather that this prescription was a symptom indicating that the status of this East Slavic koiné as language for official purposes and in public life had begun to be undermined by the expansion of Polish and thus needed to be protected (cf. Žuraŭski 1982: 28f.).

The influence of Polish increased especially during the 16th century. This sociolinguistic process was paralleled by the tightening of political bonds with Poland, and this development eventually led to the establishment of a real (or constitutional) union between the Kingdom of Poland and the GDL in 1569. That Polish was gaining more and more ground at that time can in part be explained by the same circumstance which had contributed to the establishment of the Prosta Mova: the 15th–16th centuries were a period when secular authorities slowly began to give up the use of "dead", imported language varieties (such as Latin, Greek or Church Slavonic) and for administrative, jurisdictory and other public purposes attempted to use varieties which were more deeply rooted in local vernaculars, but also allowed for refinement in written expression. Although Polish for sure was not an endogenic variety of the GDL (see below), the onset of its influential role inside the GDL (the first half of the 15th c.) immediately precedes the time when Latin in Poland ceased to be regarded as the exclusive means of expression for the purposes mentioned above and was gradually replaced by Polish (cf. Zinkevičius 1996b: 82). This, however, is rather a minor factor. A convergent and certainly more important reason for the spread of Polish in the GDL was the predominant role of the nobility, in particular the "small noblemen" (Pol. 'drobna szlachta', henceforth called simply 'gentry'), which was unusually numerous (in comparison to other European states of that time), settled in the countryside and enjoyed a politically and economically privileged position. These privileges had arisen in Poland proper and became an important factor of social life in the GDL after the marriage of Jogaila with Jadwiga (see above), since Lithuanian and East Slavic boyars were given the same kind of rights as noblemen in the Polish Kingdom (cf. Davies 1986: 291–306; Marcinkiewicz 2000: 60f.; Zielińska

2002b). From then on this type of political and social culture was inextricably associated with Polish culture and its language. Investigators agree that the noblemen, who first began to assimilate to Polish culture and language, were a very important driving force for the spread of Polish. For a long time they must have been bi- or trilingual (Polish-Belarusian, Polish-Lithuanian, Polish-Lithuanian-Belarusian),[13] but Polish increasingly became the language used for representation. This sociolinguistic distribution proved to be a reality until the 20th century (see Sections 4.5 and 5–6). For a more detailed account of the Polonisation process before and after the Lublin Union (1569) see the classical work by Martel (1938: Ch. 1).

Polish also began to be used in Letgalia, more precisely: in the region of Daugavpils / Pol. Dyneburg, Krāslava / Pol. Krasław and Rēzekne / Pol. Rzeżyca (so-called Polish Livonia), since the second half of the 16th century, when members of the Polish gentry and Polish peasants started to settle there together with Belarusians. Some Russians (mainly traders) probably had appeared there earlier, and from the end of the 17th century Old Believers from the neighbouring region around Pskov and Velikie Luki fled from persecution to Letgalia (see 4.1).[14] The contact conditions with the GDL on this small piece of land (which in part can be traced back to the early Middle Ages) thus became more intense. Influences from Polish, Russian and Aukštaitian dialects of Lithuanian have since then contributed to some of the marked structural differences of Letgalian (often called also 'High Latvian') in comparison to standard and Low Latvian. Among these distinctive features we find: (a) a full-fledged correlation of palatalisation, (b) phonological neutralization of syllabic tones, (c) the inclusion of [ɨ] as an allophone of /i/ into the phonetic inventory, (d) the use of *jis/jys*, *jì/jèi* instead of *viņš*, *viņa* as 3rd person personal pronouns, (e) the frequent use of the genitive with negation and as a means of indicating indefinite quantity, (f) the use of the verb *turēt* 'to hold, have' in predicative possession (cf. Balode/Holvoet 2001a: 9f., 19f., 33, 36–38; Koptjevskaja-Tamm/Wälchli 2001: 649, 676).

The role of Belarusian (or more appropriately: of koinés based on western varieties of East Slavic) in official language use faded away, until the joint Sejm (Parliament) decreed in 1697 that Belarusian be abandoned and Polish remain the only administrative language within the Polish-Lithuanian Commonwealth. One important fact on Prosta Mova is that it disappeared quite abruptly almost without any traces, as soon as its use in administration was no longer considered to be justified. Although we actually do not know what the genuinely East Slavic vernaculars of that time were like, nor how they developed in the countryside until the midst of the 19th century, we can be sure that

Prosta Mova differed from them quite remarkably. Anyway, by no means can it be regarded as a predecessor of the codified Belarusian language of the 20th century (see 4.2), which rests on a different dialectal base than the Prosta Mova (cf. Kramko et al. 1968: 13ff.; Podlužnyj 1997: 191; Pryhodzič 1998: 15).

Similarly, we have hardly any data which would allow for a characterisation of the development of Lithuanian dialects up to the same period, and we cannot submit ourselves to definite judgements as for the rise of the Polish varieties in south-eastern Lithuania from the 15th century, the probable onset of more intense Polish-Lithuanian contacts.[15] In general, no clear judgements concerning the demographic situation in the pertinent area can be made, and in particular no ultimate judgement is possible as for the time from which Polish-speaking people settled on Lithuanian territory, nor which role captives taken by Lithuanian warriors during numerous raids onto Polish territory might have played.[16] A significant role can be ascribed to Podlasie, the region east and north-east from Warsaw, which – abundant in forests, lakes and swamps – since the Middle Ages was a kind of transmitter from Mazovia towards Lithuania proper. The largest percentage of Polish speaking settlers moved towards the Lithuanian part of the GDL from Mazovia.[17] Podlasie belonged to the GDL during the 15th century and until 1569, when almost all of it was ultimately incorporated into the territory of the Polish Crown. This incorporation was preceded by a continuous Polonization on all levels of life. The Podlasian gentry was among the first who voted for an abolition of the East Slavic 'Prosta Mova' as language of administration (for the background cf. Błaszczyk 2002: 117–136).

There is reason to believe that more considerable Polish settlement began in towns like Vilnius (Pol. Wilno, Bel. Vil'nja), Kaunas / Pol. Kowno, Novahrudak / Pol. Nowogródek and some others.[18] In any case, not until the declaration of the Lublin Union in 1569 were foreigners (including Poles) permitted to settle in the GDL countryside[19] (Kurzowa 1993: 19), so that we cannot assume larger numbers of Polish immigrants into the GDL until the second half of the 16th century. Eventually, it even remains unclear to which extent linguistic and cultural Polonisation took place as a consequence of immigration from Poland, or rather on the basis of a gradual, but massive language switch of the autochthonous boyars, who governed in the countryside.[20] We may, however, suppose that this process started with the cultural and, thus, linguistic assimilation of the ethnically Lithuanian (in part also Ruthenian) boyars; their orientation towards Polish culture must have already set in during the 15th century (cf. Marcinkiewicz 2000: 55–57); see above.

A further significant factor for the establishment of Polish in the GDL was the Reformation as well as the Counterreformation (16th c.). From the beginning of the 17th century Polish served as a medium for both movements, which eventually led to the foundation of colleges and similar institutions with Polish as the language of instruction (cf. Zielińska 2002a: 28f.). The close affiliation of the Catholic Church with Polish (and Poles) was, inter alia, reflected by the fact that "there have always been relatively few Catholic priests of Lithuanian origin in the Duchy" (Marcinkiewicz 2000: 57); cf. also Gaučas (1993: 43f.) and Suchocki (1983: 60).

Numerous wars and plagues during the 17th century, which decimated and even partially eradicated the peasantry of these areas, also must be viewed as reasons for the retreat of Lithuanian and its replacement by Belarusian in the eastern and south-eastern parts of Lithuania (around Vilnius). The devastated lands were then repopulated by settlers from neighbouring regions, among which Belarusian speakers most probably constituted the largest percentage (cf. Jurkiewicz 1994: 249; Zdaniukiewicz 1992: 276; Zielińska 2002b). An analogous case was Suvalkija, where Lithuanians were superset or assimilated by Polish newcomers after an epidemic in 1710–1711 (Marcinkiewicz 1997: 1615). Nonetheless, even in the 18th century peasants from Poland did not come in greater waves, but rather in smaller groups scattered across the countryside (parts of which may well have been assimilated). Not until a later period of time and only thanks to the continuous migration of individuals, did the presence of peasants and poor gentry lead to a certain degree of Polish settlement in the GDL, which might have played a role in the mass Polonization process of the late 19th century (see below). This role, however, was at best an indirect one and must not be overestimated (cf. Jurkiewicz 1994: 250, 253f.).

Therefore, the Polish varieties which came into existence in southern and eastern Lithuania cannot be considered a "natural" prolongation of the genuinely Polish-speaking territory; it is separated from it by more than 100 kilometres (from south-west to north-east).[21] PolKres is thus an exogenous variety. By no means is it a homogeneous monolith (see Section 4), and the influences from an East Slavic (Belarusian) substratum are, by and large, much more obvious than the rather few traits of Lithuanian (East Baltic) influence.

4. The main ethno–and sociolinguistic changes after 1795 until WW I

4.1 Urban vs. rural varieties

After the partitions of the Polish-Lithuanian Commonwealth ('Rzeczpospolita Obojga Narodów') Russian became the dominant official language on the whole territory of the former GDL, and after the first Polish insurrection in 1831 the Czarist authorities began to take rigid measures in order to Russify the Lithuanian-Polish (as well as Belarusian and Ukrainian!) inhabitants.[22] This policy became even more severe after the insurrection in 1863–1864. For instance, Lithuanian texts were allowed to be printed only in Cyrillic letters, Polish was ultimately removed even from elementary schools, and parish schools (in all of which Polish was the language of instruction) were altogether closed (Šapoka 1990 [1936]: 482). This oppressive policy lasted until 1905.

As stressed in Čekmonas (2001a, b) – which contain the most systematic account of Russian varieties in the former GDL to date – one should distinguish between urban and rural varieties. The former was practically co-extensional with the language of the Czarist authorities, mainly in Vilnius, the capital of the newly created 'Vil'na province', after 1831 also of the so-called 'Northwest region' (Russ. 'severo-zapadnyj kraj'). Contrary to this, practically the only Russian dialect which we can find in the countryside of the former GDL is the dialect of the Russian speaking Old Believers, who fled from the Orthodox authorities and the Czarist regime starting in the 1680's and during the 18th–19th centuries. The original "homelands" of the Old Believers are the regions of Pskov and Velikie Luki – an area which from very ancient times (5th–6th centuries AD) had been connected to the northern part of the later GDL by trade, migrations and wars (see Section 1). Since the Old Believers were persecuted for their refusal to accept the reform of the Russian Orthodox Church initiated by Patriarch Nikon (1605–1681) and adhered to many older aspects of their faith, they were anxious to isolate themselves from contacts with their surroundings, even in those countries which they emigrated to. Linguistically this has repercussions in the conservative character of the Old Believers' speech, which preserved many features of the Pskov dialect region of Russian,[23] and in the mutual lack of deeper influences between Old Believers' Russian and the language varieties by which they were surrounded. From the sociolinguistic perspective we may assume that, as a rule, Old Believers did not become bilingual themselves, although they were surrounded by Lithuanian and Belarusian peasants under conditions of insular dialects (cf. Čekmonas 2001b: 101–110 for more detailed information). Although we do not know whether Old Believers on the territory of the GDL (and in Letgalia) were influenced by Belarusian speakers to a more considerable degree, we cannot reject the possibility that a certain number of Old Believers were competent in Belarusian as well. At least these two dialects are very close to each other in structural, phonetic and geographical terms, and it seems implausible to suppose that Old Believers could have altogether avoided contacts with Belarusians. Karskij (1962:435), who also described the Old Believers' self-chosen isolation, seemed to consider this kind of bilingualism more likely than not. Later, a large proportion of Old Believers went through governmental schools during the inter-war period, when basic school education was compulsory and the medium of instruction was Polish (Čekmonas 2001b:129). To a large degree, the corresponding generation of Old Believers became Russian (dialectal)-Polish bilinguals (and there are still such informants alive; cf. Kardelis et al. 2003: Section 5).

In comparison to the Old Believers, the amount of Orthodox (= non-Old Believer) settlers from Russia was less remarkable. Larger waves of settlers from Russia were a consequence of the Russification policy of the 19th century. As noted by Čekmonas (2001b:107), "practically nothing is known about the dialects of the 19th century Orthodox Russian migrants who seem to have vanished into thin air after 1914". Some larger groups of Russian-speaking peasants seem to have remained after 1918 in Letgalia (cf. Poljakov 2000:54), i.e. the south-eastern corner of Latvia, which borders with the Russian and Belarusian dialect continua to the east and south. Nothing is known, however, about the degree of interference of Russian with Belarusian and the general impact of Belarusian on Russian. Nor have hardly any investigations been conducted concerning the influence of East Slavic varieties on Polish, which has "survived" in this area after the 16th century.[24] By and large, we can say that Letgalia (including its urban centre Daugavpils) has remained heavily Slavicised; only recently has Latvian begun to gain "sociolinguistic territory" in this area, because it has now become the only state language and compulsory language taught at school.

Let us now turn back to urban East Slavic (Russian and Belarusian). Russian in Vilnius was basically an exclave of the Russian standard language of that time as it was used in Russia proper. There was a much earlier population of 'Russians', or 'Orthodox', in Vilnius, which, however, must have spoken a dialect much closer to the surrounding vernaculars (which then became part of Belarusian) than to Russian proper. Even together with the amounts of Russian newcomers, the proportion of Russians proper in Vilnius (which practically coincided with the number of Orthodox) was lower than the number of Poles and, in particular, Jews (Yiddish speakers); Belarusians themselves were notoriously underrepresented in the towns (see 4.2). Guthier (1977:45), in his analysis of the 1897 Czarist census, gives the following figures on the proportions of native speakers of these languages spoken in Vilnius: 4,2% Belarusians, 20% Russians, 30% Polish, and 40% Jews. On the basis of some scarce statistics and observations made on the language of fictional literature Čekmonas (2001a: 83–85) comes to a similar result: he induces that Russians must have made up about 3% at the beginning of the 19th century and about 20% at its end, and that "Russian was not the everyday spoken language of the common people in Vil'na". On the basis of these data it is practically impossible to decide which language was predominant in Vilnius.[25] In fact, the role of Belarusian was probably larger than the small number of Belarusian speakers living in Vilnius itself would suggest. According to the same census data, in the countryside the percentage of Belarusian native speakers was higher than of any other of the mentioned groups: for the whole Vilnius district Guthier (1977: 42) adduces 25.8% Belarusians, 10.4% Russians, 20.1% Poles, 21.3% Jews, and 20.9% Lithuanians. Thus, it cannot be excluded that Belarusian played some significant role as a "low variant" in the public life of Vilnius. In the countryside Lithuanian and Belarusian competed for the role of the main everyday medium of communication, whereas in the immediate surroundings of Vilnius Belarusian had been gradually gaining ground against Lithuanian (cf. Gaučas/Vidugiris 1983: 29–34 for a detailed account, but also Vidugiris 1993: 116) – until Polish began to expand (see 4.5). In Vilnius itself conditions of language use most probably changed in 1905, when many of the restrictions introduced after the two insurrections against Polish and Lithuanian (see above) were relinquished. After that time the role of Polish, but partly also of Lithuanian, must have begun to increase in official and cultural life.

Finally, the written sources of Russian, as used in Vilnius, remained virtually uninfluenced by Lithuanian, and, in turn, Russian did not have any remarkable impact on the phonetics and grammatical structure of Lithuanian or Polish of the region (Čekmonas 2001a: 86). Two (probably complementary) reasons can be purported for this: first, the literature and other sources which reflect Russian proper of those days were diligently edited and purified from dialectal traits; second, Lithuanian-East Slavic bilingualism was one-sided, since basically only Lithuanian peasants were forced to use a Slavic idiom which made it possible for them to communicate with the Slavic speaking authorities and neighbours. The Slavic idiom chosen must have been a regional variety of Belarusian, with which they and their preceding generations had been familiar for centuries (see Sections 2–3, 4.5). Consequently, Russian and Lithuanian did not come into any direct contact with each other.[26]

4.2 Belarusian

In general, the status of Belarusian (more accurately: of those East Slavic dialects which now are united under that linguistic heading) remarkably differed from both Polish and Lithuanian. According to the official Czarist policy Belarusian was not acknowledged as a separate language apart from Great Russian, but considered as a group of local Russian dialects. On the one hand, this might have hampered the evolution of a Belarusian standard language in its own right, insofar as such a policy occurred as a factor lowering national and linguistic self-confidence among genuine Belarusians (which, like Lithuanians, were mainly peasants). National awakening among Belarusians, and subsequent language planning, did not emerge until the verge of the 20th century (cf. Lindner 1999: 27–41; Sipovič 1973; Wexler 1985: 37–39). On the other hand, this peculiar status prevented Belarusian from being prohibited as an idiom of (oral) public interactions (as was the case with Polish). Furthermore, from a merely structural viewpoint Belarusian dialects can be regarded as intermediate between Russian (East Slavic) and Polish (West Slavic), so that Polish and Russian speech was probably always mutually intelligible with Belarusian. Since knowledge of Belarusian already must have been widespread among Lithuanians in the areas bordering with Belarusian-speaking territory for a long time, we may assume that Belarusian functioned as a kind of uncodified koiné on a vernacular level in many places (see above).

As for the beginning of unification and codification of written Belarusian, we have to admit that during the 19th century there were several authors from different parts of Belarus' who started to write in their local or some more unified variety. The political events of the early 1860's initiated an intensive, though short-lasting production of publications in Belarusian, written both by supporters of the Czarist regime (inside the former GDL) and by those who rose up against it (mostly after emigration to western Europe or those parts of Poland which were not under Czarist rule); cf. Kramko et al. (1968: 60ff.). After the suppression of the resurrection in 1863 no texts in Belarusian could be printed (unless in exile) until 1889 (Kramko et al. 1968: 85f.). At the end of the 1880's Belarusian (as well as Ukrainian) was officially permitted in print, but in practice no newspapers or periodicals in this language appeared. This was not possible until 1906, when the first Belarusian publishing house in St. Petersburg and the first Belarusian newspapers (*Naša dolja* 'Our Lot', *Naša Niva* 'Our Cornfield') in Vilnius began their work.[27] Actually their role for the spread of Belarusian cannot have been very significant, since "only about one quarter of the Belorussians between the ages of 10–49 were literate" (Wexler 1985: 38);

solely the regions of Vilnius and Hrodna / Pol. Grodno showed a higher percentage of literate Belarusians. By and large, at the end of the 19th century Belarusians lagged behind all other ethnic groups (perhaps with the exception of Lithuanians) in those areas where they themselves constituted a majority: besides being mostly illiterate, they were clearly underrepresented in towns, more than 90% gained their living on the basis of agriculture, forestry, hunting and fishing or as small artisans in villages (for a detailed account of the basis of the 1897 Czarist census cf. Guthier 1977: 40–50). In 1912–1915 other Belarusian newspapers started their work in Vilnius and Minsk. Notwithstanding these signs of "liberalism" Belarusian remained banned from official life and almost all kinds of schools, an exception being a small number of private schools (Kramko et al. 1968: 112–115).

The specific sociolinguistic position of the uncodified Belarusian vernacular, which was outlined above, also played a significant role in the spread of Polish in the countryside. This rapid spread most probably started in the second half of the 19th century and continued until WW II. This part of the "multilingual story" of the territory at stake here will be addressed in Section 4.5.

4.3 Lithuanian

The territory of today's Lithuania can be divided into Aukštaitija, Žemaitija and parts of former East Prussia. This last part is sometimes called 'Lithuania Minor', from the Middle Ages it was under German (Prussian) rule. The first two parts constituted so-called 'Lithuania Maior' and formed part of the GDL, namely: its ethnically Baltic part. In former times only the part to the east from Kaunas and Panevėžys, i.e. Eastern and Southern Aukštaitija, was called Lithuania proper, the part west from this line belonged to 'Samogitia'. These historical names do not coincide with the accepted dialect division, since from this last viewpoint Žemaitija is smaller than the territory referred to by the same term (Engl. *Samogitia*, Pol. *Żmudź*, earlier also *Żmujdź*) in works of historians. In any case, here we are interested only in the Aukštaitian dialects.[28]

We do not know much about the linguistic structure of Lithuanian (in particular Aukštaitian) dialects until the end of the 19th century (Zinkevičius 1996a: 210f.). The written history of Lithuanian also sets in late, after the spread of the Prosta Mova (see Section 3) and at the beginning only in German-ruled Ducal Prussia during the Reformation. Specialists in the history of the Lithuanian literary (and then also standard) language differentiate three centres of normification: an East Prussian variant, a "Samogitian" variant (which actually was located in west and middle Aukštaitija, around Kaunas) and an East Aukštaitian (so-called "Lithuanian" proper) variant. Only the two latter ones are of interest here, and both developed after the "Prussian" one. It is important to note that, contrary to the Prosta Mova, written varieties of Lithuanian in the 16th–18th centuries did not fulfil a secular, administrative function, but served predominantly as a means of missionary activities, first by the Protestant clergy (especially Calvinists), then also by the Catholic Counterreformation. This fact explains the lack of a truly stabilised norm and the considerable number of translated texts of the 16th–17th centuries. The west and east Aukštaitian written "koinés" differed from each other insofar as they reflected phonetic and morphological traits of the dialects on which they were based (cf. Palionis 1967: Ch. 1–2; [2]1995: 19–23, 35–101; Zinkevičius 1996a: 224f., 227–255). These traits were more or less identical with the dialectal differences between the same dialect areas in the 20th century. The west Aukštaitian ("Samogitian") variant was less influenced by Slavicisms, and especially the system of declensions, stresses and syllabic tones was considered the most conservative one. This dialect group (on the north-western edge of the GDL) belonged to the most archaic ones probably because it had never been in direct contact with East Slavic, while contacts with Polish (from the south) started late and were not very intensive, inter alia because of topographical obstacles (swamps and other wasteland); the Teutonic and Livonian Orders (form the west and north) relatively seldom reached this region (Zinkevičius 1996a: 206).

The significance of the two early written koinés mentioned above should not be overestimated, and they practically did not play any role in language contacts. They were not multifunctional, as most of the Lithuanians (in the countryside) were not able to read, and if they were taught to read and write, the languages of school instruction were mainly Latin and Polish (with an increasing dominance of the latter until the first half of the 19th century; see 4.1). The Lithuanian standardised varieties came into oblivion during the 18th century,[29] partly because the Catholic clergy increasingly oriented itself towards Polish, and partly because of various diseases and devastation by wars, which decimated the peasant population especially in the region around Vilnius (south-east Lithuania). However, during the 19th century (in particular in its second half), with the appearance of a somewhat belated national awakening among Lithuanians, the west Aukštaitian written variant began to serve as a model for a unified standard language, and ultimately west Aukštaitian dialects became the principal basis on which the modern Lithuanian standard language (Lith. *bendrinė kalba*) has been formed since the end of the 19th century. This did not happen by accident: the main stimuli for the creation of a standardized language came from west Aukštaitija and the eastern part of Suvalkija,[30] i.e. from a region with a lower degree of contacts with Slavic varieties and, thus, multilingualism (see above). This region was also healthier economically, and the level of education of its inhabitants is considered to have been higher. This is linked to the fact that the rights of serfdom had been abandoned there in 1807 already by Napoleon, whereas in the southern and eastern regions of ethnic Lithuania serfdom was not abolished until 1861. Furthermore, west Aukštaitija was closer to the border with East Prussia, from where Lithuanian books (printed in Latin, not Cyrillic letters) were smuggled into south-eastern Lithuania; seldom did such books reach the region of Vilnius (Zinkevičius 1996a: 288f.). Thus, taken together these circumstances make it plausible why Lithuanian peasants in the eastern and southern corners of Lithuania, where code-mixing with and language-switches to East Slavic (Ruthenian, Belarusian) had already taken place for centuries, were considerably less apt to conceive notions of nation-building. The poor peasant population apparently did not associate actual language use with an incipient national identification.[31] Basically the same seems to be true with respect to the Belarusian peasant population (see 4.2; cf. Guthier 1977; Lindner 1999: 27–41).

Turning now to the eastern and southern Aukštaitian dialects, hardly any reliable statistical data on the number of Lithuanian-speaking people in this part of the former GDL exist (see Note 25). We may, however, refer to an important map designed by Chomiński in the late 1920s on the basis of an earlier account by Rozwadowski (from 1901), who had investigated the entire Lithuanian-Belarusian borderland area with the exception of the Braslaŭ district and Letgalia (in the very north-east corner of the territory discussed here; see Map 1). Chomiński thoroughly researched the whole area which belonged to the Second Polish Republic from 1920 until WW II, i.e. with the exclusion of Letgalia (the region around Daugavpils / Pol. Dyneburg and Krāslava / Pol. Krasław). In his view there were about 105.000 Lithuanian speakers in the ethnically Lithuanian part of the Second Polish Republic in 1930. Their largest agglomeration was to be found in the district of Švenčionys / Pol. Święciany (approx. 50.000 persons). This area did not embrace the Braslaŭ district, situated farther to the north-east; see Bednarczuk (1999: 97f.).

Zinkevičius (1996a: 287) draws attention to the fact that at the end of the 19th century the vitality of Lithuanian (vs. its replacement by Polish) was to a large degree determined by the linguistic practice of the priests in their parishes:

> In 1893 out of 62 Lithuanian parishes (excluding those which were Polonized) Lithuanian sermons were given in only 28, in both languages in 11, and only in Polish in the remaining 23, even though their parishioners were Lithuanians, spoke Lithuanian and most did not understand Polish. Those parishes which did not allow Lithuanian to be used in church became Polonized much faster. The reverse occurred in those parishes which reintroduced Lithuanian or had never abandoned it: they were hardly affected by Polonization.

The assertion that the dominant (or even exclusive) language of the respective community depended mainly on the language used by priests in their parishes can basically be confirmed from our own fieldwork with informants remembering the 1920's and 1930's in that region (see Section 6). Let us now come to the dynamics of the Lithuanian-Belarusian transition zone (4.4), before turning to the question where the Polish rural varieties arose from (4.5).

4.4 Diachronic changes of the borders between Lithuanian (East Baltic) and Belarusian (East Slavic) dialects

Today's transit (or: overlap) area between Belarusian and Lithuanian dialects approximately coincides with the present-day border between Lithuania and Belarus. On the Belarusian side, there were and still are a few enclaves of Lithuanian speakers (Opsa/Apsas, Gervjaty/Gervėčiai, (†)Lazduny/Lazūnai, †Dzjatlava/Zietela, Peljasy/Pelesa; see Map 2). In the 1930s the number of speakers was somewhere between 12.000 and 13.000 (Bednarczuk 1999: 97ff.).

In the first half of the 19th century, the Belarusian-Lithuanian language border in its central, the broadest, segment could be characterised as following (according to Klimčuk 1981: 214; Vidugiris/Klimčuk 1978: 20f.); see Map 1:

– Lithuanian had noticeably been pushed back east and south from Druja, to the west of the river Daugava / Pol. Dźwina (= pre-WW II and today's border with Latvia), where only small groups of speakers of Lithuanian continued to live for some time. According to census data east from Braslaŭ (Pol. Brasław, Lith. Breslauja) there were still some Lithuanian speakers in 1919. Then the linguistic borderline went southwards, where it passed Pastavy / Pol. Postawy / Lith. Pastovys in the west, turned towards Smarhon', ran along the Berezina up to the Neman (Lith. Nemunas, Germ. Memel). Then it passed by Lida from the north, ran to the north-west passing Ščučyn, Žaludak and Hrodna / Pol. Grodno from the north and eventually turned to the north-west up to Sopockin / Poln. Sopoćkiny and Sejny (now in north-east Poland).

– The line, west and north of which Lithuanian still dominated, can be outlined the following way: west from Braslaŭ and Drysvjaty / Pol. Dryświaty / Lith. Drūkšiai towards Soly, Astrovec / Pol. Ostrowiec and Vilnius. Then southwards past Ašmjana to the underflow of the Berezina (Nemanskaja Berezina) and Iŭ'e to the west till Sejny.

Bednarczuk (1999: 103) assumes that this transitional zone was even broader before the 20th century. At the turn from the 19th to the 20th century Belarusian was already spoken even to the west and north-west of Vilnius (in Trakai / Pol. Troki and Riešė / Pol. Rzesza). We may assume that all these changes reflect continuous language-switches of Lithuanians to Belarusian. Particularly intensive switches to Belarusian took place south-west of Vilnius in the region of Eišiškės / Pol. Ejszyszki, Pariečė / Pol. Porzecze and Peljasa / Lith. Pelesa (see Maps 1 and 2); cf. Zinkevičius (1996a: 288).

As further indicated by Bednarczuk (1999: 103), Lithuanian and Belarusian dialects of this area share a phonological feature, namely: the so-called "dzekanne, cekanne". This entails that the etymological consonants [d] and [t], when palatalized ([d', t']), are pronounced like highly palatal affricates [dz", c"].[32] This observation allows for the hypothesis that the centre of this zone more or less coincides with an isogloss that constitutes an innovation both in east and south Aukštaitian and in (north-west) Belarusian dialects. Problems begin, however, when one wants to determine whether East Slavic dialects (precursors of Belarusian) took over this feature from Baltic speakers or the other way round. Zinkevičius (1996a: 196–199) argues for the former alternative, i.e. a Baltic substratum in Belarusian. He indicates that the speakers of the (now extinct) Lithuanian insular dialect of Dzjatlava (Lith. Zietela, Pol. Zdzięcioł), halfway between Lida and Slonim, did not have this feature, although they were surrounded on all sides by Slavic speakers and had lost contact with the Lithuanian "mainland" a long time before. Whether this can be regarded as a plausible argument, cannot be decided here. Anyway, another specific feature of south Aukštaitian dialects, testifying close contact with Slavic varieties (and this time clearly indicating an influence from Slavic), is the hardening of /r'/, /š'/, /ž'/ and the affricates (these are always velar in the relevant Belarusian dialects and in Polish); cf. Zinkevičius (1996a: 209).

Most remarkable, however, is the observation that north of Švenčionys up to the line (from west to east) of Naujasis Daugėliškis, Kačergiškė, Tverečius / Pol. Twerecz (see Map 1) and farther east along the contemporary border of Lithuania and Belarus virtually no Belarusian (nor Polish) has been spoken at all. This fact was marked on Chomiński's map (see above), and we were able to confirm it on the basis of interviews with informants of the region north of Švenčionys, conducted in 2000 and 2001. The explanation probably lies in the fact that priests of that region more or less consistently used Lithuanian in church and in conversation with their parishioners (see Section 6).

4.5 The appearance of Polish rural varieties in the Lithuanian–Belarusian borderlands

Nitsch (1925) was the first to lance the hypothesis that rural varieties of Polish must have arisen on both sides of the Lithuanian–Belarusian linguistic border not earlier than during the 19th century, but with a subsequent rapid spread. Turska aimed to elaborate on his reasoning and was about to publish a systematic investigation of this phenomenon in 1939. Unfortunately, the manuscript, which had already been prepared for distribution, was destroyed when WW II broke out, and only the first third part of it was passed down to us. It has been published twice: first in "Studia nad polszczyzną kresową I" (1982), and as a photomechanic reproduction of that edition printed 1995 in Vilnius; here I will refer to the 1995 edition.

Let us begin with the geographical extension. Turska (1995 [1939]) pinpointed three main Polish-speaking regions. These are (see Maps 1 and 2):

i. the Vilnius region, surrounding Vilnius / Pol. Wilno, but not encompassing it.[33] It stretched along the right (northern) banks of the river Neris / Pol. Wilia approximately from Kernavė / Pol. Kiernów (west from Vilnius) till Švenčionėliai / Pol. Nowe Święciany, where it turned to the east until more or less Pastavy / Pol. Postawy.
ii. the region of Smalvos / Pol. Smołwy, which reached in the north from Zarasai / Pol. Jeziorosy and Turmantas / Pol. Turmonty just along the Lithuanian-Latvian border and the Daugava / Pol. Dźwina until more or less Pljusy / Pol. Plusy (now in Belarus) and in the south from Kaltanėnai towards Vidzy / Pol. Widze and the lakes of Braslaŭ / Pol. Brasław / Lith. Breslauja (now also in Belarus).
iii. the region north and north-east from Kaunas / Pol. Kowno, approximately in the triangle of Kaunas, Panevėžys and Ukmergė, in particular along the little river Lauda (north of Kaunas), a tributary of the Nevežis.

These areas of the northern polszczyzna kresowa (henceforth PolKres) have been more or less compact until WW II. The Vilnius region (i) increased after WW I (during the Second Polish Republic) to the south to include more or less the whole territory from the south-west of Lida towards north-east along today's border between Lithuania and Belarus up to Švenčionys / Pol. Swięciany in the north (see Map 1).

The role of larger towns in the rapid switch to Polish in the countryside might have been different. The role of Vilnius was amazingly insignificant. This is due to the fact that the immediate surroundings of Vilnius did not participate in this rapid change in the midst of the 19th century, rather considerably later (Turska 1995:4). It is likewise arguable whether the spread of Polish in the Smalvos region (ii) (as well as in the Krāslava region, Letgalia) can be ascribed to the role of Daugavpils as a cultural and trading centre, as Gaučas/Vidugiris (1983:43) assert. It should be further stressed that these rural varieties of PolKres, which presumably did not arise (or, at least, rapidly spread) until after the second half of the 19th century, are by no means homogeneous insofar as they are characterised by partly different types of structural interferences (see Section 5), and each of them has been full of ideolectal differentiation.

How did Polish spread in these areas? According to Turska's reconstruction, based on extensive fieldwork in regions (i) and (ii) and the analysis of documents in archives of Vilnius, Polish experienced a noticeable rise after the abolition of serfdom in 1861, because more and more Lithuanian and Belarusian peasants, who had been given the freedom of profession and mobility, associated Polish with the medium of education and with social careers. The paradoxical situation to be explained is the following: Polish had been being under severe suppression after the 1831 uprising, and Russian was the only language allowed in education and administration. So, why should people who were eager to abandon a poor life in the countryside choose Polish, not Russian? First of all, the command of Russian in the Lithuanian countryside was most probably very poor (even poorer than in Vilnius; see 4.1). Second, Russian was associated with the language of the occupant, whereas Polish from the times of the GDL had left behind itself a renommé of a culturally prestigious language.[34] On the one hand, after the abandonment of the Prosta Mova (in 1697) as an official language, Belarusian also eventually ceased to play any role in education. On the other hand, Lithuanian books, printed in Latin characters in Lithuanian-speaking Prussia (under German rule) and illegally distributed from there, reached the Lithuanian-Belarusian borderlands much less frequently than other, more central parts of Lithuania and those parts in a more favorable position in terms of economy and education. As a result, Lithuanian peasants in the eastern regions were less influenced by the awakening of national consciousness, which emanated from the Prussian part of Lithuania, Suvalkija and western Aukštaitija (see 4.3). Third, Polish was also the language traditionally associated with the Catholic Church. From the times of the Lublin Union (1569) Lithuanians had been almost exclusively Catholic, and the clergy predominantly used Polish (see Section 3). Thus, an important factor was the language used by the clergymen in their parishes: the "agglomeration" of (rather) Polish- vs. (rather) Lithuanian-speaking areas more often than not coincided with the location and distribution of the parishes (Turska 1995: 54). This fact has repercussions until today (see Section 6). Fourth, one cannot dismiss the purely linguistic fact that Belarusian is quite an intermediate language between Russian and Polish. Therefore, if Belarusian already was the most wide-spread medium of communication (at least) in the countryside and used also by Lithuanians, it might well have served as a spring-board towards Polish. Turska (1995: 52) herself notes that Polish began to spread particularly rapidly in those areas where (in the first half of the 19th century) Lithuanians had "belaruthenized" immediately beforehand.

The most controversial among Turska's statements is her hypothesis that after the abolition of serfdom Lithuanians switched to Polish directly, without the "intermedium" of Belarusian, whereas Belarusians themselves remained reluctant about a switch to Polish. Their sociolinguistic behaviour, as she argues, changed only after WW I, when Polish (again) became the official language of the authorities and education. To motivate her hypothesis Turska argues that Belarusians did not feel a need for another language to communicate with their immediate surroundings: their language was not forbidden (although considered only a "dialect" of Great Russian) and understandable both for Polish- and for Russian-speaking people, and Lithuanians always had adapted to Belarusians instead of vice versa (see 4.1–4.2). Furthermore, Belarusians were predominantly Orthodox and to a greater degree influenced by Czarist propaganda concerning their "historically founded membership to the (Great) Russian nation". In the remaining part of her book Turska provides a detailed discussion of interference features which, according to her, speak in favor of a direct Lithuanian substratum. Those traits which can be recognised as Belaruthenisms, she argues, are common to all Polish varieties in the former GDL; they can be found in particular in the Polish variety of the towns and the members of the gentry as well, which has another genesis and is considerably older (see Section 3). She argues further that many Belarusian features entered the new Polish variety in the countryside directly either from that older variety of Polish or from the Lithuanian substratum, which previously had adopted those elements from Belarusian.

At this point Turska's argumentation is in danger of becoming circular, and in any case we have to look attentively at each of the features mentioned by her in order to make our own judgement concerning their sources. Here I can only signal that this question remains open for further research. Anyway, even a superficial survey of Turska's catalogue of interference features discloses a general problem in deciding where a particular interference feature really originated from: a given feature very often turns out to be common to most of, or even all, the varieties in the contact area, and more often than not one cannot reconstruct even a relative chronology of the borrowing or structural influence (as the case may be). Therefore, if the investigator has a conception of the direction and manner of language switch and corresponding substrata, but encounters examples contradictory to this conception, it is not very difficult, but, as a rule, not convincing either, to try to prove that these elements originate from a third, structurally closer variety (as the two local Polish varieties of different origin in the former GDL). This unsatisfying argumentive approach reveals itself even in Turska's otherwise ground-breaking investigation – not to mention many other publications after WW II (and after Turska) dealing with the origin and peculiarities of PolKres.

Despite this drawback, it is one of Turska's merits that she tried to distinguish as clearly as possible between a mixed Belarusian–Polish speaking population, which used Polish only for public purposes, but not at home, and a population in which Polish was the dominant if not sole language (at least in the private sphere). The problem, however, is that one cannot really be certain as for (and reconstruct) the degree of mixture between these two (and other) languages. It is unlikely that Belarusian was abandoned altogether even if a switch to Polish occurred; in other words: it is quite likely that those people remained competent in both languages. Besides this, one must recall for Belarusian that it had been moving north-westwards through the assimilation of the Lithuanian-speaking population. By this very fact it had somehow set the stage for language-switches as such.

5. The inter-war period

Among the three regions outlined following Turska (1995) in 4.5, region (i) is the largest one and it is also the one best investigated up to date. Region (iii) is the smallest one; from a linguistic viewpoint it is somewhat set apart from the other two regions. The reasons for this are evidently the following: first, this region has never been in direct contact with Slavic-speaking territory. Second, from 1920, when eastern and southern Lithuania (the so-called Vilnius region, Pol. *Wileńszczyzna*, Russ. *vil'njusskij kraj*, Lith. *Vilniaus kraštas*) was incorporated into Poland and diplomatic contacts with the Lithuanian Republic did not exist until 1938, it had been hermetically separated from the other two regions up to 1939. Region (iii) constituted a Polish-speaking minority within the interbellum Lithuanian Republic, and for the political reason just mentioned contacts with the regions (i) and (ii), belonging to the Polish Republic, were virtually impossible. Regions (i) and (ii), to the contrary, after 1920 found themselves within a state, in which Polish was the only official language and the language used for education. Both in interbellum Lithuania and in interbellum Poland language policy was restrictive, inter alia with regard to Polish and Lithuanian speaking minorities, respectively.[35]

Interference features (including their relative frequency) found in the speech of the last representatives of the Polish-speaking region along the Lauda river (region (iii)), differ to some extent markedly from interference patterns in the other two regions, which were investigated by Turska herself. These differences can be explained only with reference to different conditions of contact to which Polish-speaking multilinguals have been exposed. Here we cannot discuss entire catalogues of traits of interferences in the three regions of rural varieties of Polish, all the more as we do not dispose of such a catalogue for the "Kaunas variety" in the interbellum period (let alone for an earlier time). It suffices to adduce just some contemporary features from this variety, which are discussed by Zielińska (2002a: 102, 109ff.; 2002c) and are supposed to have existed there already before WW II: (a) the use of the feminine personal endings instead of the masculine ones in the past tense forms of verbs (lam, aś / aš in place of {em, eś}), (b) non-discrimination of [i] and [ɨ], (c) use of a possessive pronoun without distinction of gender and number, (d) use of the preposition *od* 'from' instead of *z* 'id.' for the indication of a person's birth or living place (e.g., *on* ***od*** *Kiejdan* 'he is from Kiejdany'; compare the equivalent Lith. *jis* ***nuo*** *Kėdainių*). All these features can be explained as interferences from Lithuanian. On the contrary, in the Kaunas region we encounter the following features not at all or only sporadically. These are very common in the two other PolKres regions, which can be explained as interferences from Belarusian (or East Slavic in general): (e) mixing of [v] and [u] (and [u̯]) in different positions,[36] (f) lack of person marking in past tense forms of verbs, (g) dative plural ending {am} instead of {om}, (h) analytical superlative (e.g., *samy starszy* instead of "synthetic" *najstarszy* 'the oldest'). The absence (or, at least, lower frequency) of these features in the "Kaunas variety" can be explained by the lack of direct contact with East Slavic (Belarusian).

A few words on the Polish variety in Letgalia, based on Ostrówka (2001: Ch. 2–3). Although Letgalia was part of a sovereign Latvian state after WW I and Polish became a minority language, speakers of Polish did not experience pressure from the authorities. Until 1934 many schools with Polish as language of instruction were founded in that area, although there were no compact territories (or villages) inhabited exclusively by speakers of Polish. Russian was a dominant language in public life and at people's working places; some variety of Belarusian was used for communicative intercourse between neighbours. In poorer peasant families, who worked on farmsteads or rented pieces of land in the summer, there was practically no need to communicate in any other language than Polish. The situation changed quite dramatically in 1934 after the upheaval, when the new president Ulmaņis lanced a rigorously Lettonizing policy with discriminating consequences for ethnic and linguistic minorities.

As for Polish in interbellum Soviet Belarus (from 1926) we dispose of even less data. According to a census conducted in 1926 (when Belarus became a Soviet Republic) 97.500 persons declared themselves as Poles, but only 42,2% of them really used Polish. From 1937 onwards the number of speakers of Polish began to be drastically decimated by Stalinist "purges" and the consequences of WW II (cf. Grek-Pabisowa 1997: 152f.).

6. Pieces of reconstruction on the basis of some most recent findings

I wish to finish this survey with some results of fieldwork conducted in 2000 and 2001 in the north-eastern corner of contemporary Lithuania, during which we interviewed people of different linguistic backgrounds, but who were born and/or raised in that area before WW II. This area, according to Turska's division, almost entirely belongs to the region of Smalvos / Pol. Smołwy (= region (ii)); only a limited part around Adutiškis / Pol. Hoduciszki should be referred to the most northern part of Turska's Vilnius region (= region (i)). This area has remained poorly investigated. Thanks to our interviews (and some additional sociolinguistic material gathered in 2000–2001) we can now attempt to reconstruct some significant pieces of the sociolinguistic situation of that region during the interbellum period (when this area was under Polish rule).[37] The following findings have been included into our report Kardelis et al. (2003). The area under discussion is now divided by the state boundary between Lithuania and Belarus. Before WW II most of it belonged to the district of Braslaŭ / Pol. Brasław (today mainly in Belarus). It bordered with Latvia in the north (along the river Daugava down to Daugavpils) and with the USSR in the east (at Leonpol). In interbellum Poland it belonged to the regions with the poorest infrastructure and level of education, industrialization and agriculture.

The distribution of Lithuanian and Polish in this area has clearly been conditioned by the distribution of parishes. There are now 13 "Lithuanian" and 3 "Polish" parishes (the latter are the parishes of Gaidė / Pol. Gajdy, Puškos / Pol. Puszki, Kačergiškė / Pol. Kaczergiszki). In "Lithuanian" parishes only newcomers from Vilnius or ethnic Poland and representatives of the state administration made use of Polish. Within Lithuanian families normal language transition to the younger generation basically remained intact. By and large, mixed marriages were infrequent. According to our Lithuanian informants, non-Lithuanians who married a Lithuanian switched to Lithuanian in their spouse's family; this rule, however, worked also in the opposite direction (towards Polish) in villages in which Polish was the dominant language.

The area of Smalvos was separated from the Vilnius region in the south-west by a strip of practically entirely Lithuanian-speaking land stretching from Švenčionys / Pol. Święciany in the south to Tverečius / Pol. Twerecz in the north (see 4.4). Our informants remember that even to the north of that strip of land, i.e. in the Smalvos region, Lithuanian was the normal language used in church during services. Only later was Polish introduced as an alternative language of liturgy and sermons. As for school education the situation was worse almost through the whole interbellum period: although officially allowed and encouraged, the foundation and work of schools with Lithuanian as language of instruction was hampered by the Polish authorities. Lithuanian schools and libraries were often closed, teachers were not confirmed and the possibility of preparing teachers themselves was limited by the nearly total lack of appropriate institutions. Thus, even in predominantly Lithuanian-speaking villages and parishes schooling basically took place in Polish; on an unofficial (later also illegal) level Lithuanian parents began to organize some private schooling (so-called Lith. *mokyklos nuo tėvų* lit. 'schools from the parents').

As for East Slavic varieties, it was very hard to find informants who indicated that Belarusian was spoken by anyone in their childhood. Belarusian was usually spoken only farther to the south, around Adutiškis / Pol. Hoduciszki (see Map 1). Characteristically, only old *men* were remembered to have occasionally spoken Belarusian among each other. This assertion of our informants agrees with a remarkable fact related by Turska (1995:34–36): she observed that the crucial driving force in the quick change from Lithuanian to Polish after 1861 were Lithuanian peasant mothers. They were eager not to expose their children to a non-prestigious language, which would not increase chances of some sort of social career, and therefore would prefer to speak broken Polish to their children than use their native tongue. Both observations indicate that men (fathers) seem to have behaved more conservatively than women (mothers).

Before WW II Russian was also almost unknown. It did not become more popular until 1944 under the Soviet regime, with the influx of a large amount of people from various Soviet republics to the kolkhoz and sovkhoz farms.

From these observations we may induce the following:

i. Despite the fact that Turska and other Polish investigators have characterised the Smalvos region as a continuous Polish speaking area, most of the territory north from Švenčionys up to the Latvian border had remained predominantly Lithuanian. This may not be a contradiction if we admit for the possibility that Lithuanians, but not Polish newcomers were bilingual. Therefore:
ii. At least young Lithuanian speakers of the interbellum period by majority must have become to some extent bilingual, since they often were schooled in Polish (officially) and Lithuanian (unofficially).
iii. The role of Belarusian seems to have been less significant than in the regions around Vilnius.

All these points, however, should yet be investigated more thoroughly.

7. Concluding remarks

In this paper I have tried to give a report on the state of the art of our knowledge about the intricacies of the multilingual situation in the territory of (or related to) the Grand Duchy of Lithuania, which existed until 1795. In doing so I have attempted to give insights on a considerable part of the sociolinguistic complexities in the borderlands of Lithuania and Belarus and occasionally also some of the neighbouring regions now belonging to Latvia or Poland. In this whole area we can observe a remarkable amount of, partly exclusive, isoglosses transgressing boundaries of "genetic" affiliation between the involved varieties. These isoglosses are to a large degree located within the northern part of the former GDL and must have arisen due to ancient contacts between speakers of East Slavic and East Baltic. Only during the GDL and after its ultimate fall did Polish begin to gain weight as an exogenous variety. I have only very fragmentarily and superficially addressed linguistic convergences and interference phenomena, because the primary aim of this contribution has been to demonstrate how painstakingly investigators have to "filter" information pertinent to multilingualism (multidialectism) from various sources dealing more with history, demography, ethnic culture and identity, education and the policy behind all them. Since more often than not no reliable information on language use can be obtained, or can be inferred only indirectly, the sociolinguistic picture "composed" here must necessarily remain unsatisfying. It becomes even more intricate because of rather frequent changes of administrative and political boundaries and of demographic cataclysms. The lesson to be learned from this is that we must be much more cautious than has hitherto been practiced in drawing conclusions on language behaviour, in particular on individual and group multilingualism, from facts foremost pertaining to demography, ethnic and religious identity, political borders and their changes in history. Even more caution is necessary when our knowledge about the social, political and cultural background of speaker populations is rather fragmentary and often not based on facts, but instead on circular judgements on the relation between extra-linguistic factors and real language use.

Appendices

Abbreviations of languages (varieties)

Bel.	Belarusian (Byelorussian, according to earlier conventions)
Engl.	English
Germ.	German
Lith.	Lithuanian
Pol.	Polish
PolKres	(northern) polszczyzna kresowa
Russ.	Russian

Maps

Map 1: Borders and regions relevant to the regional Polish (polszczyzna kresowa) during and after the GDL

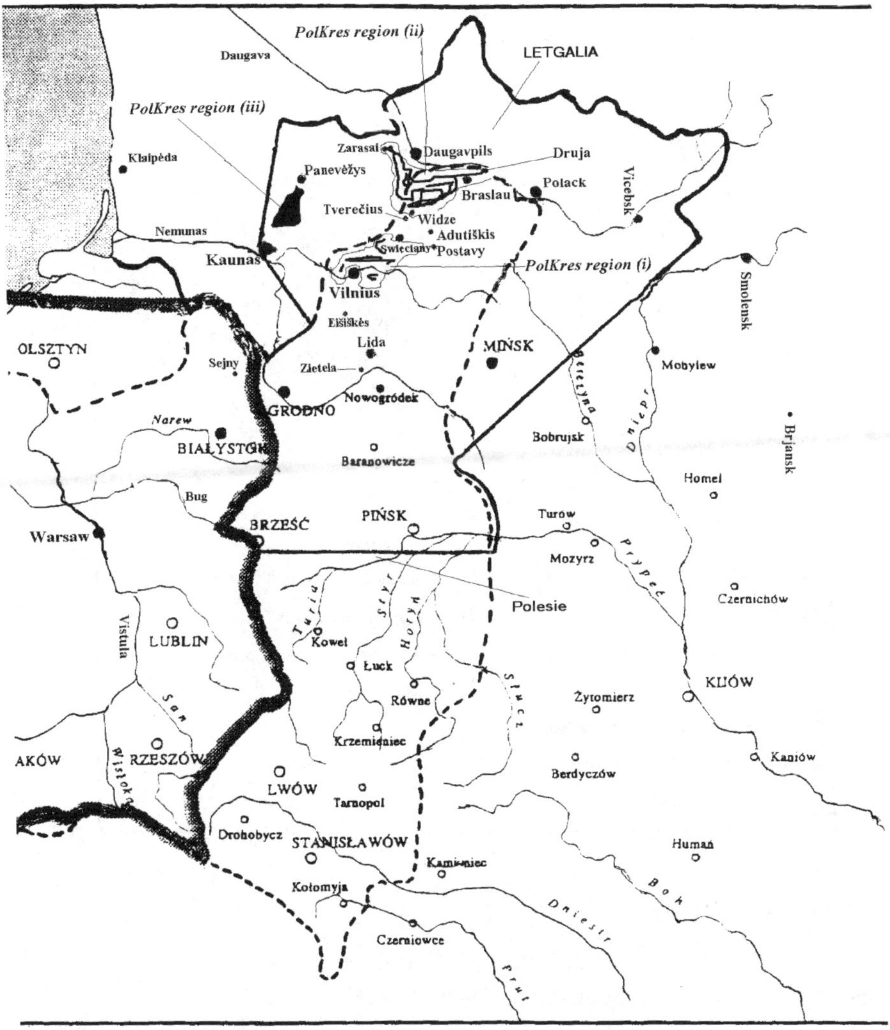

contemporary border of Poland

Polish border from 1920 to 1939

range of impact of the northern polszczyzna kresowa before World War I

Map 2: **The ethnolinguistic situation in the Lithuanian–Belarusian borderland**

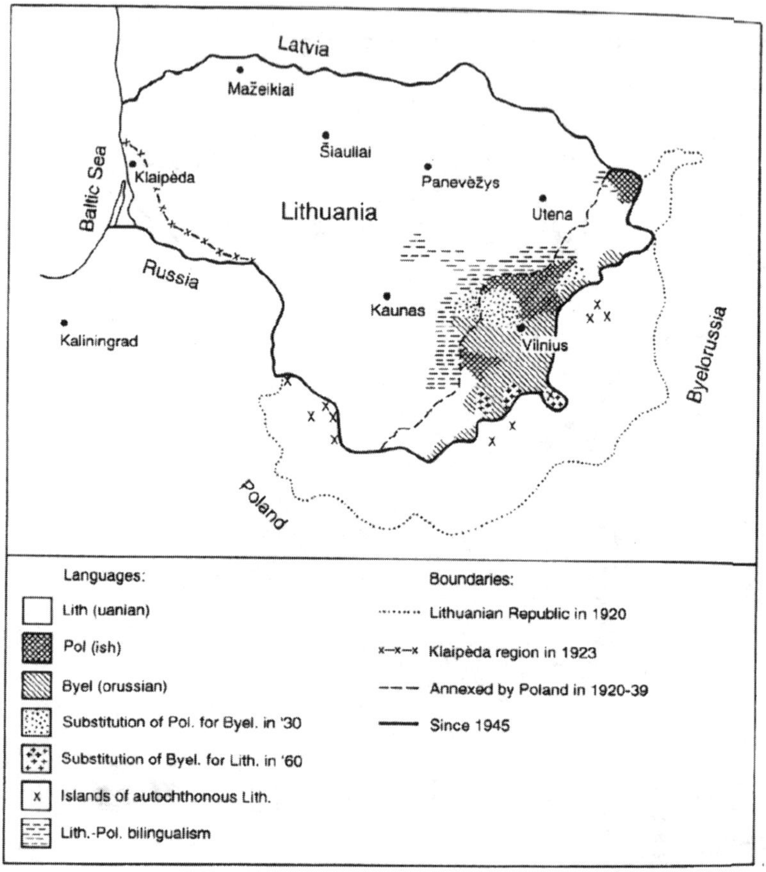

Sources of maps

Map 1: Grek-Pabisowa (1997:179), modified
Map 2: Grumadienė/Stundžia (1997:1914)

Notes

1. The only real exclusion to this rule are a couple of publications by Sudnik, in part together with colleagues, based on fieldwork in in the 1960's and 1970's (cf. first of all Sudnik 1975

and Nevskaja/Sudnik 1978) as well as some fieldwork conducted by Čekmonas (Czekman), which, as far as I can judge, has remained unpublished for the most part. The appeal of looking at the linguistic situation of the Grand Duchy as an area of considerable structural convergences caused by long-lasting multilingualism and language contact was lanced by Bednarczuk (1993, 1994). However, only rather recently serious attempts have been made to analyse how and why contacts between linguistic populations have been leading to such convergences in Slavic, Baltic, Fennic and varieties of some other languages spoken in that particular area. For such analyses of various structural features in the broader context of the CBA see the contributions in Dahl/Koptjevskaja-Tamm (2001), in particular Koptjevskaja-Tamm/Wälchli (2001). For the smaller area of the GDL such investigations are basically still lacking.

2. This research was conducted at Konstanz University in collaboration with colleagues from Poland, Lithuania, Belarus and Russia under the auspices of the SFB 471 "Variation and evolution in the lexicon" (project B-4) at the University of Konstanz. For some brief information see the URL http://ling.uni-konstanz.de/pages/proj/sfb471/naveng.html and Wiemer (2000).

3. For the problem of demography and migrations such uncritical approaches were pointed out by Jurkiewicz (1994), who himself gave a careful survey of the existing literature on this topic. Cf. also Zejmis (1999).

4. I am very much indebted to Mathias Niendorf (Kiel), who, by discussing some historical details and supplying me with some more literature on the subject, helped me avoid some shortcomings in the presentation of the historical background of language contacts in the territory discussed here. I thank him and two anonymous reviewers, who read an earlier version of this article, for remarks which I have taken account of in this revised version. Of course, neither they nor anybody else should be made responsible for mistakes or misinterpretations which might have evaded my attention. Nonetheless, keep in mind that this paper is written, first of all, from a (socio)linguistic perspective.

5. For an overview and information on minor languages of this region cf. Bednarczuk (1994), Grek-Pabisowa (1997:146–152) and various contributions to the two volumes by Dahl/Koptjevskaja-Tamm (2001).

6. Here and in the following place and river names will be adduced in the version according to the official language of the state in which they are located at present. If an alternative calling will be used after a slash, the respective language will be indicated by an appropriate abbreviation (see list of abbreviations in the appendix).

7. This assimilation had been taking place for more than 1000 years, since the Slavs spread from the south of the river Prypjat' (Poles'e) and, among others, gained more and more of the originally Baltic territory in today's Belarus, "pushing away", as it were, the Baltic (Lithuanian) territory from south-east to north-west and north. For more detailed information cf., inter alia, Sedov (1994).

8. It has been a topic of considerable debate whether the GDL's real centre of power and expansion originated in its parts now belonging to northern Belarus. In particular some Belarusian historians have defended the view that the dominant role in the GDL was played by East Slavic leaders. Since this discussion does not give any hints on real language use (cf.

also Niendorf 2003: 117), I will refrain from details and remind the reader about the caveat raised at the end of the Introduction. For a recent survey of the historiographic details cf. Zejmis (1999) and the systematic investigation Lindner (1999).

9. On the gradual assimilation of Balts by (east) Slavs from the first centuries AD cf. Sedov (1994).

10. Zinkevičius (1996b: 62f.), without going into any details, maintains that the élite was formed by Lithuanians; but cf. also Gudavičius (1999: 35f., 48–59, 70–83, 101–145) and Ochmański (1990: Ch. 3) for a detailed account, whereas many Belarusian authors dispute this opinion (see Note 8).

11. The term 'Polish-*Lithuanian* commonwealth' is thus justified not on linguistic grounds, but based on the fact that the entire gentry of the GDL, regardless of its ethnic or religious affiliation, considered themselves as 'Lithuanians'. It was this "upper class" that constituted the basis for what was to become the 'political nation' (cf. Błaszczyk 2002: 297ff.; Suchocki 1983: 74f.). Again mind about the caveat uttered at the end of the Introduction.

12. The different labels for this variety are partly due to its different chronological stages and regional provenience, partly due to ideological attitudes (cf. Bieder [3]1998: 123). Its earliest (14th century) form betrayed linguistic features not from the central (north-east Belarusian) parts of the GDL, but from a region situated much more to the south (Poles'e) (Stang 1939: 94–103). Church Slavonic elements entered this variety mainly in the 16th century, when it became a means of polemics for theological disputes between representatives of the Catholic, the Russian Orthodox and the Uniate Church. Cf. Moser (1998: 15, 19f.) and Uspenskij (1987: 260ff.) as the basic sources, Zinkevičius (1996b: 77f.) for a critical discussion of the term 'starobelorusskij' ('Old Belarusian') as well as Pryhodzič (1998: 13).

13. As pointed out by Uspenskij (1987: 265), the noblemen east from the river Bug certainly were bilingual in Prosta Mova and Polish, and the "mixture" between both varieties must have been considerable. Beside Prosta Mova, however, there must have been in the first place other vernacular predecessors of Belarusian (i.e. western East Slavic, Ruthenian) which members of the gentry spoke as their native tongue.

14. For an account of the history of the role of Polish and a linguistic analysis of the contemporary Polish spoken in Letgalia cf. the yet unpublished thesis Ostrówka (2001).

15. The first possible direct contacts in Suvalkija (today's north-east Poland) cannot date earlier than from the beginning of the 14th century: in 1278–1283 the Crusaders smashed the tribe of the Yatvingians (cf. Zinkevičius 1993: 12). This tribe was situated between Lithuania proper and the north-eastern parts of Poland. But even then contacts between Poles and Lithuanians must have remained sparse, because the devastated zone was full of swamps and forests (cf. Błaszczyk 1998: 26). Not until the end of the 16th century did Polish settlement (mostly from Mazovia) become more intense (cf. Marcinkiewicz 1997: 1615).

16. On this question see the thorough analysis of historical data by Błaszczyk (1998: 179–192) and the survey in Jurkiewicz (1994: 240–244).

17. Cf. the historical account by Wiśniewski (1964: 121ff.) and the synthetic evaluation in Jurkiewicz (1994: 245f.).

18. Cf. Jurkiewicz (1994: 246f.) for a careful discussion and Zielińska (2002a: 27).

19. In fact, this permission was withdrawn in 1588 by the 3rd Lithuanian Statute, so that the respective paragraph in the Statute and the constitutional law from 1569 contradicted each other (!). In practice, however, either one of these two laws was circumvented as the regional authority liked, and Poles continued to settle in the GDL (M. Niendorf, p.c.).

20. See the concise overview in Zielińska (2002b). For a critical assessment of theories concerning the origin of the Polish varieties in the former GDL cf. Rieger (1995). The fact that Lithuanian (as well as East Slavic) noblemen (and other representatives of the political élite of the GDL) quite willingly assimilated themselves to Polish, is also acknowledged by Lithuanian scholars; cf., for instance, Gaučas (1993:43), Gudavičius (1999:454f., 460), Vidugiris (1993:119f.), Zinkevičius (1993:12, 1996a:244).

21. For the sake of exhaustiveness, we should also mention the hypothesis according to which the Polish varieties along the Lithuanian-Belarusian borderland are a natural continuation of a dialect which allegedly was spoken by a West Slavic tribe (called 'Old Podlasians') in the 5th–10th centuries AD; cf. Maryniakowa (1992). Besides on archaeological findings she bases her opinion on similarities in morphology and syntax shared by the polszczyzna kresowa and Polish dialects in east and north-east Poland. This hypothesis is far-fetched and built on weak grounds, because it ultimately rests on archaeological findings, the assumption that ethnic and linguistic reconstructions can be directly correlated and the neglect of possible (and, indeed, very likely) language contact results which must have blurred the original distinction between East and West Slavic dialect continua. Indeed, one of the serious flaws in Maryniakowa's argumentation is that she does not really account for the consequences of secondary convergencees, which certainly have taken place during more than thousand years in an area of quite vivid contacts between speakers of West and East Slavic dialects.

22. Until that time Polish had been permitted for administrative and educational purposes (Pryhodzič 1998:15; Žuraŭski 1982:39f.); see above.

23. Not until the second half of the 20th century did these features begin to vanish in consequence of the liquidation of traditionally compact settlements and the growing number of mixed marriages of Old Believers with adherents of other faiths.

24. See however, Ostrówka (2001:Ch. 4) for some structural description of Letgalian Polish. After 1568 a large part of Letgalia was added to the GDL for a few years. Then it remained part of the Polish-Lithuanian commonwealth (so-called Polish Livonia, Pol. 'Inflanty').

25. In general, statistical data ought to be met with great caution. For the reasons see the criticism on statistical data in the 18th–19th centuries in Sipovič (1973:4), for ethnic Lithuania at the turn from the 19th to the 20th century in Gaučas (1983, 1993:54ff.); concerning the interbellum situation cf. Guthier (1977:52ff.) for Soviet Belarus and Poland, Karaś et al. (2001:26ff.) for Lithuania.

26. Čekmonas (2001a:87) comments on this as follows: "Bilingualism in Polish or Lithuanian and Russian or trilingualism in Polish, Lithuanian and Russian were not characteristic of certain social strata, but rather of local educated individuals." And he continues: "It is natural to suppose that the number of bilingual and trilingual people was growing rapidly after the Russification of educational establishment (...)."

27. Cf. Sipovič (1973:30) and Lindner (1999:96–109) for some more details on these and similar newspapers.

28. For a concise overview of the Lithuanian dialect division see Balode/Holvoet (2001b: 41–43).

29. Interestingly, this happened immediately after the abolition of early Belarusian (i.e. Prosta Mova) as official language (see 4.2).

30. A large part of Suvalkija was incorporated into Poland after WW I. This part is situated north of Augustów and west, southwest of Marijampolė down to more or less Ogrodniki (situated on the Polish side of the contemporary Lithuanian-Polish border). Practically nothing is known about Polish-Lithuanian bilingualism in this area until the end of WW II.

31. The first literary journals (*Aušra* 'The Dawn', *Varpas* 'The Bell' and others) started appearing in the 1880's (they were printed in East Prussia), but they tell us virtually nothing about the influence of multilingualism in south-eastern Lithuania, because this part of the country was simply not very much involved in these publications and most of the articles printed there were practically re-written by editors of west Aukštaitian or East Prussian origin. After the abolition of the press ban (in 1904) the first Lithuanian newspaper began to appear in Vilnius; but this does not give any reliable hints at interferences from East Slavic or Polish either. On the history of Lithuanian national awakening and its consequences for printed publications and codification cf. Zinkevičius (1996a: 286–294) and the detailed account in Palionis ([2]1995: 165–278).

32. In Lithuanian dialectology this is one of the two features called *dzūkavimas.*

33. The immediate surroundings of Vilnius and the broader regions south from it showed a rather continuous change from Lithuanian to Belarusian (see 4.1).

34. This fact is underlined by every Polish investigator on this topic, but cf. also Čekmonas (2001a: 88).

35. On the Lithuanian policy towards the Polish minority in the Kaunas–Panevėžys region cf. Karaś et al. (2001: 26–34) and Zielińska (2002a: 25f., 30f.), on the Polish policy directed towards the Lithuanian population cf. Zinkevičius (1996a: 299–302), Grumadienė/Stundžia (1997: 1916) and Section 5.

36. In most Belarusian dialects the distribution of [v], [u] and [u̯] is regulated by phonotactic rules, in particular whether a vowel precedes and a consonant follows.

37. The aim of these expeditions was not just to collect language data of all the language varieties spoken there, but also to systematically question residents about the present sociolinguistic situation and its historic background. Due to the lack of reliable demographic and historic material, this is the only possibility to attempt a reconstruction of the highly complex sociolinguistic situation in these regions. During our expeditions information on the larger part of that area was tape-recorded at length and is being archived.

References

Avanesaŭ, R. I., Atraxovič, K. K., & Mackevič, Ju. F. (Eds.). (1968). *Linhvistyčnaja heahrafija i hrupoŭka belaruskix havorak.* Minsk: Navuka i tėxnika.

Balode, L. & Holvoet, A. (2001a). The Latvian language and its dialects. In Ö. Dahl & M. Koptjevskaja-Tamm (Eds.), *Circum-Baltic Languages, vol. 1: Past and Present* (pp. 3–40). Amsterdam–Philadelphia: Benjamins.

Balode, L. & Holvoet, A. (2001b). The Lithuanian language and its dialects. In Ö. Dahl & M. Koptjevskaja-Tamm (Eds.), *Circum-Baltic Languages, vol. 1: Past and Present* (pp. 41–79). Amsterdam–Philadelphia: Benjamins.

Bednarczuk, L. (1993). La communauté linguistique du Grand Duché de Lituanie. *Linguistica Baltica, 2*, 5–13.

Bednarczuk, L. (1994). Stosunki etnolingwistyczne na obszarze Wielkiego Księstwa Litewskiego. *Acta Baltico-Slavica, 22*, 109–124.

Bednarczuk, L. (1999). Litewsko-słowiańskie pogranicze językowe w pierwszej połowie XX wieku w świetle badań Olgierda Chomińskiego. *Acta Baltico-Slavica, 24*, 95–105.

Bieder, H. [3](1998). Das Weißrussische. In P. Rehder (Ed.), *Einführung in die slavischen Sprachen (Mit einer Einführung in die Balkanphilologie)* (pp. 110–125). Darmstadt: Wissenschaftliche Buchgesellschaft.

Błaszczyk, G. (1998). *Dzieje stosunków polsko-litewskich od czasów najdawniejszych do współczesności, t. 1: Trudne początki*. Poznań: Wydawnictwo Naukowe UAM.

Błaszczyk, G. (2002). *Litwa na przełomie Średniowiecza i nowożytności (1492–1569)*. Poznań: Wydawnictwo Poznańskie.

Čekmonas, V. (2001a). Russian varieties in the southeastern Baltic area: Urban Russian of the 19th century. In Ö. Dahl & M. Koptjevskaja-Tamm (Eds.), *Circum-Baltic Languages, vol. 1: Past and Present* (pp. 81–99). Amsterdam–Philadelphia: Benjamins.

Čekmonas, V. (2001b). Russian varieties in the southeastern Baltic area: Rural dialects. In Ö. Dahl & M. Koptjevskaja-Tamm (Eds.), *Circum-Baltic Languages, vol. 1: Past and Present* (pp. 101–136). Amsterdam–Philadelphia: Benjamins.

Čekmonas, V. (2001c). On some Circum-Baltic features of the Pskov-Novgorod (North-western Central Russian) dialect. In Ö. Dahl & M. Koptjevskaja-Tamm (Eds.), *Circum-Baltic Languages, vol. 1: Past and Present* (pp. 339–359). Amsterdam–Philadelphia: Benjamins.

Dahl, Ö. & Koptjevskaja-Tamm, M. (1992). *Language typology around the Baltic sea: A problem inventory*. Stockholm (= Papers from the Institute of Linguistics, University of Stockholm. Publication 61).

Dahl, Ö. & Koptjevskaja-Tamm, M. (Eds.). (2001). *Circum-Baltic Languages, vol. 1: Past and Present; vol. 2: Grammar and Typology*. Amsterdam–Philadelphia: Benjamins.

Davies, N. (1986). *Heart of Europe (A Short History of Poland)*. Oxford–New York: Oxford U.P.

Gaučas, P. (1983). Lietuvos gyventojų skaičius 1897–1914 m. *Geografija, XIX*, 74–92.

Gaučas, P. (1993). Lietuvių-gudų kalbų paribio etnolingvistinė situacija 1795–1914 m. In K. Garšva & L. Grumadienė (Eds.), *Lietuvos rytai* (pp. 42–100). Vilnius: Valstybinis leidybos centras.

Gaučas, P. & Vidugiris, A. (1983). Ėtnolingvističeskaja situacija litovsko-belorusskogo pograničʼja s konca XVIII po načalo XX v. *Geografija, XIX*, 26–73.

Grek-Pabisowa, I. (1997). Językowa rzeczywistość na dawnych polskich Kresach północno-wschodnich. In K. Handke (Ed.), *Kresy – pojęcie i rzeczywistość* (pp. 145–179). Warszawa: Slawistyczny Ośrodek Wydawniczy.

Grumadienė, L. & Stundžia, B. (1997). Lithuania. In H. Goebl et al. (Eds.), *Kontaktlinguistik (Ein internationales Handbuch zeitgenössischer Forschung)*, 2. Halbband (pp. 1912–1919). Berlin–New York: Mouton de Gruyter.

Gudavičius, E. (1999). *Lietuvos istorija, t. 1: Nuo seniausių laikų iki 1569 metų*. Vilnius: Akademinio skautų sąjūdžio Vydūno fondas Čikagoje / Lietuvos rašytojų sąjungos leidykla.

Guthier, S. L. (1977). The Belorussians: national identification and assimilation, 1897–1970. *Soviet Studies, XXIX* (1), 37–61.

Jacobs, N. G. (2001). Yiddish in the Baltic region. In Ö. Dahl & M. Koptjevskaja-Tamm (Eds.), *Circum-Baltic Languages*, vol. 1: *Past and Present* (pp. 285–311). Amsterdam–Philadelphia: Benjamins.

Jurkiewicz, J. (1994). Osadnictwo polskie w Wielkim Księstwie Litewskim w świetle badań historycznych. *Acta Baltico-Slavica, 22*, 237–255.

Karaś, H. et al. (2001). *Język polski na Kowieńszczyęnie (Historia. Sytuacja socjolingwistyczna. Cechy językowe. Teksty)*. Warszawa–Wilno: Elipsa.

Kardelis, V., Sinočkina, B., Wiemer, B., & Zielińska, A. (2003). Sytuacja językowa na terenie od Wisagini do Hoduciszek na Litwie. Raport z badań terenowych. *Acta Baltico-Slavica* 27 (to appear).

Karskij, E. F. (1962). K voprosu o granice belorusskix govorov. In E. F. Karskij (Ed.), *Trudy po belorusskomu i drugim slavjanskim jazykam* (pp. 435–440). Moskva: Izdatel'stvo AN SSSR. [Reprint from: *Russkij Filologičeskij Vestnik, LIII* (1905), 55–61.]

Klimčuk, F. D. (1981). K istorii rasprostranenija belorusskix govorov v jugo-vostočnoj Litve. *Balto-slavjanskie issledovanija, 1980*, 214–220. Moskva: Nauka.

Koptjevskaja-Tamm, M. & Wälchli, B. (2001). The Circum-Baltic languages: An areal-typological approach. In Ö. Dahl & M. Koptjevskaja-Tamm (Eds.), *Circum-Baltic Languages, vol. 2: Grammar and Typology* (pp. 615–750). Amsterdam–Philadelphia: Benjamins.

Kramko, I. I., Jurėvič, A. K., & Janovič, A. I. (1968). *Historyja belaruskaj litaraturnaj movy*, t. II. Minsk: Navuka i tėxnika.

Kurzowa, Z. (1993). *Język polski Wileńszczyzny i kresów północno-wschodnich XVI–XX w.* Warszawa–Kraków: Państwowe Wydawnictwo Naukowe.

Lemchenas, Ch. (1970). *Lietuvių kalbos įtaka Lietuvos žydų tarmei*. Vilnius: Mintis.

Lindner, R. (1999). *Historiker und Herrschaft (Nationsbildung und Geschichtspolitik in Weißrußland im 19. und 20. Jahrhundert)*. München: Oldenbourg.

Lojka, P. (2001). Die weißrussischen Territorien als Teil des Großfürstentums Litauen (13. bis 16. Jahrhundert). In D. Beyrau & R. Lindner (Eds.), *Handbuch der Geschichte Weißrußlands* (pp. 80–92). Göttingen: Vandenhoeck & Ruprecht.

Marcinkiewicz, J. (1997). Polnisch-Litauisch. In H. Goebl et al. (Eds.), *Kontaktlinguistik (Ein internationales Handbuch zeitgenössischer Forschung)*, 2. Halbband (pp. 1614–1622). Berlin–New York: Mouton de Gruyter.

Marcinkiewicz, J. (2000). Processes of linguistic integration in the Grand Duchy of Lithuania in the light of the theory of communicative networks and other sociolinguistic concepts. In G. Błaszczyk & M. Hasiuk (Eds.), *History, Culture and Language of Lithuania (Proceedings of the International Lithuanian Conference, Poznań 17–19 Sept. 1998)* (pp. 47–63). Poznań: Wydawnictwo Naukowe UAM.

Martel, A. (1938). *La langue polonaise dans les pays ruthènes. Ukraïne et Russe Blanche 1569-1667*. Lille. (= Travaux et Mémoires de l'Université de Lille. Nouvelle série: Droit et Lettres, No. 20.)

Maryniakowa, I. (1992). Północno-wschodnie obszary polszczyzny wobec języków wschodniosłowiańskich i bałtyckich. In J. Siatkowski (Ed.), *Z polskich studiów slawistycznych*. Seria 8: *Językoznawstwo* (pp. 153–158). Warszawa: Wydawnictwo PAN.

Moser, M. (1998). *Die polnische, ukrainische und weißrussische Interferenzschicht im russischen Satzbau des 16. und 17. Jahrhunderts*. Frankfurt/M. etc.: Lang.

Moser, M. (2002). Čto takoe 'próstaja mova'? *Studia Slavica Hungarica, 47* (3/4), 221–260.

Nevskaja, L. G. & Sudnik, T. M. (1978). Dialektnye kontakty v zone sovremennogo baltijsko-slavjanskogo ėtnojazykovogo pograničja. *Slavjanskoe jazykoznanie. VIII meždunarodnyj s"ezd slavistov (Doklady sovetskoj delegacii)*, 285–307. Moskva: Nauka.

Niendorf, M. (2003). *Studien zur Nationsbildung in der Frühen Neuzeit. Das Großfürstentum Litauen 1569–1795*. Kiel (unpublished manuscript of postdoctoral thesis).

Nitsch, K. (1925). Język polski w Wileńszczyźnie. *Przegląd Współczesny, 12*, 25–32.

Ochmański, J. (1990). *Historia Litwy*. Wrocław etc.: Wydawnictwo Ossolińskie.

Ostrówka, M. (2001). *Współczesna polszczyzna mówiona na Łotwie*. Warszawa. (unpublished ms. of doctoral dissertation)

Palionis, J. (1967). *Lietuvių literatūrinė kalba XVI–XVII a.* Vilnius: Mokslas.

Palionis, J. [2](1995). *Lietuvių rašomosios kalbos istorija*. Vilnius: Mokslo ir enciklopedijų leidykla.

Podlužnyj, A. I. (1997). Belorusskij jazyk. In V. N. Jarceva et al. (Eds.), *Jazyki Rossijskoj Federacii i sosednix gosudarstv. Ėnciklopedija v trex tomax*, t. I: *A–I* (pp. 189–201). Moskva: Nauka.

Poljakov, O. (2000). Die russische Sprache im Baltikum (Geschichte und Gegenwart). In B. Panzer (Ed.), *Die sprachliche Situation in der Slavia zehn Jahre nach der Wende (Beiträge zum Internationalen Symposion des Slavischen Instituts der Universität Heidelberg vom 29. Sept. bis 2. Okt. 1999)* (pp. 49–66). Frankfurt/M. etc.: Lang.

Pryhodzič, M. P. (1998). Z historyi belaruskaj movy i jae vyvučėnnja. In A. A. Lukašanec et al. (Eds.), *Belaruskaja mova* (pp. 13–24). Opole: Uniwersytet Opolski, Instytut Filologii Polskiej.

Rieger, J. (1995). W sprawie genezy i ewolucji polszczyzny w Wielkim Księstwie Litewskim. *Studia nad polszczyzną kresową, 7*, 31–38.

Sedov, V. V. (1994). Vostočnoslavjanskaja ėtnojazykovaja obščnost'. *Voprosy jazykoznanija, 1994* (4), 3–16.

Sahanowitsch, H. (2001). Der Eintritt des Großfürstentums Litauen in die polnische Adelsrepublik: Weißrußland im 16. und 17. Jahrhundert. In D. Beyrau & R. Lindner (Eds.), *Handbuch der Geschichte Weißrußlands* (pp. 93–105). Göttingen: Vandenhoeck & Ruprecht.

Sipovič, Č. (1973). The Language Problem in the Catholic Church in Byelorussia from 1832 to the First World War. *The Journal of Byelorussian Studies, 3–1*, 3–40.

Stang, Chr. S. (1935). *Die westrussische Kanzleisprache des Großfürstentums Litauen*. Oslo: Dybwad.

Stang, Chr. S. (1939). *Die altrussische Urkundensprache der Stadt Polozk*. Oslo: Dybwad.

Stolz, Th. (1991). *Sprachbund im Baltikum? Estnisch und Lettisch im Zentrum einer sprachlichen Konvergenzlandschaft*. Bochum: Brockmeyer.

Suchocki, J. (1983). Formowanie się i skład narodu politycznego w Wielkim Księstwie Litewskim późnego Średniowiecza. *Zapiski historyczne, 48* (1/2), 31–78.

Sudnik, T. M. (1975). *Dialekty litovsko-slavjanskogo pograničʼja (Očerki fonologičeskix sistem)*. Moskva: Nauka.

Šapoka, A. (Ed.). (1990). *Lietuvos istorija*. Vilnius: Mokslas. [Reprint of the 1936 edition, Kaunas: Švietimo Ministerijos knygų leidimo komisija.]

Turska, H. (1995). *O powstaniu polskich obszarów językowych na Wileńszczyęnie*. Vilnius: Mintis. [photomechanic reprint from *Studia nad polszczyzną kresową* I. pod red. J. Riegera i W. Werenicza. Wrocław etc.: Wydawnictwo Ossolińskie, 1982. (19–122). Originally prepared for print in 1939.]

Uspenskij, B. A. (1987). *Istorija russkogo literaturnogo jazyka (XI–XVII vv.)*. München: Sagner.

Vidugiris, A. (1993). Etnolingvistinė pietryčių Lietuvos padėtis XX a. pirmojoje pusėje. In K. Garšva & L. Grumadienė (Eds.), *Lietuvos rytai* (pp. 115–131). Vilnius: Valstybinis leidybos centras.

Vidugiris, A. & Klimčuk, F. D. (1978). Nekotorye voprosy ėtno-jazykovyx processov na balto-vostočnoslavjanskom pograničʼe. In V. V. Ivanov et al. (Eds.), *Konferencija: Ėtnolingvističeskie balto-slavjanskie kontakty v nastojaščem i prošlom, 11–15 dekabrja 1978 g. (Predvaritelʼnye materialy)* (pp. 10–35). Moskva: Nauka.

Wälchli, B. (2000). Infinite predication as a marker of evidentiality and modality in the languages of the Baltic region. *Sprachtypologie und Universalienforschung, 53* (2), 186–210.

Wexler, P. (1985). Belorussification, Russification and Polonization. Trends in the Belorussian Language 1890–1982. In I. T. Kreindler (Ed.), *Sociolinguistic Perspectives on Soviet National Languages (Their Past, Present and Future)* (pp. 37–56). Berlin: Mouton de Gruyter.

Wiemer, B. (2000). Semantisches und grammatisches Verhalten von Verben in Kontaktvarietäten des südlichen Litauen (Präsentation eines Projekts). *Acta Baltico-Slavica, 25*, 51–75.

Wiemer, B. (2003). ʻmowa prostaʼ – Präliminaria zu einer strukturellen Beschreibung. In R. Blankenhorn, J. Błaszczak, & R. Marzari (Eds.) *Beiträge der Europäischen Slavistischen Linguistik (POLYSLAV) 6* (pp. 227–237). München: Sagner.

Wiemer, B. (in prep.). ʻMowa prostaʼ w literaturze naukowej – od pojęcia potocznego do naukowego.

Wiśniewski, J. (1964). Rozwój osadnictwa na pograniczu polsko-rusko-litewskim od końca XIV do połowy XVII wieku. *Acta Baltico-Slavica, 1*, 115–135.

Zdaniukiewicz, A. A. (1992). O powstaniu i rozwoju języka polskiego na kresach wschodnich – polemicznie. In J. Siatkowski (Ed.), *Z polskich studiów slawistycznych*. Seria 8: *Językoznawstwo* (pp. 271–276). Warszawa: Energeia.

Zejmis, J. (1999). Belarusian National Historiography and the Grand Duchy of Lithuania as a Belarusian State. *Zeitschrift für Ostmitteleuropa-Forschung, 48* (3), 383–396.

Zielińska, A. (2002a). *Polska mniejszość na Litwie Kowieńskiej (Studium socjolingwistyczne)*. Warszawa: Slawistyczny Ośrodek Wydawniczy.

Zielińska, A. (2002b). The sociolinguistic situation of the Polish language of the Slavic-Lithuanian borderlands (the region of the present-day countries: Byelorussia, Lithuania and Latvia). *Folia Linguistica, 36* (3–4), 359–380.

Zielińska, A. (2002c). O łączeniu metod socjolingwistycznych i dialektologicznych w badaniach nad językiem polskim na Litwie i Białorusi. In J. Siatkowski (Ed.), *Z polskich studiów slawistycznych*, seria X, *Językoznawstwo* (Prace na XIII Międzynarodowy Kongres Slawistow w Lublanie 2003) (pp. 281–289). Warszawa: Energeia.

Zinkevičius, Z. (1993). Pietryčių Lietuva nuo seniausių laikų iki mūsų dienų. In K. Garšva & L. Grumadienė (Eds.), *Lietuvos rytai* (pp. 9–29). Vilnius: Valstybinis leidybos centras.

Zinkevičius, Z. (1996a). *The History of the Lithuanian Language*. Vilnius: Mokslo ir enciklopedijų leidykla.

Zinkevičius, Z. [Zinkjavičjus] (1996b). *Vostočnaja Litva v prošlom i nastojaščem*. Vilnius: Mokslo ir enciklopedijų leidykla.

Žuraŭski, A. I. (1982). Dvuxmou̯e i šmatmou̯e u historyi Belarusi. In M. V. Biryla & A. J. Suprun (Eds.), *Pytanni bilingvizmu i u̯zaemadzejannja mou̯* (pp. 18–49). Minsk.

Swedish and Swedish

On the origin of diglossia and social variation in the Swedish language

Lars Wollin
Åbo Akademi University Turku, Finland

Some one hundred years ago the Swedish poet Erik Axel Karlfeldt (1864–1931) coined a set expression for a particular, socially discriminating, linguistic capacity characterising his alter ego *Fridolin*, a poet of peasant stock. This man is able, Karlfeldt implies, to comfortably cross barriers that are not crossed by everybody:

> och han talar med bönder på böndernas sätt, / men med lärde män på latin
> 'and he speaks to peasants in the peasants' way, but to learned men in Latin'

The idea of easy linguistic variation in approaching different interlocutors was thus given a fixed poetic expression by Karlfeldt. Ever since, this concept has been frequently referred to in Swedish discussions on linguistic behaviour.

At the turn of the 20th century, among a broad mass of the Swedish population, an important condition of personal success in society was, or was thought to be, the capacity for individual, socially determined linguistic variation. People working or appearing with reasonable credibility in an "educated" context were expected to adapt their spoken language to the rather strictly defined variety of current Swedish prevalent in that particular context. Mixing up levels of usage occured at their peril. It is generally argued that this kind of capacity lost its urgency during the 20th century, in a Swedish language that had grown constantly more levelled and stylistically homogeneous. This modern phase of linguistic development in Sweden will not, however, be focused upon in the present paper.[1]

To the historical linguist who is interested in the external conditions of long-term linguistic development, the Fridolin case – however poetically fictitious – naturally gives rise to some other questions. If a demand for individual flexibility in speaking was a reality around 1900, how long had it been so? And, more generally, how old are the origins of distinct functional and social varieties of spoken and written Swedish? When, where, and in which genres of written texts are we able to trace the first evidence of a variation in linguistic form that is not based on mere geographical differences in the language system or purely accidental, but which, besides being systematic, is also *deliberate*? Which grammarians, or others reflecting theoretically upon language, first showed some kind of awareness of such matters? A few scattered observations on this topic will be put forward and discussed in the present paper – though without pretensions to provide conclusive answers; my object is rather to point out problems and to suggest some directions for further research. It should be mentioned at once that the thread through history will be followed back as far as the late medieval monastic "typing pool" at Vadstena, where my argument will be presented and concluded in more detail.

Research concerning stylistic, situational and social variation in 17th, 18th and 19th century Swedish has not been infrequent in the last three decades.[2] Central concepts that are often referred to are "the court language" (*hovspråket*) and "bookish Swedish" (*boksvenska*). These are higher varieties of spoken language, though principally based on different genres of writing. The former was supposedly used by the upper classes in the 17th and 18th centuries, the latter by the peasantry in the 19th century; in both cases we may generally assume a variation of a diglossic nature.

A very prominent contribution to our present knowledge about different aspects of this topic is a number of articles by Gun Widmark. My argument in Sections 1 and 2 below is based on the same material as that adduced by Widmark in her important study *Boksvenska och talsvenska* ('Bookish Swedish and spoken Swedish'; 1991/2000).

1. Stratification in language: Education and condescension. Noreen's stylistic scale

A highly useful basis for this survey is provided by certain concepts launched by Karlfeldt's contemporary *Adolf Noreen*, the leading Swedish scholar at that time within the field of Scandinavian philology and linguistics. In addition, this brings to the fore the concept of *diglossia*.

First, it is fairly safe to presuppose that Karlfeldt did not imply that Fridolin was *literally* speaking to learned men in Latin; that would have been hardly credible in late 19th century Sweden. It is quite certainly a question of a "learned" variety of Swedish, i.e. the language of scholarly discourse, as we would put it today. At that time as well as later, this variety of spoken (and of course written) Swedish held an important and conspicuous position in stylistic variation. Fridolin's "genuine" idiom was of course the Dalecarlian dialect of his own native district. The kind of linguistic conduct thus sketched out here by Karlfeldt in poetical terms actually satisfies the requirements of a rather strictly defined *diglossic* variation, even in a modern sociolinguistic sense (such as that of the concept of diglossia introduced in 1959 by Charles A. Ferguson, who also coined the term).[3] Two distinct varieties of the same language are used by the same individual in a complementary fashion dependent on situation; the governing speech situations differ in degree of formality, often also of prestige.

In the first volume, published in 1903, of his grand work *Vårt språk* ('Our language'), Adolf Noreen defines some basic dimensions of the "essence" of language, such as "structure" (*struktur*), "applicability" (*användbarhet*; referring to 'function') and "atmospheric value" (*stämningsvärde*; roughly referring to 'style'). The "national language" (*nationalspråket*) is characterized by its structure, whereas a central category defined in terms of applicability is that of "standard language" (*riksspråk*), as opposed to the dialects (*dialekter, landsmål*). A standard language is "not tied to any particular part of the country but current as a common means of communication, i.e. is usable and as such acknowledged and aimed at, within the entire territory of a national language"; the dialects are confined to smaller areas and, consequently, less "applicable".

The stylistic variation of the standard language is outlined by Noreen in an elaborated scale, comprising in its first subdivision the three traditional levels of style: "higher", "middle" and "lower". But Noreen goes further, subdividing each level into two stages. The result is six stylistic varieties of written and spoken Swedish, defined according to their use. The two varieties at the top of the scale are confined to the written language (and to speaking on the basis of written text), whereas the four others are principally spoken (though with a few instances of more or less familiar writing, such as private letters). See Table 1.

Again, it should be emphasized that Noreen's style scale is exclusively a matter of the *standard* language; it implies full "applicability". Regional, even local, features certainly occur within the boundaries of that language – particularly in the varieties of lower style, where they may be quite frequent – but their occurrence must not be confused with the relation between standard language and dialect, which is principally a different distinction. Accordingly, to Noreen

Table 1. Adolf Noreen's levels of style and stylistic varieties and their fields of application in *Vårt språk* I (1903: 27ff.)

Higher style for *public* social intercourse "language of reading and lecture"	1. oratorical style: *solemn speech, preaching, tragedy* 2. normal style: *debate, lecture, ordinary play, officia- lese, science*
Middle style for *educated private* social intercourse "language of educated conversation"	3. refined style: *polished conversation, intimate letters* 4. familiar style: *simple and unforced conversation, e.g. in the immediate family*
Lower style for *less educated private* social intercourse "language of humble or even uneducated conversation"	5. simple style: *less educated peoples' conversation, educated peoples' conversation with the less educated* 6. vulgar style: *coarse conversation, jargon, slang*

Table 2. Some discriminating variants, typical of Noreen's stylistic varieties in *Vårt språk* I (1903: 30)

1	*I stoden*	*de äro ej/icke*	*husen*	*gifva och taga*
2	*ni stodo*	*de äro ej/icke*	*husen*	*ge och ta(ga)*
3	*ni stod*	*de ä(r)inte*	*husena*	*ge å ta*
4	*ni sto(d)*	*di ä inte*	*husena*	*ge å ta*
5	*ni stog*	*di ä inte*	*husena*	*ge å ta*
6	*ni stog*	*di/dom ä (i)nte*	*husena*	*ge/gi å ta*
	'you stood'	'they are not'	'the houses'	'give and take'

1	*hafver han tagit det*	*jag sade henne*	*blott / endast*
2	*har han tagit det*	*jag sa(de) henne*	*blott / endast / bara*
3	*ha(r)hantagi(t)de(t)*	*ja(g)sahenne*	*endast / bara*
4	*ha(h)antagedet*	*ja sa henne*	*bara / endast*
5	*ha an tatt et*	*jag sa na*	*bara*
6	*ha'n tatt/taji/teji e(t)*	*jag sa na*	*bara(ste)*
	'has he taken it'	'I said her'	'only', 'merely'

the standard Swedish language is not only an idiom that is functionally and socially strictly regulated; in its rich variation it is also complete.

This stylistic variation in the standard Swedish of 1900 manifests itself rather precisely in the linguistic system. More or less complete sets of distinctly marked variants are frequent on all levels of analysis. Some of Noreen's examples on the morphological and lexical level are given in Table 2.

With this stylistic scale, Noreen offers a framework for identifying variants in diglossic as well as other kinds of variation in contemporary Swedish. He points out two particular, highly frequent instances that discriminate very clearly between the "normal" stage on the higher level and the educated conversation on the middle level, i.e., generally, between (ordinary) writing and (educated) speech. These are, first, definite plurals of neuter nouns ending in a consonant and, second, number congruence of the finite verb. The style of the written language is signalled by forms like, respectively, *husen* ('the houses') and *de äro* ('they are'), that of educated spoken language by *husena* and *de är*. From a modern sociolinguistic perspective of diglossia, we could as well term *husen* and *de äro* "H-variants" and *husena* and *de är* "L-variants" (H standing for 'high', L for 'low' prestige) within different varieties of standard Swedish at about 1900. Though Noreen himself of course could not put his thoughts into those words, it is obvious that the linguistic variation described by him in terms of style bears an unmistakable stamp of diglossia.

Of course, the notion of "education" was a very tangible one in Sweden at the time when Noreen constructed his stylistic scale; it was a dimension of linguistic variation that he could quite naturally refer to. Its ideological basis was German humanism, prevalent in northern Europe, and not least in Scandinavia, in the 19th and early 20th century and reaching its peak in the epoch of the German empire, or roughly in the half-century period between 1870 and 1920. In the spirit of this ideology, "educated" people not only represented Noreen's "middle" level of style in their genuine speech, thereby reflecting the cultivation imparted to them by upbringing and formal training. Noreen's very turn of expression (*bildades språk med obildade*, 'educated peoples' conversation with the uneducated') indicates that the educated also possessed – or were expected to possess – a specific kind of linguistic competence: the abitility to *move*, easily and assuredly, up and down the scale of stylistic variation, naturally adapting their speech to the several differing social situations in which circumstances happened to place a speaking citizen. This also included the natural use of variants on the lower stylistic level when speaking to the "less educated".[4]

This kind of condescending linguistic behaviour is an additional nuance to the more general picture of strict social stratification of spoken standard Swedish among Noreen's contemporaries. It is rather unlikely to occur today. One would very much like to know how far back in history it may be attested. A glance at some 18th century evidence indicates that it is not too far.

2. Educated speech – and honourable: Noreen and Hof

In his famous treatise *Swänska språkets rätta skrifsätt* ('The correct way of writing the Swedish language'), printed in 1753, *Sven Hof*, a senior schoolmaster, native of Västergötland, presents a description of variation in contemporary Swedish. Hof's conception is strikingly similar to that of Noreen. Nevertheless it differs from it at a few crucial points.

Despite the title of his work, Hof seems to aim at describing essentially the variation of *spoken* language. Unlike Noreen, regarding speech as the basis of writing, he searches for the rules of "correct speech". Like Noreen, Hof is working with the classical three levels of style, distinguishing between "public speech" (*offenteligit tal*), "the speech of social intercourse" (*omgiängestal, gement tal*) and "the speech of ordinary people" (*gemene mans tal*). A certain terminological confusion of the two lower levels, otherwise easy to fall into (caused by the common use of the adjective *gemen*, in this context meaning 'ordinary'), is cleverly avoided in the corresponding Latin terms: *sermo publicus...*, *sermo familiaris* ... and *sermo plebejus*, respectively. See Table 3.

The two higher levels are related to situation: public speech is used, according to Hof, "when making a full speech in front of a multitude of people" (*när man inför en myckenhet folk håller ett utförligit tal*), whereas the colloquial variety is used "in everyday talk and social intercourse" (*i dageligit tal och omgiänge*). The distinction of the third and lowest level, however, reflects a social variation: "The masses pronounce, with change of sounds and syllables, many words in the maternal tongue differently from what is usual among the honourable; this may be termed ordinary people's speech (sermo plebejus)" (*Gemene hopen uttalar, med förändring af liudämnen och stafvelser, många ord i modersmålet annorledes, än af de hederliga brukeligit är; hwilket må kallas gemene mans tal* (*sermo plebejus*)).

Accordingly, in Hof's and Noreen's systems, the three levels of style are related to each other in the same basic pattern: the "middle" level is distin-

Table 3. Sven Hof's structuring of language in *Swänska språkets rätta skrifsätt* 1753

offenteligit tal *sermo publicus, oratorius, panegyricus*
omgiängestal / gement tal *sermo familiaris, popularis*
gemene mans tal *sermo plebejus*

Table 4. Some situational variants in Sven Hof's conception of linguistic variation in *Swänska språkets rätta skrifsätt* 1753

public	*sade, sedan*	*bord, världen*	*däm*	*dät, mäd, vid*	*huset, kunnat*
colloquial	*sa, sen*	*bol, välen/välan*	*dåm*	*dä, mä, ve*	*huse, kunna*
	'said'	'table', 'the world'	'they'	'it', 'with', 'at'	'the house', 'been able to'

public	*stått*	*knappt*	*upp*	*av*	*dätta*	*stolarna*	*böckerna*
colloquial	*staji*	*knafft*	*opp*	*åv*	*dä här*	*stolana*	*böckren*
	'stood' (part.)	'hardly'	'up'	'of'	'this'	'the chairs'	'the books'

guished from the highest in terms of situation, and from the lowest in terms of social distinction. However, there is nothing in Hof's system corresponding to Noreen's two-stage gradation on each level; his "stylistic scale" is a simpler one. Nor do we find anything in Hof's conception fully equivalent to Noreen's "education" postulate, including the versatile command of the entire stylistic scale.

The substance of situational linguistic variation as described by Hof consists to a large extent in using "harder, longer and more voluminous words" (*hårdare, längre och vidlyftigare ord*) when speaking publicly. By contrast, "the shorter, more easily made words" (*kortare och lättare giorde ord*) are used in colloquial speech. This difference is most frequently reflected in contrasting long and short word forms, like *sade* : *sa* ('said') and *sedan* : *sen* ('then'). These are, then, the typical H- and L-variants of the diglossia implied by Hof. Certainly other more frequent phonological, morphological and lexical differences also include the social variation between "sermo familiaris" and "sermo plebejus", whereby the diglossic pattern of the variation may appear less distinct.

Some examples of situational variation in speech as described by Hof (irrespective of its possible social implications) are shown in Table 4.

Comparing more closely Sven Hof's conception of linguistic variation to that of Adolf Noreen is a very intriguing undertaking. First, it is obvious that the three levels cannot be matched in a simple analogy. As very discerningly pointed out by Gun Widmark (1991/2000), the "sermo plebejus" on the lowest level in Hof's system must be equivalent to the dialects; this is clear from his way of exemplifying his speech variants. Accordingly, Hof includes the dialects in the linguistic variation he is describing, unlike Noreen, who wants to isolate a variation of the standard language, keeping the dialects out. At the same time it is evident that Hof does not differentiate between two levels of private speech, so that Noreen's "middle" and "lower" style both correspond roughly to Hof's second, colloquial level, the "sermo familiaris" of "honourable" people. Table 5 helps to make the pieces fall into place.

Table 5. Sven Hof's and Adolf Noreen's structurings of linguistic variation

Hof 1753: function, social distinction	Noreen 1903: "style"	Noreen 1903: "applicability"
sermo publicus …	*higher style*	
	middle style	*standard language*
sermo familiaris …	*lower style*	
sermo plebejus …		*dialects*

In comparison with Hof's division, Noreen's analysis of linguistic reality obviously may appear the more complex and nuanced one. Particularly the situational – more or less diglossic – variation on the two higher levels is given a far more refined description by Noreen. This is due to his subdivision of each level into two, distinctly defined stages, as well as his distinction of two separate levels of colloquial speech, socially differentiated on the basis of "education", but both falling under the same concept of "standard language", alongside, not including, the dialects. At the same time, it is equally obvious that, by the very exclusion of the dialects from his discussion on "stylistic" variation, Noreen provides a description of more limited scope than does Hof.

However, this interpretation is probably a partly anachronistic one. As correctly maintained by Widmark (2000:24), we may reasonably assume that the dialects played a considerably more important part in the linguistic society in Hof's time than they did in Noreen's; particularly in the major cities they probably still held a strong position, in distinct contrast to later conditions. The dialects simply *were* the language that ordinary Swedish people spoke in the mid-18th century. On the other hand, at that time the humanistic concept of "education", referred to by Noreen as the principal basis of social distinction, was not yet part of the common view on life. One notes with interest the two scholars' differing choice of words: whereas Noreen distinguishes "the educated" (*de bildade*) from "the less educated", Hof talks about "the honourable" (*de hederliga*) as opposed to "the crowd" (*gemene hopen*).

Linguistic description certainly reflects ideas in the describer's own mind, as well as conceptions current at the time and in the cultural settings in which he is living and working. It also reflects, we may assume, something of "reality", the state of the linguistic material being described. Trying to trace the origins of social and situational differentiation by language in Sweden, we may proceed about one century further back in history, relying exclusively on sources providing this kind of double evidence.

3. Pioneers of grammar: The oldest explicit testimony of diglossia

In the light of what has been said above, a certain state of diglossia may be attested in Swedish usage since at least the early 18th century. Widmark (2000) even points out some late 17th century evidence of the same state of affairs. An important name in this context is the university teacher and poet *Petrus Lagerlöf*, who seems to have been the first scholar to give academic lectures in Swedish; he did this at Uppsala in 1691 (Widmark 1997). It is probable that speakers of some social distinction at that time already discriminated rather sharply between public and private speech domains.

As for variation on the level of morphology, we may complete this evidence with a few sources that have hardly been noticed previously in this context. The first is a work by *Eric Aurivillius*, a professor of law at Uppsala in the late 17th century, with the title *Grammaticæ Suecanæ Specimen* ('Specimen of a Swedish grammar'), written in Latin. The work was interrupted in 1684 and never published; it has been left in a partly unfinished manuscript, edited (rather unsatisfactorily) in 1884. Nonetheless, this is the oldest comprehensive account of Swedish grammar to have been handed down to posterity.

As a grammarian, Aurivillius was working from a difficult starting position. Principally, he describes the system of the Swedish language in the categories of Latin grammar. He was thereby linking up, as was usual at this time, with a powerful European medieval and Renaissance tradition, deeply rooted in Hellenism and Late Roman antiquity. The grammatical structure of Latin was still regarded as given by a higher power or by the laws of Nature. On the other hand, Aurivillius could not entirely disregard facts. One of these phenomena were the articles, the state of which he failed to make out conclusively, despite astute and penetrating attempts at a theoretical analysis (Teleman 1984; Wollin 1984). Another was the declension system of the noun. Here, however, he eventually arrived at a solution that fits Swedish into the context of historical linguistics just as neatly as it places Aurivillius himself in that of the history of learning.

Aurivillius operates, explicitly and consistently, with *two separate systems* for the inflection of Swedish "nouns". He terms the systems the "older inflection" and the "newer inflection" (*flexio antiquior* and *flexio recentior* respectively). According to the older system, he distinguishes forms in the four cases of medieval Swedish (today called Old Swedish) – though, interestingly enough, he obviously did not understand them quite "correctly". The newer system is simpler, particularly in the identification of the older dative form (*konunge, konungom*, 'king, kings') with a "head form" (*konung, konungar*). As a result, the newer system is identical with the modern two-case system (including only head form and the genitive), which was fully established in living usage in Aurivillius' time.

It is important to note that Aurivillius, discerning the "older inflection" of the noun, was by no means aiming at any kind of historical description. His grammar is an entirely synchronic one; moreover, it is written in a normative perspective. The two declension systems are presented as entirely equal to one another. Both are regarded as important parts of living Swedish, and, the author stresses, a foreigner who wants to understand and use the Swedish language correctly has to learn both. Differentiating between them is to Aurivillius a question of function: the older system mainly belongs to printed written language, the younger to private written and spoken language. The grand Reformational bible of 1541 is explicitly mentioned as also setting the standard for contemporary writing in the more serious genres.

A contemporary speaker and writer of Swedish, substantiating this description or following these recommendations, was obviously practising a diglossic variation not unlike that of Hof, or even that of Noreen. Aurivillius was probably on firm ground here: the grammatical structure of the medieval "Old Swedish" – with e.g. its four-case system, however inconsistently or erroneously conceived – still very frequently served as a guide to serious writers of the Caroline epoch. The inspiration probably emanated equally from the example of a stylistically conservative Reformational bible and from chauvinistic Swedish-"Gothic" ideology.

It appears a reasonably well-established fact, then, that a linguistic variation of considerable range, bearing the distinct stamp of diglossia, was prevalent in Sweden as early as the mid-17th century. In fact, as early as that, it seems also to have been regarded as an important dimension of Swedish linguistic culture. The question arises, whether the origins of this kind of variation may be traced to still older periods. Holm (1984) argues in favour of this possibility. How else, he wonders, could it have been feasible in the early 16th century for the young Gustav Eriksson (later to become king Gustav Vasa) – a native of central Sweden, speaking a Mälar dialect – to communicate effectively with the Dalecarlians, inhabiting a distant and linguistically remote province? The access to some kind of neutral supraregional variety of spoken Swedish, argues Holm, must be assumed here.

I believe that such a variety, and probably also a diglossic relationship between it and the "dialects", is even older than that. The evidence for this, however, cannot be looked for in explicit statements of the kind we have been discussing thus far, since it is more indirect.

4. The Reformation Bible: A deliberate mix of standards?

In his distinction between an older and a more recent system of declension, Aurivillius, as we have seen, based the older system on the *Reformation Bible.* This of course tells us quite a lot about the immense authority that was attached in the first centuries of the New Swedish period to the Reformers' great translation of the Scriptures, first printed in 1541. Yet this monumental text – in some aspects the most important one ever written in Swedish – provides no self-evident basis for an archaising word inflection. In fact, the linguistic form of the "Vasa Bible" varies to a considerable extent within the text. This is perhaps particularly apparent on the level of morphology, in the use of older and modern nominal forms side by side. Look at the section below: the story of the Tower of Babel in the Old Testament (Gen. 11:1–9). Certainly, distinguishing here between "archaic" and "modern" linguistic form is not a straightforward exercise. Nevertheless, indisputably archaizing grammatical word forms are set in bold, modern forms (i.e. forms not to be expected in classical Old Swedish) are underlined.

> Och all werlden hadhe enahanda **tungo** och måål. [2]Tå the nu drogho öster
> vth, funno the en plaan vthi Sinear land, och boodde ther, [3]och sadhe til *hvar*
> *annan*: **Kommer**, **låter** oss slå teghel och brenna. Och togho teghel för steen,
> och ler för kalk, [4]och sadhe: **Kommer låter** oss byggia en stadh och itt torn,
> **huess** högd skal reckia vp j himmelen, at wy måghe göra oss itt nampn, för ty,
> wij warde til ewentyrs sprijdde vthi **all land.** [5]Tå steegh HERREN nedher at han
> skulle see stadhen och tornet som ***menniskionnes*** barn bygde. [6]Och HERREN
> sadhe: Sij, thet är enahanda folk, och enahanda måål j bland them *alla*, och
> haffua thetta begynt at göra, the **warda** icke **afflåtandes** aff *alt thet* the haffua
> sigh företaghit at göra. [7]**Kommer**, **låter** oss stijgha nedher och förbijstra ther
> *theras* tungomåål, så att ingen skal förstå *then* **annars** måål. [8]Och så skingradhe
> HERREN them tädhan j **all land**, så at the återwende byggia stadhen, [9]och ther
> före kalladhes hans nampn Babel, ty at HERREN ther förbijstradhe *all* landz
> tungomåål, och sprijdde them tädhan vthi **all land.**
>
> (*Gustav Vasa's Bible* 1541)
>
> 'And the whole earth was of one language, and of one speech. [2]And it came
> to pass, as they journeyed from the east, that they found a plain in the land
> of Shi´när; and they dwelt there. [3]And they said one to another, Go to, let us
> make brick, and burn them thoroughly. And they had brick for stone, and
> slime had they for morter. [4]And they said, Go to, let us build us a city and a
> tower, whose top may reach unto heaven; and let us make us a name, lest we
> be scattered abroad upon the face of the whole earth. [5]And the LORD came
> down to see the city and the tower, which the children of men builded. [6]And

> the LORD said, Behold, the people is one, and they have all one language; and this they begin to do: and now nothing will be restrained from them, which they have imagined to do. [7]Go to, let us go down, and there confound their language, that they may not understand one another's speech. [8]So the LORD scattered them abroad from thence upon the face of all the earth: and they left off to build the city. [9]Therefor is the name of it called Ba´bel; because the LORD did there confound the language of all the earth: and from thence did the LORD scatter them abroad upon the face of all the earth.'
>
> (*Authorised Version*)

As we can see, the two "systems" get on well together in the text. The quantitative proportions are roughly equal. In the form *menniskionnes* we could talk about a hybrid of old and modern inflections (to the Old Swedish two-syllable ending *-onne*, "correctly" signalling the oblique case of the definite singular of a feminine noun, is "incorrectly" added the genitive ending *-s*, which was originally restricted to masculine and neutral nouns).

The distribution at this point in the total text of the Swedish Reformation Bible has been previously described and discussed by a few scholars, particularly in the former half of the 20th century (most recently by Ståhle 1968: 517ff., with further references), though never in the perspective applied here.[5] My general impression, though, is that the example above gives a reasonably representative picture of the morphological variation in the "classical" New Swedish bible language; at any rate, it provides a good starting-point for hypothesizing.

Unlike the regularizing variation according to function and genre, suggested by Aurivillius in his grammatical description, this variation of the biblical language is not one of diglossia. Rather, two partly differing systems are used alongside of one another within the same text, in a mixture apparently unregulated by any rules, or even by any general principles; or, at least, it is based on principles so far undetected by anyone doing research on the matter. There has been speculation on the possible importance of prosodical factors in oral delivery, such as demands for the rhythm and euphony of the text when read aloud, as well as the proper balance of stressed and unstressed syllables when echoing under high church vaults. But there is no clear-cut or explicit evidence for this.

Accordingly, it is on the basis of its mere *occurrence* – in fact irrespective of the frequency, perhaps even of the causes, of its actual use – that an older system of word inflection in the Reformational Bible has been able to inspire archaizing tendencies in written language. Later on, the users of the Bible have arranged this sanctioned but loose variability in their own patterns of diglossia, varying over epochs and genres. Anyhow, this appears a reasonable hypothesis.

Patterns of this kind, I will argue, may have entered vernacular writing in medieval epochs.

5. The Vadstena friars: Deliberate selection?

"The new philology" is the designation perhaps somewhat pretentiously affixed to a vital research tradition that was founded in recent decades in Europe and is well established today in Scandinavia. Very important here is the "codicological" orientation of studies of manuscripts, especially medieval ones. The point is the close study of the particular manuscript, the "codex". This document tells us something – not primarily about a textual tradition, defined in terms of "stemmatic" relations, as is the usual way of dealing with these things in traditional philology – but rather about the scribes once working behind them: their background, competence and intentions. In a wider perspective, of course, the needs and interests – including linguistic ones – once governing the creation of the manuscripts are brought to the fore. The particular manuscript bears witness to the time and the cultural setting in which it first appeared, rather than to the text which it represents. In Sweden this kind of philological research has been chiefly devoted to the study of the general book and writing culture, the so-called *literacy*, of the Middle Ages. Important empirical achievements within this theoretical framework are indicated by fairly comprehensive, more or less recent investigations of medieval collections of sermons in the vernacular (Andersson 1993, 2000), the Old Swedish legends of saints (Carlquist 1996) and late medieval Swedish legal language (Wendt 1997).

This "new philological" perspective may be a fruitful one for the study of a situational, sometimes diglossically directed linguistic variation of the kind we have been discussing above. Something of a pattern for such variation may, hypothetically, be looked for in the particular form of linguistic and stylistic *revision* that – according to our present knowledge[6] – was carried out on a considerable scale at the late medieval monastery of Vadstena. The literary activity at this institution was multi-faceted, and by no means restricted to the brothers' translating from Latin and the sisters' consecutive copying of the brothers' Swedish products. In fact, the vernacular texts resulting from these translations were copied over and over again, and were not always intended for the same readers or users. The handwritten documents produced by the copyists could vary in linguistic form as well as in external shape, according to the specific demands of the target group – or of an orderer, paying for it – in each particular case.

Setting out from these and similar assumptions but basing their arguments principally on observations by previous researchers (e.g. Ståhle 1956; Wessén 1976; Wollin 1991b), today's Swedish philologists face a great task in investigating the tradition of linguistic and stylistic revision at Vadstena. A few major studies on this field, partly new philologically orientated, have already been done (Morris 1991; Lindell 2000). Some further hints of what is possible will be given below.

5.1 St. Birgitta's Revelations

In a very late manuscript containing the main bulk of St. Birgitta's *Revelationes*, the *Cod. Ups. C 61*, the second chapter of the seventh book of Revelations begins as follows:

> Oppa kyndilsmæsso dagh nar christi brwdh war j the kirkione i rom / som kallas sancte marie maioris war hon gripin j andelike syn seandhe j hymmelenom alla redhas til stora høghtiidh.
> 'On the Candlemas day when Christ's bride was in the church in Rome, that is called Sanctæ Mariæ maioris, she was rapt by a spiritual vision, seeing in Heaven everything being prepared for a great feast.'

The Latin source text here reads:

> In purificatione beate Marie virginis, dum esset sponsa Christi in Roma in ecclesia que dicitur Sancte Marie Maioris, rapta fuit dicta domina in spiritualem visionem, videns in celo quasi omnia ad magnum festum preparari.
> 'In the purification of the Blessed Virgin Mary, when Christ's bride was in Rome in the church that is called Sanctæ Mariæ maioris, the said lady was carried into spiritual sight, seeing in Heaven as though everything were being prepared for a great feast.'

It seems obvious that the translator has left the syntactic arrangement of his source text substantially intact: the finite verb with its predicate, *rapta fuit*, is rendered *war hon gripin*, and the loosely connected participial phrase *videns in celo* ... is copied in an equivalent Swedish participial phrase: *seandhe j hymmelenom* ...

The manuscript that stands out today as something of the principal version of the Revelations text in Old Swedish, written down at a considerably earlier time than the Cod. Ups. C 61, is the *Cod. Holm. A 5 a*. Here the same passage runs:

> A Kyndilsmässo dagh nar christi brudh var j the kirkio j rom som callas sancte marie Var hon gripin j andelike syn ok oplypt j gudhelike skodhan, tha syntis

> hänne j himpnenom at alle reddo sik til stora höghtidh.
> 'On the Candlemas day, when Christ's bride was in the church in Rome that is called Sanctæ Mariæ, she was rapt by a spiritual vision, and elevated into divine beholding, then it was seen to her in Heaven that all [people] prepared themselves for a great feast.'

The relation to the Latin source text is considerably looser here: a coordinated phrase *ok oplypt j gudhelike skodhan* has been added without obvious support in the Latin source, the predicate phrase *Var hon gripin j andelike syn* has been changed, and the equivalent of the latinizing participial phrase *seandhe j hymmelenom* ... in the Cod. Ups. C 61 is the new main clause *tha syntis hänne j himpnenom* ...

There can be no doubt whatsoever that we face one and the same translation. Nor can it be questioned that this translation is better reflected in the *Cod. Ups. C 61*. The linguistic form, then, of the *Cod. Holm. A 5 a* obviously seems to be the result of some kind of *revision* of an older Swedish text, which was closer to the translation from Latin, or even identical with it; presumably it was more or less similar to the version of Cod. Ups. C 61. It is generally argued, that the alleged reviser has tried to obtain an easier, more fluent, natural or informal, maybe even a less latinizing, more "genuinely Swedish", tone as compared to the one presumably prevailing in the older version (Ståhle 1956; Wessén 1976: 47ff.). No comments or explicit statements on the matter from contemporaries have been recorded. In any case, whatever the underlying intentions, even this minor sample is enough to prove that some deliberate operations have, indisputably, been undertaken on a substantial scale in the Old Swedish version of St. Birgitta's Revelations, resulting in linguistic differences within the textual tradition that cannot be accidental. This justifies the subsequent use of the term "revision".

The state of things in the quoted passage is highly representative of the relation between these two important manuscripts in a significant part of the large bulk of Revelations text. In contrasting the two Swedish versions with the Latin original this becomes immediately apparent in differences like those exemplified, i.e., in the *syntactic* structure. However, the relation is almost equally easy to read on several other levels of analysis as well.

Another salient feature of the revision, then, is a general tendency towards increased *redundancy* in the text. The added coordinated phrase *ok oplypt j gudhelike skodhan* in the example above, which contributes to nothing but variation, is a very typical manifestation of this effort to leave nothing unsaid. Often demonstrated and discussed (though not represented in the example) are the lexical doublets, which appear in considerably higher frequencies in the Cod. Holm. A 5 a than in the Cod. Ups. C 61. So, the phrase *lechamleghin styrk* ('bodily strength') in the latter document has been expanded into *licamlik styrk ok makt* ('bodily strength and power') in the former, as has with the analogous representation in the two manuscripts, *blindher till mich syn gwdh* ('blind to me his God') into *blindir oc darottir til mik sin gudh* ('blind and foolish to me his God') and *köthzsens twingh* ('the compulsion of flesh') into *kötzsins thuang ok dröuilse* ('the compulsion and grief of flesh'). In such cases, the expansion into a doublet is normally the work of the reviser, not of the translator: in the corresponding places in the Latin original, this kind of coupled synonym is comparatively rare.[7]

The age distribution between these manuscripts, then, is an intriguing one. The more latinizing Cod. Ups. C 61 is, as mentioned, the more recent of the two, written down after 1500, whereas the revised and "freer" Cod. Holm. A 5 a is generally thought to be some one hundred years older, as prepared in the early 15th century. As a result, the relation between them is inconsistent with any idea of the Vadstena Swedish having become more "modern " in the course of time. At any rate, this conclusion is valid provided the concept of "modern" is taken as anything in the sense of 'delatinized', 'more genuinely Swedish', 'more fluently redundant' or the like.

However, there is a third interesting tendency in this revision, that has hitherto never been observed. Unlike the two others, it is seemingly adducible in favour of the hypothesis of a certain linguistic modernization related to time in the Birgittine Swedish. It manifests itself on the morphological level, lacking any apparent relation to the Latin original. It is the matter of an inclination strictly to adjust the inflection, particularly of nominal words, to the system of "classical" Old Swedish, to use the "correct" case forms with reasonable consistency. It is obvious that the older document, the Cod. Holm. A 5 a, in this particular respect presents the "stricter" and accordingly, at first sight, the older linguistic form: the frequency of these "correct" forms is higher here, whereas the more recent Cod. Ups. C 61 bears a distinct stamp of the formal dissolution that is generally characteristic of late medieval Swedish. Some examples from the 5th and 7th book of the Revelations are given in Table 6a.

To "classical" Old Swedish forms in the nominative case like *vili* ('will'), *sorghin* ('the sorrow') and *then rätuise* ('the just', adjectival, weak declension in the masculine singular) in the old document correspond forms in the more recent one that are incompatible with this system in the given grammatical context: *vilia*, *sorghena* (actually the accusative form) and *then ræthwiisa*. Similarly, forms in the genitive singular case like *världinna* ('of the world') and

Table 6a. Some examples of "correct" and "incorrect" case forms in the 5h and 7th book in two manuscripts of St. Birgitta's Revelations

Cod. Holm. A 5 a	Cod. Ups C 61
min eghin ***vili*** *är* ('my own will is')	*myn* ***vilia*** *är* ('my will is')
The ***sorghin*** *teknadhis* ('the sorrow was described')	*the* ***sorghena*** *teknades* ('the sorrow was described')
then ***rätuise*** *symeon spadhe* ('the honest simeon told')	*then* ***ræthwiisa*** *symeon spaddhe* ('the honest simeon told')
världinna *glädhe* ('the world's joy')	***wärldhenne*** *glädhy* ('the world's joy')
världinna *snille* ('the world's genius')	***världhene*** *snille* ('the world's genius')
til ***världinna*** ('to the world')	*till* ***wärldhenne*** ('to the world')
världinna *hedhir oc* ***hänna*** *glädhe* ('the worlds's honour and its joy')	***wärldhenne*** *hedher och* ***henne*** *glädhy* ('the worlds's honour and its joy')
Gønom ***hänna*** *siäl* ('through her soul')	*genom* ***hænne*** *syæll* ('through her soul')
gudz ***hälghra*** *manna skipilse* ('God's holy men's order')	*gwdz* ***hælga*** *manna skypilsse* ('God's holy men's order')
hälghra *siäla* ('of holy souls')	***hælga*** *syæla* ('of holy souls')
offra ***han*** ('offer him')	*offra* ***hanom*** ('offer him')
saa hon jomfru ***mariam*** ('she saw the Virgin Mary')	*sagh hon jomffrw* ***mariæ*** ('she saw the Virgin Mary')

Table 6b. Some examples of "incorrect" and "correct" forms in the 5th and 7th book in two manuscripts of St. Birgitta's Revelations

Cod. Holm. A 5 a	Cod. Ups C 61
jak hawir världinna glädhe ok ***ära*** ('I have the world's joy and honour')	*iach haffwer wärldhenne glädhy och* ***äro*** ('I have the world's joy and honour')
Ther til at ey ***skal*** *nakor villas* ('lest anyone should be misled')	*ther till ath ey* ***skwle*** *noghor villas* ('lest anyone should be misled')

hänna ('her', 'hers') and in the genitive plural like *hälghra* ('of the holy') are "distorted" into forms ending in *-e* and lacking the *-r* – respectively, and the accusative form of the personal pronoun *han* ('him') is replaced by the modern *hanom* (which is originally the dative form). Even the correct Latin inflection in proper names, which is normally observed in Old Swedish and early New Swedish writing, is involved in this variation: it is observed in the older manuscript but phased out in the more recent, where *mariæ* is set instead of the correct accusative *mariam*.

Certainly, instances to the contrary do not entirely fail, as shown in Table 6b.

Here, it is in the more recent manuscript that we come across a regular Old Swedish case form like the accusative *äro* ('honour') and a verbal form in the present subjunctive like *skwle* ('shall', 'will') in a final subordinate clause, whereas the reviser seems to have inserted the modern "principal" form *ära* and the indicative *skal* respectively. Cases like these, though, at a hasty perusal of some scattered sections of the large Birgittine text, seem to be considerably less likely to occur. The general impression of a morphology in the older document reflecting an older stage of linguistic development prevails.

But appearances are deceptive. A reviser, deliberately "modernizing" the language on different levels, is not very likely to have left intact an older morphological system, rather consistently observed, like that of the Cod. Holm. A 5 a. More reasonably, it is a question of adjusting a vacillating contemporary usage to a comparatively strict older norm. This adjustment, then, appears to be nothing but another element of the same revision. In fact, though certainly taking a conservative direction, it may even be part of the same "modernizing" strategy. The restitution of a classical morphological system was not carried out as a programmatic opposition to another, modern system, irresistibly gaining ground. No such system was theoretically perceptible at that time. The decisive fact is probably the mere adjustment, the consistent endeavour to establish a formally strict variety of the written vernacular, sharply marked off from other, looser, contemporary varieties. Increased formal stringency, conceived in terms of reduced variation – irrespective of the character of the actual variants – in a particular variety of usage, may as such be regarded as a step forward in the development of a situationally and socially stratified language.

This conclusion is of course very well compatible with the "new philologist" view of the different versions being directed to different users and, accordingly, distinctly adapted to the expected needs of particular target groups. Apparently, there were at least two such groups related to this literary activity: a secular public outside the monastic sphere and the monastic people themselves. A linguistic form differentiated according to these two principal categories of receivers has been attested and described quite recently in other genres of text production at the Monastery of Vadstena, such as preaching (Andersson 1993, 2000) and legends (Carlquist 1996). The Cod. Holm. A 5 a, then, is obviously addressing the former category, people attracted by a looser, less latinizing and heavy, more fluent style, possibly even by a linguistic form that was more formally consistent and, accordingly, more easily accessible. The Cod. Ups. C 61, on the other hand, may have been intended for the latter, exclusively monastic group, whose tolerance in this respect was greater, and so reflecting a linguistic form that was less elaborated. Both categories were probably equally relevant in the monastery at least up to the Reformation in the early 16th century. Consequently, the chronological relation between these two particular documents is entirely accidental.

If this interpretation holds water, we can perhaps even see the outlines of the ideology and the particular view of language that have guided the reviser of the Cod. Holm. A 5 a. Behind the extant result, it should be possible to uncover certain distinct conceptions of a linguistic form adequate for his purpose. His efforts apparently ended in an attempt to make the text *fluent* to the intended readership. In this particular case, it seems to imply three principal strategies: (1) replacement of heavy latinizing structures in syntax by simpler, more "natural" or "genuine" modes of expression; (2) extension with elucidatory material on the levels of clauses and phrases as well as of single words; (3) adjustment of word inflection to a fixed system, in practice the classical Old Swedish.

This brings us to the question of whether a linguistic ideology of this or a similar nature can be attested in other revision undertakings performed in the Monastery.

5.2 The Pentateuch paraphrase

The number of demonstrable linguistic revision undertakings at late medieval Vadstena, similar to the one discussed above, is modest. Nevertheless, one of those that can actually be proved will be brought forward here for a suggested comparative analysis. It concerns the two extant manuscripts of the so-called *Pentateuch paraphrase*, the large text making up the oldest layer of the medieval Swedish bible tradition. This work, generally designated *MB I* ('Medieval Bible, first phase') by philologists, belongs to the literary "golden age" of medieval Swedish literature, which flourished in the 13th and 14th century. Its relation to the Latin text of the Vulgate is characterized by the same older, paraphrazing type of "translation" as that which occurs in major parts of the great West Norse biblical work *Stjórn*. The Old Swedish paraphrase also presents fundamentally the same compilatory arrangement of the material as does its West Norse sister text.[8]

The two medieval manuscripts containing the MB I are both of Vadstena provenance. They are related to one another in a way that is strikingly similar to that prevailing between the two Birgitta manuscripts discussed in the previous section. The older document (Cod. Thott 4), which is often, so also here, designated *MB I A*, was written down before 1435; the more recent (Cod. Holm. A 1), called *MB I B* , is dated to the year 1526 (Hesselman 1927; Thorell 1951, 1959). Despite several minor divergences in linguistic form, these two manuscripts obviously reflect the same compilation and translation enterprise.

Consequently, they can be traced back to one and the same Swedish source, which today is lost. The origin of this archetypal text, though, belongs to an older epoch than that of the Vadstena Monastery, founded by St. Birgitta. Accordingly, only the subsequent late medieval text tradition is "Birgittinian".

Scholars early on observed that the MB I A and MB I B are not only two mutually independent copies of the same original. In addition, the *more recent* MB I B presents the *more archaic* language. The latter fact has generally been ascribed to a presumably naive and true-hearted attitude governing the female scribe behind the MB I B: she has been supposed to have, in ignorance or from pious zeal, rendered the original literally and uncritically. The older, male MB I A scribe on the other hand, it has been argued, shows a more independent and deliberate stylistic ambition, resulting in a certain amount of change of the linguistic form, with a tinge of modernizing (Hesselman 1927: 10ff.; the MB I B text is discussed also by Thorell 1951: passim and 1959: xixf.). Accordingly, the version of MB I A bears the unmistakable stamp of *revision*, performed largely at the same time and precisely in the same monastic Vadstena setting as the one underlying the Revelations manuscript Cod. Holm. A 5 a. Like this, the MB I A is also open to immediate comparison with a more recent document presenting an older linguistic form.

This comparison between the two linguistic revisions at Vadstena is a task that might be expected to have tempted Swedish philologists. Strangely enough, however, up to now it has not.[9] The question remains to be answered: may the two revisions have even been performed by the same man?

A possible outcome if one were to test this hypothesis systematically will here be suggested (without focussing, however, on the question of personal authorship). As material for a minor pilot study I select, first, the same Old Testament text as in Section 4 above on the Reformation Bible, i.e., the famous story of the Tower of Babel (Gen. 11: 1–9):

MB I A	MB I B	
Nw war tha et maal i iordhrike Oc talar nw nemrot wi maghom rædhas at æn komber tholik flodh som war i wars forfadhurs daghum Farom til oc byggiom swa høghan stadh at høgxsta tornith nalkas himpnenom allom thykte thz radh oc brændo leer oc giordho tighel oc hafdhe thz for stenana Æn i thy lande hittis swa segh iordh at hona løser enkte watn oc the iordh hafdho the for liim	Nw war eth mæle innan iorderikis oc talar Næmroth: Wi maghom rædas at æn komme slik flodh som war j waars fadhurs daghom. Farom til oc byggiom swa høghan stadh at høgxta tornet nalkis himblenom. Allom totte thz raad oc brænde taghar ther nær oc giordho tegil, oc haffdo thz før stena. J the lande hittis swa segh iordh at hona løsir enkte rægn ællir vatn. Oc the iordh haffdo the før lim.	'Now there was one language on earth and Næmroth speaks: We may fear that still comes a flood such as was in our father's days. Come on, let us build a city so high that the highest tower may approach the sky. Everybody liked that advice and lit fires down there and made bricks, and used them for stones. In that land is found so hard soil that neither rain nor water dissolves it. And that soil they used for mortar.
Thenne same nemrot war swa mykin daare at han trøste sik at wardha iæmwallogher i himpnenom som han war a iordhinne	Thænne samme Næmrot war swa mykil daare at han trøste sik maaga varda iæm valdugan j himblom som han var a iordhinne.	This same Næmroth was so much a fool that he trusted himself able to become as powerful in Heaven as he was on earth.
Nw som the byggia fast oc stadhin wæxte mykin oc høgher Tha talar war herra til ænglanna Seen hwilken daara gærdh the gøra oc trøsta sik at fulkompna sin wilia Nw wiliom wi skilia them mz thy at ængin vndestander annars maal Oc swa fik hwar slækt sina tungo	Nw som the bygdo fastas oc stadhen væxte dighir oc høghir, tha talar var hærra til ænglanar: Sen hulkir dara oc huilka dara gærdh the gøra oc trøsta sik at fulkomna sin wilia. Nw viliom wi skilia them mz thy at enghin thera wndirstande annars maal. Oc swa fik huar slækt sina thungo.	Now as they were building fast and the city increased powerful and high, then Our Lord speaks to the angels: Behold, what fools [they are] and what a foolish work they are doing and trust themselves to fulfil their will. Now we will scatter them, so that none of them may understand the other's language. And so each race got its [own] tongue.

Tho haffdho the swa mykith giort før æn the skildos at mwrin war fæmptighi alna bredher oc hundradha alna høgher æn tornith siælfft twæggia rasta høght breet nidhan oc miot owan æn stadzsens widhleker om kring war siæxtighi raster oc et thz wældoghasta watn ther i wærldinne ær lop wt genom stadhin oc genom mwrana Hær sigher aff sanctus gregorius at the ære badhin iæmp ond at thænkia hwru tholikt matte gøras oc hurw tholikt matte nidherbrytas	Tha haffdo the swa mykit giort før æn the skildos, at mwrin war fæmtighi alna bredhir oc c alna høghir, æn tornit siælfft twæggia rasta høct, bret nidhan oc miot owan. æn vidlekir stadzsins om kringh var lx rastir, oc eth thz vældugasta vatn ther j værildinne ær, lop vt gønom stadin oc gønom mwrana. Ther sighir aff sanctus ieronimus at the æru badhin æm wærd at vænta huru slik gærningh matte gøras oc huru hon matte nidhir brytas.	Then they had done so much before they were separated, that the wall was fifty ells wide and one hundred ells high, and the tower itself two "rastir" high, broad from below and narrow from the top, and the cicumference of the city was 60 "rastir", and a stream, the most powerful that is in the world, ran out through the city and through the walls. Of this says Saint Jerome that they are both equally worth [waiting=] imagining how such a work might be done and how it might be pulled down.'
(*Cod. Thott 4 4:o, ed. Klemming 1848: 175f.*)	(*Cod. Holm. A 1, ed. Thorell 1959: 134*)	(translated close to MB I B: *Cod. Holm. A 1.*)

The result is essentially negative. None of the three important strategies that were demonstrated in the revision of the Revelations is apparent in the MB I A reviser's repertory. On the whole, the picture here is a far more diffuse one: even this minor inventory of linguistic divergences between the two MB I versions results in a considerably larger number of instances that are difficult to define in grammatical or linguistic terms. As a result, no indication can be brought forward in support of the idea that the same reviser was at work in both cases.

There is, however, *one* tendency in the MB I A revision that stands out quite clearly in this particular section of the text. Provided the observation can also be generalized as valid for larger sections, or for the entirety of the MB I A, it certainly may place the revision on the same line as the other one in the general historical context we are looking for here. It is manifested in an overall inclination, discernible on several levels of the linguistic form, to insert more "modern" words and inflected forms. A few examples are given in Table 7.

The replacement of *mæle* with *maal*, *dighir* and *mykil* with *mykin*, *slik* with *tholik*, *innan* (as a preposition, taking the genitive case of the noun) with *i* and *totte* with *thykte* probably reflect efforts, within different parts of speech, to achieve a vocabulary better adjusted to contemporary "normal" language. An

Table 7. "Modern" and "archaic" words and inflected forms in two manuscripts of the Pentateuch paraphrase

MB I A	MB I B
et ***maal*** ('one language')	*eth* ***mæle*** ('one language')
mykin *oc høgher* ('mighty and high')	***dighir*** *oc høghir* ('mighty and high')
swa ***mykin*** *daare* ('that much a fool')	*swa* ***mykil*** *daare* ('that much a fool')
Tholik *flodh* ('such a flood')	***slik*** *flodh* ('such a flood')
hwru ***tholikt*** *matte* ('how such [things] could')	*huru* ***slik gærningh*** *matte* ('how such a work could')
i *iordhrike* ('on earth')	***innan*** *iorderikis* ('within earth')
Allom ***thykte*** *thz radh* ('everybody liked that advice')	*allom* ***totte*** *thz raad* ('everybody liked that advice')
hwilken *daara gærdh the gøra* ('which foolish thing they are doing')	***huilka*** *dara gærdh the gøra* ('which foolish thing they are doing')
oc ***hafdhe*** *thz for stenana* ('and had that for the stones')	*oc* ***haffdo*** *thz før stena* ('and had that for stones')
rædhas at æn ***komber*** ('fear that again comes')	*rædas at æn* ***komme*** ('fear that again [may] come')
swa høghan stadh at høgxsta tornith ***nalkas*** *himpnenom* ('so high a place that the highest tower approaches the sky')	*swa høghan stadh at høgxta tornet* ***nalkis*** *himblenom* ('so high a place that the highest tower [may] approach the sky')
mz thy at ængin ***vndestander*** *annars maal* ('so that nobody understands the other's talk')	*mz thy at enghin thera* ***wndirstande*** *annars maal* ('so that nobody [may] understand the other's talk')

analogous adjustment on the grammatical level shows itself in a modernized case inflection of the pronoun when the phrase *huilka dara gærdh* is replaced with *hwilken daara gærdh*, in the absence of number congruence in the preterite tense of a weak verb as in *hafdhe* for *haffdo*, as well as, above all, in the preference for the indicative mode in finite verbal forms in the present tense in *at*-clauses, such as *komber*, *nalkas* and *vndestander*, rather than the subjunctive *komme*, *nalkis* and *wndirstande*. – Some counterevidence does not fail, however, as in noun forms in the dative singular case like *himpnenom* (twice) in the MB I A, where the MB I B has *himblenom*, *himblom* (mod. Swedish *himlen*), possibly even *i thy lande* and *J the lande* respectively.

Irrespective of the balance between evidence and counterevidence, no general conclusions should be based on these observations, however conspicuous in this particular section of the text. An equally limited inventory for another passage in this extensive work (p. 319 in Klemming's edition of the MB I A and p. 246f. in Thorell's edition of the MB I B respectively) results in a still more obscure picture: the general tendency towards modernizing the linguistic form, the only possible distinctive feature in the example above, is difficult to prove at all here, and the number of hardly definable instances is even larger.

The so-called Pentateuch paraphrase (MB I) is, as mentioned, a compilatory work, comprising several, rather distinctly separated major sections (Wollin 2001:232ff.). The strictly biblical part of it, the actual paraphrase of the Pentateuch, takes up just a full half of the work, and the other section investigated here falls outside this biblical main part. The lack of agreement in general tendency in the revision of two separated sections of the text, as examined here, possibly indicates that the revision task was entrusted to more than one actor. Of course only a more thorough inquiry can make clear whether this may be the case and, in that case, what distribution of work may reasonably have been applied.

To the extent that the tendency actually observed in the revision of the section on the Tower of Babel could also be proved to be relevant to other major sections of the text (e.g. to biblical text as opposed to non-biblical, or to text delimited on some other, more or less accidental principles), it is arguable that a certain, *very general ambition towards modernizing* the linguistic form is common to the revisions of the Bible and the Revelations texts. If so, this ambition is working on different levels. The linguistic reviser who gave the Birgittine Revelations a partly new linguistic shape in the Swedish vernacular seems to have been guided by a more complex, in certain respects even a more sophisticated, perhaps a more deliberate and well-reasoned program than the one or ones behind the MB I revision. Yet the fundamental intention may very well have been the same. Even though the revisers of the two texts can hardly have been identical, their products are likely to have served the same non-clerical target group. In an essential sense, the two – or several – revisers of these two central Vadstena texts have, after all, worked in the same spirit, their products pointing forward in history in the same direction.

6. Conclusion

What is decisive is the specific linguistic competence of this text producing institution, i.e. the Monastery of Vadstena, to which our comparisons testify: the readiness and capacity strategically to vary the products of the scriptorium according to the varying interests of their users. This work was an extensive one; in certain respects the Vadstena monastery dominated late medieval Swedish literacy. Obviously its bookish and linguistic achievements continued more or less directly in the Reformers' important biblical work; the Reformation movement was a bridge rather than a break. In these cirumstances it is perhaps not unreasonable to see, in the varying linguistic strategies of the Monastery's professional "selling" of St. Birgitta's Revelations and of biblical text in the vernacular, the germ – or at least one of the germs – of the rich, partly diglossic variation that was to become a prominent feature of Swedish usage for several centuries to come.

The early developed habit and skill of professional writers in putting this variation into practice may have been a powerful driving force in the erection of the high linguistic barriers that seem to have existed in Swedish society right up to modern times. These barriers discriminated between language and language just as effectively as between people and people.

Notes

1. For a good survey, see e.g. Andersson (1985: 70ff.).

2. An instructive brief survey of this research is given by Nordberg (2002: 207).

3. For a recent survey on the state of the art concerning 'diglossia' see Kaye (2001) [editors' note].

4. For the latter, correspondigly, to "adapt themselves upwards", was apparently an idea beyond Noreen's imagination.

5. For the Swedish reformers' biblical language, see latest Wollin (1991a), with further references.

6. See latest Wollin (1991b), with further references.

7. For the use of "word pairs" in Swedish literature, see generally Bendz (1967). With special reference to the occurrence in Old Swedish translations from the Latin, the phenomenon is discussed in Wollin (1983: 146ff.)

8. For these Old Norse biblical compilations and the relations on different levels between them, see the recent Wollin (2001), with further references.

9. The suggestion is made, quite en passant, by C. I. Ståhle, in an oft-cited article on the Cod. Ups. C 61, where he conclusively points to the similar relationships between, on the one hand, both of the Birgitta manuscripts treated above and, on he other, the two manuscript versions of the MB I (Ståhle 1956: 18).

References

Andersson, L.-G. (1985). *Fult språk. Svordomar, dialekter och annat ont.* Stockholm: Carlsson.

Andersson, R. (1993). *Postillor och predikan. En medeltida texttradition i filologisk och funktionell belysning.* [Sällskapet Runica et Mediævalia. Scripta minora 1.] Stockholm.

Andersson, R. (2000). *De birgittinska ordensprästerna som traditionsförmedlare och folkfostrare. En studie i svensk medeltidspredikan på den 8:e söndagen efter trefaldighet.* [Sällskapet Runica et Mediævalia. Scripta minora 4.] Stockholm.

Bendz. G. (1967). *Ordpar.* 2. uppl. Stockholm.

Carlquist, J. (1996). *De fornsvenska helgonlegenderna. Källor, stil och skriftmiljö.* [Svenska Fornskriftsällskapets Samlingar. Häfte 262, band 81.] Stockholm.

Hesselman, B. (1927). *Språkformen i MB I eller Fem Mose böcker på svenska, tolkade och utlagde vid medlet av 1300-talet.* [Skrifter utgivna av K. Humanistiska Vetenskaps-Samfundet i Uppsala. 24:17.] Uppsala.

Holm, G. (1984). Kritiskt bidrag till läran om nysvenska rikstalspråket. In *Festskrift til Einar Lundeby. 3. Oktober 1984* (pp. 177–183). Oslo: Novus.

Kaye, A. S. (2001). Diglossia: the state of the art. *International Journal of the Sociology of Language, 152,* 117–129.

Klemming, G. E. (Ed.). (1848). *Svenska medeltidens bibel-arbeten* 1: *Fem Mose böcker på svenska, tolkade och utlagde vid medlet af 1300:talet.* [Samlingar utgivna av Svenska Fornskriftsällskapet 9.] Stockholm: Norstedt & Söner.

Klemming, G. E. (Ed.). (1860–1861). *Heliga Birgittas uppenbarelser* 2, 3. [Samlingar utgivna av Svenska Fornskriftsällskapet 14.] Stockholm: Norstedt & Söner.

Lindell, I. (Ed.). (2000). *Heliga Birgittas uppenbarelser bok 7 efter Cod. Ups. C 61. Diplomatarisk utgåva med kommenterande inledning.* [Samlingar utgivna av Svenska Fornskriftsällskapet 84.] Uppsala.

Morris, B. (Ed.). (1991). *Book V of St. Birgitta's Uppenbarelser. Edited from Ms Cod. Ups. C 61.* [Samlingar utgivna av Svenska Fornskriftsällskapet 80.] Lund.

Nordberg, B. (2002). Nordic language history and sociolinguistics. In O. Bandle et al. (Eds.), *The Nordic Languages. An International Handbook of the History of the North Germanic Languages* (pp. 198 –212). Berlin and New York: Walter de Gruyter.

Noreen, A. (1903). *Vårt språk. Nysvensk grammatik i utförlig framställning.* 1. Lund: C. W. K. Gleerup.

Sjögren, G. (1949). *Om språket i de svenska bibelöversättningarna 1526–1541.* Lund: Gleerups.

Stjernström, G. (Ed.). (1884). *Eric Aurivillius' Grammaticae Suecanae Specimen (1684).* (Manuscript belonging to the University Library of Linköping.) [Uppsala Universitets Årsskrift 1884.] Uppsala.

Ståhle, C. I. (1956). Ett fragment av den fornsvenska Birgitta-översättningen. *Filologiskt Arkiv* 2. [Kungl. Vitterhets Historie och Antikvitets Akademiens Handlingar.] Stockholm.

Ståhle, C. I. (1968). Några drag i det svenska bibelspråkets historia 1526–1917. In *Nyöversättning av Nya testamentet. Behov och principer* [Statens offentliga utredningar 1968: 65] (pp. 501–567). Stockholm. (Also published separately under the title *Svenskt bibelspråk från 1500-tal till 1900-tal* [Skrifter utgivna av Nämnden för svensk språkvård 40. 1970.] Stockholm.)

Teleman, U. (1984). Bestämt och obestämt. Fem 1600-talsgrammatiker på upptäcktsfärd bland modersmålets artiklar. In *Festskrift til Einar Lundeby. 3. Oktober 1984* (pp. 96–111). Oslo: Novus.

Thelander, M. (1985). *Sven Hofs Swänska språkets rätta skrifsätt (1753). Med ordstatisik och flera register i ny utgåva.* [Skrifter utgivna av Institutionen för nordiska språk vid Uppsala universitet 16.] Uppsala.

Thorell, O. (1951). *Fem Moseböcker på fornsvenska. En språklig undersökning på grundval av de bevarade handskrifterna.* [Nordiska texter och undersökningar 18.] Uppsala.

Thorell, O. (Ed.). (1959). *Fem Moseböcker på fornsvenska enligt Cod. Holm. A 1.* [Samlingar utgivna av Svenska Fornskriftsällskapet 60.] Uppsala.

Wendt, B.-A. (1997). *Landslagsspråk och stadslagsspråk. Stilhistoriska undersökningar i Kristoffers landslag.* [Lundastudier i nordisk språkvetenskap A 53.] Lund: Lund University Press.

Wessén, E. (1976). *Svensk medeltid. En samling uppsatser om svenska medeltidshandskrifter och texter. III. De fornsvenska handskrifterna av Heliga Birgittas Uppenbarelser.* Stockholm: Almqvist & Wiksell International.

Widmark, G. (1991/2000). Boksvenska och talsvenska. Om språkarter i nysvenskt talspråk. In *Boksvenska och talsvenska. Ett urval uppsatser samlade till författarens 80-årsdag 31 Juli 2000* [Skrifter utgivna av Institutionen för nordiska språk vid Uppsala universitet 50] (pp. 19–56). (First published in *Språk och stil* NF 1, 1991 [pr. 1992], 157–198.)

Wollin, L. (1983). *Svensk latinöversättning.* II. *Förlagan och produkten.* [Lundastudier i nordisk språkvetenskap A 35. Also in Samlingar utgivna av Svenska Fornskriftsällskapet fasc. 252.] Lund.

Wollin, L. (1984). Donatus och den svenska grammatikens pionjärer. In L. Wollin (Ed.), *Tiällmannstudier.* [Nordlund 4.] Lund.

Wollin, L. (1991a). Kring det svenska bibelspråkets historia. In *Den svenska bibeln. Ett 450-årsjubileum* [Svenska bibelsällskapet. Samfundet Pro Fide et Christianismo 13] (pp. 225–241). Stockholm: Proprius.

Wollin, L. (1991b). Två språk och flera skikt: uppenbarelsernas texttradition. In T. Nyberg (Ed.), *Birgitta, hendes v¿rk og hendes klostre i Norden* (pp. 407–434). [Odense University Studies in History and Social Sciences vol. 150.] Odense: Odense Universitetsforlag.

Wollin, L. (2001). Stjórn och Pentateukparafrasen. Ett samnordiskt dominikanprojekt? *Arkiv för nordisk filologi, 116,* 221–299. Lund.

Did Latin influence German word order?

Aspects of German-Latin bilingualism in the Late Middle Ages

Diana Chirita
Lincoln

1. Behaghel's theory

In 1892 Otto Behaghel published a two-page article in *Zeitschrift für den deutschen Unterricht* in which he claimed that the predominant placement of verbs into last position in German subordinate clauses since the second half of the 16th century emerged under Latin influence. This short article started a long debate about the role of Latin in the formation of New High German word order rules, a debate that is still far from being over. Behaghel revisited the subject twice: in 1900, basing his conclusions this time on a much larger text corpus than in his previous article, and again in 1932, when he published the fourth volume of his *German Syntax*, the volume about word order, in which he seemed more convinced than ever that modern German word order emerged under the influence of Latin (Behaghel 1932: XIII, 21, 144).

Behaghel's reasoning was the following: Looking at two text categories which in his opinion represented very authentic German, *i.e.* older texts produced before the 16th century and newer texts from the dialects, he noticed that in both of these text types the verb placement rules which are typical for written German since the 16th century are frequently violated. He concluded that the modern rules are not based on spoken German but must have evolved under foreign influence, and only Latin could have provided the model for them. The use of verb-last in subordinate clauses increased under Latin influence while the spoken language allowed many deviations from this rule. The fact that some 16th century authors extended verb-last to the main clauses of narrative parts, but rarely placed the verb into last position in the dialogue parts of their writings (Behaghel 1932: 20–21) seemed to be an additional very strong argument in favor of the theory of Latin influence. This is essentially Behaghel's theory of Latin influence on German word order. Behaghel has never claimed that verb-last became the only acceptable verb position in subordinate clauses.[1] Nor has he claimed that the final position of the verb was foreign to older Germanic dialects.[2] He was also aware that there was a difference in verb positioning between main and subordinate clauses since the oldest times (Behaghel 1929: 279). His theory of Latin influence refers to the formation of the German standard language and to the increase of verb-last usage in subordinate clauses from the 16th century on. Although this theory seems to make perfect sense, there remain two major problems with it, two problems Behaghel was well aware of, but for which he was not able to provide satisfactory solutions.

The first problem concerns the flexible, almost free word order of Latin. Although it is generally accepted that basic Latin word order is SOV, Latin texts show many deviations from this word order type, thus creating the impression of great word order flexibility. Because of its word order flexibility, it seems unlikely that Latin could serve as a model for the fairly strict SOV ordering type of German subordinate clauses. To overcome this problem, Behaghel modified his theory in his 1900 article on word order. Behaghel argued that because the verb is not always in last position in Latin, the influence would not come directly from Latin texts but rather from Latin school grammars of the Middle Ages, which must have required the placement of verbs into final position, much as they did in his own time. It was the knowledge of such rules that would have had an impact on German word order (Behaghel 1900: 246).

The second problem with Behaghel's theory concerns the fact that in modern German main clauses word order is different from that in subordinate clauses, the verb being placed consistently into second position. How could one Latin model result in two different German word order types? Why would Latin selectively influence only subordinate clauses but not main clauses as well? Behaghel's solution to this problem was to claim that something similar to verb last was done in German main clauses by placing the non-finite forms of the verbs into last position, while the inflected form of the verb kept its inherited second position in the sentence (Behaghel 1900: 245).[3]

In spite of its weaknesses, Behaghel's theory of Latin influence on German became the dominant explanation for the New High German word order requirements and made it into many 20th century handbooks on the history of the German language.[4] Its weaknesses, however, did not remain unnoticed and were the subject of several studies published in the latter half of the 20th century. Hartmann (1970: 6–7) criticized the authors of the cited handbooks.

He accused them of adopting an unfounded theory without sufficient reflection. Fleischmann (1973: 35) called Behaghel's theory on German word order a "völlig unbewiesene Behauptung"[5] and argued that it "stützt ... sich im wesentlichen auf einige Vermutungen und Kombinationen"[6] (Fleischmann 1973: 42) and even called Behaghel's statement about Latin influence on German word order a completely unproved assertion (Fleischmann 1973: 35). Even more devastating to Behaghel's position, data presented by Schildt (1968, 1972), Lühr (1985) and Hartmann (1970) seemed to prove that Latin had an opposite effect on German word order than the one assumed by Behaghel. According to their evidence, Latin would have interfered with the formation of the sentence frame in main clauses and with verb last positioning in subordinate clauses, thus delaying a language change that had started in spoken German. I have discussed these studies in detail (Chirita 1997) and, without intending to prove that Behaghel was right, I was able to show that the arguments presented were not able to refute Behaghel's theory. Still, these studies had ample time to impact newer research and therefore it is not surprising that more recent handbooks either completely ignore Behaghel's theory or else mention it with reservation and even skepticism.[7] However, several more recent publications dealing with certain aspects of Early New High German (ENHG) syntax, such as Lötscher (2000) and Speyer (2001) revisit the possibility of Latin influence. Certain of the AcI constructions attested in earlier German that were analyzed by Speyer seem to have been borrowed from Latin. And, according to Lötscher, main clause verb last placement in German 15th and 16th century prose, although unlikely to be an imitation of some hypothetical Latin verb placement rules (Lötscher 2000: 167), should nevertheless be recognized as a characteristic of an elevated style for which Latin provided the model (Lötscher 2000: 167, 183). Burridge (1993: 116) links the fact that in the Middle Dutch legal documents examined by her the "rate of exbraciation is considerably lower" than in other texts to Latin or Latinate style, confirming thus earlier findings by Hammarström (1923), who believed that the new word order rules had developed in chanceries under the influence of Latin. However, Ebert (1980), whose study on the ENGH sentence frame in main and subordinate clauses in the city language of Nuremberg is very accurate and meticulous, while confirming "that chancery usage served as a model for the very high rates of full frames" (Ebert 1980: 388), could not explain his findings through Latin influence: "The results of the investigation of individuals' usage gives no support to a hypothesis of direct Latin influence" (Ebert 1980: 388). As becomes apparent, the circumstances under which modern German word order emerged are still not perfectly understood and deserve continued attention. As I have pointed out before (Chirita 1997:20), this discussion would benefit from both a thorough understanding of the presence and role of Latin in medieval and late medieval Germany and from a closer inspection of Latin word order. Likewise, the relationship between Latin and ENHG chancery language needs to be explored and evaluated. While not attempting to resolve all of these problems, I would like to contribute to the discussion of Latin influence on ENHG word order by addressing the mentioned issues in the following order:

1. The presence and role of Latin in the German Middle Ages,
2. Some notes on the word order of Latin,
3. Some notes on Early New High German word order.

2. The presence and role of Latin in the German Middle Ages

I mentioned in Chirita (1997:20) that in order to evaluate the plausibility of Latin's influence on the emerging New High German syntax rules in the Late Middle Ages, the role and presence of Latin would have to be evaluated first. The Early New High German field of study, as it emerged and developed in the past several decades, focused its research mainly on the many regional and stylistic variants of German, showing how these influenced each other and how they contributed in different ways to the development of the written standard language.[8] In such a context the continued use of Latin could only be seen as an impediment and a delay in the emergence of the German national language.[9] Only lexical borrowings from Latin into the vernacular were acknowledged at many different stages of the history of the German language, while the overall influence of Latin on the emerging standard German language did not receive proper attention.

I would like to shift focus briefly to the presence and role of Latin in the Middle Ages to establish that the most striking characteristic of Medieval and Late Medieval written culture in the German regions is its German-Latin bilingual nature.

Through their written sources, the German Middle Ages present themselves to us predominantly as the creation of bilingual individuals. With few exceptions we can assume as a rule that until the end of the 16th century everyone who knew how to write also knew Latin. Everything that came down to us is the creation of someone who mastered Latin in addition to his Germanic mother tongue. Even the rare authentic Germanic poems, such as the *Hildebrandslied* and the *Nibelungenlied*, which antedate the arrival of Latin into Central Europe and were handed down during centuries of oral tradition, found their written expression through the hands of scribes well versed in Latin. The Latin text production exceeds the vernacular one throughout the Middle Ages and well into the age of printing, with Latin books outnumbering German books until the end of the 17th century (Stopp 1978: 251).

This situation came about through the historical circumstances of the early Frankish kingdom. With the conquest of Gaul, the hitherto illiterate Franks came into contact with the Roman Empire's "practice of government and administration by means of the written word" (McKitterick 1992: 89) and discovered that this was a powerful tool for their own administrative needs. The conversion of the Merovingians to Christianity at the end of the fifth century established Catholicism based on the *Vulgate* and other Latin translations as a state religion and thus extended the role of Latin to theology and religious rite. While in the western regions of the growing Frankish kingdom there was at first little difference between written and spoken language, in the eastern regions literacy implied Germanic-Latin bilingualism.[10] Here the production of documents of every type required the constant employment of translation skills and translation techniques. In the West, Latin and Old Romance evolved together for a while with the effect that Latin started to move away slightly from the classical models. This development was stopped during the Carolingian Renaissance, which brought a new awareness of correct Latin based on antique sources and triggered an abundant production of manuscripts from classical Roman authors. This might have been the moment in which a firm and permanent difference between Romance and Latin in the western parts of the Frankish Empire was established.[11] Latin as a mother tongue had died out. But it continued to exist for several centuries in both east and west in mainly, but not only, written form as the language of learning, religion and administration.

In order to supply both public and ecclesiastic administration with competent literate clerks, a system of schooling was put into place, with monasteries as the first centers of education, to which parish and cathedral schools were added from the 11th century on (Henkel 1988: 13–14). Learning to write and read Latin, and to understand Latin texts of varying degrees of difficulty, was the main and often the only educational task in most institutions of learning.

At first, education was intended exclusively for those who would enter the clergy. Members of the nobility, whose main ambitions were excellence in fighting, jousting and hunting, looked with contempt upon such activities as reading and writing (Wendehorst 1986: 27).

In spite of school curricula in which Roman authors such as Horace, Virgil, Cicero, Sallust and Ovid played a major role (Henkel 1988: 11, 56–64), medieval Latin took on a life of its own and started to drift away from the classical models. But it survived in an arguably somewhat diminished form in its previous function as the language of public life up to the centuries of European humanism, when the attention of educated Europe turned once again with great fascination towards the Roman (and Greek) antiquity, language and culture.

The 15th and 16th centuries, the centuries of German humanism, are of particular interest for the matter at hand out of two reasons: (1) we witness a huge expansion of education and (2) classical Latin is brought again into focus as a language of unequaled beauty and perfection.

The humanistic ideal of morality and self-perfection through education reached Germany in the 15th century and sparked a great interest in learning, triggering a wide scale secularization of education and the foundation of a large number of institutions of learning at every level. Many new schools were founded in the growing and prosperous German cities in order to educate not only those whose goal it was "das sie schreiben und lesen lernen"[12] or those who wished to become "gelart oder gaistlich",[13] but also others "damit sie nit müssig und auf der Gassen umlaufen, sundern bei und neben den andern Knaben Zucht lernen und des kundiger und geschickter werden"[14] as the city council of Nuremberg decreed in 1500 (Endres 1983b: 180). But even for the period before 1500, Endres concluded in a different study that illiteracy could not have been wide spread in the city of Nuremberg (Endres 1983a: 150). The situation in other cities was similar, as studies such as Schindling (1984) or Rapp (1983) indicate, and we can assume that around 1500 most townships had a Latin school (Henkel 1988: 14).

With regard to higher education, the 15th century is extremely prolific in the creation of new universities in Germany. To the five oldest ones, founded in the 14th century, Prague, Vienna, Heidelberg, Cologne and Erfurt (Seifert 1997: 198), fifteen new ones were added in the 15th century, a larger number than in any of the following centuries prior to 1900 (Boockmann 1985: 13).[15] Around 1500, the number of people with a university education was higher than ever before, a number that would not be matched again until the 19th century (ibid.).

A large number of classical Latin texts was rediscovered, copied and circulated by the Italian humanists. With the discovery of antique texts, classical Latin was once again brought into focus, studied in great detail and taught in schools and universities. Lorenzo Valla's mid 15th Century *De elegantia linguae latinae libri VI*[16] emphasized with great passion the efficiency and elegance of the Latin language and was in wide use until the 19th century (Gerl 1985: 327–328). For Valla, Latin was the language of a world culture, of science and of the arts (Füssel 1986: 82). Erasmus and Celtis followed Valla in believing that the values and the knowledge of the antique culture could be acquired through the adoption of the Latin language (ibid.: 78). And Celtis, who refused to use the "barbaric" German language in his writings, wanted to see the mother tongues abandoned in favor of perfect Latin and thus of a higher education (Füssel 1986: 84).

To sum up: During the period of German humanism the number of highly educated people who were also rigorously trained in classical Latin reached numbers never seen before. They were active in all areas of public life and participated at the creation of an increasingly written culture whose language they helped shape. Modern German, as it was created and standardized especially in the 15th and 16th centuries, is the product of these German-Latin bilingual individuals, many of whom had a great admiration for the "elegance" of the Latin language and a firm belief in its superiority. This must have created a great openness and eagerness for the adoption of Latin syntactic patterns into the written German language of the time. During the 17th century when language societies were created and general interest turned towards the vernacular, most of the modern German syntactic patterns were already in place.

3. Some notes on Latin word order

3.1 General remarks

Behaghel critics such as Fleischmann (1973) and Hartmann (1970) have contended that Latin word order is not SOV, while other scholars such as Lötscher were careful not to link their findings of verb last patterns in ENHG to some "in der Realität nicht existierenden grammatischen Regel des Lateinischen"[17] (Lötscher 2000: 165). However, it would not make sense to continue this discussion if it could not be shown that Latin word order was indeed SOV.

Unfortunately, statements about the word order of Latin are almost nonexistent both in antiquity and in the Middle Ages. This is understandable because of the great flexibility of Latin word order. It is difficult to imagine Latin sentences in which a certain word order sequence would seem ungrammatical making it thus necessary to formulate rules for correct word order usage. From antiquity we have Quintilian's famous quote about the position of the verb: "Verbo sensum cludere multo, si compositio patiatur, optimum est: in verbis enim sermonis vis est"[18] (Quintilian 1975: 375). Medieval grammarians, like all other medieval scholars, were highly interested in the natural order of things, the *ordo naturalis*, which is a philosophical, not a grammatical, concept. Medieval grammarians are eager to discuss the natural order of letters (e.g. a precedes b), grammatical categories (e.g. the singular precedes the plural), parts of speech (e.g. the noun precedes the verb) and more. In this sense Fleischmann's conclusion that Medieval Latin word order was SVO is based on a misinterpretation of Priscian's and Melanchthon's grammars, in which recommendations are made to interpret sentences by ordering them starting with a noun or pronoun and having the verb follow immediately after it (Fleischmann 1973: 48–49).

> Interestingly, the two new aspects of linguistic study introduced by Priscian's *Institutiones*, the philosophical implications of grammatical concepts and the study of syntax, are closely associated in early medieval analysis. The very definitions of the noun and the verb, based on the notions of substance and action, impose an order on the principal parts of speech: the noun, the substance, precedes the verb, the action, which is one of the accidents of the substance.
> (Luhtala 1993: 146–147)

The real order of Latin words in a sentence, which was never confounded with the *ordo naturalis,* seems to have been of little interest to both medieval and humanistic grammarians.[19]

As for modern Latin grammars and school grammars, they are in agreement that unmarked Latin word order is SOV, but that there are many deviations from this pattern in order to satisfy syntactic, pragmatic, stylistic and poetic requirements (Hofmann & Szantyr 1972: 397; Scherer 1975: 218; Pinkster 1988: 268, 282; Wheelock 2000: 19–20).

Two aspects regarding Latin syntax deserve further consideration and could shed light on the problem of Latin influence on German word order better. The first is the remarkable difference between archaic and classical Latin, and not only with respect to word order; the second, is the significant difference in constituent order between Latin main clauses and Latin subordinate clauses. This latter aspect raises questions about the function and marking of main and subordinate clauses, which, although not directly related to the topic at hand, should be mentioned briefly.

3.2 Archaic and classical Latin

The reason why the difference between archaic and classical Latin is of interest to the current topic as will be seen later, is the fact that similar differences can be found between standardized German from the 16th century on and some of the earlier German texts.

Courtney (1999: 3–6) lists certain features that are distinctive for archaic Latin and illustrates them with numerous examples from Latin texts produced before 100 B.C. While I do not believe that they "characterize an early stage of thought" (ibid.: 3), I do agree that they are typical for an "early stage of expression" (ibid.) or, more precisely, written expression. They are the following:

a. The paratactic style (ibid.: 3–4). Complex sentences are made up of small, coordinated units; subordination is rarely used.
b. The *guttatim* or drop-by-drop style (ibid.: 4–5). Little use is made of grammatical means to tie small isolated units of thought together.
c. The standardization of word order as SOV or at least as V-final (ibid.: 5).
d. The coexistence of competing grammatical forms (ibid.: 5–6).

Archaic Latin sentences seem to overuse demonstratives in order to connect sentences, while relative clauses are clumsy and rare (ibid.: 7–8; Kroll 1934: 11–12). Koch and Oesterreicher (1990: 10) propose a very interesting distinction between *Nähesprache* 'language of proximity' and *Distanzsprache* 'language of distance'. According to this distinction, the paratactic style, the *guttatim* style and the overuse of deictic devices are typical for a language of proximity. Classical Latin, on the other hand, with its great syntactic complexity, is a language of distance (ibid.: 129).

A typical example of Latin of proximity or archaic Latin would be the following passage from Ennius' *Euhemerus*:

> *Deinde Pan eum deducit in montem, qui uocatur Caeli sella. Postquam ascendit, contemplatus est late terras, ibique in eo monte aram crea<ui>t Caelo, primusque in ea Iuppiter sacrificauit. in eo loco suspexit in caelum quod nos nunc nominamus, idque quod supra mundum erat, quod aether uocabatur …*
> (Courtney 1999: 28)[20]

The transition to classical Latin happened, according to Neumann (1968: 89), between roughly 200 and 43. B.C., the year of Cicero's death. Ennius (239 to 169 B.C.), whose *Euhemerus* is written in an archaic style and is included by Courtney (1999: 26–39) in his book on archaic Latin prose, is one of the first writers to suggest an orthographic reform (Neumann 1968: 90) and is considered by Neumann to be at the beginning of the process of standardization that would eventually result in classical Latin (ibid.: 89). Cicero's works mark the completion of this process (ibid.). We do not have many details about how the standardization of Latin was achieved, and although some names of reformers such as Scipio Aemilianus, Ennius, Lucilius, Accius and a certain Sp. Carvilius have come down to us, many other poets, grammarians, politicians and orators involved in the reform remain anonymous (ibid.: 89–90). What we do know is that it was a conscious effort on the part of many over several generations, aimed, as Neumann (1968: 91) sums up, at a language characterized by simplicity, precision, transparency of words and logical connections between its different elements. The creation of such a precise and efficient language, in which, moreover, words had great syntactic autonomy, makes it possible to master many levels of subordination and allows exploiting constituent placement for the implementation of special nuances and effects.

3.3 Word order in Latin main and subordinate clauses

In the discussion of Behaghel's theory there is one aspect that has not received enough attention and that must have escaped even Behaghel himself. It is the fact that there is a remarkable difference between verb positioning in Latin main clauses and subordinate clauses, with verbs being much more consistently placed into last position in subordinate clauses. This has been pointed out in several studies of Latin word order and might be the strongest argument in favor of Behaghel yet.

Linde (1923: 154–156) presents statistics for verb-last placement from classical and early medieval authors showing that in each single one of them verb-last is more common in subordinate clauses. However, there seems to be a slight decline in verb-last ordering in later texts (ibid.: 156).

One of the aims of Koll's 1965 study is to analyze a fairly large number of classical, late antique and early medieval texts which span the period from 63 B.C. to 843 A.D., in order to show how the proportion OV/VO changes during the centuries in which Old Romance is considered to have evolved from Latin. To his own surprise, there are few differences between older and younger texts (ibid.: 262). VO order appears with similar frequency throughout the nine centuries, and, moreover, the reasons for its use do not seem to have changed since classical Latin: It is to avoid obscure sentences when objects are heavy or are expanded by participial constructions, infinitives or relative clauses (ibid.: 252). In the texts he studied, OV is more frequent in subordinate clauses than in main clauses (ibid.: 246–247).[21] Interestingly, he finds what he called Romance word order or SVO only in texts translated from Greek or in biblical texts. In Early Medieval legal texts, the classical word order or SOV predominates (ibid.: 265). In Koll's opinion this cannot be a reflection of spoken old Romance but must be linked to the survival of an older tradition of composing legal documents (ibid.: 265). And a little later he adds:

> ... *denn die Dokumente und Formulare des beginnenden MA, nach deren Muster ja die Urkunden im mittelalterlichen Europa z. T. noch bis weit über die Jahrtausendwende angefertigt wurden, lehnen sich ja in Aufbau und Formulierung wahrscheinlich an ähnliche Texte der römischen Kaiserzeit an.*
> (ibid.: 267)[22]

Fankhänel (1938) and Marouzeau (1938) produced extensive and detailed studies on verb placement in classical Latin. Starting from the premise that verb-last is the normal or unmarked order, they both try to analyze the special effects produced by other ordering patterns. For both authors it is evident that verb-last is more common in subordinate clauses than in main clauses (Fankhänel 1938: 17; Marouzeau 1938: 49).

Most interesting among all studies on Latin word order is a short paper by Perrochat, published in 1926. It examines verb placement in subordinate clauses in the second book of Tacitus' *Historiae*. Out of 361 subordinate clauses, only 58 or 14% are exceptions to the verb-last order (Perrochat 1926: 53). Perrochat then examines each of these instances closely and discovers that most of them fall into one of three categories. The first category consists of the so-called extended subordinate clauses in which a group of words is added after the verb either as an apposition to the whole clause, or as an afterthought, or in order to convey special emphasis to them (ibid.: 53–56). The second category comprises a few cases in which an overly monotonous discourse is avoided by breaking up verb-last patterning (ibid.: 56). The third category is made up of verbal expressions which contain nouns or infinitives, but which should be regarded as a verbal unit (ibid.: 57). By eliminating each of these special groups he is left with just 20 exceptions from the normal word order or roughly 6% (ibid.). Even among these, further study reveals that some don't have a truly subordinate character (ibid.). Perrochat concludes:

> *Ainsi, variable dans les propositions principales, la place du verbe est à peu près fixe dans les subordonnées, et la stabilité de la construction diminue à mesure que le caractère de subordination s'affaiblit.* (Perrochat 1926: 58)[23]

I would like to conclude with Marouzeau's explanation for this character of the subordinate clause, an explanation essentially borrowed from Perrochat (1926:59):

> *La subordonnée a un caractère d'enoncé second, complément ou complété; elle est une donnée de l'énoncé, elle n'en est pas l'essentiel et le but; il s'ensuit qu'elle se prète moins que la principale à l'expression des nuances et des reliefs, et s'accommode mieux d'un type de construction inexpressive.*
>
> (Marouzeau 1938:49)[24]

3.4 Clause marking

Both Perrochat's and Marouzeau's conclusions suggest that there is a link between the function or "character" of subordinate clauses and word order. The SOV word order of the subordinate clause is preserved even during the time of transition from Latin to Romance, as Raible (1992:328) points out. These observations raise questions and invite a discussion about the necessity of marking subordination by means of word order regulations. Such a discussion is not directly related to the topic at hand, but I would like to point out a few things. There is a fairly important difference between text styles with regard to word order. Similar to Tacitus, Caesar uses predominantly SOV constructions, 84% in main clauses and 93% in subordinate clauses, in the texts evaluated by Linde (1923:154). His contemporary, Cicero, on the other hand, is much more flexible in his word order usage, although in his texts, too, there is a difference between main and subordinate clauses, with SOV varying between 35% and 54% in main clauses and 61% and 70% in subordinate clauses according to Linde (ibid.). Traditionally, Caesar is considered monotonous while Cicero is considered to be one of the greatest masters of classical Latin. The subtleties of Cicero's language and the power of persuasion of his texts and orations are achieved at least in part by word order variation. If we think of the transition from archaic to classical Latin, or from Latin of proximity to Latin of distance to use Koch's and Oesterreicher's (1990) terminology, then breaking up the standardized SOV order is one of the innovations. The fact that SOV is abandoned in the main clause first suggests to me that illocutionary force might be a factor in the rearrangement of these clauses, but certainly not the only one, since subordinate clauses, which do not have illocutionary force, can also be subjected to rearrangement. No doubt these problems deserve further attention. Similarly, Perrochat's (1926:58) intuition of a continuum from clauses with weaker subordinate character to clauses with stronger subordinate character and the accompanying increase in word order rigidity needs to be evaluated with data from other authors. Lehmann's (1989) beautifully developed typology of clause linkage could serve as a guide for more rigorous and diversified studies and promises good insights into the nature of Latin subordination.

3.5 Summary

In the 2nd and 1st century B.C. Latin became a literary language of great consistency and precision. Written Latin was used in the administration of the growing Roman Empire. "Written communication lacks the aid of the situational context. Thus it has to be much more precise, explicit, and exact than oral communication" (Raible 1992:300). In Latin main clauses writers could make use of the great syntactic autonomy of Latin words by arranging them in many different ways in order to create the desired precision and stylistic effects. Latin subordinate clauses preserved the original unmarked verb-last ordering to a great extent and – against the variable word order in the main clause –, SOV might have become an "additional signal for subordination" (ibid.:328).

4. Some notes on Early New High German word order

4.1 Introduction

When we are looking at older Germanic texts in order to establish their word order, we are immediately confronted with problems almost impossible to resolve. Many Old High German and Middle High German texts are either poetic works, intended for recitation, in which word order is subjected to constraints like rhythm and rhyme, or else translations, mainly from Latin, in which the word order of the original is followed more or less closely. Thus, even certain of Behaghel's conclusions about the word order of older Germanic dialects must be rejected, because they are based on the evaluation of translations such as those of Tatian, in which the word order of the Latin original is almost never changed (Behaghel 1932:14).

So the best we can do is conjecture what the starting point of the development might have been that led to Modern German word order with its unusual coexistence of two types, Vf-second Vi-last in the main clause and SOV in the subordinate clause. Even for later stages, for which original German texts are increasingly abundant, we have to bear in mind that most authors were educated bilingual individuals, who first learned to write Latin and only subsequently adapted their spoken German mother tongue to learned written patterns, circumstances that provide little solid evidence about the word order of their spoken German.

In order to further evaluate the possibility of Latin influence on German word order, I would like to revisit the data brought against Behaghel;[25] then I would like to inspect some samples of German prior to the emergence of standard German; and, finally, I would like to discuss briefly the role and influence of the German chancery language, since it seems that the new word order patterns are followed here closer and earlier than in other text types.

4.2 The data against Latin influence

Fleischmann (1973) contests Behaghel's theory of Latin influence with four interesting arguments. However, his strongest argument, the claim that medieval Latin word order was SVO, is based on a misinterpretation of the following passage from Melanchthon's grammar:

> *Orditur sententiam nominativus, aut quod vice nominativi fungitur, hunc proxime sequitur verbum finitum, deinde adiicitur obliquus, alicubi et adverbia, et adtexunt saepe plura nomina, praepositiones, saepe aut integra commata, aut verba singula, coniunctiones. Hunc ordinem verborum in interpretando utile est a pueris exigere, ut animadvertant, quot voces sententiam absolvant, quomodo singulis nominibus singula verba respondeant.* (Melanchthon 1854:373)[26]

I argued in Chirita (1997:12–14) that the order proposed by Melanchthon is the *ordo naturalis*, which had a long tradition in Latin classrooms as a didactic device. Melanchthon follows this tradition when he recommends that students should number the Latin words in sentences according to this order. Once the above quotation is put back in its context, there remains no doubt about Melanchthon's didactic intention when recommending the numbering of words to be used 'in interpretando' (ibid.). Fleischmann's other arguments are weaker and lose even more of their power, once this first argument has been invalidated. I have discussed all of Fleischmann's arguments in Chirita (1997:12–16) and would like to refer to that study for further details.

Also in Chirita (1997:16–19) I have discussed other studies presenting data against the theory of Latin influence. Schildt (1968, 1972), Hartmann (1970), and Lühr (1985) investigate different aspects of ENHG syntax. Schildt (1968, 1972) examines the sentence frame in main clauses, Hartmann (1970) studies direct object clauses within the framework of Heringer's dependency model, while Lühr (1985) investigates the syntax of subordinate clauses in Luther's language with particular focus on the *September Bible* and the *December Bible* of

1522. Only Hartmann undertakes to challenge Behaghel's thesis of Latin influence (1970: 17), while Schildt (1968, 1970) and Lühr (1985) do not state such a goal. All four studies are based on ENHG Bible translations. By comparing such translations with the *Vulgate* they reach the same surprising conclusion: Latin interfered with the development of verb-last in subordinate clauses and the sentence frame in main clauses. Hartmann (1970: 193) finds that verb-last is more common in German than in Latin; Lühr (1985: 48) discovers that in Luther's language verb-last in subordinate clauses is quite common in most of his writings, but not in the Bible in which the verb is often placed into middle position; Schildt (1968: 195; 1972: 240) does not give any specific evidence for his conclusion, but we must trust it to be based on his good knowledge of other ENHG texts. Thus Behaghel's theory seemed to be definitively refuted.

I tried to show in Chirita (1997: 17–19) that, actually, these studies could not be considered convincing evidence against Behaghel for several reasons. First, biblical Latin is very different from both Classical Latin and Early Medieval Latin, making wide use of uncommon word order sequences such as verb-object rather than object-verb and verb-subject rather than subject-verb. In Koll's (1965: 250) opinion these uncommon sequences must originate in biblical Hebrew or Greek. This is consistent with St. Jerome's testimony on the translation of the Holy Scriptures:

> *Ego enim non solum fateor sed libera voce profiteor me in interpretatione Graecorum absque Scripturis sanctis, ubi et uerborum ordo mysterium est, non uerbum e uerbo sed sensum exprimere de sensu.* (St. Jerome [1950]: 26)[27]

Therefore the *Vulgate* is not a suitable text for word order comparisons between Latin and German.

Furthermore, if we inspect more closely the sequence verb-subject in the examples quoted by Hartmann, we discover that it is often changed in the German translation leaving the German verb in last position:[28]

(1) a. *ne videant oculi eorum*
that.not see.3rd.PL.SUBJ.PRES. eyes theirs
'that their eyes don't see'

b. *das ir augen nit gesechent*
that their eyes not see
'that their eyes don't see' (Hartmann 1970: 32)

(2) a. *ut non peccet justus*
that not sin [the] just.SUBJ
'that the just man should not sin'

b. *das der gerecht nit sünde*
that the just.SUBJ not sin
'that the just man should not sin' (Hartmann 1970:32)

However, if we look at examples like (3) and (4) which also contain a post verbal prepositional object, it is clear that the change in German takes place according to a rule of subject placement rather than verb placement, since only the subject position is changed while the prepositional object following the verb retains its place:

(3) a. *quia vere complebuntur sermones mei contra vos*
that truly shall be fulfilled words.SUBJ my against you
'that my words shall stand against you'
b. *das mein rede werdent derfullt wider euch*
that my speech.SUBJ shall be fulfilled against you
'that my words shall stay against you' (Hartmann 1970:32)

(4) a. *quod dominetur Excelsus in regno hominum*
that rules Highest.SUBJ in kingdom of men
'that the Highest rules in the kingdom of men'
b. *das der Hoechst herscht in dem reich der menschen*
that the Highest.SUBJ rules in the kingdom of.the men
'that the Highest rules in the kingdom of men' (Hartmann 1970:45)

It becomes apparent that it is the postposition of the subject that bothers the translator, not the position of the verb.[29] In a significant number of examples in Hartmann's dissertation, the verb-last position in German against verb-middle in Latin can be explained this way. A few other sequences such as verb-pronominal object are also often changed into pronominal object-verb:

(5) a. *ut sanctificaret eum*
that sanctify.3rd.SG.SUBJ.PRES. him
'that he sanctify him'
b. *das er in geheiligte*
that he him sanctify.3rd.SG.SUBJ.
'that he sanctify him' (Hartmann 1970:36)

These, too, need to be evaluated carefully, and might indicate yet another group of examples in which the German verb seems to be moved into last position, where in reality the postposition of the short pronoun might be unacceptable to the translator as (6) could indicate:

(6) a.

ut	*facerem*	*eis*	*malum*	*hoc*
that	I.would.do	to.them	harm	this

'that I would do this harm to them'

b.

das	*ich*	*in*	*tete*	*ditz*	*ubel*
that	I	to.them	would.do	this	harm

'that I would do this harm to them' (Hartmann 1970: 52)

This would be consistent with Behaghel's "Gesetz der wachsenden Glieder," the 'law of increasing constituents' (Behaghel 1932: XII, 6), which received ample confirmation by Hartmann (1970: 193).[30]

We can conclude, therefore, that although in biblical language the verb tends to occupy a position that is unusual to both ENHG and Latin, this might not be quite as offensive to ENHG translators as unusual noun or pronoun placement, thus indicating that the verb might not have found its definitive position in the sentence yet.

4.3 German syntax prior to standardization

For Behaghel there was no doubt that verb-last in ENHG subordinate clauses was a characteristic of an elevated style (Behaghel 1932: XIII). In order to compare this elevated style to what he considered a more "authentic" German, Behaghel inspected older German texts and modern German dialect texts in both his 1892 and his 1900 papers, finding in both of them that the rule of verb-last placement in subordinate clauses is frequently violated (Behaghel 1900: 242). In 1932 he also examined dialogue parts of several 16th century narratives and found additional evidence for his claim that verb-last could not have originated in the spoken language (Behaghel 1932: 20–21). Hammarström (1923: 3) considered that the language of the *Volksbücher* was less influenced by foreign models and compared two of them, *Till Eulenspiegel* and *Doktor Faust*, to a large number of chancery documents. His investigation confirmed Behaghel's findings. The language of the *Volksbücher* is much less strict in implementing the standard German word order rules than the chancery language (Hammarström 1923: 177–178, 190). In spite of their name, most of the *Volksbücher* are not genuine folk productions, but were written by certain authors for the entertainment of the upper classes (Wilpert 1979: 888). Some of them, however, such as *Till Eulenspiegel*, the *Lalebuch* and *Doktor Faust*, seem to be genuine (ibid.: 889), so in this sense Hammarström's selection was fortunate. The language of the *Volksbücher* is quite different from contemporaneous and later literary texts and might indeed be very close to spoken ENHG. Here is an example from *Till Eulenspiegel* as printed in 1515 by Johann Grüninger in Strasburg:

> *Da nun Ulenspiegel wider geen Brunschwick kam / zů der beckerstuben / da wont ein becker nach darbei / der růfft im in sein hauß vnd fragt in was er für ein gesel oder für ein handtwerckß man wer. Vlenspiegel spruch / Ich bin ein beckerknecht. Der brotbecker der sprach. Ich hab eben kein knecht wiltu mir dienen Vlenspiegel sagt ia.* (Kettmann 1971: 176)[31]

This sample contains two subordinate clauses (7) and (8), of which (8) has the verb in last position while (7) doesn't:

(7) *Da nun Ulenspiegel wider geen*
As then Ulenspiegel again to
Brunschwick kam / zů der beckerstuben /
Brunschwick came to the bakery
'As Ulenspiegel came again to Brunschwick to the bakery'

(8) *vnd fragt in was er für ein gesel ... wer*
and asked him what he for an apprentice were
'and asked him what kind of an apprentice ... he was'

This is consistent with both Behaghel's and Hammarström's findings. However, more interesting about this sample are the short sentences, the rudimentary subordination, the paratactic and *guttatim* style, the overuse of demonstratives (*da, darbei, der, der*) and the lack of grammatical devices other than demonstratives to link the individual clauses. These features make up almost all the characteristics listed for archaic Latin or for a language of proximity and might indeed be general characteristics of languages not intended and developed for written communication. While in the Eulenspiegel this style is certainly intentional by mimicking the spoken language of uneducated people, we find similar unintentional features in many of the 13th century parallel Latin-German legal documents examined by Schulze (1975). Thirteenth century German was by no means as well suited for written communication as was Latin:

> *Do bischolf Rudeger vom bistům ze bassowe mit recht vñ mit sin selbes willen gescheiden wart, nach dem wart bischolf Berhtolt, der heute ist gewaltiger bischolf. zu dem furen sine man, di von sinem goteshause lehen heten, vnde namen daz von im. Also tet ouh herre Hertenide von altenhoven daz sine.* (Schulze 1975: 24)[32]

In spite of the one conjunction (*do*) and the two relative pronouns (*der, di*), the linking of clauses is clumsy and demonstratives are again overused. The corresponding Latin text is made up of just one well-constructed and well-linked complex sentence:[33]

> *Cum post depositionem dñi Rudegeri quondam Patauieñ epi, quam ipse R. tandem uoluntarius admittebat, veñ? dñs B. Patavieñ epc per iustam sui assumptionem episcopatus eiusdem regimina suscepiscet et eccẽ Patauieñ vasalli pro sumendis eorum ab ipso feodis suam presenciam accederent, uenit et ad ipsum homo nobilis Hertnidus de altenhoven et suum ab eo sumpsit feodum ...*
>
> (Schulze 1975: 24)[34]

Of the three German subordinate clauses, two have the verb in last position while the third one does not. In the main clauses, the verb is consistently in second place. More interesting, however, are the findings for Latin: all three quite extensive subordinate clauses have the verb in last position, but not the main clause, which has the verb in second position.

The number of examples of "authentic" German could be increased at will. For Ebert's Nuremberg sample, it is the language of secular women "whose usage may be considered closest to the spoken language" (Ebert 1980: 382). It hardly surprises that they "had the lowest rates of full frames" (ibid.). Overall this "authentic" language is characterized by short sentences, clumsy linking, prevalent parataxis and most of the other features listed for archaic Latin. Unlike archaic Latin, in which word order was standardized to SOV for both main and subordinate clauses, German word order in subordinate clauses seemed more flexible. Main clauses are standardized to verb-second, but the implementation of a sentence frame is not yet fully established. As German evolved into a precise and efficient written language comparable to Latin, these "archaic" features disappeared.

4.4 The chancery language

In his 1923 dissertation, Hammarström examined verb position in a large number of chancery documents from the 14th to 16th century, as well as in two *Volksbücher*, the *Eulenspiegel* and *Doktor Faust*. Hammarström found that chancery documents implement the sentence frame in main clauses (Hammarström 1923: 107) and verb-last in subordinate clauses much earlier and more consistently than the *Volksbücher* (ibid.: 115–120). While he did not explain the emergence of the sentence frame in main clauses through the influence of Latin (ibid.: 108), Hammarström was convinced that verb-last in subordinate clauses emerged in the chancery language under Latin influence. Since subordination was not widely used in the spoken language, (for Hammarström the language of the *Volksbücher*), Latin would have provided the model for constructing such clauses. German subordinate clauses modeled after Latin subordinate clauses would have the verb in last position (ibid.: 199). Unfortunately, Hammarström's study is limited to just two text styles, which are, moreover, at opposite ends of the range of possible styles, thus leaving unexamined word order usage in other text types. However, his work received full confirmation through Ebert's meticulous study on word order in Nuremberg texts of the period from 1300–1600 (Ebert 1980). Ebert's study, diversified by social and stylistic factors, reaches the conclusion that "chancery usage served as a model for the very high rate of full frames which developed in the written usage of individuals in the course of the 15th and 16th centuries" (Ebert 1980: 388). This development is more pronounced in subordinate clauses than in main clauses (ibid.: 385–386). However, his findings "give no support to a hypothesis of direct Latin influence" (ibid.: 388), nor can they explain "how and why chancery usage itself became characterized by very high rates of full frames" (ibid.: 386). We might be dealing with the survival of very old chancery traditions, as Koll (1965: 265) believes. If indeed the legal documents up to the turn of the millennium and well beyond were based on old Roman models (Koll 1965: 267), there is no reason to assume that this tradition stopped suddenly. Indeed, when examining collections of old documents such as Böhmer (1870), it becomes apparent that the main change that took place in the imperial and royal chanceries over the centuries is the slow and gradual replacement of Latin by German. However, Latin is still present in Maximilian's imperial chancery as Chmel's (1845) collection demonstrates. It is quite likely that the chanceries were responsible for developing many of the modern German syntactic patterns such as verb-last in subordinate clauses using Latin as model. A superficial look at the chancery usage in Böhmer (1870) seems to confirm this, but detailed studies are needed. Since chancery language, and especially the language of the imperial chancery, enjoyed a very high reputation (Josten 1976: 146–151), it is hardly surprising that individual writers adopted syntactic patterns of chancery usage, as Ebert (1980: 385) noticed.

4.5 Summary

Tracing the emergence of Modern German word order is a difficult enterprise because it is almost impossible to define a starting point. Written German was influenced by Latin from its earliest manifestations, and this influence might be reflected in word order usage. Late medieval text samples that are close to the spoken language reveal that, similar to archaic Latin, German does not make use of a wide array of syntactic devices for clause linking, using instead a paratactic style and a large number of demonstratives. Verb-last in subordinate clauses is implemented earlier in chancery documents than in any of the other text types examined by Hammarstöm (1923) or Ebert (1980) and could have developed here under the influence of Latin. The origins of the sentence frame in the main clause remain unclear. The findings of Schildt (1968, 1972), Hartmann (1970), and Lühr (1985) against the possibility of Latin influence on German word order could not be confirmed.

5. Conclusion

When Latin and German first came into contact, Latin was a written language of great complexity and precision, while German had no written tradition. Latin became the language of public life throughout the German Middle Ages. As German itself developed gradually into a precise and complex written language, Latin was present, well known and admired and most certainly served as a model for writing. Many syntactic patterns of Latin, such as the AcI, extended participial constructions, the use of multilevel subordination and more, might have been borrowed from Latin into German and into most other European languages, as Blatt who speaks of "Latin loan-syntax" (Blatt 1957: 33) tried to demonstrate. I tend to agree with Hammarström (1923: 199) who argued that originally subordination was only rudimentary developed in German, and its increased use was triggered by Latin models. Latin subordinate clauses are characterized by verb-last, and the habit of placing the verb into last position in German could have been adopted from Latin as German authors adopted the technique of building complex sentences with many levels of subordination. Among the different text styles, the chancery language had a very high prestige and might have had much wider exposure than other styles. Therefore, its impact on the developing German syntax might have been quite substantial. Latin syntactic patterns developed with insight and purpose in the 2nd and 1st centuries B.C. might have continued in an unbroken tradition until today.

Notes

1. Cf. e.g. the numerous examples for for postposed constituents in subordinate clauses in Behaghel (1900: 246–252).
2. Cf. e.g. the discussion of Old English and Old Norse word order in Behaghel (1929: 278).

3. Interestingly enough, Behaghel did not try to explain German word order with Wackernagel's law (Wackernagel 1892), published in 1892 and therefore already available to him at least by 1900. Wackernagel's law has received ample support in recent years and is still considered a good explanation for V2 in German main clauses (cf. e.g. Betten 1987:122 or Harris & Campbell 1995:215). Surprisingly, Behaghel considers Wackernagel's law to be a good explanation for V3, which is attested by him in older Germanic dialects (Behaghel 1932:12–13).

4. Cf. Bach (1965:286): "Unter der Einwirkung des Lat. ergab sich die Regelung, daß das Verbum an das Ende des Nebensatzes tritt ... Im 16./17. Jh. wird dann nicht selten auch im Hauptsatz die lat Wortstellung nachgeahmt ..."; Watermann (1966:121): "Perhaps the most notorious of Latin syntactic borrowings from this era is reflected in the practice of transposing the verb to the end of a clause introduced by a subordinating conjunction or by a relative pronoun."; Moser (1965:135): "Nach lateinischem Einfluß stellt man auch gern das Zeitwort and den Satzschluß *zu kainer zyt uns wol ist* (Wyle 58,20). Dies wird wichtig für die neuhochdeutsche Endstellung des Verbums." For further examples cf. Hartmann (1970:6–7).

5. A completely unproved assertion (author's translation).

6. Is essentially based on some speculations and combinations (author's translation).

7. E.g. Wells (1985) does not mention Latin influence on German word order, Betten (1987:121–135), Polenz (1991:200), Ebert (1978:41–42), Ebert (1986:110–111), Ebert (1993:431) discuss it with reservations.

8. For a documentation of theories on the emergence of Modern German cf. e.g. Wegera (1986).

9. Cf. e.g. Wells (1985:142) "In the sixteenth century the explosion of printed material hastened this development, but on the other hand the lack of political (and then of religious) unity impeded it, as did the continued use of Latin for important political and administrative purposes." Cf. also Schildt (1972:240): "Diese Entwicklung, in deren Verlauf die Zahl der Sätze mit einer Klammer anteilmäßig ständig zunimmt, ist gleichbedeutend mit dem Prozeß der Befreiung von den Fesseln der Fremdsprache, die Übersetzer gewinnen mehr und mehr Distanz zu ihrer Vorlage und bieten in dem Maße, wie sie dieses syntaktische Kennzeichen gebrauchen, eine dem Wesen der deutschen Sprache gemäßere Übertragung."

10. Cf. McKitterick (1989:22): "Bilingualism on the part of those involved in public life at every level would have been required."

11. Cf. McKitterick's discussion of Wright's thesis that written Latin and spoken Romance were the same language up to about 800 (McKitterick 1989:10).

12. That they learn to read and write (author's translation).

13. Learned or clerical (author's translation).

14. That they wouldn't run uselessly on the streets but would learn manners next to the other boys and would become more knowledgeable and skilled (author's translation).

15. According to Boockmann (1986:13) an equal number of universities, namely 15, was founded in the 17th century, but three of them were closed soon after, while only one of the 15th century universities would not last.

16. Six 'books' about the elegancy of the Latin language (author's translation).

17. To some in reality non-existent grammar rule of Latin (author's translation).

18. It is by far best to close a unit of meaning with a verb if the composition allows it. For in the verbs lies the power of the language (author's translation).

19. Cf. Jellinek (1914: 426–427) "Daß die Humanisten den *ordo naturalis* von der wirklichen Wortstellung unterschieden, ist von vornherein klar."

20. And then Pan led him down the mountain, which is called the seat of Caelus. After he climbed it, he surveyed the lands far and wide, and on that mountain her created an altar to Caelus upon which Jupiter was the first to sacrifice. In this spot he hung in the sky what we now call and that which is above the earth, which was called Heaven ... (author's translation).

21. Koll's statistics (1965: 246–247) have to be read with caution so that texts with just few instances of OV or VO do not get overinterpreted.

22. Because the legal records and forms of the beginning Middle Ages, which served as examples for documents in Medieval Europe until far after the turn of the millennium, are probably modeled in structure and form after similar texts of the Roman Empire (author's translation).

23. Thus variable in main clauses, the position of the verb is pretty much fixed in subordinate clauses, and the stability of this construction diminishes as the power of subordination weakens (author's translation).

24. The subordinate clause is characterized as a secondary statement, complementing or completing; it is a given in an utterance, it is not the essential and the goal; it follows that it is less suitable than the main clause in expressing nuances and depth, and is better suited for an inexpressive construction type (author's translation).

25. Cf. Chirita (1997: 17–19).

26. The nominative or what functions as a nominative begins the sentence. The finite verb follows immediately thereafter; then the oblique cases and adverbials are placed and often prepositions attach several nouns, or cammas and conjunctions attach single words. It is useful to request this order of words from pupils in interpreting, so that they notice how many words make up the sentence, and how single verbs correspond to single nouns (author's translation).

27. I do not just admit it, I acknowledge it openly that in the translation of Greek texts, with the exception of the Holy Scriptures in which even word order is holy, I have not translated a word by a word but expressed a [textual/referential] meaning by a[n equivalent] meaning (author's translation).

28. All examples quoted after Hartmann compare the text of the *Vulgate* with Mentel's Bible translation of 1466.

29. Cf. also Hammarström (1923: 191) about the postposition of the subject in subordinate clauses: "Der echt deutschen konstruktionsweise der volkstümlichen literatur ist diese stellung fremd." ['This position is foreign to the authentic German composition of folk literature' (author's translation).]

30. Cf. Behaghel (1932:6): "dieses bedeutsame Gesetz [...] macht sich besonders im Satzschluß geltend".

31. As Ulenspiegel came again towards Brunschwick to the bakery, there lived a baker close to it, this one called him into his house and asked him what kind of an apprentice or craftsman he was. Ulenspiegel answered, I am a bakers helper. The breadbaker he said. Just now I don't have a helper, would you like to work for me. Vlenspiegel said yes (author's translation).

32. When bishop Rudeger of the diocese at Passau had left rightly and of his own will, after this Berhtolt became bishop, who today is a powerful bishop. To him came his men, who had feuds from his church and they took that from him. Likewise did also Sir Hertenid of Altenhoven his own (author's translation).

33. I acknowledge that it is slightly unfair to reproduce this sentence from Schulze's *Lateinisch-deutsche Parallelurkunden des 13. Jahrhunderts*, since she lists it in order to criticize Lhotzky's commentary of the two versions. Lhotzky admires the complexity of the Latin sentence and states that, while Modern German would not have any difficulty in rendering this sentence, Medieval German struggles with it and breaks it up into isolated components. Schulze, who throughout her book is eager to find original German syntactic patterns in 13th century legal documents, explains that there is no real evidence that the German translates the Latin rather then the other way around, and that Medieval German uses its own quite appropriate means to render the same content (Schulze 1975:24–25). I tend to agree with Lhotzky.

34. When, after the deposition of Sir Rudeger formerly bishop at Passau, which R. himself accepted voluntarily, the venerable Sir B. bishop of Passau took over the rule of that same diocese through just claim and the vassals of the church of Passau came up to him in order to receive their feuds, a noble man Hertnidus of Altenhoven also came to him and received his feud (author's translation).

References

Bach, A. (1965). *Geschichte der deutschen Sprache*, 8th ed. Heidelberg: Quelle & Meyer.

Behaghel, O. (1892). Zur deutschen Wortstellung. *Zeitschrift für den deutschen Unterricht, 6*, 265–267.

Behaghel, O. (1900). Zur deutschen Wortstellung. *Wissenschaftliche Beihefte zur Zeitschrift des Allgemeinen Deutschen Sprachvereins, 17/18*, 233–251.

Behaghel, O. (1929). Zur Stellung des Verbs im Germanischen und Indogermanischen. *Zeitschrift für vergleichende Sprachforschung, 56*, 276–281.

Behaghel, O. (1932). *Deutsche Syntax*. Vol. 4. Heidelberg: Carl Winter.

Betten, A. (1987). *Grundzüge der Prosasyntax*. Tübingen: Max Niemeyer.

Blatt, F. (1957). Latin influence on European syntax. In *The Classical Pattern of Modern Western Civilization* [Travaux du cercle linguistique de Copenhague 11] (pp. 33–69). Copenhagen: Nordisk Sprog- og Kulturforlag.

Böhmer, J. F. (Ed.). (1870). *Acta imperii selecta: Urkunden deutscher Könige und Kaiser.* Innsbruck: Wagner.

Boockmann, H. (1986). Wort und Bild in der Frömmigkeit des späteren Mittelalters. In S. Füssel (Ed.), *Bild und Wort: Mittelalter-Humanismus-Reformation* [Pirckheimer-Jahrbuch 1985] (pp. 9–40). München: Fink.

Burridge, K. (1993). *Syntactic Change in Germanic* [Current Issues in Linguistic Theory 89]. Amsterdam: John Benjamins.

Chirita, D. (1997). Latin influence on German word order: A discussion of Behaghel's theory". In G. F. Carr & I. Rauch (Eds.), *Insights in Germanic Linguistics II: Classic and Contemporary* [Trends in Linguistics. Studies and Monographs 94] (pp. 9–27). Berlin and New York: Mouton de Gruyter.

Chmel, J. (Ed.). (1845). *Urkunden, Briefe und Aktenstücke zur Geschichte Maximilian I. und seiner Zeit* [BLV 10]. Stuttgart: Literarischer Verein.

Courtney, E. (1999). *Archaic Latin Prose* [American Classical Studies 42]. Atlanta: Scholars Press.

Ebert, R. E. (1978). *Historische Syntax des Deutschen.* Stuttgart: J.B. Metzlersche Verlagsbuchhandlung.

Ebert, R. E. (1980). Social and stylistic variation in Early New High German word order: The sentence frame (>Satzrahmen<). *Beiträge zur Geschichte der deutschen Sprache und Literatur (Tübingen), 102*, 357–398.

Ebert, R. E. (1986). *Historische Syntax des Deutschen II: 1300–1750.* Bern: Peter Lang.

Ebert, R. E. (1993). Syntax. In R. P. Ebert, O. Reichmann, H.-J. Solms, & K.-P. Wegera (Eds.), *Frühneuhochdeutsche Grammatik* (pp. 317–488). Tübingen: Max Niemeyer.

Endres, R. (1983a). Die Bedeutung des lateinischen und deutschen Schulwesens für die Entwicklung der fränkischen Reichsstädte des Spätmittelalters und der frühen Neuzeit. In L. Kriss-Rettenbeck & M. Liedtke (Eds.), *Schulgeschichte im Zusammenhang der Kulturentwicklung* [Schriftenreihe zum Bayerischen Schulmuseum Ichenhausen 1] (pp. 144–165). Bad Heilbrunn: Julius Klinkhardt.

Endres, R. (1983b). Das Schulwesen in Franken im ausgehenden Mittelalter. In B. Moeller, H. Patze, & K. Stackmann (Eds.), *Studien zum städtischen Bildungswesen des späten Mittelalters und der frühen Neuzeit* [Abhandlungen der Akademie der Wissenschaften in Göttingen, Phil.-hist. Klasse, 3. Folge, Nr. 137] (pp. 173–214). Göttingen: Vandenhoeck & Ruprecht.

Fankhänel, H. (1938). *Verb und Satz in der lateinischen Prosa bis Sallust.* Berlin: Junker und Dünnhaupt.

Fleischmann, K. (1973). *Verbstellung und Relieftheorie.* München: Fink.

Füssel, S. (1986). Barbarus sermo fugiat . . . ': Über das Verhältnis der Humanisten zur Volkssprache. In S. Füssel (Ed.), *Bild und Wort: Mittelalter–Humanismus–Reformation* [Pirckheimer-Jahrbuch 1985] (pp. 71–110). München: Fink.

Gerl, H.-B. (1985). Zwischen faktischer und numinoser Gültigkeit: Lorenzo Vallas Theorie vom Vorrang der lateinischen Sprache. In R. J. Schoeck (Ed.), *Acta Conventus Neo-Latini Bononiensis: Proceedings of the Fourth International Congress of Neo-Latin Studies* [Medieval & Renaissance Texts & Studies 37] (pp. 327–336). Binghamton: State University of New York.

Hammarström, E. (1923). *Zur Stellung des Verbums in der deutschen Sprache*. Lund: Håkan Ohlsson.

Harris, A. & Campbell, L. (1995). *Historical Syntax in Cross-Linguistic Perspective*. Cambridge: CUP.

Hartmann, W. (1970). Zur Verbstellung im Nebensatz nach frühneuhochdeutschen Bibelübersetzungen. Ph.D. Dissertation, Heidelberg University.

Henkel, N. (1988). *Deutsche Übersetzungen lateinischer Schultexte* [Münchener Texte und Untersuchungen zur deutschen Literatur des Mittelalters]. München and Zürich: Artemis.

Hofmann, J. B. & Szantyr, A. (1972). *Lateinische Syntax und Stilistik*. München: C. H. Beck.

Jellinek, M. H. (1914). *Geschichte der neuhochdeutschen Grammatik von den Anfängen bis auf Adelung*. Vol. 2. Heidelberg: Carl Winter.

Josten, D. (1976). *Sprachvorbild und Sprachnorm im Urteil des 16. und 17. Jahrhunderts* [Europäische Hochschulschriften 152]. Bern: Herbert Lang and Frankfurt/M: Peter Lang.

Kettmann, G. (Ed.). (1971). *Frühneuhochdeutsche Texte*. Leipzig: VEB Bibliographisches Institut.

Koch, P. & Oesterreicher, W. (1990). *Gesprochene Sprache in der Romania: Französisch, Italienisch, Spanisch* [Romanistische Arbeitshefte 31]. Tübingen: Max Niemeyer.

Koll, H.-G. (1965). Zur Stellung des Verbs im spätantiken und frühmittelalterlichen Latein. *Mittellateinisches Jahrbuch, 2*, 241–272.

Kroll, W. (1934). Die Entwicklung der lateinischen Schriftsprache. *Glotta, 22*, 1–27.

Lehmann, C. (1989). Latin subordination in typological perspective. In G. Calboli (Ed.), *Subordination and Other Topics in Latin* [Studies in Language Companion Series 17] (pp. 153–179). Amsterdam and Philadelphia: John Benjamins.

Linde, P. (1923). Die Stellung des Verbs in der lateinischen Prosa. *Glotta, 12*, 153–178.

Lötscher, A. (2000). Verbenstellung im Hauptsatz in der deutschen Prosa des 15. und 16. Jahrhunderts. *Sprachwissenschaft, 25*, 153–191.

Lühr, R. (1985). Zur Syntax des Nebensatzes bei Luther. *Sprachwissenschaft, 10*, 26–50.

Luhtala, A. (1993). Syntax and dialectic in Carolingian commentaries on Priscian's Institutiones Grammaticae. In V. Law (Ed.), *History of Linguistic Thought in the Early Middle Ages* [Studies in the History of the Language Sciences 71] (pp. 145–191). Amsterdam and Philadelphia: John Benjamins.

Marouzeau, J. (1938). *L'ordre des mots dans la phrase latine: II – le verbe*. Paris: Les belles letters.

McKitterick, R. (1995). *The Frankish Kings and Culture in the Early Middle Ages* [Variorum Collected Studies Series; CS 477]. Aldershot: Variorum.

McKitterick, R. (1992). The written word and oral communication: Rome's legacy to the Franks. In I. R. North & T. Hofstra (Eds.), *Latin Culture and Medieval Germanic Europe, Germania Latina* (pp. 89–112). (reprinted in McKitterick 1995)

McKitterick, R. (1989). *The Carolingians and the Written Word*. Cambridge: CUP.

Melanchthon, Philipp (1854). Opera quae supersunt omnia [Corpus Reformatorum 20]. Brunsvigae: Schwetschke et Filium. (Reprinted 1963)

Moser, H. (1969). *Deutsche Sprachgeschichte*, 6th ed. Tübingen: Max Niemeyer.

Neumann, G. (1968). Sprachnormung im klassischen Latein. In *Sprachnorm, Sprachpflege, Sprachkritik* [Schriften des Instituts für deutsche Sprache 2] (pp. 88–97). Düsseldorf: Pädagogischer Verlag Schwann.

Perrochat, P. (1926). Sur un principe d'ordre des mots: la place du verbe dans la subordonnée. *Revue des etudes latines, 4*, 50–60.

Pinkster, H. (1988). *Lateinische Syntax und Semantik.* Tübingen: Francke.

Polenz, P. von (1991). *Deutsche Sprachgeschichte.* Vol. 1. Berlin and New York: Walter de Gruyter.

Quintilian, M. F. (1975). *Institutionis oratoriae libri XII.* Vol. 2. Edited and translated by H. Rahn. Darmstadt: Wissenschaftliche Buchgesellschaft.

Rapp, F. (1983). Die Lateinschule von Schlettstadt – eine große Schule für eine Kleinstadt. In B. Moeller, H. Patze, & K. Stackmann (Eds.), *Studien zum städtischen Bildungswesen des späten Mittelalters und der frühen Neuzeit* [Abhandlungen der Akademie der Wissenschaften in Göttingen, Phil.-hist. Klasse, 3. Folge, Nr. 137] (pp. 215–234). Göttingen: Vandenhoeck & Ruprecht.

Raible, W. (1992). The pitfalls of subordination: subject and object clauses between Latin and Romance. In B. Brogyanyi & R. Lipp (Eds.), *Historical philology: Greek, Latin and Romance: Papers in honor of Oswald Szemerényi II* [Current issues in linguistic theory 87] (pp. 299–337). Amsterdam and Philadelphia: John Benjamins.

Scherer, A. (1975). *Handbuch der lateinischen Syntax.* Heidelberg: Carl Winter.

Schildt, J. (1968). Zur Ausbildung des Satzrahmens in Aussagesätzen der Bibelsprache (1350–1550). *Beiträge zur Geschichte der deutschen Sprache und Literatur (Halle), 90*, 174–197.

Schildt, J. (1972). Die Satzklammer und ihre Ausbildung in hoch- und niederdeutschen Bibeltexten des 14. bis 16. Jahrhunderts. In G. Feudel (Ed.), *Studien zur Geschichte der deutschen Sprache* [Bausteine zur Geschichte des Neuhochdeutschen 49] (pp. 231–242). Berlin: Akademie-Verlag.

Schindling, A. (1984). Die humanistische Bildungsreform in den Reichsstädten Straßburg, Nürnberg und Augsburg. In W. Reinhard (Ed.), *Humanismus im Bildungswesen des 15. und 16. Jahrhunderts* (pp. 107–120). Bonn: Acta humaniora.

Schulze, U. (1975). *Lateinisch-deutsche Parallelurkunden des 13. Jahrhunderts* [Medium Aevum 30]. München: Fink.

Seifert, A. (1997). Das höhere Schulwesen: Universitäten und Gymnasien. In N. Hammerstein (Ed.), *Handbuch der deutschen Bildungsgeschichte*, Vol. 1 (pp. 197–374). München: C.H. Beck.

Speyer, A. (2001). Ursprung und Ausbreitung der AcI-Konstruktion im Deutschen. *Sprachwissenschaft, 26*, 145–187.

St. Jerome (1950). Epistula LVII. Ad Pammachivm. De optime genere interpretandi. In C. Favez (Ed.), *Sancti Eusebii Hieronymi Epistulas Selectas* [Collection Latomus 4] (pp. 23–38). Brussels: Latomus.

Stopp, H. (1978). Verbreitung und Zentren des Buchdrucks auf hochdeutschem Sprachgebiet im 16. und 17. Jahrhundert. *Sprachwissenschaft, 3*, 237–261.

Valla, L. (1532). *De elegantia linguae latinae libri sex.* Paris: Simon Colinaeus.

Wackernagel, J. (1892). Über ein Gesetz der indogermanischen Wortstellung. *Indogermanische Forschungen, 1*, 333–436.

Waterman, J. T. (1966). *A History of the German Language*. Seattle: University of Washington Press.

Wegera, K.-P. (Ed.). (1986). *Zur Entstehung der neuhochdeutschen Schriftsprache*. Tübingen: Max Niemeyer.

Wells, C. J. (1987). *German: A Linguistic History to 1945*. Oxford: Clarendon Press.

Wendehorst, A. (1986). Wer konnte im Mittelalter lesen und schreiben? In J. Fried (Ed.), *Schulen und Studium im sozialen Wandel des hohen und späten Mittelalters* (pp. 9–33). Sigmaringen: Jan Thorbecke.

Wheelock, F. M. (2000). *Wheelock's Latin*, 6th ed. New York: Harper Resource.

Wilpert, G. von (1979). *Sachwörterbuch der Literatur*. Stuttgart: Alfred Kröner.

From unity to diversity in Romance syntax

Portuguese and Spanish*

Ana Maria Martins
Lisboa University, Portugal

1. Introduction

In the 15th and 16th centuries in Portugal the literates and in general the aristocracy cultivated Spanish-Portuguese diglossia as a distinctive feature of culture and high class status. The appeal of the robust and innovative Castillian literature induced an increasing number of Portuguese authors to write a significant part of their works in Spanish. As an example we can mention the dramatic production of the outstanding poet and playwright Gil Vicente whose plays were performed between 1502 and 1536. In a total of forty-six plays, nineteen are bilingual, twelve are written in Spanish, fifteen in Portuguese.

In the court circle spoken Spanish would be heard at the festive occasions when poetry would be sung and theatre performed. But possibly there would be room for spoken Spanish in day-to-day life as well, since most of the Portuguese kings' consorts were Castillian then and their entourage would include some Spanish native speakers. Spanish-Portuguese diglossia was thus the manifestation of a desired closeness between the Portuguese court and the Castillian court, between their cultural inclinations and literary productions. But this approach was unilateral as the Spanish-Portuguese diglossia did not emerge on the Castillian side. Moreover, the Portuguese authors were in general unable to see their works printed in Spain – although in contrast to the state of affairs in Portugal, several centers of Spanish printing were producing books on a high scale. The Spanish or bilingual production of the Portuguese writers thus circulated in the limited circle of the Portuguese literates. Its inward transmission and reproduction would have consolidated what has been called *Castillian of Portugal*. This was a variety of Spanish permeated in a quite systematic way by some features of the Portuguese grammar and having vis-à-vis standard Spanish an old fashioned and slightly dialectal flavour.

Borrowing a perspective developed by creolists, we can think of this 15th and 16th centuries 'Spanish of Portugal' as a *relexified* Portuguese, which resulted in a variety of Spanish given the broad syntactic identity between the *substrate language* (i.e. Portuguese) and the *superstrate language* (i.e. Spanish).[1] *Relexification* is to be understood as a "mental process that builds new lexical entries by combining new phonological forms with the syntactic and semantic information of lexical entries that are already established" (Lumsden 1999: 129). The existence in the period under consideration of an extensive cognate lexicon between the two languages (see Castro (forthcoming)) smoothed and presumably acelerated the relexification process. A less distinct phonology eased the task of recognizing lexical correspondences. It was the unity of syntax, however, that would have provided a particular context of second language acquisition at a distance (through literary sources and reduced contact with native speakers) which led to the creation of an autonomous grammar by an unusual community of speakers.

In his reference work on the literary language of Gil Vicente, Paul Teyssier (1959) identifies one clear case of syntactic interference of Portuguese in Vicente's Spanish. This is the frequent use by the author in his Spanish writings of the Portuguese inflected infinitive, which the excerpts in (1) and (2) below exemplify.

(1) *Penitencia seraa harta*
penitence will-be-3SG enough
***pensares** en mi tormento.*
think-INFL.INFIN-2SG in my torment
'You will have enough penitence thinking of my torment'
(*Floresta de Enganos* 301–302. Taken from Teyssier 1959: 377)

(2) *porque tenéis gran razón*
because have-2PL big reason
*de **llorardes** vuestro mal.*
of cry-INFL.INFIN-2PL your misadventure
'…as you have every reason to cry about your misadventure'
(*Comédia do Viúvo* 84–85. Taken from Teyssier 1959: 378)

Teyssier (1959: 385–387) also points out that Gil Vicente uses interpolation often when he writes in Spanish (see Section 2.2), and, on the other hand, does not make enough use of the preposition *a* 'to' before a personal object. It should be noted however that interpolation and the lack of the preposition *a* before a personal object were grammatical options both in Spanish and Portuguese in the first half of the 16th century. Differently from the inflected infinitive, which the grammar of medieval and early Renaissance Spanish did not allow, those two other cases only reflect some variation between Spanish and Portuguese with respect to the frequency of use of structures which were grammatical in both languages.

There are two points of interest in the results of Teyssier's work (in 1959) with respect to the syntax of Vicente's Spanish. As for the slimness of the syntactic interference between Portuguese and Spanish, it shows that the syntax of Spanish and the syntax of Portuguese were much more alike at the beginning of the 16th century than they are today. The other relevant point is that Vicente's transfer of the inflected infinitive from Portuguese to Spanish was not an individual move. As Teyssier (1959: 379–380) accentuates all Portuguese authors of the time when writing in Spanish used the inflected infinitive "as if it was a normal construction". Teyssier goes on to comment: "And so we can see, by observing a particular case, how this Castillian of Portugal that we are describing had developed: this branch grown from the hispanic stem had already got at the beginning of the 16th century its originality, its own life, and even its own traditions" (Teyssier 1959: 380).[2]

In order to evaluate whether the unity of Spanish and Portuguese syntax at earlier times was as critical as I am suggesting to define the contours of the 15th and16th centuries diglossia in Portugal,[3] we will need to have a clear image of such unity and of its ulterior partial breakdown. My aim in this paper will be to give a contribution to the assemblage of such an image.

I will be dealing with a case of syntactic splitting (between Portuguese and Spanish) after the 16th century. Clitic placement and other related phenomena will be the topic of the paper. In Section 2 I will describe clitic placement in finite clauses in medieval and early Renaissance Portuguese and Spanish and will additionally bring into consideration the fact that the order OV with non clitic objects is attested in both languages in this period. In Section 3 I will sketch the diachronic paths which led from medieval and early Renaissance Portuguese and Spanish to Modern Portuguese on the one side and Modern Spanish on the other. In Section 4 I will bring into play new empirical data and will show how the medieval and early Renaissance postverbal placement of clitics in finite clauses (*e agora llaman le Barcilona* – and now (they-)call it Barcelona), which persists in Portuguese but was lost in Spanish, correlates with the availability of a pattern of minimal answer to a *yes/no* question consisting of a bare verb (¿*Quieres lo saber*? –'Do you want to know it?'; *Quiero*. – want – 'I do').

Moreover, section 4 offers an integrated account of all the facts of variation and change considered in the paper. Section 5 concludes the paper.

The divergent syntactic evolution of Portuguese and Spanish after the 16th century (which the issues addressed in this paper illustrate) shows that the 15th and 16th centuries Spanish-Portuguese high class diglossia did not influence the historical development of the Portuguese syntax. Under the hypothesis that the 15th and 16th centuries 'Spanish of Portugal' is not just a learned foreign language but rather a relexified Portuguese this is an expected result.

2. Unity: Clitic placement in medieval and early Renaissance Portuguese and Spanish

From the earlier texts through the first half of the 16th century Portuguese and Spanish display similar patterns of clitic placement in finite clauses. The contemporary contrast between Portuguese and Spanish with respect to clitic placement is the result of later change. In the present section it will be shown how Portuguese and Spanish behaved alike in medieval and early Renaissance times. Further word order facts will be brought into consideration which reinforce the view that up to the 16th century Portuguese and Spanish shared significant grammatical features in the domain of syntax. In this section ample exemplification would be needed to support the intended descriptive generalizations. In order to not overload the text with data, however, I will use a limited number of examples and at times refer the reader to a final appendix for further empirical evidence.

2.1 Unmarked main clauses: Enclisis and proclisis as variant patterns

Medieval and early Renaissance Portuguese and Spanish display variation between enclisis and proclisis[4] in the kind of sentences where enclisis is obligatory in Modern Portuguese while Modern Spanish only allows proclisis.[5] This variable placement of the clitic with respect to the verb (either preverbal or postverbal) is found in affirmative main clauses without proclisis triggers (namely wh-phrases, focused constituents, quantifiers and certain adverbs). I will refer to such clauses as *unmarked main clauses*.[6] Example (3) below, and (40) to (43) in the appendix, taken from Spanish texts, as well as example (4) below and (44) to (46) in the appendix, taken from Portuguese texts, illustrate how through the period under consideration enclisis (see sentences a.) and proclisis (see sentences b.) alternate in similar syntactic contexts. I give one example per century per language.[7] Each example contains two sentences extracted from the same literary source[8] and emerging as much as possible from analogous textual environments. The medieval and early Renaissance variation between proclisis and enclisis which sentences (3) and (4) below exemplify is not attested in verb initial sentences where enclisis was obligatory.[9]

(3) a. *e agora llaman* ***le*** *Barcilona*
and now (they-)call **it** Barcilona
'Nowadays, it is called *Barcilona*'
(Spanish. Thirteenth century. Menéndez Pidal 1978: 10b)

b. *e oy.en.dia* ***le*** *llaman Tarraçona*
and nowadays **it** (they-)call Tarraçona
'Nowadays it is called *Tarraçona*'
(Spanish. Thirteenth century. Menéndez Pidal 1978: 10b)

(4) a. *à pessoa que vos tall dise ou espreveo, pergumte****lhe***
to-the person that you-DAT such-thing told or wrote, ask-**him**-DAT
vosalteza omde estava syman afomso
Your-Highness where was Syman Afomso
'Your majesty should ask the person that told you or wrote such thing where Syman Afomso was'
(Portuguese. 16th century. Pato 1884: 99)

b. *aos que imda lá sam,* ***lhe*** *tenho dado seguros e*
to-those that still there are, **them**-DAT I-have given safe-conducts and
lhe mando agora noteficar ho voso perdam
them-DAT (I-)send now notify-of the your pardon
'I have been giving protection to the people that are still there and now I will notify them of your pardon'
(Portuguese. 16th century. Pato 1884: 94)

In agreement with the empirical evidence given above, Barry (1987) observes that in Old Spanish "clitic pronouns may be either postverbal (...) or preverbal", then adding: "The principles governing their placement have remained elusive (...). The present study is one more attempt to understand the fluctuation in pronoun placement" (Barry 1987: 213). Space considerations preclude me from reviewing the heavily extensive literature dealing with this concern.[10] Nevertheless, I will propose a semantic motivation for this case of word order variation in Section 2.3.

2.2 Subordinate finite clauses and main clauses with proclisis triggers: Proclisis, interpolation, and OV order

In subordinate main clauses clitics are preverbal in all stages of the history of Portuguese and Spanish.[11] In the medieval and early Renaissance period however clitics occur either adjacent or non-adjacent to the verb – the phenomena of non adjacency is known as *interpolation* in the Romance philological literature. During the period along which interpolation can be attested,[12] this word order is optional. Compare sentences a. to the minimally contrasting sentences b. in the pairs (5) to (7) below and (47) to (48) in the appendix. In the former, some material could have been interpolated, but was not; the latter are examples of interpolation.

(5) a. *como nesta carta* ***se*** *cõthẽ*
how in-this letter **itself** contains
'how it is stated in this letter'
(Portuguese. Year 1532. Martins 2001: 554)

b. *como* ***se*** *nesta carta contem*
how **itself** in-this letter contains
'how it is stated in this letter'
(Portuguese. Year 1538. Martins 2001: 318)

(6) a. *si tu* ***lo*** *otorgares*
if you **it** concede
'if you concede it'
(Spanish. Thirteenth century. Cf. Chenery 1905: 106)

b. *se* ***lo*** *tu mandasses*
if **it** you would-order
'if you would-order it'
(Spanish. Thirteenth century. Cf. Chenery 1905: 107)

(7) a. *Et si uos* ***lo*** *touieredes por bien*
and if you **it** have for good
'And if you consider it good'
(Spanish. Thirteenth century. Cf. Chenery 1905: 111)

b. *Et si* ***lo*** *el rey por bien toviere*
and if **it** the king for good has
'And if the king considers it good'
(Spanish. Thirteenth century. Cf. Rivero 1991: 244)

As sentences (5b) and (7b) also show, and is further illustrated by sentences (8) to (10) below, medieval and early Renaissance Portuguese and Spanish allow IP-scrambling of non-clitic objects, therefore deriving the order (S)OV. (In Section 4 it will be shown how object scrambling, interpolation, and the possibility of enclisis in finite clauses are to be interpreted as correlated grammatical options.)

(8) *Se* ***me*** *Deus enton a morte non deu*
if **me**-DAT God then the death not gave
'If then God didn't give me death'
(Portuguese. Fourteenth century. Nunes 1932: 225 (text 109))

(9) *quem* ***vos*** *tall cousa disse, mentivos mui grande mentira*
whoever **you**-DAT such thing told, lied-you-DAT very big lie
'Whoever told you that, lied to you'
(Portuguese. 15th century. Cf. Pádua 1960: 73)

(10) *Et de mas mando al omne que* ***vos*** *esta mj carta mostrara que*
and of more (I-)order to-the man who **you** this my letter would-show that
enplase a todos los que ***lo*** *contra ella fizjeren*
(he-)cites to all those that **it** against her [the letter] would-do
'Moreover, I order the man showing you this letter of mine to call before a court of law all those acting against it'
(Spanish. Year 1440. Menéndez Pidal 1919: 309 (text 234))[13]

Interpolation structures give us the means to clearly identify OV sentences displaying object scrambling (in contrast to OV resulting from left dislocation or focusing). This is so because the clitic signals the border between left-dislocated and focused constituents on one side and scrambled constituents on the other. That is, while the former surface to the left of the clitic, the latter occur to its right. The word order found in subordinate clauses with interpolation is indicated under (11) and exemplified by sentences (12) to (15). The pre-clitic constituents are marked by a double-underline in sentences (12) to (15), being respectively a left-dislocated object in (12), a sentential adjunct in (13), a focused object in (14), and a left-dislocated object followed by a focused object in (15). Scrambled objects, occurring to the right of the clitic, are underlined in sentences (12)–(13). Scrambled objects in the relevant kind of structure are concomitantly interpolated constituents, but interpolation is not restricted to them; preverbal subjects are frequently interpolated – see (13) and (14).

(11) "Comp – topic (or sentential adjunct) – focus[14] – clitic – scrambled / interpolated XPs – verb"

(12) *E com todas as pertenças que aos ditos casaaes* ***lhes***
and with all the belongings that to-the mentioned properties **them**-DAT
dereitamẽte *perteẽçe*
rightly belongs
'and with everything which according to the terms of the contract is a part of the mentioned properties'
(Portuguese. Year 1522. Martins 2001:306)

(13) *E sse pela uẽtujra* ***uos*** *alguẽ a dita vỹa enbargar*
and if by chance **you**-DAT someone the mentioned vineyard blocks
'And if by chance someone blocks the vineyard from you'
(Portuguese. Year 1296. Martins 2001:377)

(14) *So cierto que tan buen entendimiento* ***vos*** *Dios dió...*
(I-)am sure that so good understanding **you**-DAT God gave
'I am sure that God gave you such a good mind'...
(Spanish. Fourteenth century. Cf. Rivero 1997:180)

(15) *E aos outros tres, suas moradas* ***lhes*** *avyam ja dadas*
and to-the other three, their lodgings **them**-DAT (they-)had already given
'And they had already given a place to stay to the other three of them'
(Portuguese. Fourteenth century. Cf. Ogando 1980:259)

Some types of main clauses behave similarly to subordinate clauses with respect to clitic placement. Those are sentences introduced by wh-phrases, focused constituents, quantifiers and certain adverbs (such as *ja*, *ya* 'already' in (16) below and (50) in the appendix; *sempre* 'always' in (49) in the appendix; or *asi* 'so' in (51) in the appendix). In these sentences, when a clitic occurs, it is obligatorily preverbal; on the other hand, in these *proclitic-pattern* main clauses, interpolation as well as scrambled objects can be found. In both respects, such sentences contrast with the unmarked main clauses, where enclisis is a grammatical option and interpolation or object scrambling are not attested. This is shown by sentences (16)–(17) below and (49) in the appendix, from medieval Portuguese, as well as by sentences (18) below and (50)–(51) in the appendix, from medieval Spanish.

(16) *E ja* ***m'*** *El tanto mal fez*
and already **me**-DAT he so-much harm did
'He has done me a lot of harm already'
(Portuguese. Fourteenth century. Nunes 1932:209 (text 102))

(17) *Dom Froyaz amaua-a muyto e numca* ***lhe*** *tamtas cousas pode*
don Froyaz loved-her-ACC much and never **her**-DAT enough things could

fazer que a podesse fazer fallar
do that her-ACC could make speak
'Don Froyaz loved her heartily but he wasn't able to do enough to get her to speak'
(Portuguese. Fourteenth century. Cf. Pádua 1960: 53)

(18) *Todos se luego ayuntaron*
all **themselves** immediately assembled
'Everybody assembled at once'
(Spanish. Fourteenth century. Cf. Chenery 1905: 123)

2.3 A gradual change in clitic placement through the medieval period

When we look at Portuguese texts corresponding to the period between the thirteenth and 16th centuries, we realize that a slow and gradual change took place during this period with regard to clitic placement in unmarked main clauses – the kind of clause where the clitic could precede or follow the verb. In the thirteenth century, proclisis was possible but rare; in the 16th century, the situation is reversed: the occurrences of enclisis are very infrequent. This change takes place step by step (although there is perhaps some rupture point between the fourteenth and the 15th century, a matter I will not go into here) Table 1 provides the relevant data (see Martins 1994b).

Studies on clitic placement in Medieval Portuguese based on literary texts (see Lawton 1966; Ogando 1980; Silva 1989; Salvi 1990; Lobo 1996) make it possible to confirm the tendency showed by Table 1, whose data come from legal documents only. As for the 16th century, I examined several letters, chronicles, and technical texts (cf. Martins 1994b). The order clitic-verb appears generally to dominate over the order verb-clitic, but the situation is not as extreme as in the legal documents. The rate of enclisis appears to oscillate between approximately 1% and 30%.

I do not know of comparable data concerning medieval and early Renaissance Spanish. I nevertheless have some information on the proportion of pro-

Table 1. Data from Portuguese legal documents

	1250–99	1300–49	1350–99	1400–49	1450–99	1500–49
Clitic-Verb	7.1% (4/56)	24.6% (15/61)	41.9% (18/43)	78.9% (30/38)	92.7% (38/41)	98.8% (80/81)
Verb-Clitic	92.9% (52/56)	75.4% (46/61)	58.1% (25/43)	21.1% (8/38)	7.3% (3/41)	1.2% (1/81)

clisis and enclisis at the fringes of the relevant period. Barry (1987) who studies thirteenth century Spanish points out that at that time "the overwelming majority of main clause clitics are postverbal" (Barry 1987:215). On the other hand, Keniston (1937), describing clitic placement in 16th century Spanish, observes that "already in the 16th century the representation of [the principles which govern pronoun position] in speech was establishing, by virtue of frequency of usage, a set of patterns which in contemporary speech have been elevated into grammatical rules" (Keniston 1937:90). In line with Keniston, but bearing more explicitly on the issue under consideration, Lesman (1980) states that in the 16th century Spanish authors "place the pronouns before or after the verb" but "there is a preference for proclisis" (Lesman 1980:92).[15] Hence I presume that a similar changing path developed in Spanish and Portuguese through the medieval period.

The change that takes place between the thirteenth and the 16th centuries patterns like a change in use. In fact the option between preverbal and postverbal placement of the clitics in main clauses of the relevant kind was never lost. Only the clear preference for the order verb-clitic in the thirteenth century was little by little dropped in favor of the preference for the order clitic-verb that became dominant in the 15th and 16th centuries. The change was slow and progressive, as is characteristic of changes in use. Therefore, although in the 16th century the order verb-clitic is sparsely attested, I assume it was grammatically possible.

In former work, I suggested that sentences showing the order clitic-verb would be emphatic, in contrast to neutral sentences with the order verb-clitic. The alternative orders displayed by sentences like (19) and (20) below would thus correspond to the following semantic contrast:

(19) *E Rotas* ***lho*** *outorgou*
and Rotas **him-it** conceded
'And Rotas did concede it to him'
(Portuguese. Fourteenth century. Cintra 1954:36)

(20) *E elle outorgou****lho***
and he conceded **him**-it
'And he conceded it to him'
(Portuguese. Fourteenth century. Cintra 1954:36)

Under this interpretation the variant clitic positions exhibited by unmarked main clauses would be semantically motivated. The change that developed between the thirteenth and the 16th centuries may accordingly be described as a case of increasing preference for the emphatic construction (with the order clitic-verb) over the non-emphatic verb-clitic construction, until the point that the verb-clitic order showed up very infrequently. The result of such a process is that speakers lose the possibility of contrasting the neutral and the marked constructions and come to interpret the emphatic one as neutral. This type of scenario may explain the ensuing changes in clitic placement in Portuguese and Spanish. As a consequence of the weakening of evidence for two positions available for clitics, each of them with a particular interpretative effect, a fixed word order ended up being acquired by a new generation of speakers. Note that this kind of approach accounts not only for the loss of variation between proclisis and enclisis in unmarked main clauses but also for the loss of variation between interpolation and adjacency to the verb in subordinate clauses and in main clauses introduced by wh-phrases, focused constituents, quantifiers and certain adverbs. Both types of word order variation depended on the availability of the option to place the clitic in one of two distinct positions in clause structure (see Section 4).

As the hypothesis I am suggesting to account for the variant patterns of clitic placement found in medieval and early Renaissance Portuguese and Spanish can hardly be tested against the available historical data (being mainly supported on a theoretical basis), I will bring into consideration a different kind of data. Variation between enclisis and proclisis in unmarked main clauses can still be attested, although rarely, in contemporary Portuguese dialects. The example given below, taken from a corpus of spoken language, appears to support the suggested semantic interpretation of the variant word orders. The dialogue reproduced in (21) took place during a session of field work conducted by researchers engaged in a project of developing a linguistic atlas. The misapprehension behind the speech interaction between the interviewer and the interviewee is motivated by the unexpected phonetic form of the word *nascente* 'orient', which the informant pronounces with rhotacism of the coda segment in the initial syllable. When at request of the interviewer the informant repeats for the third time the same information, he changes the enclitic pattern in (21b) for the proclitic pattern in (21f). It seems legitimate to conclude, given the discourse situation in point, that the informant wished to reinforce his assertation by using proclisis as a strategy to add emphasis to the sentence.

(21) a. – *Como é que chama?*
'How do you call it (the direction from which the sun rises)'?

b. – *A gente chama-**lhe** o nascente* [nɐrsẽtɨ].
the people call **it** the (sun-)bearing(-point)
'We call it orient'

c. – Como?
'What?'

d. – *O nascente* [nɐrsẽtɨ]. *O nascente* [nɐrsẽtɨ].
the (sun-)bearing(-point) the (sun-)bearing(-point)

e. – *Diga lá outra vez, faz favor.*
'Could you say it again, please?'

f. – *A gente **lhe** chama o nascente* [nɐrsẽtɨ].
the people **it** call the (sun-)bearing(-point)
'We call it orient'.
(Portuguese dialect of Serpa. In CORDIAL-SIN: *Corpus of Portuguese Dialects Syntactically Annotated*)[16]

3. The broken unity: Divergent outcomes of syntactic change

In Section 2 it has been shown that at an earlier stage (which I will refer from now on as *Stage I*) similar facts are attested in Portuguese and Spanish with respect to clitic placement. At this stage (up to the 16th century) Portuguese and Spanish share interpolation, object scrambling and the possibility of enclisis in finite main clauses. See examples (3) to (18) above. As for interpolation, however, it should be noted that in Spanish it is well attested up to the 15th century but rare afterwards (see Kenison 1937: 101) while in Portuguese it remains fairly productive in the 16th century. The high frequency of interpolation which Teyssier (1959: 385–386) identifies in the Spanish and bilingual plays of Gil Vicente is one example of the syntactic interference of Portuguese in the 16th century 'Spanish of Portugal'. Cf. Section 1 above, and the examples below.

(22) *Assi como **o** vós fazeis*
so as it-ACC you-NOM-2PL do-2PL
'in the way that you do it'
(Portuguese. *Tragicomédia pastoril da Serra da Estrela* 676. Taken from Teyssier 1959: 385)

(23) *Como **la** vos desseáis*
as **it**-ACC you-NOM-2PL wish-2PL
'(I will do it) as you wish'
(Spanish. *Amadis de Gaula* 1166. Taken from Teyssier 1959: 385)

(24) *Este he o didal do menino*
this is the thimble of the boy
que ***me*** *tu aqui trazias*
that **me**-DAT you-NOM here brought-2SG
'This is the boy's thimble which you brought me here'
(Portuguese. *Auto da Lusitânia* 254–255. Taken from Teyssier 1959:385)

(25) *Que se* ***nos*** *isto no val*
because if **us**-DAT this not help
'because if this cannot help us'
(Spanish. *Auto da Festa* 146. Taken from Teyssier 1959:385)

In the ensuing chronological period (which I will refer from now on as *Stage II*, from the second half of the 16th century) enclisis nearly disappears, except in V1 sentences where the Tobler-Mussafia constraint remains active (see Footnote 9). Proclisis then becomes the regular pattern of clitic placement in finite main clauses. On the other hand, medieval and early Renaissance interpolation (of both heads and XPs) is not an option anymore. Object scrambling is concomitantly lost. At this point Portuguese and Spanish seem to be evolving in the same direction.

After the seventeenth century the obligatory adjacency between clitic and verb resulting from the loss of interpolation is consolidated.[17] In Portuguese, however, enclisis reappears strongly, soon becoming the only allowed pattern of clitic placement in unmarked main clauses (Portuguese *Stage III*).[18] See Table 2 below.

Differently from Portuguese, Spanish stabilizes proclisis and after the seventeenth century extends it to verb initial sentences getting rid of the Tobler-Mussafia constraint. Hence the contemporary contrast between Spanish and Portuguese with respect to clitic placement, which sentences (26) vs. (27) below exemplify.

(26) Spanish: *El rojo* ***te*** *queda bien*
the red **you**-DAT goes fine
'Red suits you'

(27) Portuguese: *O vermelho fica-****te*** *bem*
the red goes **you**-DAT fine
'Red suits you'

Table 2. Clitic placement in Portuguese from the 16th century to the 19th century

	Proclisis[19]	Enclisis	Interpolation (of heads and XPs)
Afonso de Albuquerque[20] (1462?–1515)	73.5% (119)	26.5% (43)	yes
Damião de Góis[21] (1502–1574)	97.1% (130)	2.9% (4)	yes
Fernão Mendes Pinto[22] (1510?–1583)	98.1% (102)	1.9% (2)	yes
Diogo do Couto[23] (1542–1616)	72.5% (74)	27.5% (28)	yes
Francisco Manuel de Mello[24] (1608–1666)	92.3% (36)	7.7% (3)	yes (residual)
António Vieira[25] (1608–1697)	31.6% (117)	68.4% (248)	no
António Verney[26] (1713–1792)	27.3% (18)	72.7% (48)	no
Almeida Garrett[27] (1799–1854)	19.3% (11)	80.7% (46)	no
Oliveira Martins[28] (1845–1894)	2.4% (2)	97.6% (80)	no

4. A diachronic generative syntax approach to clitic placement in Romance, with special reference to Portuguese and Spanish

VP-ellipsis (a construction which allows that verbal objects be not expressed) is found in Portuguese in replies to *yes/no* questions and in the second conjunct of coordinate structures, as examples (28) and (29) show:

(28) *A Marta deu um livro ao João? Sim, deu.*
the Martha gave a book to-the John yes gave
'Did Martha give a book to John? Yes, she did.'

(29) *O João está a ler esse romance e a Marta também está.*
the John is reading that novel and the Martha also is
'John is reading that novel and Martha is too.'

In contrast to Portuguese, Spanish does not allow VP-ellipsis in either of these contexts, as exemplified in (30) and (31) below:

(30) *¿Marta le dio un libro a Juan? *Sí, dio.*
Martha him gave a book to John yes gave
'Did Martha give a book to John? Yes, she did.'

(31) **Juan esta leyendo esa novela y Marta está también*
John is reading that novel and Martha is also
'John is reading that novel and Martha is too.'

The availability of VP-ellipsis in Portuguese makes possible that a minimal answer to a *yes/no* question consists of a bare verb. This is indeed the unmarked pattern in Portuguese, just as it was in Latin (see Hale & Buck 1903; Woodcock 1959):

(32) Portuguese: *O João fez a cama? Fez.*
the John made the bed did
'Did John make his bed? Yes, he did.'

(33) Latin: *Clodius insidias fecit Miloni? Fecit.*
Clodius-NOM plots-ACC made-3SG Miloni-DAT made
'Did Clodius plot against Milo? Yes, he did.'
(Cicero. Example taken from Pinkster 1990: 1919)

Although Modern Spanish diverges from Portuguese in this respect, medieval and early Renaissance Spanish did not, as examples (34) to (36) below show. Since sentences (34) to (36) would be ungrammatical in Modern Spanish, we have tracked down one more case of syntactic splitting between Portuguese and Spanish after the 16th century. It should be noted that sentences with VP-ellipsis were common in Spanish in the 16th century. Keniston (1937), who carried out research based on a large corpus of 16th century Castillian prose, points out that "in direct discourse object pronouns are rarely used with a verb thus repeated with sí" (Keniston 1937: 593).

(34) *¿I traedes uostros escriptos? Rei, si traemos*
and bring your books? king yes bring
'And, do you bring your books? Yes, King, we do.'
(Spanish. Twelfth century. Cf. Gifford and Hodcroft 1959: 42)

(35) *¿Sois vos alguno dellos? Si soy*
are you any of them? yes am
'Are you one of them? Yes, I am.'
(Spanish. 16th century. Cf. Keniston 1937: 593)

(36) – *Pues ¿quien esta arriba?*
'Who is upstairs? '
– ¿Quiéreslo saber?
want-it to know?
'Do you want to know it?'
– Quiero.

want
'Yes, I do'

(Spanish. Late 15th century. Cejador y Frauca 1913:62)

In this section I will take a theoretical approach (within the Chomskyan framework) to the facts which I have been describing. In that way I will be able to show how on an abstract level different apparently unrelated empirical facts depend upon common properties of grammar.

4.1 Modern Romance vs. Old Romance

In Romance, enclisis in tensed clauses correlates with the possibility of VP-ellipsis and concomitantly with a minimal answer pattern to *yes/no* questions consisting of a bare verb. The contemporary Romance languages split in two groups with respect to such correlation. Portuguese and Galician have enclisis in tensed clauses and license VP-ellipsis, as the data in Table 3 below show; in Spanish, Catalan, French, Italian and Roumanian enclisis in tensed clauses is not allowed, proclisis being pervasive, and VP-ellipsis being not permitted either, as the data in Table 4 below show. In these languages an affirmative word (but crucially not the verb) occurs in minimal answers to *yes/no* questions.

In order to account for the correlation illustrated by the data displayed above, I propose that enclisis and VP-ellipsis emerge in languages where the functional category Σ[29] which encodes polarity values, i.e., affirmation, negation, modality – bears a strong V-feature (Portuguese and Galician), whereas such phenomena are absent from languages where the V-feature of Σ is weak (Spanish, Catalan, French, Italian and Roumanian) – cf. Martins (1994a).

Table 3. Enclisis and VP-ellipsis

Portuguese:	– *(Tu) deste-**lhe** o livro?*	– <u>*Dei.*</u>	√Enclisis
	(you) gave him the book?	gave	√VP-ellipsis
	– *(**Tu) **lhe** deste o livro?*	– *Sim, dei.*	*Proclisis
	(you) him gave the book?	yes, gave	
	'Did you give him the book?'	'Yes, I did.'	
Galician:	– *(Tu) déches**lle** o livro?*	– <u>*Din.*</u>	√Enclisis
	(you) gave him the book?	gave	√VP-ellipsis
	– *(**Tu) **lle** déches o livro?*	– *Si, din.*	*Proclisis
	(you) him gave the book?	yes, gave	
	'Did you give him the book?'	'Yes, I did.'	

Table 4. Proclisis

Spanish:	– ***Le** diste el libro?*	– *Sí.*	√Proclisis
	him gave the book?	yes	*VP-ellipsis
	– **Diste**le** el libro?*	– *(**Sí,) di.*	*Enclisis
	gave him the book?	(yes,) gave	
	'Did you give him the book? '	– *Sí, **se lo** di.*	
		yes, him it gave.	
		'Yes, I did. '	
Catalan:	– ***Li** has donat el llibre?*	– *Si.*	√Proclisis
	him have given the book?	yes	*VP-ellipsis
	– **Has-**li** donat el llibre?*	– *(**Si,)he donat.*	*Enclisis
	have him given the book?	(yes,) have given	
	'Did you give him the book? '	– *Si, **l'hi** he donat.*	
		yes, him it have given	
		'Yes, I did. '	
French:	– ***Lui** as-tu donné le livre?*	– *Oui.*	√Proclisis
	him have you given the book?	yes	*VP-ellipsis
	– **As-**lui** tu donné le livre?*	– *(**Oui,) j'ai donné.*	*Enclisis
	have him you given the book?	(yes,) I have given	
	'Did you give him the book? '	– *Oui, je **le lui** ai donné.*	
		yes, I it him have given	
		'Yes, I did. '	
Italian:	– ***Gli** hai dato il libro?*	– *Sì*	√Proclisis
	him have given the book?	yes	*VP-ellipsis
	– **Hai **gli** dato il libro?*	– *(**Sì,) ho dato.*	*Enclisis
	have him given the book?	(yes,) have given	
	'Did you give him the book? '	–*Sì, **gliel'** ho dato.*	
		yes, him it have given	
		'Yes, I did. '	
Roumanian:	–***I**-ai dat caietul?*	– *Da.*	√Proclisis
	him have given pad-the?	yes	*VP-ellipsis
	– * *Ai-**i** dat caietul?*	– *(**Da,) am dat.*	*Enclisis
	have him given pad-the?	(yes,) have given	
	'Did you give him the pad? '	– *Da, **I l**-am dat.*	
		yes, him it have given	
		'Yes, I did. '	

Admitting that checking theory should not be part of a minimalist model of grammar (compare Chomsky 2000 with Chomsky 1995), I still take the 'strenghth' property of a functional category to be relevant (cf. Chomsky 2000: 132) in two ways: Strong functional categories can license null constituents. Strong functional heads are necessarily part of spelled out morphological words in the Morphology component of grammar (cf. Chomsky 1994, 2000; Halle & Marantz 1993; Harley & Noyer 1999; Embick & Noyer 2001). As for strong Σ this requisite is satisfied by merging Σ with a head related to Σ by bearing polarity features.

I take the heads which encode polarity features and therefore can agree and merge with Σ to be C, Neg and V. The merging operation may take place in the syntactic component or post-syntactically, in the Morphology component, as will be clarified farther on in this section. I assume that main clauses are usually IPs, not CPs, following ideas implemented by Boškovic (1996, 1997), and Thráinsson (1996), among others, on the non-universality of clause structure – as a corollary of principles of economy of representations. In declarative affirmative main clauses, C and Neg being not projected, strong Σ merges with V. Enclisis is the outcome of this merger between V and Σ, clitics occurring in a lower (or more rightward) position, which I will identify later on in this section. VP-ellipsis, on the other hand, is licensed by the Agree relation (cf. Chomsky 2000) between strong Σ and V, independently of the fact that Σ merges with V, C, or Neg.

Laka (1990) proposes that in Romance the lexical items that show up in minimal unmarked answers to yes/no questions incorporate in Σ. Under the analysis that I am proposing here, this is so independently of the strong or weak character of Σ. However, 'bare verb' minimal answers to *yes/no* questions can only be a property of languages where the strong nature of Σ induces merging of this head with the V head; otherwise only an affirmative/negative word will be able to give lexical content to the Σ head. Facts relating to VP-ellipsis and the patterns of answer to *yes/no* questions indicate that Σ was a strong functional category across the Old Romance languages – see Martins (forthcoming b).

4.2 Change in clitic placement in Portuguese and Spanish: From unity to diversity

The analysis that I will put forward to account for the changes in clitic placement which took place in Portuguese and Spanish (see Section 3 above) relies on the following assumptions:

a. Clitics are heads in Old and Modern Romance. Under a bare phrase structure perspective, however, clitics qualify both as minimal and maximal syntactic categories (cf. Chomsky 1994, 1995),[30] therefore clitics may move into positions unfit for regular heads.
b. Clitics move into the domain of AgrS (or of CH_{AgrS}, after AgrS moves to Σ). See Martins (2000: 171–172) for a motivation of this assumption.
c. A clitic occurs at the structural edge of the category (X^0 or XP) that contains it, that is, the clitic is dominated by the highest segment of that category. This is a reformulated version of the *Edge Principle* proposed by Raposo (2000) which I adopt in its essentials.[31]
d. Strong Σ merges with V when neither C nor Neg are projected, as is commonly the case in affirmative main clauses. In clauses that include C (like finite subordinate clauses) or a functional category belonging to the CP field (as is presumably the case in main clauses with proclisis triggers) Σ merges with C.
e. In Old and early Renaissance Portuguese and Spanish AgrS has an uninterpretable selectional feature (i.e., an EPP-feature) with an *Attract-all-F* property, in the sense of Boškovic 1999; therefore AgrS allows multiple Specs[32] – cf. Chomsky (1994), Grewendorf and Sabel (1999), Martins (2002).

Given these assumptions, variation in clitic placement in Old and early Renaissance Portuguese and Spanish, i.e. at *Stage I* (cf. Section 3 above), can be straightforwardly derived.

In unmarked main clauses proclisis results from the formation of a complex head derived from movement of the clitic to Σ after AgrS, containing V, has moved to Σ: $[_{\Sigma}$ clitic$[_{\Sigma}$ $[_{AgrS}$V,T,AgrS$]$ Σ$]]$. Given the Edge Principle, the clitic must "meet AgrS" in Σ; if the clitic would left-adjoin to the AgrS head, AgrS would be unable to move into Σ carrying the verb along.[33]

In subordinate clauses and in main clauses introduced by wh-phrases, focused constituents, quantifiers, and certain adverbs proclisis with adjacency arises when the verb and the clitic are incorporated in AgrS. Recall that in subordinate clauses as well as in main clauses introduced by proclisis triggers Σ merges with C, not with V.[34]

Both enclisis and interpolation, on the other hand, involve movement of the clitic to (the most external) Spec, AgrSP, a position accessible to clitics given its minimal/maximal nature. Interpolation emerges when other overtly filled Spec(s) of AgrS is/are projected and the verb does not move beyond AgrS (this being typically the subordinate clause pattern). Enclisis is derived by movement of the verb into Σ while the clitic is incorporated in Spec,AgrSP. Enclisis arises in unmarked main clauses because this is the kind of clause that does not include C nor Neg. Thus strong Σ must be licensed by merging with the verb. Recall that I am following Bošković (1996, 1997) and Thráinsson (1996), among others, on the hypothesis of the non-universality of clause structure. According to this view, Universal Grammar defines the set of functional categories which particular languages select from; so it is not the case that all functional categories are instantiated in all languages. Moreover the subset of functional categories selected by a given language may not be present in all clause types of that language. Bošković (1996: 290) formulates the Minimal Structure Principle (MSP) as shown under (37) below:

(37) Provided that lexical requirements of relevant elements are satisfied, if two representations have the same lexical structure, and serve the same function, then the representation that has fewer projections is to be chosen as *the* syntactic representation serving that function.

According to the MSP, main clauses will be C(omplementizer)P(hrases)s only if their CP status is imposed by lexical requirements (e.g., wh-questions). Otherwise, since (unmarked) main clauses are not introduced by a complementizer, CP will not be projected.

As for the kind of unrestricted IP-scrambling displayed by Old Portuguese and Old Spanish, it directly correlates with interpolation and enclisis because like interpolation and enclisis it depends on AgrS being associated with an Attract-all-F EPP-feature, therefore projecting multiple Specs.

The historical period identified as *Stage II* in Section 3 emerges when AgrS loses the ability to select multiple Specs (see Martins 2002 on this matter). At this point, AgrS is associated with an *Attract-1F* EPP-feature, making available one Spec for the subject.[35] This change implies the concomitant losses of enclisis, interpolation, and IP-scrambling. The only options for clitics at this point will be incorporating in AgrS where the verb is also incorporated (in subordinate clauses and main clauses with proclisis triggers) or moving into Σ after AgrS containing the verb has merged with Σ (in unmarked main clauses). In both situations proclisis and adjacency are derived.

As for the generalized enclitic pattern of Portuguese *Stage III*, we could admit that it would reflect the emergence of excorporation as a grammatical option. In this scenario, enclisis would be derived by movement of the head $[_{AgrS}$V,T,AgrS] into Σ leaving the clitic incorporated in AgrS. Once excorporation would come into play, the clitic (which in Standard Modern Portuguese does not have features relating it to Σ) would not be allowed to move into

Σ– cf. Boškovic (1997). However, I will take here Kayne's view (in 1991) that excorporation is not a grammatical option.

As an alternative approach, I hypothesize that at Portuguese *Stage III* AgrS ceases to select an EPP-feature; so AgrS does not project a Spec.[36] This change makes possible that Σ merges with V post-syntactically, that is, in the Morphology component. Once this option becomes available, it appears to exclude the option for syntactic merger.[37] Morphological merger takes place under adjacency (cf. Bolbajik 1995; Embick & Noyer 2001). Since at this stage there is no Spec intervening between Σ and 'V-in-AgrS', the two heads can in principle undergo morphological merger. If a clitic has left-adjoined to AgrS (in the Syntax component), however, the clitic breaks the required adjacency between Σ and 'V-in-AgrS' inhibiting morphological merger. This is so given the ambiguity of the relevant configuration with respect to the phrase structure status of both the category $[_{AgrS}$V,T,AgrS] and the clitic adjoined to it. Because $[_{AgrS}$V,T,AgrS] does not project a Spec position, it can be interpreted as a maximal projection to which a maximal category, the clitic, is adjoined. So the clitic is not clearly an X^0 incorporated into an X^0, that is a *morphological subword* (differently from T and V, which carry morphological features identifying them as a suffix and a root, respectively). This is the reason why the clitic has to be "removed" in order to permit merger of Σ with 'V-in-AgrS' under adjacency. I propose that enclisis is the outcome of *Local Dislocation merger with inversion* (cf. Embick & Noyer 2001) between the clitic and AgrS.[38] Then Σ undergoes *Local Dislocation merger* with 'V-in-AgrS'.

Local Dislocation merger is an operation that takes place after Linearization applies, converting the hierarchical structure received from Syntax into a linear structure. Therefore at this point (in the absence of syntactic hierarchical structure) the Edge Principle does not apply, being not violated by the inversion operation between clitic and Agr.[39]

In Spanish the pattern of clitic placement represented by Portuguese *Stage III* is not attested. *Stage III* was not reached in Spanish because in this language Σ lost the strong property which induced merger between Σ and V in unmarked main clauses.

It is a well known fact that Proto and Old Romance morphology shows a tendency towards debilitation. The fact that the V-features of Σ become weak in Spanish (as well as in Catalan, French, Italian and Roumanian) is to be seen as part of this general process of morphological debilitation. Because there is no merging between Σ and V in Modern Spanish, enclisis is not derived. On the other hand, in minimal unmarked answers to *yes/no* questions Σ has to have lexical content; once the verb does not merge with Σ it cannot fulfill this role.

It is the former adverbial *sí* 'yes', which optionally co-occurred with the verb in affirmative replies to *yes/no* questions, that takes the role of 'lexical-filler' of Σ. The structures associated with the proposed change are given below (V_S = strong V-features; V_W = weak V-features).

(38) Affirmative replies to *yes/no* questions in Old Spanish:

$$\text{(sí)} \; [_{\Sigma P}\ \Sigma\ [_{AgrSP}\ \text{AgrS}\ [_{TP}\ \text{T}\ [_{AgrO}\ \text{AgrO}\ [_{VP}\ \text{V}$$
$$+V_S \quad +V_S \quad +V_S \quad +V_S \qquad [V_{root}\text{-AgrO-T-AgrS-}\Sigma]$$
$$\uparrow \quad \uparrow \quad \uparrow \quad \uparrow \; \rule{4em}{0.4pt} \lrcorner$$

(39) Affirmative replies to *yes/no* questions in Modern Spanish:

$$[_{\Sigma P}\ \text{sí}\ [_{AgrSP}\ \text{AgrS}\ [_{TP}\ \text{T}\ [_{AgrO}\ \text{AgrO}\ [_{VP}\ \text{V}$$
$$+V_W \; +V_S \quad +V_S \quad +V_S \qquad [V_{root}\text{-AgrO-T-AgrS-}\Sigma]$$
$$\uparrow \quad \uparrow \quad \uparrow \; \rule{4em}{0.4pt} \lrcorner$$

The reanalysis of *sí* as a Σ-head may in fact have triggered the change which resulted in the loosening of the relation between V and Σ, with the consequence that these heads ceased to merge together (i.e. the V-features of Σ became weak).[40] Besides the loss of the pattern of 'bare verb' minimal answer to *yes/no* questions, other instances of VP-ellipsis became ungrammatical in Modern Spanish as well since the null VP in the VP-ellipsis construction is only licensed by strong Σ (just as a null subject is licensed by a strong Agr-head).

5. Conclusion

A comparative approach to the syntax of two neighbouring languages of the Romance familiy, Portuguese and Spanish, shows how their historical development resulted in syntactic splitting in some respects. While in the medieval and early Renaissance period Portuguese and Spanish are alike with regard to clitic placement and share a similar way of answering to *yes/no* questions (which directly relates to the availability/unavailability of VP-ellipsis), Modern Portuguese and Modern Spanish group apart with regard to such properties. The two changing features taken under scrutiny (which were nevertheless interpreted as distinct manifestations of an identical syntactic change at a more abstract level) illustrate a 'divergence' pattern which is expected to reappear in a larger picture (still to be assembled). A better knowledge of the extent of the syntactic unity between Portuguese and Spanish at earlier times will be needed to fully understand how a 'Spanish of Portugal' emerged in a diglossic context at the late Middle Ages. Under the view that this variety of Spanish resulted largely from a relexification of Portuguese, it comes as no surprise that the

15th and 16th centuries Spanish-Portuguese diglossia did not have any visible impact in the ensuing historical development of Portuguese syntax.

6. Appendix

(40) a. *el rey dio**les** fideles*
the king gave-**them** judges
'The King appointed judges to decide the result of the competition between them.'
(Spanish. Twelfth century. Menéndez Pidal 1946: 1159 (line 3593))

b. *El rey **lo** ha uedado*
the king **it** has forbiden
'The King forbade it.'
(Spanish. Twelfth century. Menéndez Pidal 1946: 910 (line 42))

(41) a. *e mando**las** fenchir de arena*
and (he-)sent-**them** fill of sand
'And he sent to fill them with sand.'
(Spanish. Fourteenth century. Menéndez-Pidal 1965: 325)

b. *e **le** desamo de allj adelante*
and **him** (he-)disliked from then on
'And from that moment he despised him.'
(Spanish. Fourteenth century. Menéndez-Pidal 1965: 324)

(42) a. *y acabada su habla respondió**le***
and finished his speech (she-)anwered-**him**
'Once he finished what he had to say, she anwered him.'
(Spanish. 15th century. Gili-Gaya 1950: 155)

b. *en el fin de su habla **me** desesperó*
at the end of his speech **me** (he-)tormented
'After he spoke, I was driven to despair.'
(Spanish. 15th century. Gili-Gaya 1950: 137)

(43) *otro en la noche fue**se** el Duque con su gente, e yo con ellos (...)*
the-other(-day) in the night left-**himself** the duke with his people and I with them (...)
*y otro día de mañana **nos** hecimos a la vela*
and other day in morning **ourselves** went on the sail
'The next day at night the duke left with his people and I went with them (...) and the next day morning we set sail.'
(Spanish. 16th century. Keniston 1937: 94)

(44) a. *E a donzela foi-**se** e deu àgua à rainha*
and the damsel went-**herself** and gave water to-the queen
'And the damsel left and brought some water to the queen.'
(Portuguese. Thirteenth century. Piel and Mattoso 1980: 23)

b. *E a donzela **lhe** disse entom que achara um mouro doente*
and the damsel **him** said then that (she-)had-met a Muslim sick
'And the damsel told him that she had met a sick Muslim.'
(Portuguese. Thirteenth century. Piel and Mattoso 1980: 28)

(45) a. *E elle outorgou**lho***
and he conceded-**him-it**
'And he conceded it to him.'
(Portuguese. Fourteenthth century. Cintra 1954: 36)

b. *E Rotas **lho** outorgou*
and Rotas **him-it** conceded
'And he conceded it to him.'
(Portuguese. Fourteenth century. Cintra 1954: 36)

(46) a. *E a aguia feze-**o** assy*
and the eagle did-**it** so
'And the eagle did it that way.'
(Portuguese. 15th century. Cf. Huber 1933: 179)

b. *E o asno **lhe** deu dous couces*
and the donkey **him** gave two kicks
'And the donkey gave him two kicks.'
(Portuguese. 15th century. Cf. Huber 1933: 179)

(47) a. *de quem quer que sobre elles algũ embargo ou Inpedimento **lhes** poser*
from who.ever that over them some obstruction or constraint **them** puts
'[protecting the renters] from whoever tries to block them [the lands] from them'
(Portuguese. Year 1544. Martins 2001: 561)

b. *de quem quer que **lhe** sobre elle (...) algũu embarguo ou empedymento puser*
from who.ever that **him** over it some obstruction or constraint puts
'[keeping him free] from whoever tries to block it [the land] from him'
(Portuguese. Year 1540. Martins 2001: 556)

(48) a. *E si él mejor* **lo** *faze*
and if he better **it** does
'And if he does it better.'
(Spanish. Fourteenth century. Cf. Rivero 1997: 171)

b. *si* **las** *omne faze a entençion que dios sea ende seruido*
if **them** man does with intention that god be of-it served
'If people do it in order to serve God.'
(Spanish. Fourteenth century. Cf. Chenery 1905: 116)

(49) *E sempre* **m'** *eu mal acharei*
and always **myself** I bad will-feel
'And I will always feel myself bad.'
(Portuguese. Thirteenth/fourteenth century. Lapa 1965: 155 (text 93))

(50) *¡Ya nunca* **vos** *yo mas veré!*
already never **you**-ACC I more will-see
'I will never see you again.'
(Spanish. Fourteenth century. Cf. Chenery 1905: 123)

(51) *Asi* **les** *Dios aluengue los dias de las vidas*
so **them**-DAT God extends the days of the lives
'May God extend their lives.'
(Spanish. Fourteenth century. Cf. Chenery 1905: 123)

Notes

* The research reported here was partially funded by the Collaborative Center on Multilingualism – 538 – Sonderforschungsbereich Mehrsprachigkeit (University of Hamburg) and by FCT – *Fundação para a Ciência e a Tecnologia* through the European Community programme POSI. I wish to acknowledge the Collaborative Center on Multilingualism for the very stimulating research environment that I was offered during my stay in the Center in October 2001. FCT provided the financial support that enabled me to attend *Going Romance 2001* where part of this research was presented. Last but not least, thanks are due to the two anonymous reviewers who commented on this paper.

1. I follow here creolists in taking the terms *substrate* and *superstrate* to reflect the power relationships among groups in contact. As for the different uses of the terms *substrate* and *superstrate* in creole studies and in historical linguistics, see Goodman (1964), among others.

2. Cf. the original French text by Teyssier (1959: 379–380): "Ceux-ci [tous les Portugais d'expression castillane] l'utilisent [l'infinitif conjugué] sans la moindre gêne ni le moindre repentir, comme s'il s'agissait d'un tour normal. Et nous voyons par là, sur un cas précis, comment s'était constitué ce castillan du Portugal que nous sommes en train de décrire: ce

rameau sorti du tronc hispanique avait au début du XVIe siècle son originalité, sa vie à part, et déjà ses traditions".

3. Spanish-Portuguese diglossia extends into the seventeenth century, not only while the kings of Spain (Philipe I, Philipe II, Philipe III) rule over Portugal (from 1581 to 1640) but even afterwards, reaching the eighteenth century. The Spanish of seventeenth century Portuguese authors however seems to be just standard Spanish, not the former variety of Spanish. See Castro (forthcoming).

4. I leave the issue of phonological cliticization out of the scope of this paper. Thus I use the terms 'enclisis' and 'proclisis' in a purely distributional vein to refer to the position of the clitic in relation to the verb.

5. With futur and conditional forms of the verb mesoclisis can be found in medieval and early Renaissance Portuguese and Spanish as well as in Modern Portuguese. "Mesoclisis" terms the situation in which a clitic is placed inside a morphological word, namely a verb, surfacing in between the verbal root and the inflectional suffixes (T+Agr). Mesoclisis is a particular instance of enclisis with the clitic leaning on the verbal root. Therefore, mesoclisis is found in the same type of clauses where enclisis arises; it is allowed in Modern Portuguese but not in Modern Spanish because only in Portuguese enclisis in finite clauses persisted.

6. *Marked main clauses* which like subordinate clauses induce obligatory proclisis will be considered in Section 2.2.

7. As for twelfth century Portuguese, the written sources are too scarce to permit the intended exemplification.

8. The set of texts from which the sentences are taken is listed below, in chronological order:[Portuguese texts] *Livro Velho de Linhagens*; *Crónica Geral de Espanha de 1344*; *O Livro de Esopo*; *Cartas de Afonso de Albuquerque*; [Spanish texts] *Cantar de Mio Cid*; *Primera Crónica General de España*; *Crónica de Castilla*; Diego de San Pedro, *Cárcel de Amor*; Afonso Enríquez de Guzmán, *Libro de la Vida y Costumbres.*

9. The constraint against placing clitics in first position is known by the name of *Tobler-Mussafia* (see Mussafia 1886; Tobler 1875, 1889; Meyer-Lübke 1897). In thirteenth and fourteenth century Portuguese, the Tobler-Mussafia constraint excludes clitics not only from the absolute sentential left-periphery but also from the immediate first position after a Left Dislocated constituent, a clausal adjunct (namely an adverbial clause), or a coordinate conjunction. In the 15th century, however, the interdition against placing clitics sentence initially appears to be restricted to the absolute sentence-peripheral position. From the second half of the fourteenth century, clitics can be attested following a coordinate conjunction. In the next century clitics are also found following a left adjoined adverbial clause or a Left Dislocated phrase. Similar facts (with variable chronology) are attested in the other Romance languages – see Labelle and Hirschbühler (2002). Whatever the nature of the Tobler-Mussafia constraint is (be it syntactically or prosodically motivated), I take these facts to show that there was a weakening of this constraint at some point in the medieval period, instead of three near simultaneous changes affecting the syntax of coordinate structures, the syntax of complex sentences integrating adverbial clauses, and the syntax of Clitic Left Dislocation structures – but see Benincà (1995) for a different view.

10. The variable pattern of clitic placement observed in unmarked main clauses in most medieval Romance languages has been motivated in prosodic, syntactic, and semantic terms. Although much extensively debated the issue is not settled, the current investigation on this topic being far from leading to some consensual result.

11. Some apparent exceptions to the regular proclitic pattern of subordinate clauses can be found in particular contexts. Complement clauses selected by declarative verbs, for example, may allow enclisis (see Martins 1994b: 98–102). Torrego and Uriagereka (1993), however, claim on independent grounds that these are instances of *parataxis* not 'true' subordination (i.e. *hypotaxis*). On the other hand, enclisis appears to be also attested in coordinate structures within embedded domains – relevant examples are found not only in Old Portuguese and Old Spanish but in other Old Romance languages, as pointed out for Old French by Labelle and Hirschbühler (2002). Since in the medieval texts punctuation does not signal syntactic boundaries in the way it does in contemporary texts, the level at which coordination applies is not always easily identified. Still we will possibly be left with a handful of clear examples of enclisis in clauses involving coordination below CP.

12. In Portuguese, interpolation remains fairly productive in the 16th century while in Spanish interpolation is well attested up to the 15th century but rare afterwards. A few examples of residual interpolation in 16th century Spanish prose are given by Keniston (1937: 101).

13. The sentence in (10) is found in Rivero (1991: 244). I quote from Menéndez Pidal (1919) because the example is incorrectly dated in Rivero (1991).

14. In Focus-movement configurations, the focused constituent is not 'information' focus associated with new information but rather identificational focus associated with an exhaustive and exclusive reading.

15. Cf. Lesman (1980: 95): "Proclisis is the norm in the 16th century when the subject, the direct or indirect object (...), or an adverbial clause (...) precede the verb, but there is always the possibility of enclisis, triggered by a variety of factors. In the seventeenth century proclisis dominates in these sentences, with just very few exceptions".

16. See http://www.clul.ul.pt/sectores/cordialsin/projecto_cordialsin.html. The project CORDIAL-SIN has been funded by *Fundação para a Ciência e a Tecnologia* through the European Community programmes PRAXIS XXI and POSI (PRAXIS/P/PLP/13046/1998; POSI/PLP/33275/1999).

17. Some contemporary Portuguese dialects still allow interpolation; it differs from medieval and early Renaissance interpolation, however, as only heads (not XPs) can be interpolated.

18. In fact *Stage III* emerges in Portuguese already in the seventeenth century but at the time the large majority of authors/texts still reflect the *Stage II* grammar. See Martins (1994b) for details.

19. The values for proclisis and enclisis given in Table 2 refer to clitic placement in unmarked main clauses. Since focused phrases are difficult to identify in the written sources, however, I admit that some of the percentage of proclisis obtained for each one of the authors represented in Table 2 comes from clauses introduced by focused phrases (i.e. a proclisis trigger). The relevant emphatic/identificational focus-construction appears to be more productive until the 18th/19th centuries than it is nowadays.

20. See Pato (1884: 1–21, 65–90).

21. See Góis (1566: 1–50).

22. See Pinto (1614: 1–60).

23. See Couto (1616: 1–57).

24. See Lapa (1937: 1–52).

25. See Vieira (1679–1784 vol. 1: 87–142, 365–447, 1039–1118; vol. 2: 1–26, 309–345; vol. 4: 210–247; 491–549; vol. 7: 305–332; vol. 15: 1–47).

26. See Verney (1746: 17–81).

27. See Garrett (1938).

28. See Martins (1885: 1–50).

29. Cf. Laka (1990: 86): "I argue here that, similarly to the way in which the head **Neg** can head its own functional projection (...), there is also a X^0 **Aff**, which projects an Affirmation Phrase. These two heads (Neg and Aff) are further argued to belong in the same syntactic category, which I will call Σ. Thus, both NegP and AffP are claimed to be different instantiations of a more abstract projection: the Σ Phrase".

30. "A category that does not project any further is a maximal projection XP, and one that is not a projection at all is a minimal projection X^{min}; any other is an X', invisible at the interface and for computation. As we proceed, I will qualify the conclusion somewhat for X^0 categories, which have a very special role" (Chomsky 1995: 242–243). "A consequence is that an item can be both an X^0 and an XP. Does this cause problems? Are there examples that illustrate this possibility? I see no particular problems, and one case comes to mind as a possible illustration: clitics. Under the DP hypothesis, clitics are Ds. Assume further that a clitic raises from its θ–position and attaches to an inflectional head. In its θ–position, the clitic is an XP; attachment to a head requires that it be an X^0 (on fairly standard assumptions)" (Chomsky 1995: 249).

31. Cf. Raposo (2000: 290–291): "Clitics cannot appear embedded in a functional category that contains them. This is explicitly formulated in the following principle, which I take to be a primitive of the morphological component of UG: (...) *The Edge Principle* [:] A clitic occurs at the structural edge of a head H that contains it".

32. This selectional property of AgrS varies parametrically across languages and when available is optional.

33. Cf. Raposo (2000: 289–291) for a clarification of why, given the Edge Principle, a (functional) head with an incorporated clitic is frozen in place.

34. Therefore in subordinate clauses $[_{AgrS}$V,T,AgrS$]$ does not move into Σ.

35. Maybe Spec,AgrSP is still ocasionally available for the clitic (when it is not taken by the subject). This would explain why enclisis, although sparsely attested, is not totally absent from non-V1 structures during *Stage II*.

36. As for Modern Spanish, it is irrelevant whether AgrS selects a Spec position. Within the approach that I am proposing here the fact that enclisis is not a grammatical option in finite clauses in Spanish is independently motivated. An anonymous reviewer suggests that Modern Portuguese and Modern Spanish should be similar with respect to the EPP

properties of AgrS because they are both null subject languages. I consider that the licensing of null subjects does not depend on the availability of the Spec of AgrS position. Space considerations, however, preclude me from going into the arguments which support this view. See Alexiadou and Anagnostopoulou (1998) on this matter.

37. An anonymous reviewer notes that the analysis proposed in this paper derives in different ways Old Portuguese and Modern Portuguese enclisis (in finite clauses). I think this is a welcome result because Old Portuguese enclisis and Modern Portuguese enclisis are in fact dissimilar, even though many authors have thought differently (cf. Barbosa 1993, 1996, 2000; Benincà 1995; Galves 1997, 2000; Salvi 1990, 1991, 1993, 1997, among others). It is worth to stress, with respect to the relevant type of clauses, that Modern Portuguese enclisis is obligatory while Old Portuguese enclisis is optional, displaying variation with proclisis. See Martins (forthcoming a).

38. Brazilian Portuguese contrasts with European Portuguese in that this inversion operation does not take place. So Brazilian Portuguese displays generalized proclisis although Σ bears a strong V-feature in Brazilian Portuguese, as shown by the fact that VP-ellipsis is a grammatical option. I interpret these facts as indicating that clitics in Brazilian Portuguese are verbal prefixes adjoined to the Vroot; therefore clitics in Brazilian Portuguese do not block the adjacency between Σ and V that morphological merger requires. (Cf. the account given by Embick and Noyer (2001:590) of the contrast between constituent negation and prefixal negation in relation to *do*-support.)

39. Using as a diagnosis test the position of adverbs, Costa (1998) proposes that in contemporary European Portuguese the verb does not move beyond T. The analysis presented in this paper to account for enclisis in Modern European Portuguese can be harmonized with Costa's proposal. Admitting that the verb stays in T in contemporary European Portuguese, enclisis would be derived following morphological Lowering of both clitic and AgrS to T (cf. Costa 2001). There are some complications to this picture though, and I will not be able to go into details here.

40. Spanish *sí* 'yes'can express emphatic affirmation in declarative sentences whereas Portuguese *sim* 'yes' cannot. Consider the translation of the emphatic affirmative statement: *She* DID *come*. In Spanish one can say *Ella sí vino*, but in Portuguese **Ela sim veio* is ungrammatical. This contrast shows that Spanish *sí* is a Σ-head whereas Portuguese *sim* is not.

References

Alexiadou, A. & Anagnostopoulou, E. (1998). Parametrizing AGR: Word Order, V-movement and EPP-checking. *Natural Language and Linguistic Theory, 16*, 491–539.

Barry, A. K. (1987). Clitic pronoun position in thirteenth century Spanish. *The Hispanic Review, 55*, 213–220.

Barbosa, P. (1993). Clitic Placement in Old Romance and European Portuguese. *Papers from the Twenty-Ninth Regional Meeting of the Chicago Linguistic Society*. Chicago: Chicago University Press.

Barbosa, P. (1996). Clitic Placement in European Portuguese and the position of Subjects. In A. L. Halpern & A. M. Zwicky (Eds.), *Second Position Clitics and Related Phenomena* (pp. 1–40). Stanford, CA: CSLI Publications.

Barbosa, P. (2000). Clitics: A Window into the Null Subject Property. In J. Costa (Ed.), *Portuguese Syntax: New Comparative Studies* (pp. 31–93). Oxford and New York: Oxford University Press.

Benincà, P. (1995). Complement clitics in Medieval Romance: the Tobler-Mussafia Law. In A. Battye & I. Roberts (Eds.), *Clause Structure and Language Change* (pp. 325–344). New York and Oxford: Oxford Universiry Press.

Bobaljik, J. D. (1995). Morphosyntax: On the syntax of verbal inflection. Ph.D. Dissertation. Cambridge, MA: Massachusetts Institute of Technology.

Boškovic, Z. (1996). Selection and the categorial status of infinitival complements. *Natural Language and Linguistic Theory, 14*, 269–304.

Boškovic, Z. (1997). *The Syntax of Nonfinite Complementation: An Economy Approach.* Cambridge, MA and London: MIT Press.

Boškovic, Z. (1999). On multiple feature checking: multiple wh- fronting and multiple head movement. In S. D. Epstein & N. Hornstein (Eds.), *Working Minimalism* (pp. 159–187). Cambridge, MA and London: MIT Press.

Castro, I. (forthcoming). Sur le bilinguisme littéraire castillan-portugais. *Arquivos do Centro Cultural Português.* Paris: Fundação Calouste Gulbenkian.

Cejador y Frauca, J. (1913). *Fernando de Rojas, La Celestina.* Madrid: Clasicos Castellanos – Ediciones de La Lectura.

Chenery, W. H. (1905). Object-pronouns in dependent clauses: A study in Old Spanish word-order. *Publications of the Modern Language Association of America, 20*, 1–151.

Chomsky, N. (1994). Bare phrase structure. *MIT Occasional Papers in Linguistics.* Reprinted in G. Webelhuth (Ed.), *Government and Binding Theory and the Minimalist Program* (pp. 383–439). Oxford and Cambridge: Blackwell, 1995. [Included in Chomsky, N. 1995.]

Chomsky, N. (1995). *The Minimalist Program.* Cambridge, MA and London: MIT Press.

Chomsky, N. (2000). Minimalist inquiries: The framework. In R. Martin, D. Michaels, & J. Uriagereka (Eds.), *Step by Step: Essays on Minimalist Syntax in Honor of Howard Lasnik* (pp. 89–155). Cambridge, MA and London: MIT Press.

Cintra, L. F. L. (1954). *Crónica Geral de Espanha de 1344: Edição crítica do texto português.* Vol. 2. Lisboa: Imprensa Nacional – Casa da Moeda.

Costa, J. (1998). *Word Order Variation: A constraint-based approach.* The Hague: Holland Academic Graphics.

Costa, J. (2001). Null vs. overt Spec,TP in European Portuguese. Paper delivered at *Going Romance 2001: Fifteenth Symposium on Romance Linguistics, Amsterdam.* To appear in the proceedings.

Couto, D. do (1616). *Da Ásia de Diogo do Couto. Decada Setima. Parte Primeira.* Lisboa: Na Regia Oficina Typografica. 1782.

Embick, D. & Noyer, R. (2001). Movement operations after Syntax. *Linguistic Inquiry, 32*, 555–595.

Galves, C. (1997). Do português clássico ao português europeu moderno: Uma análise minimalista. In R. V. Mattos e Silva (Ed.), *Estudos Lingüísticos e Literários*, 19 (pp. 105–128). Salvador: Universidade Federal da Bahia. [Included in Galves 2001.]

Galves, Charlotte (2001). *Ensaios sobre as Gramáticas do Português*. Campinas, São Paulo: Editora da Unicamp.

Garrett, A. de Almeida (1938). *Doutrinas de Estética Literária*. Lisboa: Textos Literários/Autores Portugueses.

Gifford, D. J. & Hodcroft, F. W. (1959). *Textos Lingüísticos del Medioevo Español*. Oxford: The Dolphin Book.

Gili Gaya, S. (1950). *Diego de San Pedro, Obras*. Madrid.

Góis, D. (1566). *Crónica do Felicíssimo Rei D. Manuel. Parte II*. Coimbra: Acta Universitatis Conimbrigensis, 1953.

Goodman, M. (1964). *A Comparative Study of Creole French Dialects*. The Hague: Mouton.

Grewendorf, G. & Sabel, J. (1999). Scrambling in German and Japanese: Adjunction versus multiple specifiers. *Natural Language and Linguistic Theory, 17*, 1–65.

Hale, W. G. & Buck, C. D. (1903). *A Latin Grammar* (Alabama Linguistic and Philosophical Series, 8). University of Alabama Press, 1987 (fifth reprinting).

Halle, M. & Marantz, A. (1993). Distributed Morphology and the pieces of inflexion. In K. Hale & S. J. Keyser (Eds.), *The View from Building 20: Essays in Linguistics in Honor of Sylvain Bromberger* (pp. 111–176). Cambridge, MA and London: MIT Press.

Harley, H. & Noyer, R. (1999). Distributed Morphology. *Glot International, 4* (4), 3–9.

Huber, J. (1933). *Gramática do Português Antigo*. Lisboa: Fundação Calouste Gulbenkian, 1986.

Kayne, R. (1991). Romance clitics, Verb movement, and PRO. *Linguistic Inquiry, 22*, 647–686.

Keniston, H. (1937). *The Syntax of Castillian Prose: The Sixteenth Century*. Chicago and Illinois: The University of Chicago Press.

Labelle, M. & Hirschbühler, P. (2002). Changes in clausal organization and the position of clitics in Old French. Paper delivered at *VII Diachronic Generative Syntax Conference, Girona*. To appear in the proceedings.

Laka, I. (1990). Negation in Syntax: On the Nature of Functional Categories and Projections. Ph.D. Dissertation. Cambridge, MA: Massachusetts Institute of Technology.

Lapa, M. R. (1937). *D. Francisco Manuel de Melo, Cartas Familiares*. Lisboa: Livraria Sá da Costa.

Lapa, M. R. (1965). *Cantigas d'Escarnho e de Mal Dizer dos Cancioneiros Medievais Galego-Portugueses*. Vigo: Galaxia.

Lawton, R. A. (1966). La syntaxe des pronoms personnels atones en ancien portugais: La phrase principale à sujet initial et à verbe initial. *Actas do V Colóquio Internacional de Estudos Luso-Brasileiros*. Vol. 3. Coimbra.

Lesman, A. St. Clair (1980). El pronombre Átono en la Prosa Española del Siglo XVII. Ph.D. Dissertation. University of Maryland.

Lobo, Tânia (1996). A sintaxe dos clíticos. In R. V. Mattos e Silva (Ed.), *A Carta de Caminha Testemunho Lingüístico de 1500* (pp. 85–115). Salvador: Editora da Universidade Federal da Bahia.

Lumsden, J. S. (1999). Language acquisition and creolization. In M. DeGraff (Ed.), *Language Creation and Language Change: Creolization, Diachrony and Development* (pp. 29–157). Cambridge, MA and London: MIT Press.

Martins, A. M. (1994a). Enclisis, VP-deletion and the nature of Sigma. *Probus, 6*, 173–205.

Martins, A. M. (1994b). Clíticos na História do Português. Ph.D. dissertation. Faculdade de Letras da Universidade de Lisboa.

Martins, A. M. (2000). A minimalist approach to clitic climbing. In J. Costa (Ed.), *Portuguese Syntax: New Comparative Studies* (pp. 169–190). Oxford and New York: Oxford University Press. [Reprinted, with minor revisions, from: A. M. Martins 1995, same title. In *Papers from the 31st Regional Meeting of the Chicago Linguistic Society*, 215–239.]

Martins, A. M. (2001). *Documentos Portugueses do Noroeste e da Região de Lisboa: Da produção primitiva ao século XVI*. Lisboa: Imprensa Nacional – Casa da Moeda.

Martins, A. M. (2002). The loss of IP-scrambling in Portuguese: Clause structure, word order variation and change. In D. Lightfoot (Ed.), *Syntactic Effects of Morphological Change* (pp. 232–248). Oxford and New York: Oxford University Press.

Martins, A. M. (forthcoming a). Deficient pronouns and linguistic change in Portuguese and Spanish. In J. Schroten (Ed.), *Romance Languages and Linguistic Theory 2001: Selected Papers from 'Going Romance' 2001*. Amsterdam and Philadelphia: John Benjamins.

Martins, A. M. (forthcoming b). VP-ellipsis, clitic placement and scrambling in Romance. Paper delivered at *VII Diachronic Generative Syntax Conference, Girona*. To appear in the proceedings.

Martins, J. P. O. (1885). *História da República Romana*. Vol. 2. Lisboa: Parceria António Maria Pereira, 1919 [3rd edition].

Menéndez-Pidal, R. (1919). *Documentos Lingüísticos de España*. Vol. 1: *Reino de Castilla*. Madrid: Centro de Estudios Históricos, 1929.

Menéndez-Pidal, R. (1946). *Cantar de Mio Cid: Texto, Gramática y Vocabulario*. Vol. 3. Madrid: Espasa-Calpe, 1980.

Menéndez-Pidal, R. (1965). *Crestomatía del Español Medieval*. Madrid: Gredos.

Menéndez Pidal, R. (1978). *Primera Crónica General de España, editada por Ramón Menéndez Pidal con un estudio actualizador de Diego Catalán*. Vol. 1. Madrid: Gredos, 1979.

Meyer-Lübke, W. (1897). Zur Stellung der tonlosen Objektspronomina. *Zeitschrift für romanische Philologie, 21*, 313–334.

Mussafia, A. (1886). Una particolarità sintattica della lingua italiana dei primi secoli. In G. I. Ascoli et al. (Eds.), *Miscellanea di Filologia e Linguistica in Memoria di Napoleone Caix e Ugo Angelo Canello* (pp. 255–261). Firenze: LeMonnier.

Nunes, J. J. (1932). *Cantigas d'Amor dos Trovadores Galego-Portugueses*. Lisboa: Centro do Livro Brasileiro.

Ogando, V. (1980). A colocación do pronome átono en relación co verbo no galego-portugués medieval. *Verba, 7*, 251–282.

Pádua, M. P. C. de (1960). *A Ordem das Palavras no Português Arcaico*. Coimbra: Instituto de Estudos Românicos.

Pato, R. A. B. (1884). *Cartas de Afonso de Albuquerque Seguidas de Documentos que as Elucidam*. Vol. 1. Lisboa: Academia Real das Sciencias de Lisboa.

Piel, J. M. & Mattoso, J. (1980). *Livros Velhos de Linhagens*. Lisboa: Academia das Ciências de Lisboa.

Pinkster, H. (1990). *Latin Syntax and Semantics*. London: Routledge.

Pinto, F. M. (1614). *Peregrinaçam*. Vol. 1. Porto: Portugalense Editora, 1944.

Raposo, E. P. (2000). Clitic positions and Verb movement. In J. Costa (Ed.), *Portuguese Syntax: New Comparative Studies* (pp. 266–297). Oxford and New York: Oxford University Press.

Rivero, M. L. (1991). Clitic and NP climbing in Old Spanish. In H. Campos & F. Martínez-Gil (Eds.), *Current Studies in Spanish Linguistics* (pp. 241–282). Washington, DC: Georgetown University Press.

Rivero, M. L. (1997). On two locations for complement clitic pronouns: Serbo-Croatian, Bulgarian and Old Spanish. In A. van Kemenade & N. Vincent (Eds.), *Parameters of Morphosyntactic Change* (pp. 170–206). Cambridge: Cambridge University Press.

Salvi, G. (1990). La sopravvivenza della legge di Wackernagel nei dialetti occidentali della Peninsola Iberica. *Medioevo Romanzo, 15*, 177–210.

Salvi, G. (1991). Difesa e illustrazione della legge di Wackernagel applicata alle lingue romanze antiche: La pozicione delle forme pronominali clitiche. In *Per Giovan Battista Pellegrini: Scritti degli allievi padovani* (pp. 439–462). Padova: Unipress.

Salvi, Giampolo (1993). Ordine delle parole e struttura della frase nelle lingue romanze antiche. *Alfa, 37*, 187–203.

Salvi, Giampolo (1997). From Latin weak pronouns to Romance clitics. In R. V. Mattos e Silva (Ed.), *Estudos Lingüísticos e Literários*, 19 (pp. 85–104). Salvador: Universidade Federal da Bahia.

Silva, R. V. M. e (1989). *Estruturas Trecentistas: Elementos para uma Gramática do Português Arcaico*. Lisboa: Imprensa Nacional – Casa da Moeda.

Teyssier, P. (1959). *La Langue de Gil Vicente*. Paris: Klincksieck.

Thráinsson, H. (1996). On the (non-)universality of functional categories. In W. Abrahams, S. D. Epstein, H.Thráinsson, & C. J.-W. Zwart (Eds.), *Minimal Ideas: Syntactic Studies in the Minimalist Framework* (pp. 253–281). Amsterdam and Philadelphia: John Benjamins.

Tobler, A. (1875). Review of J. Le Coultre, De L'ordre des mots dans Chrétien de Troyes. *Göttingische Gelehrte Anzeigen, Stück, 34*, 1057–1082. Reprinted in *Vermischte Beiträge zur Französischen Grammatik, 5*, 1902 and 1971 [Amsterdam: Rodopi].

Tobler, A. (1889). Pronominales Objekt zu Infinitiv oder Partizipium. *Zeitschrift für romanische Philologie, 13*, 186–191. Reprinted in *Vermischte Beiträge zur Französischen Grammatik*, 2, 1902 and 1971 [Amsterdam: Rodopi].

Torrego, E. & Uriagereka, J. (1993). Indicative dependents. Ms. University of Massachusetts at Boston and University of Maryland at College Park.

Verney, L. A. (1746). *Verdadeiro Método de Estudar*. Vol. 1: *Estudos Linguísticos*. Lisboa: Livraria Sá da Costa, 1949.

Vieira, A. (1679–1784). *Sermões* [Editio Princeps]. 15 volumes. Lisboa.

Woodcock, E. C. (1959). *A New Latin Syntax*. Cambridge: Harvard University Press.

Sardinian between maintenance and change

Rosita Rindler Schjerve
Vienna

1. Preliminary considerations

Focusing on multilingualism in European language history necessarily involves the investigation of smaller and socially non-dominant languages which have extensively been under the socio-cultural hegemony of larger national or state languages in many parts of Europe. The formation of European nation-states generally went along with the enforcement of linguistic homogeneity upon all citizens. As a consequence, smaller speech communities, located mostly at the peripheries of the state, assimilated into the larger national context; where they did not do so, they turned into ethnic minorities who were considered as deviating from the linguistic main-stream norms (cf. Heckmann 1992). These minorities were forced into bilingualism if they wanted to or had to communicate in state-controlled domains such as education, administration, military service or the judiciary.

It goes without saying that aspects of multilingualism as they arise from the asymmetrical relationship between socio-linguistically dominant majorities and their subordinate minorities result in varying status-ascriptions to the languages (high vs. low ranking) and, consequently, in varying degrees of their functional stability. In these conditions, low language status normally interacts with restricted and, hence, with recessive language use. Multilingualism of this kind thus generally relates to aspects of language shift and change.

Language shift indicates that the social compartmentalisation of bilingual language use becomes unstable, since one language, i.e. the dominant or state-language, is being increasingly used in domains where it did not apply formerly. Hence, language shift means that the use of the socially dominant language in the context of multilingual state-nations extends to and overlaps with communication domains that were previously restricted to the subordinate language.

The use of subordinate languages usually refers to informal domains in general, and to the family, which predominantly provides for the production and reproduction of the ethnic minority language in particular (cf. Nelde, Strubell, & Williams 1996). Thus, the expansion of the dominant language to these domains generally goes hand in hand with the reduction and, consequently, with the sociolinguistic disintegration of the minority language.

In most cases, language shift is a long term process which can last for several decades while the recessive language, although it is undergoing structural changes, still remains in place. This means that as long as the shift is not completed, aspects of linguistic change and disintegration interact with aspects of maintenance (Dorian (Ed.) 1989). In these contexts, the various stages of shift are generally accompanied by the structural rearrangement of the recessive language which is very often remodelled after the dominant majority language without, however, losing its linguistic and socio-pragmatic autonomy. This is the reason why in most minority languages which can be considered recessive but not dying it often appears difficult to grasp the rearrangements observed in clear-cut terms of language decay and attrition. This task is further complicated by the fact that, at the same time, this remodelling may also show signs of innovation and vitality on the part of the recessive language (cf. i.e. Gal 1989; Hamp 1989).

The phenomenon described above characterizes what is actually happening to Sardinian, which is a recessive but by no means obsolete minority language in contact with Italian. In the following chapters, we will pursue the goal of finding out how the obviously paradox dynamics of maintenance and change actually works in this language, which is the largest minority language in Italy and which has only recently been recognized as such by the Italian state (cf. Legge 15 Dicembre 1999: N. 482). In a first step, we will give a brief account of Sardinian as a Romance language in historical contact with other languages and, in particular, as a recessive minority language in contact with Italian. Here, we will refer primarily to the results of diglossia and language shift in Sardinia which have been elaborated in a first stage of our long-term case study on language contact in Sardinia (cf. Rindler Schjerve 1987). In a second and main step, we will then focus upon the preliminary results of our more recent project on mixed bilingual Sardinian-Italian speech (cf. Rindler Schjerve 1996–2002) in order to find out in how far Sardinian is actually converging with Italian and to what extent the structural integrity of Sardinian is being maintained or lost at present. From this perspective, we will finally attempt to draw tentative conclusions about the ultimate survival of this language.

2. Language contact through the ages

Throughout history, Sardinian has undergone various stages of contact and of foreign influence exercised by dominating powers such as the ancient Romans and in turn the Byzantines who reigned Sardinia in the first centuries AC.[1] In the 11th century, after a period of Sardinian autonomy which went along with the political formation of the souvereign *judicatos*, Genovese and Pisan forces established their control over the island and its population until the 14th century,[2] when finally Catalans occupied Sardinia. After the unification of Aragon and Castillia, Catalan domination subsequently changed into Spanish dominance, which was officially upheld until the 18th century (cf. Blasco Ferrer 1984: 140–162; Wagner 2002: 149–186). After 1718 when Sardinia became an integrative part of the Piemontese reign (*Regnum Sardinae*), Italian began to replace Spanish, although the latter language continued to be the *de facto* official language until well into the 19th century (cf. Blasco Ferrer 1984: 167–169, 1988: 888–890; Wagner 1951, 2002: 187–203). In 1827, the autochthonous legislation of the *Carta de Logu* (1395) was abolished, which dated from the time of the medieval *judicatos* and had been the symbol of Sardinian socio-cultural autonomy vis a vis the changing foreign dominations throughout the centuries. The abolition of this legislation was associated with the final breakdown of ethno-political autonomy and of resistance against foreign hegemony and influence.

After 1861 when the *Regnum Sardiniae* was officially integrated into the larger Italian Reign, Sardinians gradually started to assimilate into the cultural and linguistic paradigm of the Italian nation-state. As a consequence, Italian was extended as an official means of communication within domains of administration and education. Until the middle of the 20th century, the use of Italian as a national state language concentrated on urban centres. Only from the 1950s when the state started to integrate Sardinia into its national programmes of compulsory schooling, did Italian slowly begin to spread into rural areas. At the end of the 1960s, the shift from Sardinian to Italian became obvious since, by and by, rural families had begun to use Italian as a primary means of socialisation (cf. Blasco Ferrer 1988: 890–892; Rindler Schjerve 1993, 1997c, 2003a).

In the wake of the regionalist movements of the 1970s, Neosardinian autonomist forces started to struggle for cultural and linguistic autonomy, putting forward their claims for the official acknowledgement of Sardinian as a minority language within the Italian state. Several legal drafts and bills were developed in which the regional council was called upon to take steps towards Sardinization and the recognition of legal equality between Sardinian and Italian. It was also requested to revise the autonomy statute of Sardinia in order to cater for the official recognition of the Sardinian language and the introduction of bilingualism on the island (cf. Rindler Schjerve 1987: 15–78, 1993, 1997c).

Under the pressure created by a resolution of the Council of Europe on the protection of minorities, the Italian government appointed a committee for investigating the issue in 1982. In 1993, a law providing for the promotion of Sardinian within the regional administration and education was put to the vote by the regional council. But it was only in 1998, after Italy had ratified the European framework convention for the protection of national minorities (cf. Frame Work Convention), that Sardinian was officially recognised as a minority language within the Italian state. It now remains a responsibility of the state to realise this recognition in terms of the safeguard and the promotion of Sardinian (cf. Legge).

3. Sardinian as a Romance language

With some 1,6 million speakers,[3] Sardinian is the largest minority language in Italy. Sardinians form an ethnic minority since they show a strong awareness of being an indigenous group with a language and a culture of their own. Although Sardinian appears to be recessive in use it is still spoken and understood by a majority of the population on the island.

From a linguistic point of view, Sardinian is an autonomous Romance language which consists of different spoken varieties that can be defined in the larger koines of *Logudorese*, which is spoken in the northern part of the island, and of *Campidanese* in the south. Yet, it is uncertain whether the two northernmost dialects, *Sassarese* and *Gallurese* should be conceived of as Sardinian or rather as Italian dialects.[4]

Since the late Middle Ages, the collective knowledge of an autonomous Sardinian culture had primarily been transmitted and shaped by oral discourse. Due to the activities of the judicial chambers (*judicatos*), however, a variety of writing was gradually established which was exemplified in documents (*condaghes*), minutes, statutes, decrees, and family chronicles. These text types, of which the *Carta de Logu* forms a prominent example, result from the institutional structures characterising these times, and reflect the actions and interest of a growing urban bourgeoisie and of a clergy with expanding influence and power (cf. Rindler Schjerve 2003a).

Early written signs of meta-discoursive reflexions can also be found in the scarce Sardinian poetry of the 16th and 18th century (cf. Alziator 1954; Sanna 1957). These reflexions should in turn be continued in the grammars and dictionaries on Sardinian (cf. Sanna 1957). In the 19th and 20th century, Sardinian was furthermore the focus of linguistic debates with reference to the newly established Romance studies (cf. Wagner 1951, 1960–1964). Despite intensive efforts for accomplishing a unified orthographical norm, which has been discussed in connection with the "*Questione della lingua sarda*"[5] since the 1970s, however, Sardinian has presently remained a language which is only partly codified and has not yet elaborated a generally accepted written norm (vgl. Bolognesi & Helsloot 1999; Rindler Schjerve 1991b, 1993: 274–278; Rindler Schjerve 1997c).

4. Aspects of language shift

In the course of the last decades, the longstanding bilingual diglossia[6] of Sardinian and Italian has become unstable. The ongoing language shift in Sardinia has been subject to different studies which focused on the functional distribution of Sardinian and Italian in small towns and villages on the island (cf. Mercurio Gregorini 1980; Sole 1988). Furthermore, comprehensive research concentrating on the macro- and micro-structural aspects of the functional asymmetry of the two languages in contact (cf. Rindler Schjerve 1987) indicates that in the last two decades, Sardinian has become a socially recessive language which suffers from the dominance of Italian although it is by no means obsolete. Empirical studies conducted in the 1980s show that the shift to Italian had been progressing from the beginning of the 1970s when, even in rural areas which had resisted language shift so far, Italian was increasingly adopted as a primary means of socialisation within Sardinian families. The results obtained suggest that women tend to use Italian more frequently than men and that younger speakers are using it increasingly in the private domains; moreover, it appears that Sardinian has continuously been pushed into the lower social and educational strata. Although an obvious tendency towards shift was noted, the assimilation of Italian in rural areas appeared to be slowed down by factors such as closed social networks, low education rates, male language behaviour and higher age rates (cf. Rindler Schjerve 1987: 120–289). The results obtained in micro-sociolinguistic investigation of language shift in rural families showed that young women used more Sardinian within their socially restricted Sardophone networks than they would admit, despite their claims of speaking predominantly Italian. Although young women had shifted to Italian in the education of their children, they still used Sardinian nearly as often as men or as older speakers since they had to comply with the norms within the Sardophone network. Here, the pressure of network membership and group solidarity imposed the use of the ethnic language on the speaker. Case studies focusing on Sardophone families which had shifted to Italian as a primary means of socialization have shown that there is an enormous potential for conflict in these families as they respond to the pressure of assimilation into Italian (cf. Rindler Schjerve 1987:223–289).

This strand of research, which was based on predominantly variationist hypotheses (cf. Rindler Schjerve 1991a), suggests that the sociolinguistic maintenance of the threatened minority language was being achieved at the costs of a growing number of structural changes. The lexicon of spoken Sardinian was undergoing comprehensive relexification from Italian; concurrently, certain areas of syntax seemed to be remodelled on the basis of Italian, whereas morphology and phonology appeared to be more resistant to the Italian influence (Rindler Schjerve 1987:290–328). It turned out, however, that it was not possible to capture the Sardinian remodelling along parameters of Italian with purely variationist parameters (age grading, sex, schooling, social class) and that, in order to explain the current restructuring process, it was necessary to integrate detailed micro-structural analyses of actual speech performance in this language pair.

5. Codeswitching as an indicator for maintenance and shift

Since in informal everyday communication Sardinian and Italian do not figure as two entirely separate codes, conversations and, in particular, conversations conducted in Sardinian, appear to be rather mixed as far as discursive, lexical and, to a lesser degree, grammatical structure is concerned. The reasons for these mixed bilingual performances may firstly be seen in the close typological affinity between the two languages, and secondly in the fact that these two languages are relatively neutral in contexts of informal use and are not associated with a politically polarized interethnic conflict.[7] Finally, a third reason may be that bilingualism in Sardinia is so widespread nowadays that there are hardly any speakers who are not also fluent in Italian. These factors might also explain why conversation in Sardinian is generally characterised by patterns of intensive code-switching among which the intrasentential type is of particular relevance. While it appears that conversations conducted in Italian show a certain degree of codeswitching (CS) as well, Italian, however, appears to be far lesser affected in structure by the interference of Sardinian than vice versa (cf. Rindler Schjerve 1987: 329–345).

Yet, it cannot be ignored that at present many young speakers, who have frequently been brought up in Italian, have a restricted active or even a merely passive command of their ethnic language. This lack of active command is generally reflected in deficient or restricted use of Sardinian and in patterns of CS that are particularly characteristic of this restricted use.

At present, Sardinian is still a viable language, although at the same time it cannot be ignored that it is actually undergoing a process of asymmetrical restructuring which appears to be intimately associated with patterns of CS. Since switching is a salient feature of everyday bilingual conversations, we have assumed that there has been a close relationship between the ongoing restructuring and these switching patterns.

In general, CS occurs in situations of close language contact. It is considered to be a salient feature of bilingual ingroup conversation and an important communicative strategy in many bi- and multilingual communities (cf. Gumperz 1982), since it enables speakers to manipulate two or more languages simultaneously. Frequent switching, however, can favour borrowing of elements from one language to another, and it can also lead to language change. This phenomenon is mainly observed in situations of unstable diglossia as e.g. in our Sardinian case study, where the socially dominant majority language increasingly outsets the subordinate minority language. In these contexts, the transfer of foreign elements is very often asymmetric, which indicates that the socially non-dominant language is affected much more widely than the dominant one. Viewing the issue from this perspective, many empirical findings suggest that CS is an area of language use which frequently mediates change in the socially non-dominant language potentially leading to convergence or even to language decay in more advanced stages of shift (cf. Myers Scotton 1992). This point will be discussed in more detail in Chapter 5.3.1.

5.1 Data and methodology

The data collection for the study on CS in Sardinia, which was carried out in 1991–1995, involved the elaboration of a corpus of informal conversations recorded in the homes of various families in Bonorva, a market place in a rural area of Central Sardinia situated within the Logudorese area. The present data has not yet been fully analysed, therefore the results and the evaluation presented here are to be seen as preliminary conclusions. The corpus consists of 54 bilingual discourses featuring 95 persons who were distributed as evenly as possible over the respective categories of age, sex, educational background, bilingual command[8] and social network. The transliterated conversations comprise 11.483 text lines in which 3.846 instances of CS were registered (cf. Rindler Schjerve 1996, 1997a, b, 1998a, b, c, 2001a, b, c).

In line with the findings of more recent CS research we argued that CS was not the accidental outcome of code alternation or even the arbitrary mixing of two languages, but rather a systematic process resulting from the interaction between speakers' socio-psychological motivations, social norms and linguistic constraints.[9]

Consequently, we concluded that CS phenomena may relate to different motivations since, in certain contexts, they may convey social meaning and identity marking, e.g. accommodation and solidarity with another speaker or a social setting, whereas in other contexts CS may indicate conversational structuring, e.g. turn-taking, change of topic, emphasis, etc. The third type of CS, which was realised within the sentence boundaries and occurred in the guise of a one-word or constituent transfer or as transfer of grammatical structures, was to be regarded as a separate type, which would relate to bilingual command and to communicative norms of bilingual use rather than to bilingual attitudes or to the structuring of bilingual discourse.

A further result of the corpus analysis was that CS phenomena appeared in different guises: they were realized as situational code alternations or as a switch at the beginning of a conversational turn; they equally occurred within a turn at sentence boundaries or even within a sentence as a constituent or as a one-word borrowing and, in certain communicative contexts, they were realised as transfer of grammatical morphemes or as transfer of syntactic structures. And finally, if these CS occurred at high frequencies, these CS would generally represent a domain in which change and restructuring was likely to take place.

The categorisation of CS types was carried out with the purpose of finding out if the overall pattern of bilingual switching was in any way unbalanced, since hierarchies concerning the occurrence and functions of switching would suggest tendencies towards shift and language change (cf. Rindler Schjerve 1996, 1997b, 1998a, b). Particular attention was paid to the place of switching and, within this domain, especially to intrasentential CS. The reason for this focus was the assumption that switches within the sentence realized as one-word borrowing, as transfer of constituents or as elements of mixed grammar, represented a domain susceptible to the induction of language change and thus required separate investigation (cf. Rindler Schjerve 1997a, 1998c).

As CS in the Sardinian-Italian language pair was likely to correlate with factors such as age, sex, education and social network, we aimed at investigating these socio-linguistic correlations in detail, as this would enable us to gain insights into the social dynamics of ongoing linguistic shift and change. In this connection it was important to find out whether switches into Italian were more frequent than those into Sardinian since CS appeared at high frequencies in our data. As intrasentential transfers seemed to be the most salient characteristics of CS in this language pair, it was of particular interest to obtain information about the kind of switches, which were usually realised between the sentence boundaries, and about their interference with the lexical and grammatical structure of present Sardinian.

In our investigation, we assumed that the mixed bilingual conversations were conducted on the structural matrix of only one language which was supposed to be the main language of the respective conversation (cf. Myers Scotton 1993a: 113–154). The more intrasentential CS occurred in our data, the more important it was to establish this main language (see below 5.3.1). In cases of doubt, in which the bilingual CS was so prominent that it was difficult to define the matrix language on an ad hoc basis, the words in Sardinian and Italian were counted and the language with the greater number of occurring words was specified as the matrix language (cf. Myers Scotton 1993b: 20).

Consequently, the classification of the CS phenomena was undertaken in the following way.

As far as social and identity marking was concerned, we distinguished between two types of CS, which, due to thorough discourse-analytic contextualisation, were coded as switching into the preferred code [PREF] and as accommodation towards interlocutor and communicative setting [ACCO].

In addition, we established eight subtypes of CS which appeared to be most prominent in connection with the conversational structuring of our mixed bilingual data: change of topic [CTOP], emphasis [EMPH], reiteration [REIT], reported speech [RSP], back-channel behaviour [BCHB], metacommunication [METAC], particles [PART] and interjections [INTJ].

Finally, a separate category was established by defining intrasentential CS as subdivided into different types of transfer: morphologically and phonologically inadapted lexical transfers [TRANS1], partly adapted transfers [TRANS2], neologisms [TRANS3], doublet forms [TRANS4], lexical borrowings which due to their structural adaptation and frequency of use appeared to be integrated into Sardinian lexis [BORW], transfer of entire constituents [TRANS5], grammatical transfers [INTF], hybrid forms of vocative [VOC], phraseological transfers [PHRAS], and last but not least, CS which was triggered by a lack of bilingual command on the part of the speakers involved in a conversation [COMP].[10]

In addition, the different guises of CS were registered as occurring at the beginning of a conversational turn [T], within a turn at sentence boundaries [IT, in] or within a turn and within a sentence [IT,it]. And finally, coding included the direction of switching (S>I vs. I>S) as well as maintenance of switch direction (S>I-I; I>S-S) or return to initial code (S>I>S; I>S>I). The direction of switching was important in so far as it provided for information about the discreteness of the two languages and their function as a primary or secondary medium of bilingual conversations (compare 5.3.1).

The coding of the different CS types was realised as follows:[11]

a: [T:I>S]	b: [T:S>I]
c: [IT:I>S>S,in]	g: [IT:S>I>I,in]
d: [IT:I>S>S,it]	h: [IT:S>I>I,it]
e: [IT:I>S>I,in]	i: [IT:S>I>S,in]
f: [IT:I>S>I,it]	j: [IT:S>I>S,it]

1: RSP	6: CTOP	142: TRANS2	16: VOC
2: PART	7: REIT	143: TRANS3	17: BORW
3: BCHB	10: PREF	144: TRANS4	18: PHRAS
4. EMPH	12: ACCO	145: TRANS5	19: METAC
5: INTJ	141: TRANS1	15: INTF	21: COMP

The following extracts from the recorded conversations provide examples for the different functional types. Since these examples are extracted from spontaneous conversations, they do not reflect the full range of the types defined above. The examples cited below should also illustrate how CS patterns vary in accordance with the varying bilingual competences of the relative speakers.

Example number V/1994/6,5
Speakers: G.A. house wife, L.L. house wife
Topic: tax declaration

G.A.: E si a cussal barantottomizza francoso s'annu **j144 l'aggiunghese j144 d'ogni** mese sa **j141 quota fissa** de sa **j141 luce**, de su **j141 telefono** e de s'abba... cussal barantotto chi pigana a dughentoso.

L.L.: Deo po narrere non faghia mai una cosa de sol **j143 renditoso**, deo non n'appo mai fattu. Dae canno el bessida custa **j141 legge**, narramoso de sal domoso, so faghinne... però non pagaia mai nudda ca... **j2 invece** poi comente el moltu babbu e custa cosa a mie **j17 risultada** segunna **j141 casa** supera e **j145 ogni anno** devo faghere sa **j141 denuncia** 'e sol **j17 redditoso** a palte po caulese mioso, cumpresu?

(G.A.: And if to these fourtyeight thousand francs per year *you add every* month the *fixed amount* for the *light*, the *telephone* and the water ... these fourty thousand will be two hundred thousand.

L.L.: I so to say have never thought about *returns*, I never did this. Since the time when this *law* came into force, the law of the houses, I am doing ... *however*, I never paid anything because... but then when daddy died and this thing *became* my second *house* then it is more and *every year* I have to do my *tax declaration*, as far as my things are concerned, do you understand?)

Despite the extraordinarily high frequencies of CS into Italian which are produced by well-balanced bilingual speakers, this passage shows that Sardinian does not lose its function as a main language in the conversation.

Example number II/1992/2,1
Speakers: G.A. housewife, G.C. housewife
Topic: medical operation and choice of hospital

G.A.: Daghi este in Padova, menzusu non pigada a Bologna... a s'operare sunu **h145** più specializzati.

G.C.: No. Ma non c'è bisogno. Anche ad Ozieri sono specializzati. Lo stesso...non è un'operazione, dà! **c7** este una cosa chi faghene **j144** d'ogni die Giuannà, mì, si tottu anna bene in deghe diese so in domo **g4** poi non mi farannno neanche taglio /.../ **c4** non b'a bisonzo. Sa tia 'e Gianni chi tenede **h145** più di cinquanta /.../ **f15** gli hanno tolto /.../ Ozieri è specializzato nell'operazione di tagli così, infatti **c7** "deo mi cheria operare a Nuoro appo nadu " datu chi b'est issa inie micc'anno a Nuoro, **g4** c'è lei, ...

(G.A.: If she is in Padova, she'd better go to Bologna . . .to have an operation they are *more specialised*.

G.C.: No. But it is not necessary. Also in Ozieri they are specialised. The same... it is not an operation, you see! *It is a thing which they do every* day Giuanna, O.K., if everything goes well in ten days I'm at home, *then they won't even make an incision, there is no need.* Gianni's aunt who is *more than fifty years old* /.../ they have removed *her* /.../ Ozieri specializes in these kinds of operations, indeed "*I will be operated in Nuoro" I told myself since she is there and therfore I'll go to Nuoro*, she is *there*, ...)

This passage, where a Sardinian dominant bilingual (G.A.) and an Italian dominant bilingual person (G.C.) interact with each other, illustrates how in a Sardinian dominated conversation Italian interferes in the turn of the Italian dominant individual in varying degrees and manners, without compromising, though, the integrity of Sardinian.

Example number IV/1993/3b,4
Speakers: M.S. uncle, G.A. mother, F.B. father, G.B. daughter
Topic: cleaning the car

M.S.: **b16** Giovà, me la pulisci, la macchina? Tu me la devi pulire. Sabato...
G.A.: (Turning to M.S.) **a12** Sappadu tenede..
F.B.: Giovanna tenede s'esame, non el faghinne nudda mancu in domo, Mariu!
M.S.: Eggià l'ischid issa itte devel faghere. (to G.) **g21** Stasera che no ti veda in piazza passeggiando, allora..
G.B.: Già non mi vedi
F.B.: (to M.S.) **a10** Bò, bò..e si essidi?
M.S.: Giovanna, will you clean the car for me? You must clean it. Saturday.
G.A.: On Saturday she has...
F.B.: Giovanna has an exam, she does not do anything in the house either, Mario
M.S.: She knows what she has to do. Don‘t let me see you on the promenade tonight, or else...
G.B.: You won‘t see me.
F.B.: Oh well, .. and what if she goes out?

This conversation involved three bilingual persons and one monolingual Italian speaking person, who, however, exhibited passive competence of Sardinian. The passage illustrates the characteristics of CS behaviour under these circumstances.

5.2 Quantitative results

As far as the overall CS pattern is concerned, a first quantitative elaboration of the data showed that intrasentential CS realized as mere borrowing was most frequent (44%), followed by the conversational type of CS (34%) and by CS as social and identity marking (22%). This result shows that CS activity is heavily concentrated on phenomena of transfer and borrowing. The high rates of intrasentential CS suggest that there is a large amount of lexical rearrangements in this language pair (compare example above, number V/1994/6,5). At the same time, the relatively large amount of CS of the discursive type indicates that the use of the two languages is of a rather unmarked kind, i.e. that in informal contexts both languages may occur evenly distributed without normative restrictions (compare examples above, number IV/1993/3b,4 and number II/1992/2,1). This view of the two languages as fairly neutral and unmarked counterparts appears to be confirmed by the low degree of CS marking social status and identity, since low rates of this type of CS match the idea of neutral bilingual use.[12]

The cross-tabulation of these CS types with age, sex, educational background and bilingual competence of the speakers revealed that younger subjects and Italian dominant individuals realized more intrasentential CS than older and Sardinian dominant speakers, whereas conversational CS turned out to be more frequent with middle-aged speakers and speakers of higher educational background who appeared to be balanced bilinguals. The identity marking CS, on the other hand, proved to be most frequent with young Italian dominant and older Sardinian dominant speakers, who were rather situated at the monolingual poles of Italian or Sardinian due to their age (cf. Rindler Schjerve 1996, 1997b, 1998a, b).

As far as direction of switching is concerned, CS from Sardinian into Italian (S>I) was most frequent (64,6%). This result needs to be seen in relative terms, however, since it turned out that most of the switching into Italian occurred as one-word or constituent CS within the sentence boundaries (51%) after which the speakers generally returned to Sardinian (S>I>S 93,8%). As a consequence, switch direction turned out to be an indicator for language maintenance in Sardinian since it confirmed the hypothesis that the two codes, although interacting to mark identity, conversational structuring and borrowing, were discretely kept apart during the conversations.

This result, on the whole, confirms the hypothesis that CS in the Sardinian-Italian language pair is heavily involved in the borrowing activities which contribute to the present remodelling of Sardinian, and in particular to its lexical remodelling along parameters of Italian.

5.3 Qualitative investigation

5.3.1 *Theoretical preliminaries*

In accordance with research on language change and obsolescence in different recessive contexts (cf. Brenzinger 1992; Dorian 1981, 1989; Dressler 1988; Silva-Corvalan 1994; Thomason & Kaufman 1988; etc.), it was obvious that changes which occurred in relatively short time-spans, as e.g. in our Sardinian case, would show symptoms of heavy borrowing and loss of word formation devices associated with relexification on the one hand, and symptoms of overgeneralization, loss of rules and of grammatical convergence on the other. At the same time these findings, however, suggested that changes of this kind do not necessarily imply a loss of structure in the functionally recessive language; yet, under certain circumstances and depending on the nature of the particular contact under study, these changes could also be interpreted as rule gains and innovations on the part of the functionally recessive language (cf. Gal 1989; Hamp 1989; Huffines 1989; Hoenigswald 1989; Rindler Schjerve 2002), provided that these changes appeared with high frequencies in the handling of the languages involved.

On the basis of existing obsolescence research, the precise structural and sociolinguistic terms along which we can differentiate between phenomena of linguistic loss and gains cannot be determined, since these investigations have largely ignored the study of bilingual conversations as interactive discourse and CS. Turning, hence, to our Sardnian data which did not obviously show signs of obsolescence, it was of utmost interest to investigate in detail if the phenomena of ongoing change were indeed to be interpreted as symptoms of innovation and vitality rather than of disintegration and decay.

A major starting point for finding an answer to this question was constituted by the more recent findings of research on intrasentential CS. As mentioned above, intrasentential CS could be defined as a mechanism through which the recessive language changes. In this context, the matrix-language-frame-model (MLFM), as outlined by Myers Scotton (1993a, b), appeared to be the most promising model for our question since it opened an avenue in which intrasentential CS could be related to various stages of shift and change. The MLFM is based on the assumption that the two languages involved in intrasentential CS do not operate on equal terms. Whereas one language is the dominating matrix language (ML), both in terms of frequency of morphemes and in terms of being the expected and thus unmarked code in a particular bilingual conversation (1993a: 113–154), the other one is the embedded language (EL) from which the transfer takes place (1993b: 66–74). Moreover, it is argued that the ML provides for the grammatical framework of the bilingual conversation. In this context, it is important to note that the term ML refers to a language as being the main language of a particular conversation; it does not, however, refer to aspects of societal dominance as they are generally reflected in the relationship between majority and minority languages. It is a major point of the MLF model that the ML and the EL are viewed as two differently activated systems from which it follows that lexical transfer from the EL has to be accommodated to the structural requirements of the ML. This means that lexical transfer from the EL, which is not the main language of a particular conversation, becomes integrated into the grammatical framework of the ML. To give an example: It. *occhial-i* "spectacle-s" appears as Sard. *occhial-ese* >> It.EL+Sard.ML.

Based on these theoretical considerations, Myers Scotton (1993b: 208ff.) develops different scenarios arguing that in situations of language maintenance, i.e. of stable diglossia, the interference from the EL has different results from those realised in situations of language shift. As long as there is no shift, borrowing from the EL is normally restricted to modest lexical borrowing. However, as soon as the sociolinguistic relationship between the two languages turns into asymmetrical shift, the transfer from the meanwhile socially expanding language to the functionally recessive language undergoes changes: in an early stage of unstable diglossia, shift may be accompanied by heavy lexical borrowing into the minority ML, gradually leading to the substitution of its core lexicon without, however, seriously changing its grammatical structure. In stages of advanced obsolescence, entire grammatical subsystems may be transferred from the majority language, leading to convergence and to remodelling of the recipient recessive language on the socially dominant donor system. This process signals that the obsolete minority language loses its matrix function. In other words, it is the basic tenet of these scenarios that in progressing stages of shift, the structural system of the recessive language changes through CS, which seem to be increasingly associated with deep grammatical borrowing at these stages.

In the following chapter, we shall see whether our Sardinian data actually support these hypotheses.

5.3.2 *Intrasentential CS and change*

As far as the nature of our Sardinian data is concerned, it was clear that the language shift was not yet advanced enough to admit extensive grammatical borrowing. Rather, we expected that CS would be limited to heavy lexical borrowing associated with sporadic grammatical interferences. The results obtained from the quantified data had proved that intrasentential CS from Sardinian into Italian was very prominent (51%). Unfortunately, a more fine-grained statistical evaluation is not available at present, but the qualitatively assessed distribution of the various subtypes shows that the highest frequency rates occur for one-word lexical transfers [TRANS1] and [TRANS4], followed by grammatical transfers [INTF], and finally by multi-word or constituent transfers [TRANS5]. It turned out that one-word transfers from Italian which were morphologically integrated into Sardinian grammar [TRANS4] triggered strong relexification since they established doublet forms which progressively substituted the traditional lexical corpus of Sardinian.

(1) So pig-ada e fi [TRANS4] riemp-inne sal [TRANS4]
I-am gone-up and was-she fill-ing the
pomodor-oso...
tomato-es...
I went up and she was filling the tomatoes...
(ITAL. Riemp-ire vs. SARD. pienn-are/to fill; ITAL. pomodor-i vs. SARD. pumat-as/tomato-es)

(2) Ite ses [TRANS4] cumbin-enne ista seru?
What are-you do-ing this evening?
(ITAL. combin-ando vs. SARD. oldinz-enne/do-ing)

(3) Sa [TRANS4] poltineri-a [TRANS4] appalten-idi a sos
The porter's lodge belong-s to the
[TRANS4] inquilin-oso.
tenant-s.
(ITAL. Inquilin-i, SARD. inquilin-oso/tenant-s)

(4) ...poi [TRANS4] continu-ada a si [TRANS4] gratt-are.
...then continue-s-he to him scratch
Then he continues to scratch himself.
(ITAL. continu-are vs. SARD sigh-ire/to continue; ITAL. gratt-ar-si vs. SARD. si ratt-are/scratch oneself)

Example (3) shows that beyond morphological integration [TRANS4] there may also be phonological adaptation of CS as indicated in "*poltineri-a*" and "*appalten-idi*" (Ital. *portin-eria*, Sard. *poltin-eria*/porter's lodge; Ital. *appart-*

iene vs. Sard. *appalten-idi*/it belongs). And in example (4) we may observe that the clitic "*si*" follows postdetermination in Sardinian instead of predetermination in Italian.

As far as morphologically non-integrated transfers [TRANS1] were concerned, our data showed that CS of this type – even though they occurred at high frequencies – was restricted to contexts where the one-word transfer related to referents exclusively associated with the Italian culture:

(5) In su [TRANS1] soggiorno lu pott-o fagh-ere.
In the living-room it can-I do.
I can do it in the living-room.
(ITAL. Soggiorn-o/living-room)

(6) Lu dev-es narrere a su [TRANS1] camionista.
It must-you tell to the chauffeur.
You must tell it to the chauffeur.
(ITAL. Camionist-a/chauffeur)

(7) In su [TRANS1] portabagagli già b' ist-o.
In the boot just there stay-I.
I just stay in the boot. (ITAL. Portabagagl-i/boot)

Looking at transfer of grammar [INTF] it turned out that CS of this kind was restricted to certain subsystems of grammar such as word order of adjectives, which sometimes followed the premodification principle of Italian rather than Sardinian postmodification:

(8) Est un acc-a chie og-ada [INTF] meda latte.
Is-she a cow which carries-she much milk /
(SARD. latte meda vs. ITAL. molta latte / much milk)
This is a cow with a lot of milk.

(9) In sa [INTF] granne cittade [h145] si pag-a anche l'aria.
In the big town one pay-s also the'air.
One even pays the air in the big town.
SARD. cittade manna vs. ITAL. grande città / big town)

Furthermore, occasional incongruities were observed with regard to grammatical structures which differed in the two languages, such as prepositional accusatives in Sardinian against non-prepositional constructions in Italian:

(10) Bi a postu s'innari e non ad-a
There has-he put the money and not has-he
accuntent-adu [INTF] sa zente.
satisf-ied the people
He has put the money there and has not satisfied the people.
(ITAL. INF Accontent-are ACC la gent-e vs. SARD. INF Accuntent-are PREP.ACC a sa zent-e/satisfy people)

(11) Te lo tolg-o [d145] a azzuare [INTF] su pizzinu.
You it take-from-I to help the child.
I take it from you to help the child.
(ITAL. Aiut-are ACC il bambino vs. SARD. azzu-are PREP.ACC a su pizzinu/to help the child).

It also turned out that mixing of grammatical morphemes was extremely limited, which suggests that it still seems to be considered a violation of the norm that is consciously avoided:

(12) Eh, a itte l' [INTF]appr-idi?
Eh, to what it' opens-he
And why does he open it?
(ITAL. INF apr-ire, 3rd PERS apr-e vs. SARD. INF apperr-ere 3rd PERS apper-ede/he-opens)

As far as multi-word CS [TRANS5] are concerned, our data showed that they were generally realized as constituents:

(13) Sal [TRANS4] concessionari-asa las ten-ene sal macchin-asa
The car seller-s them keep-they the car-s
chi fini [d145] sotto pubblicità.
which were under advertising.
Car sellers keep the cars which were advertised.

(14) Babbo ha pensato [h145] chi sa macchina ne fidi
Father has thought that the car away was
ru-inne in su'e Peppinu.
glid-ing-down to Peppinu.
Father thought that the car was driving down to Peppinu.

It turned out, however, that in cases in which such more-word CS was not realized as a constituent, such switches generally occurred at points where mainly homophonous or similar sounding trigger words neutralized language boundaries (cf. Clyne 1987) and stimulated the switch into Italian. Triggering of this kind appears to be an important motivation for CS in this language pair since

Italian and Sardinian are closely related languages and there are numerous ancient Italian loans in Sardinian:

(15) Am-ol a biere, cral seru {TRIG} si el [d145]
Have-we to see, tomorrow evening one is-he
preso dal panico.
taken with-the panic.
We have to see, tomorrow evening everybody will be panicking.

(16) Poi [TRANS4] dichiaram-oso sa {TRIG} fine dei lavori.
Then declare-we the end of-the works
Then we declare the end of the work.

In connection with this triggering we have to take into account that beyond the ongoing relexification of Sardinian, CS of this kind is heavily stimulated by the close typological affinity between the two languages and by an ancient layer of Italian loans in Sardinian, which dates back to a former Italian domination in the middle ages (cf. Note 2). Thus, typological affinity and old loans constitute a common ground which triggers the alternative handling of the two languages in bilingual conversations.

Returning to the hypotheses outlined at the beginning of this chapter (cf. 5.3.1), the results obtained from our qualitative investigation suggest that the changes induced by CS in present-day Sardinian are first and foremost restricted to a lexical remodelling on the basis of Italian, i.e. that the Sardinian lexicon is actually undergoing a restructuring according to the foreign model with the result that a good deal of the indigenous core vocabulary is being substituted by Italian. Although CS occurs at highest frequencies, both systems are still kept apart showing that the matrix function of Sardinian is still uncompromised since the lexical import from Italian is generally adapted to the morphological matrix of Sardinian. On the basis of our CS data it cannot be ignored, however, that the relexification actually taking place in Sardinian is accompanied by grammatical transfers which, however, still appear to be restricted to phenomena of a rather superficial structural level without showing deep borrowing yet.

6. Conclusion

In conclusion, the evidence presented above suggests that Sardinian is a language between maintenance and change. As a socially recessive code it actually appears to be involved in profound changes associated with high frequencies of CS. Our data show that CS is a mechanism which is intimately linked to the simultaneous handling of the two languages in various ways.

On the one hand we can observe that Sardinian is still a viable language since high rates of discursively motivated CS indicate that switching is used as a device to cope with both codes in bilingual conversations which are characteristic of informal communication. At the same time, the relatively high share of young speakers engaged in identity-marking CS reflects the fact that these speakers, who are mostly raised in Italian, realise CS to signal their ethnic membership. And, finally, increased rates of younger speakers' one-word CS into Italian show that these speaker still handle both languages with a tendency of gradually accommodating Sardinian to Italian and of smoothing structural incongruencies between both languages to facilitate their simultaneous use.

Although the Sardinian lexicon is being strongly remodelled on Italian, there is no clear evidence for defining Sardinian as a disintegrative language. Sardinian grammar still appears to be resistant to the Italian influence since no wide-spread morphological mixing between the two languages could be observed yet. At the same time it cannot be ignored, though, that there is some evidence of grammatical remodelling after Italian.

Actually, the evidence of highest frequencies of intrasentential CS triggering change seems to indicate that as long as the languages in contact are not involved in escalating inter-ethnic conflicts, their speakers appear to develop strategies unconsciously to neutralise structural unevenness in order to move smoothly between the two codes. Since Sardinian is a socially subordinate and a linguistically non-codified minority language it goes without saying that neutralisation processes of this kind are asymmetrically concentrated on the minority language. Although Sardinian is a restricted language, it nevertheless appears to be a language which is still alive. As far as language change is concerned, this phenomenon cannot be interpreted as a signal of decay on the basis of our data. The data much rather suggest that this is a symptom of vitality. The restructuring processes that we have exemplified through CS point to the fact that Sardinian can only survive under the given circumstances if it adapts to Italian. Consequently, we assume that the change in Sardinian today is still to be seen as the price for its maintenance.

Notes

1. For a more comprehensive account of the historical situation cf. Blasco Ferrer (1984); Wagner (1951, 2002); for a short survey cf. Mensching (1994:10–14); Rindler Schjerve (1993, 2003a).

2. This is the period when Italian structures entered Sardinian, and in particular Sardinian lexicon, for the first time, giving rise to an old layer of lexical loans which have been maintained throughout subsequent socio-linguistic dominances from the iberique peninsula (cf. Blasco Ferrer 1984:62–132; Wagner 2002:187–203).

3. As there has not been any language census in Italy since 1921, it is difficult to give the exact figures. Estimates vary between 1,2 million and 1,6 million speakers including emigrants (cf. Euromosaic 2002).

4. As far as the debate on the typology of Sardinian varieties within the Romance languages is concerned, we refer to the survey in Rindler Schjerve (1987:41–48, 1993:286); for more extensive details cf. Wagner (1951:387–404) and Blasco Ferrer (1984:195–200).

5. The "questione della lingua sarda" relates to the debates dealing with the controversial question of a unified norm that marked the beginning of the Sardinian language renaissance, in particular since the 1970s when the language controversy moved more into the fore of Sardinian regionalism. Although there have been different attempts purporting to create a unified norm, these initiatives did not prove to be successful. At present an official proposal of standardisation is being discussed without, however, reaching consensus (cf. Rindler Schjerve 1991b; Bolognesi & Helsloot 1999).

6. At this point it seems necessary to clarify the concept of diglossia adopted in this paper as our perspective differs somewhat from the traditional view that has generally been applied within the North-American paradigm of languages in contact (Ferguson 1959; Fishman 1972). In this context, diglossia is commonly defined as a socially differentiated compartmentalisation of languages. In the Fergusonian definition, diglossia refers to a stable complementary distribution of a highly valorised standard language and its socially lower termed dialects. Fishman applied this concept to bilingual settings where diglossic functions and values appeared to be very similar. The main point is now that North-American sociolinguistics characterizes diglossia as a stable phenomenon whereas Catalan and Occitan sociolinguistics defines it as a dynamic and temporary situation which ultimately leads to monolingualism either by the substitution or by the normalisation of the low and socially subordinate variety (cf. Kremnitz 1979, 1982). Subsequently, it has been argued that diglossia refers to power related asymmetries which are reflected in terms of sociolinguistic dominance and subordination of the respective language groups. It is the latter perspective from which we view diglossia here (cf Rindler Schjerve 2001d; Rindler Schjerve & Vetter 2003b).

7. There are several hypotheses arguing that intensive intrasentential CS might be facilitated by the typological affinity between the language pair (cf. e.g. Boeschoten 1991; Clyne 1987; Giacalone Ramat 1995) and that, apart from structural determinants, it is primarily sociocultural parameters, e.g. the existence of interethnic conflicts, which influence not only the

frequency but also the specific patterns of CS (Bentahila/Davies 1991: 394; Treffers-Daller 1992).

8. In this context, we distinguished between four groups of individuals, i.e. well-balanced Sardinian-Italian bilinguals, Italian monolinguals with a passive command of Sardinian, Italian dominant bilinguals, and Sardinian dominant bilinguals.

9. Cf. Auer (1984, 1995); Poplack (1980); ESF-Papers (1990–1991); Gumperz (1982); Heller (1988); Milroy/Muysken (1995); Myers-Scotton (1993a, b).

10. It has to be mentioned though that the different subtypes of intrasentential CS as they are registered here refer to mechnisms which are quite heterogeneous from a structural point of view, since they cover a wide range of transfer including phenomena of rather diversified lexical, morphological and syntactic borrowing. In defininining these subtypes we were well aware of the problems relating to the distinction between the different phenomena commomly referred to as CS, transfer, borrowing and mixing. These problems have been widely discussed in the field of more recent CS research (cf. Romaine 1989: 110–147; Appel/Muysken, 1987: 117–172; Myers-Scotton, 1993b: 163ff.). It is against this theoretical background and the issues raised in these discussions that we decided to define CS as a cover term that includes all kinds of transfer as they occur within a particular language pair regardless of their frequency of occurrence and integration. In view of Sardinian as a non-codified language, i.e. a code without clearly defined normative references, the distinction between transfers of different levels of either structural or social integration proved to be difficult. Another reason for favouring a broad definition of CS was the fact that we attempted to assess the overall pattern of CS within the Sardinian-Italian language pair in order to account for how, in this situation of shift, the recessive Sardinian actually interacts with the dominant Italian language. Hence it proved to be important to register all kinds of CS as they were realised in our mixed bilingual conversations.

11. The categorisation is indicated by means of bold print in the text passages. The quanitative analysis was carried out using SPSS.

12. At this point it should be stressed, however, that these results do not contradict our hypothesis of an ongoing shift in the Sardinian-Italian language pair. As a matter of fact, many speakers, i.e. mostly younger and Italian dominant speakers, have shifted to Italian as a primary medium of communication although they keep using Sardinian in a more restricted and informal field of interaction with Sardinian dominant and older individuals.

References

Alziator, F. (1954). *Storia della letteratura di Sardegna.* Cagliari: La Zattera.

Appel, R. & Muysken, P. (1987). *Language Contact and Bilingualism.* London–New York–Melbourne–Auckland: Edward Arnold.

Auer, P. (1984). *Bilingual Conversation.* Amsterdam: Benjamins.

Auer, P. (1995). The pragmatics of code-switching: a sequential approach In L. Milroy & P. Muysken (Eds.), *One speaker, two languages. Cross-disciplinary perspectives on code-switching* (pp. 115–135). Cambridge: CUP.

Bentahila, A. & Davies, E. (1991). Costraints on CS: A look beyond grammar. *ESF-Papers, 1991c*, 369–403.

Blasco Ferrer, E. (1984). *Storia linguistica della Sardegna*. Tübingen: Niemeyer.

Blasco Ferrer, E. (1988). Sardisch: Externe Sprachgeschichte. Storia del sardo. In G. Holtus, M. Metzeltin, & Ch. Schmitt (Eds.), *Lexikon der Romanistischen Linguistik, Bd. IV* (pp. 884–897). Tübingen: Niemeyer.

Boeschoten, H. (1991). Asymmetrical code-switching in immigrant communities. *ESF-Papers, 1991a*, 85–100.

Bolognesi, R. & Helsloot, K. (Eds.). (1999). *La lingua sarda. L'identità socioculturale della Sardegna nel prossimo millennio.* Atti del Convegno di Quartu Sant'Elena 9–10 Maggio 1997. Cagliari: Condaghes.

Brenzinger, M. (Ed.). (1992). *Language Death: Factual and Theoretical Explorations with Reference to East Africa*. Berlin-New York: de Gruyter.

Clyne, M. (1987). Constraints on code-switching, how universal are they? *Linguistics, 25*, 739–764.

Dorian, N. (1981). *Language Death. The Life Cycle of a Scottish Gaelic Dialect*. Philadelphia: University of Pennsylvania Press.

Dorian, N. (Ed.). (1989). *Investigating Obsolescence. Studies in language contraction and death.* Cambridge: CUP.

Dressler, W. U. (1988). Spracherhaltung – Sprachverfall – Sprachtod. In U. Ammon, N. Dittmar, & J. K. Mattheier (Eds.), *Sociolinguistics* II, 2 (pp. 1551–1563). Berlin: De Gruyter.

ESF-Papers (1990). *Papers for the workshop on concepts, methodology and data*. Basel 12–13 January 1990. Strasbourg: European Science Foundation.

ESF-Papers (1991a). *Papers for the workshop on constraints, conditions, and models*. London 27–29 September 1990. Strasbourg: European Science Foundation.

ESF-Papers (1991b). *Papers for the workshop on impact and consequences: broader considerations*. Brussels 11–24 November 1990. Strasbourg: European Science Foundation.

ESF-Papers (1991c). *Papers for the symposium on codeswitching in bilingual studies: theories, significance and perspectives*. Vol. I, II. Barcelona 21–23 March 1991. Strasbourg: European Science Foundation.

Euromosaic (2002). http://www.uoc.edu/euromosaic

Ferguson, Ch. (1959). Diglossia. *Word, 15*, 325–340.

Fishman, J. A. (1972). Domains and the relationship between micro- and macrosociolinguistics. In J. Gumperz & D. Hymes (Eds.), *Directions in Sociolinguistics* (pp. 435–453). New York–Chicago–San Francisco: Holt, Rinehart, Winston.

Framework convention for the protection of national minorities; ets no: 157, 01/11/95; http://conventions.coe.int

Gal, S. (1989). Lexical innovation and loss: the use and value of restricted Hungarian. In N. Dorian (Ed.), *Investigating Obsolescence. Studies in language contraction and death* (pp. 313–331). Cambridge: CUP.

Giacalone-Ramat, A. (1995). Code-switching in the context of dialect/standard language relations. In L. Milroy & P. Muysken (Eds.), *One speaker, two languages. Cross-disciplinary perspectives on code-switching* (pp. 45–67). Cambridge: CUP.

Gumperz, J. J. (1982). *Discourse strategies*. Cambridge: CUP.

Hamp, E. P. (1989). On signs of health and death. In N. Dorian (Ed.), *Investigating Obsolescence. Studies in language contraction and death* (pp. 197–210). Cambridge: CUP.

Heckmann, F. (1992). *Ethnische Minderheiten, Volk und Nation. Soziologie inter-ethnischer Beziehungen*. Stuttgart: Ferdinand Enke.

Heller, M. (Ed.). (1988). *Codeswitching. Anthropological and Sociolinguistic Perspectives*. Berlin–New York: Mouton de Gruyter.

Hoenigswald, H. M. (1989). Language obsolescence and language history: Matters of linearity, leveling, loss and the like. In N. Dorian (Ed.), *Investigating Obsolescence. Studies in language contraction and death* (pp. 347–354). Cambridge: CUP.

Huffines, M. L. (1989). Case usage among the Pennsylvania German sectarians and nonsectarians. In N. Dorian (Ed.), *Investigating Obsolescence. Studies in language contraction and death* (pp. 211–226). Cambridge: CUP.

Kremnitz, G. (Ed.). (1979). *Sprachen im Konflikt. Theorie und Praxis der katalanischen Soziolinguistik*. Tübingen: Narr.

Kremnitz, G. (Ed.). (1982). *Entfremdung, Selbstbefreiung und Norm. Texte aus der okzitanischen Soziolinguistik*. Tübingen: Narr.

Legge 15 Dicembre (1999). n. 482 –http//www.senato.it/parlam/leggi/994821.htm

Mensching, G. (1994^{2}). *Einführung in die sardische Sprache*. Bonn: Romanistischer Verlag.

Mercurio Gregorini, R. (1980). L'Italiano e il sardo nelle scuole elementari. In F. A. Leoni (Ed.), *I dialetti e le lingue delle minoranze di fronte all'italiano* (pp. 527–554). Roma: Bulzoni.

Milroy, L. & Muysken, P. (Eds.). (1995). *One speaker, two languages. Cross-disciplinary perspectives on code-switching*. Cambridge: CUP.

Myers Scotton, C. (1992). Codeswitching as a Mechanism of Deep Borrowing, Language Shift and Language Death. In M. Brenzinger (Ed.), *Language Death in East Africa* (pp. 31–58). Berlin: Mouton de Gruyter.

Myers-Scotton, C. (1993a). *Social Motivations for Codeswitching. Evidence from Africa*. Oxford: Clarendon Press.

Myers Scotton, C. (1993b). *Duelling Languages. Grammatical Structure in Codeswitching*. Oxford: Clarendon Press.

Nelde, P., Strubell, M., & Williams, G. (1996). *Euromosaic. The Production and Reproduction of the Minority Language Groups of the EU*. Brussel-Luxemburg: European Commission.

Poplack, S. (1980). Sometimes I'll start a sentence in Spanish y termino en Espagnol: Towards a typology of code-switching. *Linguistics, 18*, 581–618.

Poplack S., Sankoff, D., & Miller, Ch. (1988). The social correlates and linguistic processes of lexical borrowing and assimilation. *Linguistics, 26*, 47–104.

Rindler Schjerve, R. (1987). *Sprachkontakt auf Sardinien. Soziolinguistische Untersuchungen des Sprachenwechsels im ländlichen Bereich*. Tübingen: Narr.

Rindler Schjerve, R. (1989). Sprachverschiebung und Sprachtod: Funktionelle und strukturelle Aspekte. In H. Beck (Ed.), *Germanische Rest- und Trümmersprachen* (pp. 1–14). Berlin–New York: De Gruyter.

Rindler Schjerve, R. (1991a). Ethnolinguistic and interpretative concepts in explaining language shift. In J. Verschueren (Ed.), *Levels of Linguistic Adaptation. Selected Papers of the International Pragmatics Conference* (pp. 223–233). Amsterdam–Philadelphia: Benjamins.

Rindler Schjerve, R. (1991b). Sardisch. In W. Dahmen et al. (Eds.), *Zum Stand der Kodifizierung romanischer Kleinsprachen* (pp. 119–137). Tübingen: Narr.

Rindler Schjerve, R. (1993). Sardinian: Italian, In R. Posner & J. Green (Eds.), *Bilingualism and Linguistic Conflict in Romance* [Trends in Romance Linguistics and Philology Vol. 5] (pp. 271–294). Berlin and New York: De Gruyter.

Rindler Schjerve, R. (1996). Cambiamento di codice come strategia di sopravvivenza overro sulla vitalità del sardo al giorno d'oggi. In D. Kremer & A. Monjour (Eds.), *Studia ex hilaritate. Mélanges de linguistique et d'onomastique sardes et romanes offerts à H. J. Wolf* [Travaux de Linguistique et de Philolgie XXXIII–XXXIV] (pp. 409–425). Strasbourg and Nancy: Klincksieck.

Rindler Schjerve, R. (1997a). Codeswitching-oder Sprachstrukturen im Konflikt? In W. W. Moelleken & P. Weber (Eds.), *Neue Forschungsarbeiten zur Kontaktlinguistik* [Plurilingua XIX] (pp. 437–446). Bonn: Dümmler.

Rindler Schjerve, R. (1997b). Funktionen des Codeswitching in der Situation des Sprachenwechsels am Beispiel des Sardisch-Italienischen. In D. Kattenbusch (Ed.), *Kulturkontakt und Sprachkonflikt in der Romania* [Ethnos 50] (pp. 31–45). Wien: Braumüller.

Rindler Schjerve, R. (1997c). Sardaigne (Sarde, Italien, Catalan) In H. Goebl, P. H. Nelde, Z. Starý, & W. Wölck (Eds.), *Kontaktlinguistik. Ein Internationales Handbuch zeitgenössischer Forschung*, Vol. II (pp. 1376–1383). Berlin and New York: De Gruyter.

Rindler Schjerve, R. (1998a). Codeswitching as an indicator for language shift? Evidence from Sardinian-Italian bilingualism. In R. Jacobson (Ed.), *Codeswitching Worldwide* [Trends in Linguistics. Studies and Monographs 106] (pp. 221–247). Berlin and New York: Mouton de Gruyter.

Rindler Schjerve, R. (1998b). Sul cambiamento linguistico in situazioni di bilinguismo instabile: aspetti del codeswitching (CS) fra sardo e italiano. In G. Ruffino (Ed.), *Atti del XXI Congresso Internazionale di Linguistica e Filologia Romanza,* vol. V, Centro di studi filologici e linguistici siciliani, Università di Palermo 18–2 settembre 1995 (pp. 589–602). Tübingen: Niemeyer.

Rindler Schjerve, R. (1998c). Codeswitching und Sprachkontaktforschung. *Grenzgänge, 9* [Beiträge zu einer modernen Romanistik], 70–93.

Rindler Schjerve, R. (2001a). Codeswitching and language shift in Sardinian. In C. Schaner-Wolles, J. R. Rennison, & F. Neubarth (Eds.), *Naturally! Linguistic studies in honour of Wolfgang Ulrich Dressler presented on the occasion of his 60th birthday* (pp. 433–440). Torino: Rosenberg and Sellier.

Rindler Schjerve, R. (2001b). Inventario analitico delle attuali trasformazioni del sardo. In *Revista de Filologìa Romànica, 17*, 229–246.

Rindler Schjerve, R. (2001c). Das Sardische- eine sterbende Sprache? In Ch. Adobati, M. Aldouri-Lauber, M. Hager, & R. Hosch (Eds.), *Wenn Ränder Mitte werden. Zivilisation, Literatur und Sprache im interkulturellen Kontext. Festschrift für F. Peter Kirsch zum 60. Geburtstag* (pp. 151–161). Wien: WUV.

Rindler Schjerve, R. (2001d). Languages in contact and competition: Lessons from diglossia. In C. de Bot, S. Kroon, P. Nelde, & H. van der Velde (Eds.), *Institutional Status and Use of National Languages in Europe* [=Plurilingua XXIII] (pp. 77–90). St. Augustin: Asgard.

Rindler Schjerve, R. (2002). Wie stirbt die Sprache? Neueste Überlegungen zur Erforschung von Sprachenwechsel, Sprachverfall und Sprachtod. In J. D. Range (Ed.), *Baltisch-deutsche Sprach- und Kulturkontakte in Nord-Ostpreußen. Methoden ihrer Erforschung* [Schriften des Instituts für Baltistik 2, Universität Greifswald] (pp. 17–42).

Rindler Schjerve, R. (2003a). Externe Sprachgeschichte des Sardischen. In G. Ernst, M. D. Glessen, Ch. Schmitt, & W. Schweickard (Eds.) *Histoire des langues romanes. Manuel international d'histoire linguistique de la Romania* [Handbücher zur Sprach-und Kommunikationswissenschaft]. Berlin and New York: De Gruyter (forthcoming).

Rindler Schjerve, R. & Vetter, E. (2003b). Historical sociolinguistics and multilingualism: theoretical and methodological issues in the development of a multifunctional framework. In R. Rindler Schjerve (Ed.), *Diglossia and Power: Language Policies and Practice in the 19th Century Habsburg Empire* [=Language, Power and Social Process 9]. Berlin- New York: Mouton de Gruyter (forthcoming).

Romaine, S. (1989). *Bilingualism.* Oxford: Blackwell.

Sanna, A. (1957). *Introduzione agli studi di linguistica sarda.* Cagliari: Valdes.

Silva-Corvalán, C. (1994). *Language Contact and Change. Spanish in Los Angeles.* Oxford: Clarendon Press.

Sole, L. (1988). *Lingua e cultura in Sardegna.* Milano: Unicopli.

Thomason, S. G. & Kaufman, T. (1988). *Language Contact, Creolization and Genetic Linguistics.* Berkeley: University of California Press.

Treffers-Daller, J. (1992). French-Dutch Codeswitching in Brussels: Social Factors Explaining Its Disappearance. *Journal of Multilingual and Multicultural Development, 13* (1–2), 143–167.

Wagner, M. L. (1951). *La lingua sarda. Storia, spirito e forma.* Bern: Francke.

Wagner, M. L. (1960–1964). *Dizionario etimologico sardo.* Vol. I, II. Heidelberg: Winter.

Wagner, M. L. (2002). *Geschichte der sardischen Sprache,* hrgg. v. Giovanni Masala. Tübingen–Basel: Francke.

Language contact and Maltese intonation

Some parallels with other language varieties

Alexandra Vella
University of Malta

1. Introduction

Maltese is assumed by many, for example Alexander Borg (1994) and Wettinger (1993), to have developed in the late 9th century, probably from a medieval variety of Arabic.[1] According to Alexander Borg (1994:27):

> [...] the Arabic vernacular of the Maltese islands evolved in line with its own internal logic and drifted away from the norms of spoken Arabic with the result that Maltese and Arabic are today not mutually comprehensible.

Influences on the evolution of Maltese, that of (Old) Sicilian in particular, as well as that of other Romance varieties, and more recently that of English, have been widely documented (cf. Brincat 2000). Alexander Borg (1994:27) contends that it is precisely "the factor of language contact, first with Italian and later with English" which served as the "catalyst for independent linguistic development".

This paper seeks to throw new light on the way Maltese has evolved in a context of language contact, paying particular attention to an area which has to date been completely neglected by scholars in this field, namely the intonation of Maltese.

The paper is organised as follows. I first describe the context within which Maltese exists, showing that a multilingual reality has, from the beginning of the existence of Maltese, served as the context for its development. Parallels between Maltese and a number of varieties of Arabic on the one hand, and Italian on the other, are then discussed with reference to its phonology. It has been suggested (cf. for example Alexander Borg 1978; Wettinger 1993) that Maltese fits in better with the Maghreb (North African) Arabic dialect group as far as features such as verbal morphology and other aspects of grammar are concerned, but with the Levantine (Eastern) Arabic dialects as far as phonological traits are concerned.[2] It is assumed that the prosody of Maltese has been shaped in ways similar to other aspects of the phonology of Maltese. This paper therefore seeks to establish to what extent the above classification can be extended to include aspects of the prosody of Maltese, in particular its intonation, and to a more limited extent its system of lexical stress. At the same time, the paper attempts to investigate the extent to which Italian varieties have left their mark on the above mentioned aspects of the phonology of Maltese. Sections 3 to 5 provide an overview of the segmental system and lexical stress before stopping to focus on intonation. Particularly in Sections 4 and 5, which deal with lexical stress and intonation in Maltese respectively, comparisons will be made, where possible, with published accounts of the intonation of two Arabic dialects, namely Moroccan Arabic, a dialect of the Maghreb (Benkirane 1998), and Lebanese Arabic, a Levantine dialect (Chahal 1999). The main source for the comparison with Italian will be Palermo Italian (Grice 1995), but work on other varieties of Italian will also be cited.

The focus of this paper is Standard Maltese, the variety of Maltese which to date has been most widely described (cf. for example, Albert Borg, & Azzopardi-Alexander 1997; Fabri 1993; Mifsud 1995; Mifsud & Albert Borg 1997). However, occasionally, reference is made to work on dialects of Maltese, including preliminary work on the intonation of dialects of Maltese, to elucidate points in the discussion.

2. Maltese and its development in the context of multilingualism

2.1 The Maltese language and bilingualism in Malta

Maltese is the national language of Malta and is spoken by the greater part of the 382,525 inhabitants of the Maltese Islands.[3] It is also still used as a first language by some Maltese emigrants, in particular, first and second generation emigrants living in large expatriate communities in Australia, Canada and the United States (cf. for example, Bovingdon 2001). In spite of its status as national language, however, Maltese does not hold sway alone, even within the shores of Malta. It shares official status with English and any "such other language as may be prescribed by Parliament" (*Constitution of the Republic of*

Malta 1974: 2). This official policy of bilingualism reflects, and is reflected in, the facts concerning language use at other levels of Maltese life.

2.2 Geographical and historical context

The Maltese Islands (area approximately 316 km^2) are situated in the central Mediterranean, a position which has often been perceived as a crossroads between East and West. In spite of their small size, the islands' geographical position has resulted in Malta playing a central role in the Mediterranean, and sometimes also in international affairs.

The British colonial period, starting in 1800, was the last in a series of foreign dominations which included Phoenician, Roman, Arab and Norman rule, a long period during which Malta was ruled by the knights of the Order of St. John, and a brief French period under Napoleon. Malta gained independence in 1964. It is a member of the Commonwealth and has been a republic since 1974. Malta is expected to become a European Union member-state in May 2004.

2.3 Origins and development of Maltese

Like much else that is Maltese, the Maltese language of today is an entity distinct from any other, having incorporated elements from various sources and subsequently transmuted them into something new.

Attempts to trace the precise origins of Maltese back to either Phoenician or Punic have, as Hull (1993: 297) comments, "been totally discredited by modern scholarship". The author concludes that there is no doubt that "Maltese derives from the Arabic introduced into Malta and Gozo some time between A.D. 870 and 1090".[4] It has been suggested by Cassola (1985: 2) that it was probably as a manifestation of what is known as Siculo-Arabic that the Maltese language of today had its beginnings:

> [...] Siculo-Arabic [...] was gradually transformed into [...] the linguistic phenomenon that is Maltese, a language whose morphology is almost entirely Semitic, and whose syntax and lexis are Romance. (Own translation)

The heterogeneity of the Maltese language has been commented on by various authors (cf. Aquilina 1958; Aquilina 1961; Mifsud 1995). In a paper called "Kattoliċità Maltija – jew il-vokazzjoni tal-ħuttaba" ("Maltese Catholicism – or the vocation of the matchmaker"), Serracino-Inglott (1989: 266) says of Maltese that:

> [...] the originality of our language lies in the melding of elements from Romance as well as other languages with an Arabic base [...]. (Own translation)

Maltese, therefore, consists of a Semitic base upon which various borrowings from other languages, English as well as the Romance languages are superimposed. Mifsud (1995: 27) describes Maltese as consisting of three strata. He describes the Semitic "stratum" as:

> [...] the basis of the phonology, morphology and to a lesser extent the syntax of Maltese, while [on the other hand] the lexis of Semitic origin constitutes a nucleus of basic concepts, with more culturally sophisticated terms generally being of Romance or English origin.

The Romance "superstratum":

> [...] is represented by a large stock of lexical, syntactic, phonological and some morphological accretions.

Lastly, the English "adstratum":

> [...] consists mainly of lexical material adapted by Maltese since 1800 in two phases roughly distinguishable in terms of the English-Maltese contact.

It has been noted that the Romance period can be divided into an early period involving greater influence from Sicilian and a later period involving greater influence from Northern dialects of Italian such as Tuscan Italian (Brincat 2000).

The success of a language can often be attributed in part to its ability to adapt in the face of ever-changing realities. Documentation of the continuing adaptability of Maltese in the face of foreign accretions is available in a number of studies. While the most obvious level for such updating is the lexical one (cf. for example Albert Borg 1986), adaptation can also be noted at other levels of structure. Thus, for example, Mifsud (1995) demonstrates that, notwithstanding constraints such as those from the morphology of Maltese on borrowing from English (Brincat Massa 1986), Maltese has developed a repertoire of successful morphological strategies for coping with borrowing from English as well as Romance. In fact, it has been suggested by Camilleri and Albert Borg (1992) that the kind of borrowing that takes place and the way it is brought about often result in further transformation of the original Semitic base. For example the often-cited example of the English plural morpheme *-s*, according to them, is rapidly becoming "an integral part of Maltese pluralising morphology" (cf. also Fabri 1993). Although most of the examples quoted in these studies involve lexical borrowing and its effect on the morphology, it seems reasonable to suppose that effects of the phenomenon referred to by Camilleri and Albert Borg (1992) as the "Englishisation of Maltese" are also present at other levels of structure such as syntax and phonology.

2.4 The rise of multilingualism

From the earliest days, one of the consequences of Malta's central position in the Mediterranean was a necessity for the Maltese to communicate both with trading peoples who visited the island in times of peace, and with unwelcome invaders in times of war. Blouet (1967:44) describes the linguistic situation in Malta during the early stages of the development of Maltese as one in which the bulk of the population spoke "a dialect of Arabic augmented by Latin, Spanish and Italian words". Such an amorphous entity could quite conceivably have functioned as "a communication link between peoples of different ethnicity and heritage" (Serracino-Inglott 1989:266, own translation).

With the continuing development of Maltese into a separate language, however, the need for the local inhabitants to resort to other languages for communicating with the stream of traders and travellers stopping in Malta would definitely have increased. In fact, Blouet (1967:44) reports "an elite group" to use "a Romance language for purposes of social, economic and legal intercourse among themselves and with the outside world". Coupled with the reported increase in the use of Maltese for local purposes, claims such as Blouet's suggest that, while one cannot exclude sections of the population amongst whom monolingualism would still have been the norm, the linguistic reality in Malta for many others could hardly have been a monolingual one. Multilingualism in Malta can therefore be considered a phenomenon stretching back at least as far as the existence of Maltese as a language in its own right, thus providing a continuing context of language contact within which Maltese developed.[5]

3. The segmental phonology of Maltese

As mentioned earlier, it has been argued, for example by Wettinger (1993) and Alexander Borg (1994), that Maltese can be firmly classified typologically with the dialects of the Maghreb (or North African) Arabic area (e.g. Tunisia, Algeria, Morocco) on the basis of formal grammatical features such as verbal morphology. However, Maltese is frequently shown to share other characteristics, particularly phonological and lexical ones, with members of the Levantine (or Eastern) Arabic dialect area (e.g. Lebanon, Palestine, Syria). In this section and the following ones I attempt to shed light on the extent to which our knowledge about Maltese phonology justifies a classification of Maltese as similar to the Levantine dialects of Arabic, and to what extent evidence of language-contact phenomena of other sorts, for example in the form of similarities to different varieties of Italian, can be detected in the sound system of Maltese.

3.1 Consonantal phonemes

Watson (2002) provides a description of the phoneme inventories of two dialects of Arabic, that of San'ani, a dialect of the Gulf Arabic type, and that of Cairene. Watson shows that the San'ani consonantal system is closer to that of eighth-century CE[6] Classical Arabic than is that of Cairene. The main differences between San'ani and Cairene occur with respect to the class of interdental and dental-alveolars of San'ani as compared to the dental-alveolars of Cairene, the latter having completely lost the distinction between the two classes which San'ani retains. It is interesting that Maltese, in fact, is similar to Cairene Arabic in this respect, but differs from Cairene Arabic and from most other Arabic dialects across the different dialect groups, in having furthermore lost the distinction between emphatic and non-emphatic versions of plosives and fricatives. Thus, whereas most dialects of Arabic make a distinction between *sajf* 'sword' and *ṣajf* 'summer', Maltese uses the same initial consonant phoneme /s/, while different vocalisations of the vowel distinguish *sejf* 'sword' from *sajf* 'summer'.

Alexander Borg (1994) compares aspects of the consonantal phoneme system of contemporary Maltese to that of Old Arabic. His comparison shows that the Standard Maltese system of consonant phonemes differs from that of Old Arabic both in having lost some of the Old Arabic consonant phonemes and in having added some new ones to the system.

The differences between the consonantal systems of Maltese and Arabic have been summarised by Brincat (2000). While Maltese utilises the non-Arabic phonemes /p/, /v/, /ts/, /dz/, /ʧ/ and /ʤ/, consonants it shares with Italian, it has lost all the Arabic pharyngeals and emphatics. It does however retain use of the glottal fricative /h/, and although Classical Arabic ç has been lost, /ʔ/ is used in Maltese in place of Classical Arabic /q/. This latter fact, according to Kaye and Rosenhouse (1997: 270), constitutes "strong evidence that [Maltese] cannot be considered a Maghrebian (North African) dialect".

Brincat (2000) argues that while it seems reasonable to conclude that, with respect to its consonantal system, Maltese appears to have moved away from

Arabic and closer to Italian, there are still many unanswered questions. For example, the original Semitic base of Maltese may, says Brincat (2000: 186):

> [...] have come in with a non-Arabic community which had learnt an Arabic already modified by [a language] substratum (Romance? Greek? Berber?) in Sicily or North Africa, and these sounds may have been present in Maltese from the beginning of its history... similarly it is difficult to put a date to exactly when those sounds which were lost were dropped. (Own translation)

3.2 Vowel phonemes

There is no doubt that Maltese differs from most dialects of Arabic in having evolved a much more fully articulated system of vowels. This system of vowels, according to Albert Borg and Azzopardi-Alexander's (1997) description of Standard Maltese, consists of 5 short and 6 long monophthongs, and 7 diphthongs. As mentioned above, vowel distinctions are often used in Maltese to make those distinctions which Arabic dialects effect on the basis of a richer consonantal inventory. Both Alexander Borg (1994) and Kaye and Rosenhouse (1997) make reference to characteristics of the vowel system of Maltese, for example the preservation of Old Arabic diphthongs, with respect to which Maltese, particularly in some of its dialectal manifestations, also seems to align more closely with the Levantine dialects of Arabic than with the Maghrebian ones.

In his comparison of the phonetics and phonology of Maltese to that of Arabic and Italian, Brincat (2000) refers to work on Maltese dialects such as that carried out by Aquilina and Isserlin (1981), Schabert (1976), Sciriha (1986) and Camilleri and Vanhove (1994). He claims that the relationship of the vowel systems of different dialects of Maltese to the vowel system of Standard Maltese on the one hand, and to dialects of Arabic on the other, has yet to be ascertained. Brincat however takes a stronger position with regard to what he considers the origins of the vowels of Standard Maltese. According to him, these derive primarily from Sicilian, although influence from Latin as well as Tuscan Italian is also suggested.

4. Lexical stress in Maltese

4.1 The case of antepenultimate stress

As in the case of its phonemic system, the influence of Italian on lexical stress in Maltese cannot be ignored, especially in the case of antepenultimate stress, a relatively recent phenomenon in Maltese.

Lexical stress in Maltese is outlined in, among others, Sutcliffe (1936), Aquilina (1959, 1965), Brame (1972, 1974) and Alexander Borg (1973, 1975). Although individual formulations differ, all the accounts agree that lexical stress in Maltese is generally either final or penultimate. While generally acknowledged, the occurrence of antepenultimate stress, especially in loan words, has often been dismissed as a "foreign-stress pattern" (Aquilina 1959: 73).

The possibility of antepenultimate stress in Maltese lexical items was recognised as early as Sutcliffe (1936: 12–13). Sutcliffe, however, also notes the tendency for stress in loan words to be regularised to native patterns. Thus:

> In Maltese words, the accent does not occur earlier than the penultimate syllable. Apparent exceptions to this rule are learned formulations or loan words which have not adapted themselves to the genius of the language, e.g. **artíkolu**, the definite 'article'. Similar words which have become really identified with the language omit the short vowel of the penultimate syllable, e.g. **kanónku** *canon* (ecclesiastical term) from Sicilian 'Canónicu', or 'Canónacu'.

It is interesting to note that Sutcliffe's very example of a non-regularised instance of antepenultimate stress has since been so regularised, to *ar'tiklu*.[7] This fact can be construed as evidence for an ongoing process of regularisation of antepenultimate stress to native patterns. On the other hand, the list of examples of antepenultimately stressed items in present day Maltese is long.[8] Amongst the examples of lexical items of Italian origin having antepenultimate stress in Maltese we find *a'naliżi* 'analysis', *'ċiniku* 'cynic' and *ka'tastrofi* 'catastrophe'. Examples from English in which the original antepenultimate stress patterning is retained include *'barbikju* 'barbecue', *'bajsikil* 'bicycle' and *'terminus* 'terminus'. An increasing number of more complex loan words, especially loan words from English, for example *il'lejbilja* 'he labelled' and *is'servisja* 'he serviced', which are modelled on the morphology of Maltese, are also pronounced with antepenultimate stress by many speakers, although penultimately stressed versions of these words are also possible (cf. Mifsud 1995 and below).

Like Sutcliffe, Aquilina (1959:73) observes a tendency for stress to be regularised in words such as *'stupidu* by deletion of the penultimate syllable and reassignment of stress to the penultimate syllable, thus resulting in the form [ˈstuːptʊ]. Other examples of this regularisation are *'mużika* with the form [ˈmuːzkɐ] and *anti'patiku* having the form [ɐntɪˈpɐːtkʊ].[9] Aquilina suggests that the regularisation of antepenultimate to penultimate stress in cases such as the above is often a marker of the less educated speaker. He suggests that the phenomenon is not widespread. However, the number of examples of lexical items orginally having antepenultimate stress which have become lexicalised as forms having penultimate stress is quite large. Examples include Maltese *abi'tudni* < Italian *abi'tudine* 'habit', *pe'riklu* < Italian *pe'ricolo* 'danger', and *'stonku* < Italian ***'stomaco*** 'stomach'. Toponyms provide additional illustrative material. Thus for example, we have *'Napli* < Italian *'Napoli* and *'Tripli* < *'Tripoli*, but *'Korsika* not **'Korska* < Italian *'Corsica*.

It is perhaps interesting to draw a parallel with what Rossi (1998:235) says about lexical stress in what he calls "Gallo-Italic dialectal varieties of Northern Italy". According to Rossi, lexical stress in these varieties is also limited to either final or penultimate position. Thus:

> Antepenultimate stress "sdrucciolo" disappears either through dropping of the post-tonic syllable as in:
>
> MANtova ⇒ MANtwa (the town "Mantova")

or through rightward stress-shift:

> PALpebra ⇒ parPEla (eyelid)
> LEvanto ⇒ liVANtu (the town "Levanto")

The processes involved in the regularisation of antepenultimate stress to penultimate described by Rossi bear a remarkable resemblance to the situation described for Maltese above. In this regard, the contact with Tuscan Italian in the middle to late sixteenth century noted by Brincat (2000) is perhaps significant. Brincat (2000:103) describes a situation extant in sixteenth century Malta at the time of the Knights during which Tuscan Italian was used alongside Maltese as the "high" variety. This was especially the case in the domains of administration and the church, as well as in the language used by professionals such as notaries, teachers and perhaps also doctors. It is usually assumed that the phenomenon of antepenultimate stress in Maltese is a relatively recent one, and one which entered the language through contact with different varieties of Italian. Oddly enough, however, the original constraint on antepenultimate stress in Maltese, operative at least until the first half of the twentieth century (but no longer so), may also have arisen out of earlier contact with dialects of Italian such as those mentioned by Rossi (above) which enforced such a restriction.

From a synchronic point of view, the phenomenon of antepenultimate stress appears to me to be far too common in present day Maltese for its dismissal as a "foreign stress-pattern" to be acceptable. While it is clear that such stress is more normally characteristic of loan words of both Italian and English origin than it is of words of Arabic origin, it is also clear that for stress to be assigned antepenultimately, the antepenultimate syllable of the word in question, regardless of its origin, must count as phonologically [+heavy], i.e. for Maltese, minimally (C)VC or (C)V: (cf. Vella 1995), thus [nɐː] in *a'naliżi* 'analysis', [ʧiː] in *'ċiniku* 'cynic', [tɐs] in *ka'tastrofi* 'catastrophe', [bɐr] in ***'barbikju*** 'barbecue', [bɐɪ] in ***'bajsikil*** 'bicycle' and [tɛr] in *'terminus* 'terminus', as well as [leɪ] in *il'lejbilja* 'he labelled' and [sɛr] in *is'servisja* 'he serviced'.[10]

4.2 Lexical stress assignment in Maltese from a comparative perspective

I will here examine the facts about lexical stress assignment in Maltese from a comparative perspective by referring to Benkirane's (1998) and Chahal's (1999) accounts of lexical stress in the Maghrebian dialect of Moroccan Arabic and the Eastern dialect of Lebanese Arabic, as well as to other accounts of lexical stress assignment available in the literature such as that of Hayes 1995 (following, amongst others, Brame 1974) on Palestinian Arabic.

Maltese makes a distinction between light (C)V syllables, heavy (C)VC and (C)V: syllables, and superheavy (C)VCC and (C)V:C syllables (cf. Hayes 1995 who makes a similar distinction, for example with respect to Palestinian Arabic). In this respect, Maltese resembles Lebanese (Chahal 1999) and Palestinian Arabic (Hayes 1995) but not Moroccan Arabic (Benkirane 1998) which only has syllables of the light and heavy types.

Lexical stress assignment in Maltese can be characterised as follows: assign lexical stress to a superheavy final syllable or to the heavy syllable closest to the end of the word; in the absence of either a final superheavy or a non-final heavy syllable, assign lexical stress penultimately. Antepenultimate stress in examples such as those quoted at the end of the previous section is assigned completely regularly given this rule. In fact, the rule given above can be said to apply to all Maltese words except loan words from Italian containing an open final heavy syllable such as *libertà* 'freedom', *verità* 'truth' and *virtù* 'truth': in these cases, it is my impression that the final stressed vowels are in fact rendered phonetically longer than is the case for non-final stressed versions of these vowels. Empirical study of this issue is yet to be carried out.

Thus, Maltese can be seen to differ from Moroccan Arabic in allowing the three-way distinction between light, heavy and superheavy syllables as in Lebanese and Palestinian Arabic. Moreover, Maltese, like both Lebanese and Palestian Arabic but unlike Moroccan Arabic normally requires a final syllable to be superheavy if it is to be assigned stress. Maltese is unlike Lebanese Arabic in one respect, however. Lebanese Arabic requires a penultimate syllable to be heavy in order to receive stress. In the absence of a syllable heavy enough to carry stress, Lebanese Arabic assigns stress to the antepenultimate syllable. By contrast, it is the penultimate syllable in Maltese which is assigned stress in the absence of the relevant superheavy or heavy syllable.

To summarize, it appears that, by and large, lexical stress assignment in Maltese follows principles more similar to those for Levantine dialects of Arabic rather than to dialects of the Maghreb such as Moroccan Arabic, as suggested by Alexander Borg (1994) and Kaye and Rosenhouse (1997) among others. Classification of Maltese with the Levantine dialect group in this respect is however not as neat as suggested by Alexander Borg and Kaye and Rosenhouse. At the same time, the discussion in Section 4.1 has shown that borrowing from English, as well as from Italian over a more extensive period, have both left their mark on the system for the assignment of lexical stress in Maltese.

5. The intonation of Maltese

Although interest in both intonation and intonational variation is increasing, work on the intonation of non-Indo European languages is still relatively restricted. Notwithstanding this, an important aim of this paper is to address the issue of how the intonation of Maltese compares to that of the varieties which have formed the basis of the comparison in the preceding sections of this chapter. On the one hand, it seems that Arabists listening to spoken Maltese are often struck by how much Maltese sounds like Arabic, in spite of the "foreignness" arising out of the stock of non-Semitic vocabulary as well as from, at a more basic level, that arising out of the absence of certain "Arabic" phonemes and the presence of other "non-Arabic" ones in the structure of many words (M. Mifsud, personal communication; cf. also Section 3.1). On the other hand, linguists working on intonational variation within dialects of Italian in particular, regularly comment on certain tunes described for Maltese sounding very much like tunes present in some varieties of Italian. While these two facts may seem contradictory, they are precisely what one would expect given the context of language contact (cf. Section 2 above) within which Maltese has evolved. Intonation, like other prosodic features, is acquired relatively early in the process of the acquisition of language. At the same time, such features appear to be highly permeable to change. It should therefore not be surprising if the prosody of Maltese turns out to be hybrid in nature, with influences from various sources having left their mark.

In what follows, I attempt to compare a number of intonation structures in Maltese to their counterparts in available descriptions of Moroccan Arabic (Benkirane 1998) and Lebanese Arabic (Chahal 1999) on the one hand, and Palermo Italian (Grice 1995) on the other. The description of intonation in Maltese given here is largely based on Vella (1995). The discussion provided in this section is couched in the terms and notation associated with the Autosegmental-Metrical (AM) model of intonational phonology (Ladd 1996) which was developed from seminal work by Pierrehumbert (1980). I have attempted to provide a "standardised" interpretation of the analyses given in the different descriptions. Schematisations of global contour shape (Figures 1, 2, 5 and 7) have, however, also been provided. These serve as an "atheoretical" anchor intended to bypass the notational inconsistencies across the different descriptions.

As in the preceding sections, the choice of Arabic dialects for the comparison has been made partly in an attempt to determine whether Maltese is more similar to the Levantine rather than to the Maghrebian dialects of Arabic at the level of phonology, in this case its prosody.

In the case of Italian, restricting the comparison to specific dialects is also important, partly because it makes it possible to bypass the difficulty arising out of the heterogeneity of Italian (cf. Rossi 1998). Given the history of the contact of Maltese with Sicilian Italian on the one hand and Tuscan Italian on the other (Brincat 2000), it makes sense to align a comparison of language contact effects between Italian and Maltese mainly to descriptions of dialects of these two areas. For various reasons, including the non-availability of literature on the intonation of different varieties couched in a comparable framework, in the following, intonation in Maltese is compared only to one Italian dialect, namely Palermo Italian as described by Grice (1995).

The discussion which follows deals first with intonation in declaratives with late focus (also referred to as "broad focus" in the literature) (5.1), yes-no questions with late focus (5.2) and wh-questions (5.3). Consideration of other aspects of the intonation of the varieties discussed here would have made it possible to draw other interesting parallels. In particular, in view of the fact that a correlation between early focus (also referred to as "narrow focus) structures and post-nuclear pitch accents has been documented for both Maltese

(Vella 1995) and Palermo Italian (Grice 1995), the intonation of early focus structures in the different varieties would have made for an interesting study. However, due to lack of space, this issue will not be discussed here.

The illustrative material from Maltese in this section is taken from data involving three adult male speakers of Standard Maltese. Each of these speakers was first asked to read a short text containing a range of grammatical structures. Two of the speakers were then recorded as they engaged in free conversation together. The initials of each speaker together with an indication of whether the example in question involves read (_R) or conversational (_C) data are placed in parenthesis following the first mention of each example.

5.1 Intonation in declaratives with late focus

According to Benkirane (1998), the "basic non-emphatic pattern" in Moroccan Arabic, i.e. the pattern in cases of late focus, involves a rise-fall with the rise occurring on the syllable carrying sentence accent. The F_0 contours provided by Benkirane (1998: 353, Figures 2–5) support the analysis he gives of a rise-fall, presumably a sequence which could be annotated as L H* L-L%. The global shape of the course of F_0 in this case is schematised in Figure 1 below.[11]

The tune in Lebanese Arabic declaratives described by Chahal (1999), on the other hand, involves a typical "hat pattern". Chahal analyses this as a sequence consisting of a H* pitch accent followed by a H* L-L%, the second H* being associated with the syllable carrying sentence accent.

Palermo Italian, as described by Grice (1995), seems to allow both a fall approached from above similar to the hat-patterned fall described for Lebanese Arabic by Chahal, and a more marked version of the fall consisting of a rise from the pre-stressed syllable to the start of the fall within the stressed syllable itself. Grice suggests analyses of HL* L^b L^B and H*L L^b L^B respectively for the two versions of the fall.[12] Either way, there is a fall from the stressed syllable, either approached from above, or approached from below. These possibilities

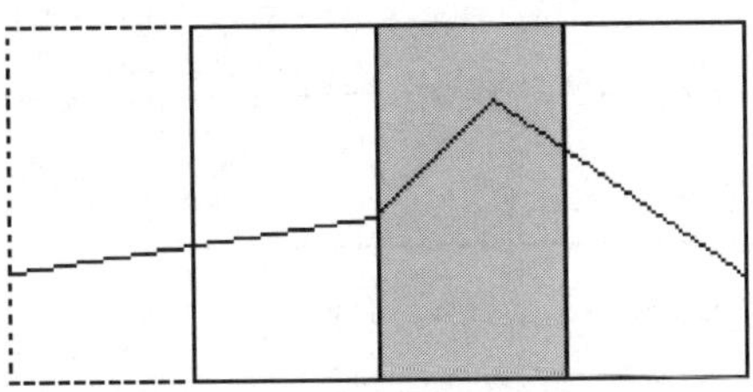

Figure 1. Rise-fall in late focus declaratives

are schematised in Figure 2 below. The broken lines in this figure represent the different possible approaches to the nuclear fall.

The late focus declarative in Maltese is described in Vella (1995) as consisting of a straightforward fall occurring within the stressed syllable, H*+L L%. The F_0 contour for *u jinterrompih.* 'and he interrupts him.' (CP_C), involving use of such a fall is shown in Figure 3 below.[13] The approach to the fall in this case is similar to the form for the more marked version of the fall described by Grice (1995) for Palermo Italian.

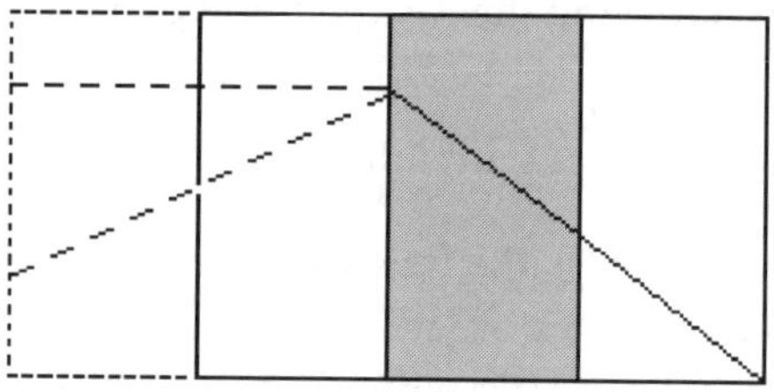

Figure 2. Falling contour in late focus declaratives

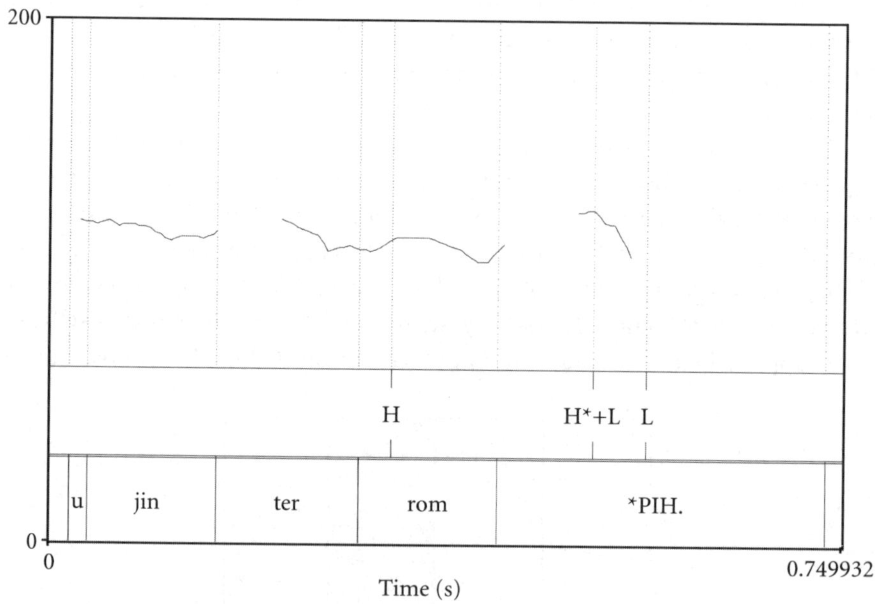

Figure 3. *u jinterrompih.* 'and he interrupts him.'

The hat pattern intonation, described by Chahal (1999) for Lebanese Arabic and by Grice (1995) for the less marked version of the Palermo Italian fall, is however also possible in Maltese. In fact, preliminary work on the intonation of the dialect of speakers from Żebbug, Gozo (Vella 1997) has noted the occurrence of such a pattern. Moreover, the analysis of declaratives in conversational data suggests that a fall approached from above also occurs frequently as the choice of tune of speakers of Standard Maltese. The F_0 contour for *April li għadda.* 'Last April.' (AB_C) shown in Figure 4 below provides a clear example of the use of a fall approached from above similar to those described by Chahal and Grice for Lebanese Arabic and Palermo Italian, respectively.

Although a more detailed study of the distribution of the two versions of the fall described above in Standard Maltese needs to be carried out, the above suggests that Maltese declaratives have the same pattern as the Lebanese Arabic and Palermo Italian one, a pattern different to that of Moroccan Arabic.

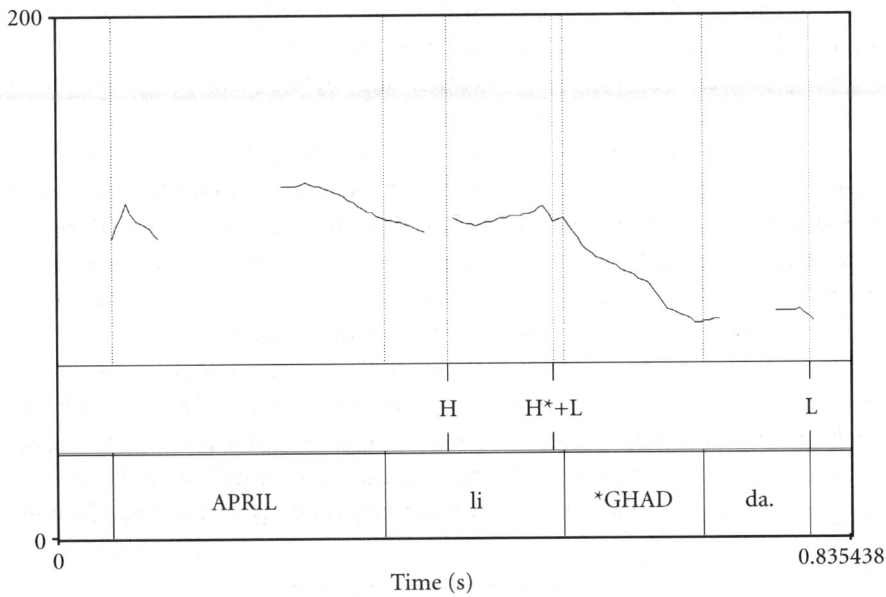

Figure 4. *April li għadda.* 'Last April.'

5.2 Intonation in yes-no questions with late focus

The intonation of yes-no questions with late focus described by Benkirane (1998) for Moroccan Arabic involves a rising movement within the nuclear syllable followed by a fall to a L tone at the boundary, something like L*H L-L% in AM notation. Although this pattern may at first appear to be very similar to that described above for Moroccan Arabic declaratives, the difference between the two patterns is, according to Benkirane (1998: 354), that while "there is an overall raising of the whole pitch register including the onset" in the case of yes-no questions, such an increase in pitch register does not happen in declaratives. A difference in timing implementation can also be noted. Although a final H boundary tone is possible, this is usually used to signal a degree of surprise.

The late focus yes-no question tune described by Grice (1995) for Palermo Italian is in fact very similar to that described by Benkirane for Moroccan Arabic. In other words, the intonation of late focus yes-no questions in Palermo Italian involves a rising movement within the stressed syllable followed by a fall in pitch to the boundary. The analysis suggested for the intonational form of such questions is L*H L^b L^B. The course of F_0 in late focus yes-no questions described by Benkirane and Grice is schematised in Figure 5 below.

Unlike what happens in both Moroccan Arabic and Palermo Italian, the yes-no question possibilities occurring in Lebanese Arabic described by Chahal (1999), notationally L* H-H% or L*+H H-H%, both involve an overall rise in pitch. The first of the two contour shapes involves a rise in pitch from a L tone reached late in the stressed syllable, the second a rise in pitch starting within the stressed syllable and continuing to the edge of the phrase.

Similarly, yes-no questions in Maltese are characterised by an overall rise in pitch. An example of the F0 contour for the utterance [*milli*] *tħalli 'il ħaddieħor jitkellem?* '[than] to allow others to speak?' (AP_C) is given in Figure 6 below.

According to Vella (1995), the tune in question, notationally L* H%, is characterised by a gradual rise to a H boundary tone associated with the edge

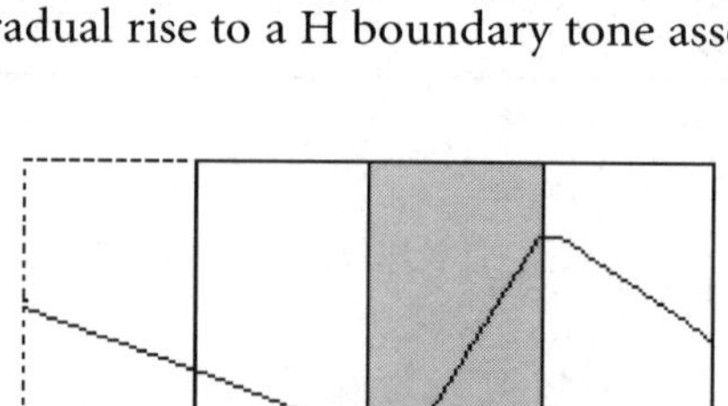

Figure 5. Rise-fall in late focus yes-no questions

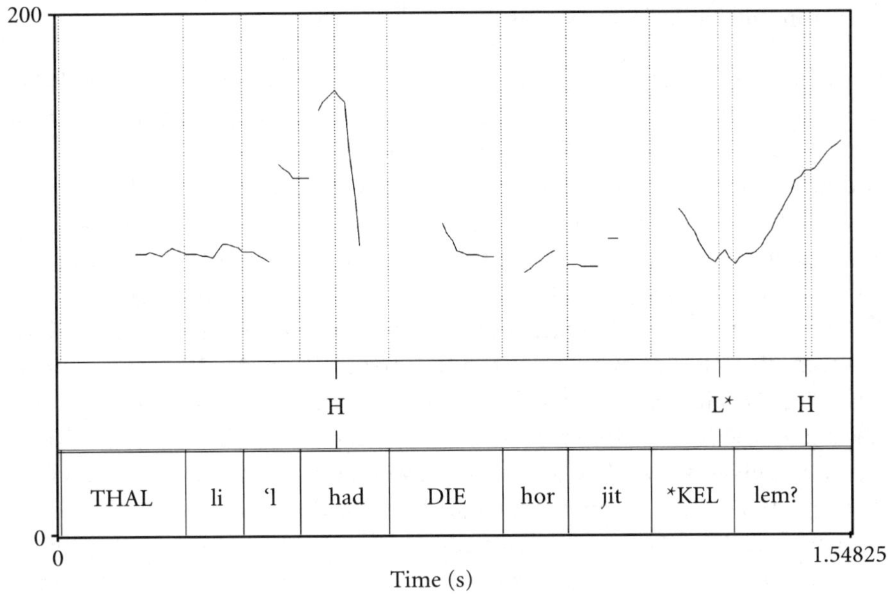

Figure 6. [*milli*] *tħalli 'l ħaddieħor jitkellem?* 'than to allow others to speak?'

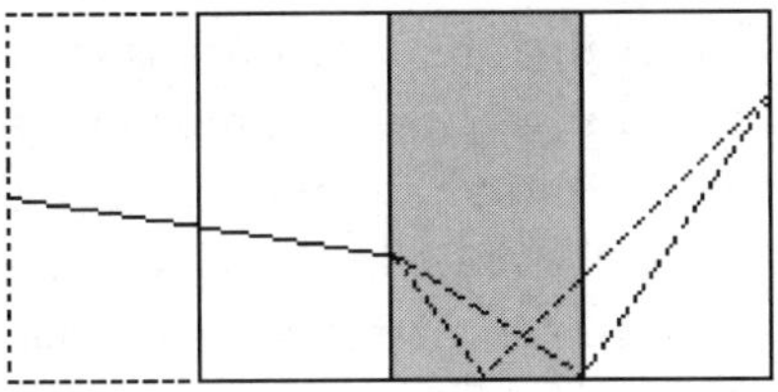

Figure 7. Rising contour in late focus yes-no questions

of the phrase. Vella (1995) suggests that the lowest point in the F_0 contour in such questions is reached late in the stressed syllable. This is similar to what happens in one of the two possibilities described by Chahal for Lebanese Arabic. A schematisation of the course of F_0 in late focus yes-no questions with a rising contour is given in Figure 7, the broken lines in the figure once again representing the different possibilities.

Thus, with regards to the intonation of yes-no question, Maltese aligns with Lebanese Arabic but not with Palermo Italian. The tune used in Palermo Italian is in this case similar to that in Moroccan Arabic but whether the similarity is due to language contact effects or not is a matter upon which one can but speculate at this stage.

5.3 Intonation in WH-questions

Reporting on a number of crosslinguistic surveys on the form of WH-questions, Cruttenden (1997) concludes that the most frequently used pattern in such questions amongst the languages surveyed is the fall. Moreover, according to the various surveys, "those languages which have a fall on question word interrogatives frequently have the same tune as declaratives except that the initial question word is very often given a specially high pitch" (Cruttenden 1997: 159). Ladd (1996) distinguishes between languages with WH-movement such as English, which do not stress the WH-word itself, and languages like Turkish without WH-movement, which do. He suggests that, cross-linguistically, languages without WH-movement tend to have intonation peaking on the WH-word wherever that word occurs in the utterance. However, although languages like Romanian have WH-movement, as does English, they nevertheless give prominence to the WH-word.

The dialects of Arabic and Italian for which descriptions are available do not seem to differ much with respect to the intonation of WH-questions. Thus, Benkirane (1998: 354) comments that "the intonation pattern of WH-questions is very similar to that found on imperatives which are also characterised by a high or rising onset followed by a rapid fall to the bottom of the speakers' range". He adds that the WH-word is made prominent by an F_0 peak, "whatever its place in the utterance". Unfortunately, there is nothing in either the description or the examples provided by Benkirane – he only provides schematisations of the examples in this case rather than F_0 contours as he does in other cases – to throw further light on the nature of such questions. Chahal's (1999) description of Lebanese intonation makes only one reference to WH-questions, suggesting that they are similar in form to yes-no questions. In the absence of illustrative material of this question type, the following brief reference to WH-questions is to be treated with caution.

A description of WH-question intonation in Italian (variety not specified) is given by Ladd (1996). The analysis suggested by Ladd for the example *Dove vai*? 'Where are you going?' is one involving a H tone associated with the WH-word, H*, downstepped to a H+L* and followed by a final L, L%. Crucial to the analysis is the assumption that the nuclear accent in Italian falls on *vai* rather than on the WH-word. In this respect, the analysis of WH-questions proposed by Ladd for Italian differs from that suggested by Benkirane for Moroccan Arabic.

In terms of global shape, WH-questions in Maltese seem to be no different from WH-questions in either Moroccan Arabic or Italian described above.

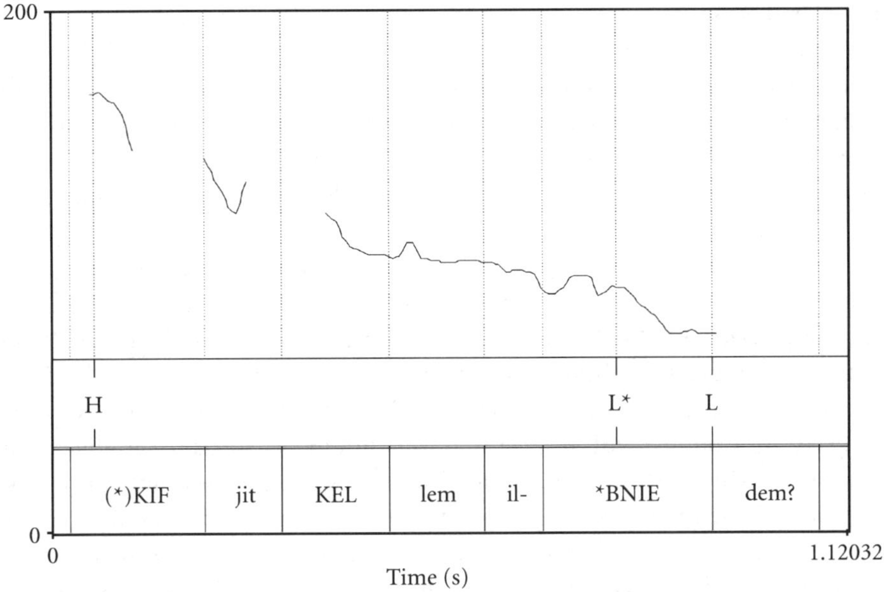

Figure 8. *Kif jitkellem il-bniedem?* 'How does man [learn to] speak?'

Such questions in Maltese seem to be characterised by a fall in pitch starting early in the intonation phrase, continuing to lower to the stressed syllable closest to the end of the phrase, from which pitch continues to fall to the end of the phrase. An example of the F_0 contour for a question of this kind, *Kif jitkellem il-bniedem*? 'How does man [learn to] speak?' (PP_R) is given in Figure 8.

The WH-question illustrated above has a form similar to that of the vocatives and imperatives described in Vella (1995) for which a H% L* L% analysis is postulated. Assuming that the analysis of the H tone at the left edge of the phrase is justified, as in Italian, sentence accent in such questions could be said to fall on the stressed syllable closest to the edge of the phrase rather than on the WH-word itself, such sentence accent being implemented as a L* pitch accent followed by a boundary L, L%. If Benkirane's analysis of intonation in WH-questions as consisting of a high falling pitch accent associated with the WH-word in Moroccan Arabic is correct, the above may serve to align Maltese to Italian with respect to intonation in such utterances.

6. Conclusion

The comparison of the sound system of Maltese to Moroccan Arabic and Lebanese Arabic on the one hand, and Palermo Italian on the other, suggests that while the categorisation of Maltese as being phonologically closer to the Levantine rather than the Maghrebian dialects largely holds, the influence of Italian cannot be ignored.

The similarity of Maltese to Lebanese Arabic with respect to the intonational patterns examined here is striking, in that it provides further support for the categorisation of Maltese with the Levantine as opposed to the Maghrebian dialects of Arabic. In addition, it is extremely interesting to note the hybrid nature of Palermo Italian: it is similar to Maltese and Lebanese Arabic in some respects, for example with respect to intonation in late focus declaratives, but is more similar to Moroccan Arabic in other respects, for example in the intonation of late focus yes-no questions. While it would be premature to draw clear conclusions from the patterns that have been identified here, this appears to be an area that warrants further investigation, using directly comparable data which may help to better exemplify the melting-pot effect on languages in contact.

Notes

1. Throughout this work, references to work by Albert Borg and Alexander Borg are distinguished in the text as well as in the References section using the respective authors' full names.

2. Dialects of Arabic are often divided into four groups as follows: *Maghreb Arabic* spoken in Tunisia, Algeria, Morocco and parts of Libya; *Egyptian Arabic* spoken in parts of Libya and Egypt; *Levantine Arabic* spoken in Israel, Palestine, Jordan, Lebanon, Syria; *Gulf Arabic* spoken in Bahrain, Kuwait, Oman, Qatar, Saudi Arabia and the UAE.

3. This figure is based on information for end of year 2000 obtained from the website of the National Statistics Office, Malta, http://www.nso.gov.mt/quarterly%20statistics/mainindicators.htm

4. For a contribution to the ongoing endeavour of illuminating what the author refers to as "the still fog-shrouded origins of our language" (own translation) cf. Brincat (1994: 138).

5. There is evidence that the Phoenicians (themselves acquainted with Greek) co-existed with the Bronze Age inhabitants of Malta. The existence of Greek inscriptions from the Punic period in fact makes it possible to hypothesise that multilingualism may have been in existence in Malta as early as the 8th–7th century BCE (Albert Borg, personal communication).

6. B/CE = Before/Common Era.

7. The spelling of examples, in all cases for which lexical entries are available, is as given in Aquilina's *Maltese – English Dictionary, Volumes 1 and 2* (1987, 1990). Aquilina makes use of the grave accent ˋ, to mark the vowel of the stressed syllable in cases where the location of stress is not self-evident. Instead of Aquilina's convention I mark stress in both citation and phonetic form examples by means of a superscript ˈ at the start of the stressed syllable. Examples from other authors in the text are also transliterated to conform to the stress-marking convention used here, although individual authors' conventions are retained in quotations.

8. A few examples such as *im'moniterja* 'he monitored' with ante-antepenultimate stress, have also entered Maltese through contact with English. Stress in this position is however extremely rare in Maltese and is therefore not discussed here.

9. Apart from the forms [ˈstuːpɪdʊ] and [ˈmuːzɪkɐ] with antepenultimate stress, possible phonetic realisations for /ˈstuːpɪdʊ/ and /ˈmuːzɪkɐ/ are [ˈstuːbdʊ] and [ˈmuːskɐ], although [ˈstuːptʊ] and [ˈmuːzgɐ] are also possible, cf. obstruent voicing rule for example Vella (1995).

10. Penultimately stressed versions of as *illej'bilja* 'he labelled' and *isser'visja* 'he serviced' would also involve [+heavy] penultimate syllables as a result of gemination of the [l] and [s] respectively, thus [ɪl.leɪ.ˈbɪl.ljɐ] and [ɪs.sɛr.ˈvɪs.sjɐ].

11. The following conventions are used in the figures in this chapter involving schematisations: each rectangular section represents a syllable; rectangular sections having broken lines for borders represent the *n* other possible syllables stretching out leftwards; stressed syllables are represented by means of shading; broken F_0 contour lines represent different possibilities for the implementation of F_0.

12. Grice (1995) uses the superscripts ^{b} and ^{B} respectively rather than the more usual % to indicate association with intermediate and intonation phrase boundaries respectively.

13. The following conventions are used in the figures in this chapter involving F_0 contours: examples are transcribed orthographically syllable by syllable; capitalisation is used to indicate lexical stress; capitalisation preceded by an asterisk is used to indicate the main stress of the phrase.

References

Aquilina, J. (1958). Maltese as a mixed language. *Journal of Semitic Studies, 3*, 58–79. Reprinted in Aquilina 1961.

Aquilina, J. (1959). *The Structure of Maltese*. Malta: Progress Press.

Aquilina, J. (1961). *Papers in Maltese Linguistics*. Malta: Progress Press.

Aquilina, J. (1965). *Teach Yourself Maltese*. London: The English Universities' Press Ltd.

Aquilina, J. (1987). *Maltese – English Dictionary, Volume 1*. Malta: Midsea Books Ltd.

Aquilina, J. (1990). *Maltese – English Dictionary, Volume 2*. Malta: Midsea Books Ltd.

Aquilina, J. & Isserlin, B. S. J. (1981). *A Survey of Contemporary Dialectal Maltese, Volume 1 – Gozo*. Leeds: University of Leeds.

Benkirane, T. (1998). Intonation in Western Arabic (Morocco). In D. J. Hirst & A. Di Cristo (Eds.), *Intonation Systems: A survey of twenty languages* (pp. 345–359). Cambridge: CUP.

Blouet, B. (1967). *The Story of Malta*. Malta: Progress Press.

Borg, Albert (1986). The maintenance of Maltese as a language: What chances? In *Council of Europe, 1988*, 89–106.

Borg, Albert & Azzopardi-Alexander, M. (1997). *Maltese* [Descriptive Grammars]. London and New York: Routledge.

Borg, Alexander (1973). The segmental phonemes of Maltese. *Linguistics, 109*, 5–11.

Borg, Alexander (1975). Maltese morphophonemics. *Journal of Maltese Studies, 10*, 11–28.

Borg, Alexander (1978). A Historical and Comparative Phonology and Morphology of Maltese. Unpublished Ph.D. Dissertation, The Hebrew University.

Borg, Alexander (1994). Language. In H. Frendo & O. Friggieri (Eds.), *Malta: Culture and identity* (pp. 27–50). Malta: Publication of the Ministry of Youth and the Arts.

Bovingdon, R. (2001). *The Maltese Language of Australia: Maltraljan*. München: Lincom Europa.

Brame, M. (1972). On the abstractness of phonology: Maltese ς. In M. Brame (Ed.), *Contributions to Generative Phonology* (pp. 22–61). Austin, TX: University of Texas Press.

Brame, M. (1974). The cycle in phonology: stress in Palestinian, Maltese and Spanish. *Linguistic Inquiry, 5*, 39–60.

Brincat, J. M. (1994). Gli arbori della lingua maltese: Il problema del sostrato alla luce delle notizie storiche di al-Himyarī sul periodo arabo a Malta (870–1054). In J. M. Brincat (Ed.), *Languages of the Mediterranean* (pp. 130–140). Malta: Malta University Press.

Brincat, J. M. (2000). *Il-Malti: Elf sena ta' storja* [Kullana Kulturali 10]. Malta: Pubblikazzjonijiet Indipendenza, pin.

Brincat Massa, M. (1986). Interferenze inglesi sulla lingua maltese. *Journal of Maltese Studies, 16*, 45–52.

Camilleri, A. & Borg, Albert (1992). Is Maltese an endangered language? Unpublished paper presented at the XVth International Conference of Linguistics, Laval University, Quebec.

Camilleri, A. & Vanhove, M. (1994). A phonetic and phonological description of the Maltese Dialect of Mġarr (Malta). *Zeitschrift für Arabische Linguistik, 28*, 87–110.

Cassola, A. (1985). La lingua maltese ieri ed oggi. *Nouvelle Europe, 48*, 21–25.

Chahal, D. (1999). A preliminary analysis of Lebanese Arabic intonation. *Proceedings of the 1999 Conference of the Australian Linguistic Society*, 1–17.

Constitution of the Republic of Malta (1974). Malta: Department of Information.

Cruttenden, A. (1997). *Intonation* [Cambridge Textbooks in Linguistics]. 2nd edition. Cambridge: CUP.

Fabri, R. (1993). *Kongruenz und die Grammatik des Maltesischen*. Tübingen: Niemeyer.

Grice, M. (1995). *The Intonation of Palermo Italian: implications for intonation theory* [Linguistische Arbeiten 334]. Tübingen: Niemeyer.

Hayes, B. (1995). *Metrical Stress Theory*. Chicago: University of Chicago Press.

Hull, G. (1993). *The Maltese Language Question: A case study in cultural imperialism*. Malta: Said International.

Kaye, A. S. & Rosenhouse, J. (1997). Arabic dialects and Maltese. In R. Hetzron (Ed.), *The Semitic Languages* (pp. 263–311). London and New York: Routledge.

Ladd, D. R. (1996). *Intonational Phonology* [Cambridge Studies in Linguistics]. Cambridge: CUP.

Mifsud, M. (1995). *Loan Verbs in Maltese: A descriptive and comparative study.* Leiden: E. J. Brill.

Mifsud, M. & Borg, Albert (1997). *Fuq l-Għatba tal-Malti* [Threshold Level Maltese]. Strasbourg: Councils of Europe Publishing.

Pierrehumbert, J. (1980). The Phonetics and Phonology of English Intonation. Unpublished Ph.D. Dissertation. Cambridge, MA: Massachusetts Institute of Technology.

National Statistics Office, Malta (2000). http://www.nso.gov.mt/quarterly%20statistics/maininidicators.htm

Rossi, M. (1998). Intonation in Italian. In D. J. Hirst & A. Di Cristo (Eds.), *Intonation Systems: A survey of twenty languages* (pp. 219–238). Cambridge: CUP.

Schabert, P. (1976). *Laut- und Formenlehre des Maltesischen anhand zweier Mundarten.* Erlangen: Palm und Enke.

Sciriha, L. (1986). A Sociolinguistic Study of Monophthongization in Maltese. Unpublished Ph.D. Dissertation, University of Victoria.

Serracino-Inglott, P. (1989). Kattoliċità Maltija – jew il-vokazzjoni tal-ħuttaba. In T. Cortis (Ed.), *L-Identità Kulturali ta' Malta: Kungress nazzjonali 13–15 ta' April 1989* (pp. 263–270). Malta: Dipartiment tal-Edukazzjoni.

Sutcliffe, E. F. (1936). *A Grammar of the Maltese Language.* Oxford: OUP.

Vella, A. (1995). Prosodic Structure and Intonation in Maltese and its Influence on Maltese English. Unpublished Ph.D. Dissertation, University of Edinburgh.

Vella, A. (1997). Intonational variation across dialects: An intonational phonology approach. In A. Botinis, G. Kouroupetroglou, & G. Carayiannis (Eds.), *Intonation: Theory, models and applications* (pp. 325–328). Athens, Greece.

Watson, J. C. E. (2002). *The Phonology and Morphology of Arabic* [The Phonology of the World's Languages]. Oxford: OUP.

Wettinger, G. Plurilingualism and cultural change in Medieval Malta. In Alexander Borg & M. Erdal (Eds.), *Mediterranean Language Review* (pp. 144–160). Wiesbaden: Harrassowitz.

Index

In the series HAMBURG STUDIES ON MULTILINGUALISM (HSM) the following titles have been published thus far:

1. MÜLLER, Natascha (ed.): *(In)vulnerable Domains in Multilingualism.* 2003.
2. BRAUNMÜLLER, Kurt and Gisella FERRARESI (eds.): *Aspects of Multilingualism in European Language History.* 2003.